C000161558

THE WRITER AND THE PEOPLE

THE ITALIAN LIST

THE WRITER AND THE PEOPLE

Populism in Modern Italian Literature

ALBERTO ASOR ROSA

TRANSLATED BY
MATTEO MANDARINI

LONDON NEW YORK CALCUTTA

Questo libro è stato tradotto grazie ad un contributo alla traduzione assegnato dal Ministero degli Affari Esteri e della Cooperazione Internazionale Italiano.

This book has been translated thanks to a contribution awarded by the Ministry of Foreign Affairs and International Cooperation of Italy.

SERIES EDITOR
ALBERTO TOSCANO

Seagull Books, 2021

Originally published in Italian as *Scrittori e popolo*
© Giulio Einaudi editore s. p. a., 1988

English translation © Matteo Mandarini, 2021

Foreword © Daniele Balicco, 2019

ISBN   978 0 8574 2 342 9

British Library Cataloguing-in-Publication Data
A catalogue record for this book is available from the British Library.

Typeset by Seagull Books, Calcutta, India
Printed and bound by Hyam Enterprises, Calcutta, India

CONTENTS

Foreword

DANIELE BALICCO

1. Alberto Asor Rosa's *The Writer and the People* (*Scrittori e popolo*) was originally published by a small Roman Trotskyist publisher in 1965. It had unexpectedly triggered a wide public debate. The book's thesis was indeed radical: it stated that Italy's literary culture, from the nineteenth-century Risorgimento to Fascism and contemporary postwar communist cultural politics, was dominated entirely by a single ideological position—that of populism. It made little difference that this 'need to know' or 'represent' popular life was embodied in mutable, even conflicting, political standpoints, because the underlying ideological choice was the same: to shape a *national* cultural tradition in a state that had only recently been formed.

This *required* an alliance between writers, intellectuals and the people. But as Asor Rosa argues in this book, it cannot be assumed that this *purely* cultural alliance, imposed from above, really defended the interests of the people or was truly beneficial for literature. According to the author, the effects were extremely negative on both sides. In the years since its unification, Italy failed to produce literature at the level of great European modernism—aside from a few notable exceptions. At the same time, it generated a form of state unable to truly modernize the country, other than through what Antonio Gramsci—an author for whom little love is shown in this volume—had called a 'passive revolution'. This is why the populist delusion is doubly deceptive and needs to be quickly overcome. The solution proposed by Asor Rosa is radical: first of all, literature should be purely literature and nothing else. Second, politics should be the space for the only true conflict at the basis of modern development: that which opposes 'workers and capital'.[1] In contrast to the

---

1 Mario Tronti, *Operai e capitale* [Worker and Capital] (Rome: Derive-Approdi, 2013 [1966]) is the key theoretical text of Italian workerism (*operaismo*). For an introduction to Tronti's thought, see Alberto Toscano, 'Chronicles of Insurrection: Tronti, Negri and the Subject of Antagonism' in *The Italian Difference: Between Nihilism and Biopolitics* (Lorenzo Chiesa and Alberto Toscano eds) (Melbourne: re.press, 2009), pp. 109–30.

concept of the people, that of the 'working class' is not a bourgeois invention but the result of an objective process. Its existence is real and does not require any sort of cultural alliance. Its unity is founded *only* on the recognition of a precise economic interest—that of exploitation. If the populist delusion can be overcome, literature will finally be able to engage with capitalism's creative–destructive effects on life; and perhaps it will be able to produce the best of itself.

With such a radically profound thesis and an elegant, caustic style of writing, the book had powerfully broken into the contemporary public debate. It elicited stark reactions: admiration to the point of enthusiasm (especially amid the nascent student movement) or outright rejection (particularly from Communist Party intellectuals). New editions followed in quick succession and it has remained in print over the years.[2] *The Writer and the People* along with Franco Fortini's *A Test of Powers*[3] are classics of Italian literary criticism and a striking emblem of the remarkable ways in which the critical tradition has reflected on the politics at the time.

This book had few immediate heirs,[4] at least within the sphere of Italian literary criticism, for two main reasons. First, the Italian Marxist wave of workerism (*operaismo*)—to which this book serves as a kind of manifesto in the literary field—has always struggled to formulate a theoretical discourse on art and literature. It comes as no surprise that at the beginning of his thesis, Asor Rosa frankly declares that we 'care nothing for literary criticism itself'. A political tradition that has revolutionary rupture as its immediate objective can, only with great difficulty, handle the staggered and enigmatic suspended time that characterizes the aesthetic dimension. It may appear to us as a bizarre objective, but Asor Rosa writes in order to *destroy* literary criticism not in order to found a new, perhaps workerist-inspired one. Without doubt his is an extreme act, certainly not without contradictions, but with an indubitable

---

2 A new, expanded edition is available, including a critical survey of contemporary Italian literature in light of the categories established by the 1965 text. See Alberto Asor Rosa, *Scrittori e popolo* (*1965*) / *Scrittori e massa* (*2015*) [The Writer and the People (1965)/ The Writers and the Mass (2015)] (Turin: Einaudi, 2015).

3 Franco Fortini, *A Test of Powers: Writings on Criticism and Literary Institutions* (Alberto Toscano trans.) (London: Seagull Books, 2016).

4 For Asor Rosa's intellectual milieu, see *Critica e progetto. Le culture in Italia dagli anni Sessanta a oggi. Studi in onore di Alberto Asor Rosa* [Critique and Project: Cultures in Italy from the Sixties Till Today. Writings in Honour of Alberto Asor Rosa] (Lucinda Spera ed.) (Rome: Carocci, 2005).

appeal.[5] The second reason is that a few years after the publication of this book, the Roman-workerist author would become one of the leading intellectuals of the Italian Communist Party (PCI) and one of the most influential figures in the institutional life of Italian literary culture. While speaking with great pride of his workerist heritage, he also considered it as a youthful, if glorious, excess:

> On more than one occasion I have stated that it was an extremist political and, above all, intellectual experience; and extremism leads inevitably—as maturity, all maturity teaches—into error. No doubt. But it must be said that for me—specifically for me, but also for many others I think—extremism was the path to truth, passing through error [. . .]. And I ask: Is there any other way?[6]

And though there were few successors of Asor Rosa's luminous legacy, the contemporary reader might be struck by a sense of familiarity on reading this book. *The Writer and the People*—also Fortini's *A Test of Powers*—presages a way of thinking politics and literature in conjunction, which would eventually become popular in the 1980s. Anyone who has read and admired Terry Eagleton's *Marxism and Literary Criticism* (1976), Edward Said's *Orientalism* (1978), Fredric Jameson's *The Political Unconscious* (1981) or Gayatri Chakravorty Spivak's *A Critique of Postcolonial Reason* (1999)—to cite only some of the best-known works of literary criticism from the last few decades—will certainly appreciate *The Writer and the People*. With a note of caution however: *The Writer and the People* was not written as an academic work. It set itself a different task—to attack the political stereotypes of the left—it was written as a symbolic weapon aimed at specific adversaries.

It will not be easy for the contemporary reader, especially a non-Italian reader, to understand how writing a book of literary criticism could have had such a powerful political significance in the postwar period. Asor Rosa himself—while presenting the expanded 50th anniversary Italian edition—felt the need to premise it with a warning:

However hard I might try, what I will never manage to explain to a contemporary audience is the immense significance that the decisions

---

5 For a critical analysis of the theoretical contradictions of Asor Rosa's literary *operaismo*, see Fortini's *A Test of Powers*.

6 Alberto Asor Rosa, *Le armi della critica. Scritti e saggi degli anni ruggenti (1960–1970)* [The Weapons of Critique: Writings and Articles of the Roaring Years 1960-70] (Turin: Einaudi, 2011), p. *lxv*.

taken in the cultural sphere had, or could have, in a more immediately political milieu, for better and worse.[7]

There is no doubt that today it is indeed difficult even to envisage how a work of literary criticism could be written in first person and understood in public debate as a truly political act, as an action that was able to determine the direction of the broader political debate. That said, sketching—even with ample brushstrokes—the peculiar position that Italy occupied in the geopolitical context of the time might make it easier to read this work as a symptom and, at the same time, as a historical document of a very precise sociohistorical reality.

2. When Asor Rosa wrote *The Writer and the People* as a thirty-two-year-old intellectual from Rome, Italy occupied a delicate frontier zone between two rival blocs. At the Yalta Conference it was placed under the umbrella of the United States, however, since it included the largest Western communist party, it presented no small problems to the frozen equilibrium of the Cold War. Germany had been divided into two separate states, whereas Italy remained united though internally it was split. Social life revolved around two warring factions who—for better or worse—were forced into cohabitation. This resulted in the exorbitant weight of politics on the cultural life of the nation, which was (even in its minor, administrative aspects) a projection of the broader problems: an infinite variation on a single theme, the global conflict between capitalism and Soviet communism. If that were not enough, from the end of the 1950s, two further elements of transformation and chaos were added to an already congested cultural landscape. The first was the economic boom that violently unsettled Italian society and *seemed* in one fell swoop to negate a millennial continuity of art, symbolic forms, popular traditions and poverty. Consumption exploded, society became affluent. Between 1956 and 1963 Italian GDP grew at a constant rate of 6 per cent; in 1961 it surpassed 8 per cent. Everything was changing at breakneck pace, while society was shedding its skin like a snake. But institutional politics refused to budge. Almost immediately the proposed reforms of the first Centre-Left government foundered, not least because of international pressures and fears. Meanwhile, the PCI ignored the radical nature of the changes underway. It was the

---

7 Alberto Asor Rosa, 'Dieci tesi sul dopo-autunno' in *Scrittori e popolo* (*1965*) / *Scrittori e massa* (*2015*), pp. 349–62; here, p. 359.

'populist' poet Pier Paolo Pasolini—subject to an unsparing criticism in this volume—who, with great foresight, would define the combined effect of the savage economic boom and the vacuum of institutional power as a 'development without progress'.[8]

It is no coincidence that in these very years a powerful working-class and student-protest movement began to take shape to the left of the PCI. This is the second element necessary to grasp this decade of Italian history—the emergent public for which a book like *The Writer and the People* was intended. It was the political protagonist of the 'long Italian '68'—that movement of radical mass politicization that would overturn the balance of forces in society and, at least in part, within the institutions of the state. But in a country with limited sovereignty such as Italy, which was uncomfortably placed in the geopolitical zone, there were limits beyond which such a movement could not proceed—as the violence unleashed against the people by the state and its Atlantic allies would testify.

Two dates can be chosen to mark the endpoint of this low-intensity civil war, fought with unequal weapons, over a decade: 1967 and 1978. They are not equivalent dates. The first prepared the future; the second would close the door to many past illusions. The protagonist of the former is a new, young protest movement, not so interested in class conflict; on the contrary, it practiced the refusal of work. It was a visionary, technologically advanced and an autonomous movement whose aim was to liberate the body, the instincts and passions: the 'movement of 1977'. It would prefigure some of the forms of resistance to the Anglo-American financialization that will be at work in the subsequent forty years.[9]

The protagonist of the second date, on the other hand, is singular: the Italian state. 1978 is the year of the kidnapping of one of its highest officials

---

8 Pier Paolo Pasolini, *Scritti corsari* (Milan: Garzanti, 1975).

9 Asor Rosa will later publish a short book on the 1977 movement and, more generally, on the political and social crisis of the 1970s that would provoke a heated debate (see Alberto Asor Rosa, *Le due società* [The Two Societies] [Turin: Einaudi, 1977]). Asor Rosa interpreted the Italian crisis of the 1970s as an effect of a profound break between two social realities in struggle with one another: the one adult, still organized according to the traditional politics of work and its defence; the other youthful, irregularly employed and disengaged from unions and parties. According to Asor Rosa, only by completing the modernization of the Italian institutional structures could this break be healed. Clearly, we are here far from the guiding tenets of the workerist tradition.

and the president of the Christian Democratic party (DC), Aldo Moro. After fifty-five days of imprisonment, a paramilitary unit of the Red Brigades, flanked by rogue elements of the state and the Atlantic secret services (CIA and NATO), executed him. The 'long Italian '68' ends there. It is almost like the final act of a Greek tragedy, which wiped away any remaining political illusion—that Italy might *truly* be changed into a 'progressive democracy'. In the same year, which is both tragic and conclusive, the author of *The Writer and the People* will be elected to the lower house of parliament as an MP representing the PCI.

3. Our discourse is political, and fundamentally *political* is the sense of our *literary* argument. We do not know if the result matches our intentions, but we certainly forced ourselves to apply to an extremely important aspect of Italian literature of the nineteenth and twentieth centuries, the *partisan workers' critique* which constitutes the final aim of our investigation.

The ultimate goal of *The Writer and the People* is to question the general framework of the PCI's cultural politics. Palmiro Togliatti's party, through a selective and tendentious reading of Antonio Gramsci's *Prison Notebooks*, always presented itself in continuity with the tradition of the Risorgimento, as the only real political subject able to transform Italy into a *nation*. In order to do this it was necessary, however, to create a whole communist people—almost from nothing.[10] It was necessary quickly to construct a desirable, progressive and democratic Italian nation, a new 'imagined community' made up of founding myths, rituals, aesthetic forms and scientific work; in other words, an entire symbolic universe that a people could identify with. The importance ascribed by the PCI to cultural work and to the organization of intellectuals follows this set of presuppositions. In truth, the strategy had precise geopolitical causes, even if these were never openly acknowledged. Togliatti was well aware that due to the division of the world into two blocks, the most the PCI could achieve for Italy was the gradual and progressive democratization of the state—and little else. The revolution would be endlessly postponed. *The Writer and the People* was written precisely so as to dismantle this broadly defined and long-term framework with a singular, imperative act.

---

10 See Sidney G. Tarrow, *Communism in Italy and in France* (Princeton: Princeton University Press, 1975). One can read a positive judgement on Togliatti's populism in Ernesto Laclau, *On Populist Reason* (London: Verso, 2005).

Asor Rosa was shaped politically by the PCI. He would leave the party after the crisis of 1956 but (as we have noted) his departure would be temporary only. In the years that precede the writing of this book he drew closer to heterodox socialist positions, reading the 'Seven Theses on the Question of Workers' Control'[11] by Raniero Panzieri and Lucio Libertini with great enthusiasm. In this seminal article, Asor Rosa would discover the new idea of 'progressive democracy', one in which victory does not come with occupying the institutions of the state (as Togliatti continued to demand) but by taking political conflict to the workplaces, inside industrial production. It was to be a decisive change of perspective: *the working class before the party*. Like Mario Tronti, he began to follow Panzieri and his curious group of researchers and trade-unionist scholars of Marx's *Capital*, moving between Rome and Turin, outside any political movements or social mandate. This was the *Quaderni rossi* group that originated Italian workerism. The year was 1961.[12]

In the meantime, social conflict began to erupt in various sites, especially in the North and, as is the case with every respectable left-wing family, *Quaderni rossi* would eventually break up. Tronti was to lead the most combative offshoot, advancing the thesis that one should not only study the new capitalism but also try to politically organize this working-class insubordination of a new type. In 1963, the first issue of the journal *Classe operaia* was published. The famous title of the opening article was unambiguous: 'Lenin in England'.[13]

It was within this radical theoretical laboratory that the eccentric and idiosyncratic work—*The Writer and the People*—was born. Economic boom and the exponential growth of the mass worker[14] opened the possibility of

---

11 Raniero Panzieri and Lucio Libertini, 'Sette tesi sulla questione del controllo operaio', *Mondo Operaio* 2 (February 1958).

12 For an introduction to Italian workerism, see Steve Wright's excellent volume, *Storming Heaven: Class Composition and Struggle in Italian Autonomist Marxism* (London: Pluto, 2002). For a broad overview of Italian radical political thought, a good starting point is *Radical Thought in Italy: A Potential Politics* (Michael Hardt and Paolo Virno eds) (Minneapolis: University of Minnesota Press, 1996). See also *The Italian Difference*.

13 Tronti, *Operai e capitale* [Workers and Capital] (1966), pp. 87–93. Available in English at: www.marxists.org/reference/subject/philosophy/works/ it/tronti.htm (last accessed on 27 February 2017).

14 Steve Wright enumerates three attributes of the mass worker: '[I]t was massified, it performed simple labour, and it was located at the heart of the immediate process of production'—*Storming Heaven*, p. 107.

revolution in Italy once again. And never mind if the PCI failed to recognize this. That is the underlying conviction that forms the basis of the book. Asor Rosa thus set out to jettison futile ambiguities and traditions, among them the one which, above all others and for far too long, had prevented the formation of a class consciousness adequate to the times: Populism.

With such a radical framing, it comes as no great surprise that only very few authors survive unscathed from the lightning strikes of this violent ideological storm: Giovanni Verga, Federico De Roberto, Luigi Pirandello, Italo Svevo, Eugenio Montale, Carlo Levi and few others. Inevitably, many of the positions taken in *The Writer and the People* appear excessively one-sided or dated. Asor Rosa himself would later correct many of his critical judgements, specifically placing them at the heart of twentieth-century Italian literary canon, three authors—Italo Calvino, Pasolini and Fortini—the first two of whom he had harshly criticized in this book, and the third whom he would turn his guns on immediately thereafter.[15]

A similar fate befell Antonio Gramsci. Asor Rosa considered him the involuntary architect of Togliattian 'populism'. Indeed, the entire Gramscian theme of the 'national-popular' appears as an ideological operation of 'prudent moderatism', of excessive political realism which all too often serves as an alibi 'for those who would have refused *in principle* any political or cultural solution of a '"revolutionary" type'. It is striking to read such severe judgements against what, on the contrary, appears today as the indisputable far-sightedness of Gramsci's research—I am thinking, above all, of the attention he showed for commercial literature ('Gramsci goes so far as to exhibit a broad interest in that lowest form of popular literature that is the feuilleton or fourth-rate melodrama'), popular tradition and folklore. Indeed, for Gramsci the starting point is knowledge of 'common sense'; one must face up to that if one wishes to *really* engage in politics. The aim is to achieve a political comprehension of the present. Asor Rosa balks at this challenge. For him it is enough for the working class to grasp the exploitation to which it is subjected. Culture and values are useless.

In his iconoclastic fury, he neglects the fact that when Gramsci composed the *Notebooks* he was in prison reflecting on the causes of the revolution's failure in the West. Gramsci's writings should be read as the hypothesis for

---

15 Alberto Asor Rosa, 'L'uomo, il poeta' [The Man, the Poet] (1965) in *Le armi della critica. Scritti e saggi degli anni ruggenti (1960–1970)* (Turin: Einaudi, 2011), pp. 95–138.

reopening the space of politics, when it would once again prove possible, and to do so from a position of strength. As we have noted more than once, however, the aim of Asor Rosa's book is not to discuss the theoretical work of the Sardinian communist leader so much as the *political uses* that Togliatti made of it through the cultural organization of the PCI:

> Attention to the discourse of populism has served to unmask the ideologues of the Italian workers' movement: mystifiers by profession even when they are in good faith; infantile caricatures of the bourgeois intellectual.

Even from these brief quotations it is clear that *The Writer and the People* is written like a war pamphlet. And yet, the landscape it sketches with quick but sure brushstrokes has the indisputable merit of placing a real problem at the heart of its analysis, the one it identifies—wrongly or rightly—as populism. The best part of Italian culture, including Asor Rosa, has grasped that there is indeed an unresolved political question haunting the history of the constitution of the Italian state, and that this problem has persisted—without undergoing radical breaks or resolutions—from the Risorgimento and turn-of-the-century nationalism all the way to Fascism and the Republic. This problem has been an abiding object of analysis, and where possible, the target of possible solutions.

After all, the explicit aim of writing *The Writer and the People* was to prepare 'a new generation of revolutionary leaders and militants'. In the subsequent fifteen years, this new generation of intellectuals and political leaders transformed the political landscape. In some ways against the intentions of Asor Rosa himself, the undoubted theoretical tenor of the 'long Italian '68' also owes much to the savage energy of this book.

4. By way of a coda, a final observation. Fifty years after the publication of the book that you are about to read, the spectre of populism has reappeared on the world stage. After the fall of the Soviet Union it has rapidly come to occupy a significant place within public discourse and theoretical research, particularly in the West. Aside from rare exceptions,[16] the term 'populist' is used to disqualify those to whom it is applied. In *The Writer and the People* it

---

16 Among these are: Christopher Lasch, *True and Only Heaven: Progress and Its Critics* (New York: Norton, 1991); Ernesto Laclau, *On Populist Reason*; and Marco d'Eramo, 'Populism and New Oligarchy', *New Left Review* 82 (July–August 2013): 5–28.

served to indicate a strategy to be countered, because it was deemed to act as an obstacle to the development of an advanced democracy capable of self-government. Today it is *also* used against those who demand self-governance. What then is the reason for this tendentious semantic slippage? What is hidden behind this illicit extension of populism's political meaning? According to Marco D'Eramo this puzzle is not so difficult to decipher: simply by changing one's standpoint one can begin to grasp that, in truth, the use of the term tells us more about those 'who utter it than those branded with it'.[17] It should therefore be read as a case of projection, in the psychological sense. It is as though this compulsive accusation allowed the political representatives of transnational financial aristocracy to try and exorcize an unconscious fear. But, fear of what? That a quarter of a century after the collapse of the Soviet Union any form of popular rebellion might organize itself into a political counter-power to their unchallenged dominion.

'We know now that Government by organized money is just as dangerous as Government by organized mob'—these are not the words of Alexander Herzen nor Leo Tolstoy, nor Jules Michelet, Giuseppe Mazzini, an Argentinian Peronist nor a revolutionary agitator. They are, rather, from a famous public address by the President of the United States Franklin D. Roosevelt at Madison Square Garden, New York, on 31 October 1936. Today such 'populist ravings' would be immediately tossed into the media pyre. Let us not then fear the possible dangers invoked by this spectre. Like every act of necromancy, it will eventually turn against those who invoke it. What is important to understand for the time being is that the semantic twist that the term 'populism' has undergone speaks about us, and the domination to which we are subjected. Indeed, it can be said, to illuminate the neo-oligarchical mutation of the forms of power in our post-democratic era.

---

17 D'Eramo, 'Populism and New Oligarchy', p. 8.

Translator's Note

From the very beginning, Alberto Asor Rosa's *Scrittori e popolo* (*The Writer and the People*) raises a thorny problem that is at once linguistic, political and even metaphysical, linked to the crucial second noun in the title: *popolo* (people). Asor Rosa's unavoidably frequent references to *il popolo* (singular) involve an immediate problem of translation: in English, the single term people can take both singular and plural forms ('the people's revolt', singular; 'those people are congregating', plural), though as singular noun it always needs qualifier— for example, 'the Italians are a resourceful people' where, in this instance, the unity is that of the nation or an ethnic group. In English, maintaining the singular form always involves some kind of qualification. This is not the case in Italian wherein *popolo* is immediately and explicitly singular.

What appears as a minor, if at times awkward, issue of translation expands into something much broader when we link the linguistic register with a more philosophico-political one, as we can see if we turn to Thomas Hobbes' reflections on the 'people'. In *De Cive* [*On the Citizen*] he writes:

> The last factor that is detrimental to a civil Régime, and particularly to a Monarchy, is that men do not make a clear enough distinction between a *people* and a *crowd*. A *people* is a *single* entity, with a *single will*; you can attribute *an act* to it. In every commonwealth the *People* Reigns; for even in *Monarchies* the *People* exercises power [*imperat*]; for the *people* wills through the will of *one man*. [. . .] in a *Monarchy* the subjects are the *crowd*, and (paradoxically) the *King* is the *people*.[1]

This notion of the people as '*unum* quid'—a '*single* entity'—is grammatically singular across Romance languages (as it is for *populus* in Latin, which

---

1 Thomas Hobbes, 'On the Internal Causes which Tend to Dissolve a Commonwealth' in *On the Citizen* (R. Tuck and M. Silverstone eds and trans) (Cambridge: Cambridge University Press, 1998), p. 137.

was the language in which Hobbes wrote *De Cive*). This allows Asor Rosa to bring out, quite naturally, one of his principal criticisms on the adoption of the notion of 'the people' among the twentieth-century Italian communist writers. This criticism is one that can be seen to draw on a much long-standing questioning of the notion of the people in the Marxist tradition.

To briefly summarize the critique, Asor Rosa argues that the notion of the people disguises the fact that it is riven by a class conflict that actively and materially unsettles and deconstructs any conceptual or real unity it might have. This critique of populism within the Marxist tradition was not new,[2] but it had been conveniently forgotten at the time when Palmiro Togliatti, leader of the Italian Communist Party, was looking for the workers' movement to build a broad, cross-class or popular consensus, and when Joseph Stalin was demanding the establishment of 'People's Democracies' across Eastern Europe. One might argue then that the *political* significance of this critique was more important than its strictly theoretical one.[3] However, this would not be entirely correct, since it did more than inconvenience the official communist parties; rather, it called for a return to Marxism as a *revolutionary* movement, politically and theoretically, against all attempts to subordinate it to the construction of the state, whether 'in one country' or more, since the state was always the *bourgeois* state.

Implicit in this challenge to the official communist discourse on 'the people' was a particularly antagonistic position to bourgeois conceptions of the nation state, which had too readily been appropriated by the workers' movement. Asor

---

2 It goes back at least as far as V. I. Lenin's critique of the Narodniks (Russian populists) and the later charge of 'social chauvinism' on the eve of the First World War. But arguably both of these positions can be said to be more or less implicit in Marx's demand for proletarian internationalism as necessary to avoid collapsing class difference into the national unity that characterizes the people, which would lead subaltern classes to identify with their national bourgeoisies.

3 Several decades later, two thinkers from the tradition of *operaismo*—in which *The Writer and the People* stands out as the only real monograph, at least, for its founding period—came back to this distinction in text that caused a sensation. In *Empire* (2001), and a number of subsequent books and articles, Michael Hardt and Antonio Negri take up again this attack on 'the people' so doggedly pursued by Asor Rosa, but they do so by going back to the Hobbesian distinction and opposing to the 'people' not 'class' but the 'crowd'—or more precisely, and with greater philological and etymological correctness—the 'multitude' (Hobbes' term '*multitudo*' is translated here as 'crowd'). See also Paolo Virno, *A Grammar of the Multitude: For an Analysis of Contemporary Forms of Life* (Isabella Bertoletti, James Cascaito and Andrea Casson trans) (Cambridge: MIT Press, 2004).

Rosa restated and concretized in the cultural realm what Mario Tronti called the specificity of the working class' position 'within and against'[4] capital. He did this by arguing that the working class might be usefully rethought of as 'within and without': that is to say, its position within the circuits of capital means that it is necessarily within capitalism, as its ineradicable presupposition, but it is only within it by virtue of being *against* it—as that counterforce that capital must perpetually reintegrate, precisely because it is *within* in the mode of being *without*. Marx had stated that 'the real not-capital is labour'.[5] For Asor Rosa this was as true in the realm of culture as it was in that of production. *The Writer and the People* is an authoritative critique of the failure of powerful sectors of the workers' movement to recognize that workers are fundamentally 'other', alien, the *parte maudite* of 'bourgeois' modernity.

I hope that this rather lengthy aside—no doubt somewhat out of place in a translator's introduction—serves to forewarn the reader as to the political and theoretical intricacies attendant upon translating (*il*) *popolo*—(the) people. Rather than force the English construction into evermore unnatural, contorted or long-winded forms, I have typically opted for fluidity. This has sometimes meant adopting the plural ('the people are . . . ')—more familiar to the English ear. However, the reader should bear in mind the underlying unity postulated by the Italian usage, a unity that points to its relation to the bourgeois nation-state and to capital's integration of an *irreducible* class difference. In some, but not all, cases where I have had to revert to a term that does not reveal the etymological link present in the Italian, I have included the Italian in square brackets after the English term. This is somewhat inelegant—so I have tried to keep this to a minimum—but I feel necessary.

All translations are mine, unless stated otherwise. Translator's notes have been marked. Finally, I have tried to provide brief notes for some of the least well-known figures and literary traditions discussed in the book.[6] These are in no way exhaustive, but I hope they will provide the reader sufficient orientation while not making this book any more unwieldy than it already is.

---

4 Mario Tronti, *Operai e capitale* (Turin: Einaudi, 1971), p. 229.

5 Karl Marx, *Grundrisse* (Martin Nicolaus trans.) (London: Penguin, 1973), p. 274.

6 Sometimes these figures are unfairly unknown, in part due to the insularity of too much of the Anglophone publishing world. Think, for example, of the only recently remedied lack of almost any of the poetry and prose of Giacomo Leopardi—quite possibly the foremost Italian poet and essayist of the last two centuries.

THE WRITER AND THE PEOPLE

Twenty Years Later[*]

The owl of Minerva begins its flight
only with the onset of dusk.

G. W. F. Hegel

This book was thought out and written between 1962 and 1964, during the years of the *Quaderni rossi*; it was published between 1964 and 1965, when *Classe operaia* was about to appear.[1] More or less twenty years have passed since then; it feels like many more. In the intervening period, an event of great importance has taken place: we had thought that the working class[2] would have taken power but, today, following the dislocation of power that took place in these twenty years, *no* class is capable of taking and managing power, for the good reason that *there is no longer* any class able to do so. However

---

[*] The preface was added to the twentieth-anniversary edition the book: *Scrittori e popolo. Il populismo nella lettereatura italiana contemporanea* (Turin: Einaudi, 1988), pp. *vii-xviii*. [Trans.]

1 *Quaderni rossi* [Red Notebooks] and *Classe operaia* [Working Class] were two of the founding journals of the heretical Marxist tradition of *operaismo*. The defining characteristic of this tradition is the claim that the working class is capitalism's driving force, the dynamic moment that capitalism continually tries to integrate and defang. For this reason, the subjective and the political can be said to lie at the foundation of historical, technical, economic and social change. [Trans.]

2 The Italian words which we translate as 'worker' and 'working class' are *operaio* and *classe operaia*. The referent of the term 'worker' in English is sociologically generic for various 'lower' social orders, from agricultural day labourers to industrial workers. In Italian the term is specific to the latter. Instead of constantly spelling out that we mean the 'industrial working class', which can become somewhat unwieldy and inelegant, we have kept it simple. But, when we speak of 'workers' or the 'working class' we refer to the class which arose with the industrial revolution, those who, as Asor Rosa writes, 'would spend much of their life at a factory assembly line'. [Trans.]

obvious this last observation might be, it is probably to this that we owe the greyness that surrounds us (but to this I shall return later).

The path we have travelled is a very long one; personally, it has, at times, felt unfathomable. In theory, this does not aid the task of understanding or appreciating a book such as *The Writer and the People*. Even at the time of writing it presented itself as (and wanted to be) violently untimely. In its basic framework, it refused all dialogue with the notable contemporaries of the time. It is certainly true that it sought to persuade. More than that, it did not merely describe, it wanted to change things. The inspiration was strictly Marxian in kind: 'The philosophers have only *interpreted* the world, in various ways; the point is to *change* it.'[3] But the reference to its milieu and the effort to persuade were a pure provocation: we did not plead to be listened to nor did we expect we would be. The right to speak was something to be exercised *in itself*—we simply took it, even if no one invited us to nor did we wish to be invited.

Today, I fear that this untimeliness has, instead of diminishing, only grown: the 'protest against the system' is decidedly unpopular. The more we have spoken of it, the more obsolete the critique of power has become, a fashionable *bavardage* that power not only tolerates but which it stokes and encourages. It might be the sign that one should go back to cultivating the untimely with all the passion that we have left. But this will perhaps be (or, rather, it is) an untimeliness that is profoundly different from that to which *The Writer and the People* bears witness.

That does not mean that self-criticism is called for. Of course, not everything stacks up. Twenty to twenty-five earth-shaking years are too many to maintain a coherent Olympian vista of the facts and, above all, of one's own ideas. But on the level of that higher coherence which consists in keeping open and undefended the complexity and problematic quality of one's subject matter, *The Writer and the People* seems as though it might have been written only yesterday. It could not have been written or rewritten today, but for this very reason it is *present*, here. Precisely because it has been neither absorbed nor assimilated, and has not created a tradition, it has not—I believe—dissolved into the omnivorous continuum of the cultural-institutional fabric. It resists not despite its untimeliness but because of it. I present it anew to the reader

---

3 Refers to Marx's famous eleventh thesis in the 'Theses on Feuerbach'. See Karl Marx, 'Concerning Feuerbach' in *Early Writings* (Rodney Livingstone and Gregor Benton trans) (London: Penguin 1975), p. 423. [Trans.]

because of its untimeliness (rather than because of its supposed demiurgic power of suggestion or its capacity to incite movements which might spring to mind on the anniversary of 1968). I would like for these readers—at least those who because of their age or for other reasons flick through its pages for the first time in 1988[4]—to approach it in the same spirit that one may look at notes made by an older brother many years ago, having dug them out long afterwards: not as a historical document of what we were, but like the Baedeker Guide of a trip that we wanted to take but did not (and, therefore, we might still take). The stations and the platforms are still there (as in a well-organized model), even if the train has now become a ghost: it would be enough for a diligent station master to lower the levers of the electric current for the railroad points to start working again. In short: barely anything remains of the historical context and the protagonists but the logical structure continues to operate.

More specifically, there are four points and a conclusion that I would like to offer to the reader who is unwilling to accept the philistine ethical principle according to which 'the world is as it is' (whereas it is, or, rather, could be— at least, in the ways that matter—as we invent it).

First, *operaismo*. Yes, today it is completely 'out',[5] but it *remains* the red thread of our interpretation. Let us put it like this: when we look at the world, we all choose an observation point. Years ago we chose a *low* vantage point: that is, we sought to look at the world as we thought did those who knew they would spend much of their life at a factory assembly line. This low, *ground-level* standpoint, does not amount to a set of contents or a manual of existential behaviours: we always knew that intellectual labour had its own laws, not easily identifiable with the labour of workers—and we can be accused of many things but not of having aped workers. This standpoint is precisely not a mimicking but, rather, a *level* or *mode* of observing. The entire cultural tradition, from the beginnings till today can be internalized (indeed, we have always sought to be if not very knowledgeable then at least well-informed); but to look at the world with all the instruments of the cultural tradition one had to demonstrate one's ability to look at the cultural tradition as well as the world, which is to say, *to be outside it*, like those whose side we had taken unequivocally.

---

4 In 1988, *Scrittori e popolo* was republished by Einaudi, this preface was added to the new edition. [Trans.]

5 In English in the original. [Trans.].

One can debate interminably whether this is a *good* method for scientific observation, but it is a method nonetheless. Had we desired to gain recognition, we might say that it appears to us as the method closest to that of scientific observation: for it is unclear how precisely one can observe something if one is not *outside* it (whereas the vast number of so-called human scientists are so frighteningly and irredeemably mixed up in the instruments they use as to not even know what they are doing—or why). However, because we are uninterested in gaining recognition, we will simply reiterate that *remaining outside* and *looking from below* has constituted for us—since the time of *The Writer and the People*—a reasonable working method of political and cultural observation. We do intellectual work and are not interested in continuing a cultural tradition (leaving aside that particularly aberrant form of cultural tradition, the national cultural tradition that—we hope—we have always succeeded in avoiding). This decision results in a number of uncomfortable outcomes, as we can see: for example, however noteworthy the prestige that one acquires as a specialist, a high coefficient of *diversity* remains, distancing one from the current practices of power and, conversely, indicating an equally high level of *diffidence*. The working class was the metaphor (I prefer to speak of 'metaphor' rather than 'symbol') for this diversity: it is the diverse class par excellence, and for this very reason regarded with diffidence by everyone.

Certainly, one can conceive of other diversities and other metaphors. In fact, there is no doubt that our unresolved search for a diversity that is able to support itself upon a material foundation, and that is at least as substantive as what working class diversity was for us, is not irrelevant to our present condition of uncertainty. We are absolutely respectful and often interested participants in the search for 'other' diversities, even when we remain unpersuaded by many current proposals. But, meanwhile, as we wait for the emergence of a broadly persuasive argument, we must acknowledge this fact: only those who inscribe within their epistemological and mental horizon a principle of the determinate angling of their perception (or at least of their predictions) by a *real dialectic* are able to escape integration (which is, definitively—on the strictly intellectual plane too—castration and loss of creativity). If this 'real dialectic' does not exist or is too weak, knowledge too atrophies. This is in part what we had alluded to at the start. Intellectual research has an infinite capacity for invention but, to begin with, it must coincide with the extremely detailed and realistic discovery of the real situations without which the *bavardage* of intellectuals takes over. This means that a *different* intellectual investigation is one that wants to go to the root of things. What the information universe transmits to it *immediately* must appear to it—at the very least—*suspect*. There are moments, therefore, when thought necessarily flags because a real dialectic struggles to emerge. In cases such as these, parading one's muscles is merely ridiculous. One needs to know how to wait for a more opportune moment. In the meantime, one can always exercise one's intelligence: that aristocratic virtue that—with less fuss—simpler folks call the ability to not be led around by the nose.

This leads us, secondly, to the critique of ideology. The Marxian source is even more evident here. This is a particular Marx, of course, which I recall from some of the most invigorating and salutary of readings that I have ever engaged with: that of *Early Writings*, of *On the Jewish Question*, of *The German Ideology*, of the *Grundrisse*, of 'Part Three' of *Capital, Volume 1*, of 'Results of the Immediate Process of Production' that were unpublished in his lifetime. But perhaps the youthful passion for this Marx already betrayed a decision and, hence, an implicit way of relating to a cultural tradition (in this case, towards the European-left cultural tradition). What emerged from this—and would subsequently be reinforced—was the predilection for a structural form of analysis of cultural phenomena which set out from the identification of their strictly material basis to then conclude with highly formalized results. We can summarize the logic as follows: ideology is the *manifestation* of material structural nodes (that is, encounters and intersections of different elements that tend to assume a certain *form*). In other words, it is the pure semblance of essence. And what is 'essence'? Essence is the mode of being of a real subject in the context of relations of force (where 'relations of force' can also be those that are established between different ideologies). The essence does not necessarily coincide with a 'class situation'; it can perfectly well be an individual condition at the outer limits of estrangement and marginalization; or it can be—more broadly—that ensemble of common and widespread relations, without a specific class label, which these days we might call an 'anthropological condition'.

But in *each of these cases*, the 'critique' is the operation of identifying the real structures underlying the different ideological stratifications (human structures, insofar as they are 'human', squirt ink like squids: one needs a good compass to orient oneself in the enveloping clouds). Inevitably, if one accepts that knowing is a multi-layered process of formalization, one must admit that so-called real structures are also nothing other than the forms of so many ideological stratifications (which cannot be disentangled). Today I would be much less sure of the distinction that—rather than postulating—I had sensed at the time and practised with force. But the problem is not whether to attribute 'reality' to the examined objects. The problem is, as far as possible, to dig down to the depths, like Marx's old mole, so as to uncover the roots concealed beneath various strata of earth—as every truly radical critique must. The problem, in other words, is to recognize that the image of itself that any cultural phenomenon offers can never be taken for granted, because in the end it is not a fact which it suffices to recognize and describe, but a set of processes that must be discovered and progressively 'defined' one-by-one (that is, never once and for all, or never all at once). Of course we know that by persistently digging one might emerge at the *antipodes*, having passed through the centre of the earth. This was effectively our dream: to arrive at a New World, where things appear reversed when compared to those that are either so banal as to leave us immediately satiated, or intolerably crude and which we are fated to encounter every day. But that is obvious. Indeed it is obvious that a utopian impulse—the effort of the *reductio* of the world to one's measure—sustains (and as far as I'm concerned, continues to do so) a radical critical intention, such as the one that has been described above.

The object of our critical-analytical interest was therefore that set of intellectual creations and images of the world that we loved calling 'bourgeois culture' (and this is the third point). *The Writer and the People* presented itself as the forerunner of an inquiry 'that aims to confront the concept and history of bourgeois culture from beginning to end' (as I wrote in the preface to the second edition of the book). We argued that modern culture is only bourgeois culture. The working class did not produce any culture because, first, it lacked the conditions to do so, and because—more importantly—it had no need of it. (What it needed was 'theory', but by definition this was a 'working-class theory' that could not be systematized within that set of fundamentally self-justifying practical and mental relations that forms the *corpus* of the cultural tradition which, *ipso facto*, from 1789 onward, presents itself as traditional bourgeois culture.) Traversing these far-flung extremities of the intellectual sphere, we came to a point not so far from the truth. Culture, particularly modern culture, was *one*, and the undeniable contradictions that traversed it were the contradictions internal to one and the same systemic universe—this we felt must have been clear to even the most disinterested observer. A progressive intellectual is much closer to a conservative one than to any worker. The unbroken continuity of that systemic universe was the best guarantee as well as the most striking proof of its internal cohesion.

In order to remain outside all of this, *The Writer and the People* attempted to be decidedly anti-evolutionary and, therefore, also anti-historicist and anti-progressive. It proposed skipping three or four phases of development in a single leap (this again shows why the lever was the working class: that eminently non-dialectical class, which refuses the mediation offered by all forms of bourgeois power, including the socialist kind). Or more precisely—and more important still—it argued that those phases had *already* been leapt over three or four times ever since populism had taken off in Italy (ever since the Restoration, more or less). The claim to be putting an end to such a long and formidable process was certainly fanciful. And yet, to declare this process over and, hence, inoperative meant something: History would certainly not be ending *because of this*; but it entirely altered the logic of judgement. It was no longer a case of collaborating intellectually towards Progress; it was a case of establishing what price we had paid (and would pay) for the myth of the unbroken continuity and perfectibility of human action. Hence the critique of History underpinned the critique of bourgeois culture and represented its secret justification; it would be pointless to deny that largely nihilist sympathies infused the anti-historicism of this position. But was there anything really scandalous at the dawn of the 1960s in pointing out a relationship between the spirit of *The Gay Science* and that of *Capital*? To us it appeared scandalous instead that for so long the two texts could be considered so profoundly opposed to each other, when it was absolutely evident that they had been born of the same world-spirit, like the Castor and Pollux of modern thought. What happened afterwards would demonstrate that without a robust element of nihilism, all progressivism withers and dies; indeed, nihilism inoculates one against ideology's illusions, and only a progressivism without ideology could rise to the battle against conservative realism.

Literature (the fourth point) was the field that we had chosen to describe the cross section of the tensions outlined above. This is not exactly the most propitious field for such a demonstration—as some people had already observed regarding the methodological and critical apparatus of *The Writer and the People*. In truth, *The Writer and the People* revealed how much literature had weighed historically (particularly in Italy) on the 'formation' of those tensions; and, in addition, it posed a deeper problem—which has continued to arise, even if in an increasingly feeble way, over the course of the two subsequent decades. The critique of committed literature, which the book made without pulling its punches, led to the re-establishment of a hierarchy of values and a foundational vision that perfectly matched the vision and values of a class struggle carried out in the name of a non-ideologized and non-ideologizable working class. Here too we can say that there had been a need for a protracted passage through distant, cold and frequently hostile regions in order to come to the heart of the problem. But to arrive at the idea that only high-bourgeois literature (in Italy: Giovanni Verga, Italo Svevo, Eugenio Montale, Carlo Emilio Gadda and, partly, Luigi Pirandello—as the end of Part One of the book argues) had expressed what mattered to us, namely, the dramatic perception of the irresolvable character of a cultural condition. This was more than a commonplace, it was the endpoint of an exhausting process of 'making coherent' all our presuppositions. The refusal of commitment and a stringent conception of literary activity furthered an analysis that had already borne fruit in its confrontation with the sacred texts of Italian populism. Some years later, in an essay dedicated to a great poet *and* great revolutionary, Vladimir Mayakovsky, I summarized the overall sense of my investigation as follows:

> Socialism was not necessary to the writing of good literature. Writers are not essential to bring about revolution. The class struggle—when it is class struggle, not populist struggle, peasant agitation, or aesthetic admiration for the virgin strength of the masses—travels a different path. It has other voices in which it expresses itself and by which it makes itself understood. And poetry cannot keep pace with it. That is because poetry, great poetry, speaks a language in which *things*— the hard things of daily struggle and effort—have already assumed the exclusive value of a symbol, of a gigantic metaphor for the world; and the often tragic price of its greatness is that what it says departs from praxis, never again to return to it.[6]

To this day, I wouldn't know what to add to or subtract from these words. The proof that this is not a case of backdating opinions arrived at subsequently lies in the fact that the conclusions of the two much-reviled chapters on

---

6 Alberto Asor Rosa, 'Rivoluzione e letteratura' [Revolution and Literature], *Contropiano* 1 (January–April 1968): 235–6. [Trans.]

Cassola and Pasolini, which conclude this volume, still appear to me to be completely correct, to the extent that they represent an affirmation of those authors' deepest and most authentic tendencies, against everything that they had thought and wanted to be, at least in certain periods of their lives (I would like these conclusions to be read or reread, with hindsight, before they are judged anew).

This was the source of the myth of my liking for conservative or reactionary authors. That is not the case: it is literature that, *in itself*, expresses a conservative view of the world insofar as it is the formalization of a discourse of an intellectual type *at the highest possible level*. Those who have used the gift of *inventive writing* to change things in the world have made an improper and inferior use of it. This does not mean that the writing of literature has not changed the world over the last two centuries; rather, literature has changed the world to the very extent that it had no desire to do so at all. It is also true, however, that this happened insofar as the authors—or, more precisely, that species which is on the path to extinction in our country, and whom for the sake of convenience we call 'bourgeois writers'—were capable of a high degree of formal and inventive sublimation; one must fly high if one wants to grasp everything as a whole (like Svevo, Kafka, Joyce, Proust—for example). Today instead, the writers—who only with great difficulty we could call bourgeois or non-bourgeois, an extremely significant sign in its own right—who are perhaps aiming to flee from a committed and instrumental view of literature, have generally become used to flying low; they too make up that cultural universe that has chosen to regulate itself according to the dictates of a philistine ethic. On the whole, the effect is negative. One might say that in the effort to become adult, literature has renounced the irreplaceable pleasures and character of youthfulness. Besides, and I say this without irony, this is something that happens to many, and even to non-writers. Until a degree of distance, that is to say, irony is achieved, a certain desire to enjoy oneself (to enjoy oneself even within the tragic), we will be confronted with an absence of realism (or, more simply, of verisimilitude) and a lack of fantasy: in other words, we will be flat, devoid of documentary or inventive qualities, neither credible nor implausible.

Finally, let us conclude. As I was gathering ideas to write this re-presentation, a passage abounding with wisdom of Hegel's (another author who had been extremely important to me) insistently came to mind:

A further word on the subject of *issuing instructions* on how the world ought to be: philosophy, at any rate, always comes too late to perform this function. As the *thought* of the world, it appears only at a time when actuality has gone through its formative process and attained its completed state. The lesson of the concept is necessarily also apparent from history, namely, that it is only when actuality has reached maturity that the ideal appears opposite the real and reconstructs this real world, which it has grasped in its substance, in the shape of an intellectual realm. When philosophy paints its grey in grey, a shape of life has grown old, and it cannot be rejuvenated, but only recognized, by the grey in grey of philosophy; the owl of Minerva begins its flight only with the onset of dusk.[7]

That is precisely what I think happened to us. We arrived once things had already happened; we were able to say (and perhaps still can) how things went, but we had no opportunity to push them one way or another. I have no doubt that Hegel, in writing those words, was thinking above all about himself: thought—to translate his image and return it to its abstract source—takes off from the real once the real is mature and no longer requires thought. Precisely for this reason, perhaps, precisely because we had at least recognized this, we saw things more clearly than others. The great flowering is a sign that the rose garden is dying. This has to do with the history of thought; but it also concerns the history of the world (to take up again Hegel's opposition); and it is much more true today than in Hegel's time.

Indeed, on closer inspection, Hegel's words describe the arc of that other great theme, the decline of the West. From time immemorial, in the West, every epochal 'passage' has taken the *form* of 'barbarians' prevailing and, at the same time, of a return to authentic 'feeling'. The 'barbarians', however, learnt from superior but weaker beings and, once they became civilized, and in turn themselves became civilizers, they too took the place of those who could be substituted, following an infinite spiral. It becomes clear that the decline of the West has always been the decline of a *determinate* phase of the formation of Western European civilization (Oswald Spengler, Julien Benda, José Ortega y Gasset); this meant that the transitions, even when they were gigantic and

---

7 G. W. F. Hegel, Preface to *Elements of the Philosophy of Right* (Allen W. Wood ed. and H. B. Nisbet trans.) (Cambridge: Cambridge University Press, 1991), p. 23. [Trans.]

dramatic, appeared as the expressions of a powerful physiological mechanism destined to sustain near-inexhaustible change.

That with which we measure civilization today is something completely different: it is the culture of the barbarians that is technologically superior, much sharper, astute, mobile, transformative and genetic than that of civilized individuals. At the same time, the value of the authenticity of feeling is decisively shunted into second place; or, more precisely, even feeling becomes the product of a technology, or handed over to solitary thinkers, those who perforce are on the side of the civilized elites, those elites who in some moments of history have learnt to 'think'. Culture, instead of just being a large brain which thinks for everyone, is pulverized into hundreds of millions of small brains that struggle to think for themselves.

Two paths are available. The first is the one indicated by the great interpreters of the twilight of the West: the indignant retirement of the scholar to the increasingly circumscribed solitude of his study. The other involves the resolute (that is, hasty) stepping into the open, imagining that a total freedom of invention is possible, which can be opposed to an equally totalizing programming of every cultural initiative: a practice of intellectual disordering raised to the level of a system and realized with both courage and method. We certainly feel no sympathy for the 'new barbarism', with its technological arrogance and its habits of power; but there is no way that we want this lack of sympathy to lead us back to the shores of the cultural tradition, in which we refused to partake twenty-five years ago. On the contrary, the 'new barbarian' seems to us preferable to the 'old scholar' *in any case*; even if he does not want to learn, he has the advantage over the other of not having yet learnt, and hence is able to learn (something different). In this way, if we cannot be dwarfs on the shoulders of giants, we will seek to be giants who hold dwarfs on our shoulders, the hundreds of millions of dwarfs of the current cultural universe. We should make clear that this programme does not and cannot have any notable practical outcome and does not develop according to a strategy defined by the desire to achieve determinate objectives because the latter could only be gradually defined as the programme succeeds in clarifying them. But there will be, at some point, a chink in the steel armour of the Technological Era through which will penetrate the ferment of critical thinking.

The protagonist of a story by Saul Bellow, an old Jewish American intellectual called Wulpy, argues—more or less—that where classes lose sight of their material interests, there is no real political struggle; and that where there is no real political struggle, all of life rots and society falls into neurosis. I am entirely in agreement. The situation in which we live is identical to that he describes with regard to the United States in the 1970s. This does not mean that we will go back to believing that politics is everything, as we did 25 years ago, when today it is almost nothing. Politics can even be a very tiny thing compared to the whole of existence. But that tiny thing must *lucidly* express the nature, contents and objectives of the interests at play. If it fails to do so, a horrible confusion arises and everything ends up being polluted and corrupted by it.

The wheel has turned and returned to the starting point—and there it has stopped for now. We can only attempt partial operations, closely supervised, carefully circumscribed and, if possible, civically laudable; alternatively, through our work we can recall the existence of a differently configured logical framework, although we cannot expect any kind of practical returns from it.

Even the concrete terrain of application of a topic such as that of *The Writer and the People*—literature—has crumbled in our hands. Were one to repeat the operation of this book on the literary production of the last 20 years, we could only smile. Lacking the sky with its fixed stars, now disappeared, we are left only with the Empyrean, the 'candid rose':[8] the 'oneself' that is the 'other' of whom one should speak today. We are more untimely today than twenty years ago. That no one has noticed is the resounding proof of just how true it is.

April 1988

---

8 Alternatively translated as the 'white rose', from Canto 31 of 'Paradise', in Dante's *The Divine Comedy*, symbolizing divine love. [Trans.]

Preface to the Second Edition[*]
(1966)

Typically, when one decides it is necessary to draft a preface to the second edition of a book, it is because one wishes to reply to critics and to clarify the fundamental points in one's argument. That is only a minimal part of the reason for doing so here. Truth be told, I cannot see any good coming from reflecting once again on the positions of progressive cultural anti-fascism. For this reason, the only serious, correct and honest decision is 'to speak of something else'. The relationship has broken down. We speak two different or, rather, opposed languages; further discussion seems pointless. It is true that anti-fascist progressivism still extends its influence over vast sectors of Italian public opinion and of the organized workers' movement. In that respect, we cannot declare the argument to be over; on the contrary, we need to furnish it with even sharper and more implacable evaluative instruments. Here the argument becomes immediately political; it no longer requires mediations or 'pretexts'. Today, it would be ridiculous to analyse a review by Carlo Salinari or a film by Luchino Visconti in order to maintain that the tendency of the communist current is towards social democracy. That period of 'immaturity', on which we have lingered too long, is over. For us, the liquidation of the cultural struggle has meant the immediate and total reassertion of the discourse of politics. The two aspects are tightly bound together. Anyone can demonstrate it. As soon as one escapes the illusion that one can overturn the system (or contribute to doing so) through the defence and affirmation of the progressive ideological *corpus*, in that very instant it becomes clear that the core of the problem lies elsewhere: essentially, in overcoming or inverting the

---

[*] Given the nature of this work no substantive modifications have been made to the text, the notes or the bibliography.

political direction of travel that has been dominant for twenty years. Everything else, we can say, is purely extraneous.

The Writer and the People, viewed in the light of these considerations, manifests real shortcomings. The book had its theme, of course, and we pursued it with meticulous honesty, so as not to open ourselves to accusations of being too casual . . . bibliographically speaking. But in pursuing the often poor and infantile paths to be found in our native populist literature, the book at times suffers from some of its constitutive limits; while being in full control of the material, we were not able to go beyond it, except in the sense, which I shall explain later, of setting out some directions for future study. For these reasons as well, *The Writer and the People* can be called an 'Italian' book: Italian, in the same way that the objects of its investigation were dismayingly Italian. Having said that—if we may be permitted to recall it here—in the specific and unsurpassable domain of the investigation, few Italian works have expressed such a level of contempt for the national culture, *precisely insofar as it presented itself and wanted to be a national culture.*

We intended to definitively close a chapter of our literary and politicocultural history. Perhaps we did. I do not think that one can reproach *The Writer and the People* with having copied the forms and intentions of a traditional ideological and cultural polemic. Nevertheless, we must recognize that the task of grinding down the populist position has involved some concessions to the old battle—in this case too, an inevitable adaptation to the matter at hand. For someone who considers it seriously dishonourable to be thought of as a 'progressive', this is no small thing. It would be worse still if some readers were under the impression that, because of some superficial and limited aspects of the argument, the book as a whole was fundamentally heading in that direction. We are not speaking of our adversaries but of our friends, our comrades, our benign appraisers; in other words, all those who agree with the need to liquidate the 'cultural heritage' of the left, *but only to substitute it with another*, which is not clearly identified but, they affirm, is ideologically more correct. We want to be entirely clear on this point: *The Writer and the People* diverges drastically and completely from that programme. It does not propose a new cultural heritage for the workers' movement and the working class; it limits itself to showing that there is an inescapable contradiction between the ideological pretences of intellectuals and the antagonistic needs of the working class. Of course, *The Writer and the People* does not exhaust what can be said even on this terrain. It examines one value specifically which embodies one of the many forms by which the mystification of the class struggle has been carried out by the progressive intellectual: precisely the value which is to be found in the mythical concept of the 'people'. Yet it should not be difficult to understand that the specificity of the investigation does not, in this case, exclude its generalizability; on the contrary, it underlies it as an essential aspect of the problem. It is not therefore a case of using criticism in its purely oppositional function which progressivism—*whatever its type*—unanimously assigns it. Nothing is more alien to us than so-called oppositional critique. We are trying to go well beyond it. At the very least we feel that we have reached the stage of needing to critique the very concepts of criticism, of literature, of culture. The maximal programme coincides with the contribution that this type of discourse, developed on the basis of such material of investigation, furnishes to the definition of an overall revolutionary strategy of the working class.

The limitations of *The Writer and the People* are, therefore, precisely the opposite of those suggested by the progressives. We have not gone too far. Our extremism still turned in a circumscribed domain. It needed to be on another scale in order to confront the decisive core of our concerns which had gradually formed through the patient work of investigation. Nevertheless, to be aware of this is already a step forward. Any advance in method is founded on observations of this sort. Today we know that in *The Writer and the People* there are only the beginnings of an investigation that aims to confront the concept and history of bourgeois culture.

Having grasped the essence of the limitations of *The Writer and the People*, it then becomes possible to understand what can be most usefully drawn from the book's conclusions. In particular we would like willing readers to recognize that if one fully assents to the liquidation of populism and progressivism, a number of false problems are set aside and, in the field thus delimited, the most serious and most advanced targets begin to stand out clearly before our eyes, as if by a natural optical effect. Through this operation, *which is not one of salvaging*, we gain access to the most important problems of intellectual work today. Once the undergrowth has been removed, we begin to glimpse the path leading to the heart of the problem.

Second, we must acknowledge that *The Writer and the People*—leaving aside the content and the aims of its investigation—is an early example of what it might mean to transform literary criticism into a critique of literature. This is a point that I have had opportunity to explain on more than one occasion, and which cannot be taken up here in its full complexity. It should, however, already be sufficiently clear that an argument such as the one found in this volume is, rightly speaking, meaningless if one approaches it from a traditional standpoint. I am not surprised that those who insisted on inserting this book into a disciplinary box failed to understand it. The spirit of this enterprise went in a different direction: the treatment of literary materials does not mean that the field within which the book operates is literary but, rather, on the contrary. In producing a particular kind of work, the task of the Marxist researcher will be that of linking both the object of study and the specific disciplinary instrument through which that object is studied to an analogous process of disaggregation. Ultimately, one will demand that, from the investigation of the cultural materials, there should emerge a result that lies entirely outside the world of culture; which is to say, a result that must be measured by the decisive yardstick of the class struggle. We care nothing for literary criticism itself. For this reason we have no intention of enriching it with new specific contents or new disciplinary standards. We are interested in penetrating into the soul and form of bourgeois art, for within it we find a profound coherence as well as an irremediable contradiction, the daunting dissimilarity from what belongs to us as revolutionary militants of the working class. That this world is split in two is not an invention of ours. To acknowledge this is not, as some say, an invitation to speak of it no more. Far from it. An enormous body of future research confronts those who have refused cultural complicity and consensus.

It is not possible to conclude with these elementary considerations. One soon realizes that a critique of literature in and for itself does not stand up, if it is not an integral part of a much richer and larger task. The argument we have developed can be repeated for all the disciplines. Needless to say, each has its *own* problem; but it also shares something in common with the others. If we turn towards the set of values—which we call 'Culture'—that cements them together, we can show that only an unconscious act of integration in the system maintains and justifies this relationship. The first step will involve revealing—outside this mystified and incoherent relationship—the *real* social and political function of the specific intellectual work we have performed. In a society such as this, only if one finds the courage to confront the questions that are paramount, at least in this field (*wherefore,* my literary criticism? my historiography? my sociology?), can one create the possibility (take note: *only* the possibility) of escaping integration, of mastering it—and even, in some cases, overturning it and using it positively.

But one must also take the reverse route. It is difficult to travel upwards from the singular disciplines to Culture, without asking oneself the decisive questions that interrogate the destination of each one of them. But it is harder still to continue justifying everything by appealing in blind faith, as though by an immediate act of communication, to the Value of values, namely, Culture. The idea that values authorize and sublimate techniques, furnishing them with a better connective fabric, is simply absurd. Therefore, if it is true that the ancient dream of intellectuals, of making reality conform to the world of ideas is not yet spent, it should at least be clear that this battle is lost and that *ideas now are made to conform with the world.* The values of spirit have become things and, as such, can be sold in the market. They are not yet quoted at the stock market but perhaps will be. Culture, transformed into a social institution, carries out its balancing function in a disciplined fashion. It guarantees order. *It is entirely within this society.*

Whoever places oneself outside this society, places oneself outside of culture. One must reaffirm that neither aboulia nor absence, nor anarchic refusal, follow from this statement; what follows instead is the most effective and *concretely destructive* of proposals. When we affirm the need for a critique of culture, we mean that the phenomenon of culture is an object enclosed within a civilization that is now over and that we, therefore, do not partake in it and are not complicit with it. It then becomes necessary to retrace *the entire* course of bourgeois cultural history, from the beginning to now, in order to confirm the non-ideological validity of our position. Precisely because culture stands before us as an object we do not share, we can and must liquidate it *from within*, without opposing the acts of faith to acts of faith, ideologies to ideologies, new mystifications to old mystifications. We must simply demonstrate that culture dies in-itself and ends up conforming to capitalist social reality, because it has *always* been, at the best of times, nothing but a—mad, desperate, at times moving—response of the bourgeois-intellectual stratum to the system's inexorable laws of development. We can even say: a mistaken or inadequate response. For it did not stem from the awareness that this is a society divided into classes. The universalism of culture tended precisely to negate or overcome this little fact. We must certainly acknowledge that the *particular* form of antagonism towards the system that belongs to much of bourgeois art and culture ensued from this sort of attitude. But this is now all water under the bridge: it is History. As such—as we have said—it must be carefully studied and reconstructed. But those who have discovered the political antagonism of the working class, cannot share in—not even from the perspective of a nostalgic return—the nature and ends of the response developed by bourgeois intellectuals. If anything, they might use the study of cultural materials in order to demonstrate this *as well*.

In this way it is possible to rediscover—but in a much more mature form—the intrinsic, profoundly political character of our position. Attention to the discourse of populism has served to unmask the ideologues of the Italian workers' movement: mystifiers by profession even when they are in good faith; infantile caricatures of the bourgeois intellectual. The general discussion on bourgeois culture will serve to reveal that not even at the highest levels is there a relationship between culture and the working class. *Tertium non datur*[1] between progressivism and bourgeois culture. So if we can call each of our acts 'political', which leads to the understanding of capitalist social reality and to the disassembly of one of its aspects (perhaps those that are made to inhere in ideologically mystified nature by the base and superstructure), that is the sense in which we consider our discourse about culture to be fundamentally political (in other words, not politico-ideological and politico-cultural). The formation of a widespread revolutionary demand will also pass through a radical demystification of the cultural illusion.

At this point, we need to be very precise. We said at the start that the liquidation of the cultural battle meant that we have fully attained the political discourse of class. We must add that we mean this *completely* and *literally*. One cannot carry out an analysis of culture in the new spirit of which we have spoken—*it would make no sense to do so*—if one is unable to carry to the very end the political work that the situation demands. We are not only referring to the plurality of levels that any serious movement must simultaneously bear in mind but also in a direct, even elementary way, to the physical coexistence

---

1 The law of excluded middle states that a proposition is either true or false, and that no third possibility is given:

> [T]here cannot be an intermediate between contradictories, but of one subject we must either affirm or deny any one predicate. This is clear, in the first place, if we define what the true and the false are. To say of what is that it is not, or of what is not that it is, is false, while to say, of what is that it is, and of what is not that it is not, is true; so that he who says of anything that it is, or that it is not, will say either what is true or what is false; but neither what is nor what is not is said to be or not to be (Book 4: 1011b, 23–30)—Aristotle, 'Metaphysics' in *The Complete Works of Aristotle*, VOL. 2 (J. Barnes ed.) (Oxford: Oxford University Press, 1984), p. 1597. [Trans.]

of the two levels within the person of our comrade researchers. We too should not entertain delusions, perhaps ones forged after our own fashion. The entire demystifying discourse on culture can once again become a final, disenchanted discourse of a cultural character, if those who articulate it do not base it on the reality of things that cannot be reabsorbed or integrated. Never has Marx's pronouncement that the arms of criticism cannot replace the criticism of arms been truer than today. It should never be forgotten, especially by those who share our stance. We start from the principle that the aim is to oppose to the objectivized world of capitalist society, to the potent concretion and stratification of things on which our reality is built, an organized material-force able to uproot and overturn the system's laws of operation. If this is the aim, fundamental decisions follow from it and the investigation into the cultural object can find within it its proper weight *and its limits*. In light of this we can point to a first, summary conclusion. We struggle so that from the darkness of a difficult situation a new generation of revolutionary leaders and militants may emerge from the working class. The immensity of the task encourages us to try everything to push this process forward. And yet ever-present in the midst of the variety of initiatives and debates is this ultimate end of our efforts. We are fully aware that it will *all* be meaningful only once the working class wins back its own political organization for struggle. So no one will be surprised that our efforts, *from whatever position they begin*, result in this single, fundamental demand. It is on this terrain that we will verify whether our words correspond in any way to reality or not. We should make this very clear: our vocation is not a prophetic one, our future interests us insofar as *we* are able to create it in the present, we prefer to risk all our honour in the most humble and circumscribed labour than entrust ourselves to the judgement of posterity. When we speak of the political organization of the working class, we speak of it in the most literal and immediate terms, namely, as a task that is realized today by patient, difficult everyday work. It's down to us, us only to combine the audacity and—if you like—the conscious abstraction of theoretical and historical language with the methodical implacability and concreteness of the task of organization. On this dual basis, there is still serious work to be done.

April 1966

Introduction

This is a rear-guard action: populism is dead and we shall explain why. But it is not useless to draw up the balance sheet and bring the business to a close. The Italian habit of venerating the past and treating national myths with reverence remains the principal cause of that climate of cautious equivocation in which we often find ourselves working and debating. To the decisive break one ends up preferring silence, to the critical reappraisal an implicit refusal that more often than not hides the confusion of convictions and intentions. Through silence and carelessness the detritus of our culture accumulates and upon its sediments one builds a new accommodation with reality. The spirit of reformism acts in the same way within literature and culture. For reformism History is a series of steps, each of which is necessary and inescapable; the present is nothing but the latest step of the past; the future, only the cautious anticipation of the present. Within this set of ideas the discovery is yet to be made that—even within literature—one can make a revolutionary leap over a number of stages or steps of this apparently unified process. If one rejects this presupposition, the laws of continuity always end up prevailing over the demands for renewal, however honest and 'committed' the latter may be; and when continuity is affirmed as the basic character of a literary and cultural experience, there is no progressive moralism that is able to hold its own. Once again the philosophy of History, in whichever of its forms, is the hidden spring of all enquiry.

From this point of view, our investigation into Italian populism can also be read as the critique of a particular manifestation of the concept of tradition. Indeed, our thesis is that there is no populist ideology without a culture of values that have their roots buried deep in the historical past of a country or a nation. The qualification 'native', which the phenomenon of populism counts as one of its fundamental characteristics, necessarily carries with it an extremely powerful conservative charge. Among the reactionary and nationalist populists, this appears to be the logical consequence of a more general political and ideological attitude. But we intend to show how this presents itself as equally logical for democratic and progressive populists—they too are all faithfully gathered around the inescapable principle of the 'national tradition'.

This book does not, therefore, analyse those writers and those literary genres that can be strictly called 'popular', and which tend to put themselves at the expressive and communicative level of the people. When it comes to that sort of material, it is only possible to carry out a contextual, folkloric or sociological analysis. Instead, we have focused our attention on the literary level, where the demand of a relationship with the people becomes an *ideological choice* and involves a precise and conscious idea of the tasks entrusted to the writer within the framework of a national ruling class. It seems to us that the definition and critique of various populist ideologies would enable us to grasp some characteristics and behaviours that are typical of the Italian intellectual *in relation to his social commitment*, which would in turn shed light on the nature of certain purely literary, stylistic and linguistic decisions. In multiple ways, the questions of 'progressivism' and of 'commitment' will appear tightly linked to populism as different faces of the same political and cultural attitude.

For these reasons, and because this does not aspire to be an exhaustive history of Italian populism, many singular figures, even important ones, have been left out. Our aim will have been fulfilled if all the principal tendencies of the populist phenomenon in Italy are contemplated and analysed in such a way as to furnish a complete picture of the possible variants within the fundamental and permanent conception of 'popular positivity'.

A need for *pure* historical reconstruction was thus very far from our intentions. On the contrary, we wanted to undertake a task whose practical utility is truly contemporary, even if only in the negative sense to which we have alluded: to determine a 'fixed point' and to clarify some thorny ambiguities. The argument was devised in its various parts so as to 'precipitate' in its entirety towards its final consequences, that is, towards the literature of anti-fascism, of the Resistance and of Gramscianism. The antecedent parts are in many ways anticipations and preparations for this final development which, moreover, comprises the most ambitious and organic moments of Italian populism. In our treatment of the writers and tendencies of the 1800s, we simply wished to provide a broad account of the ways in which populism in

Italy, as in other European countries, begins to affirm itself and elaborate its earliest, foundational ideologies; and to do so in a way that allows the non-specialist reader to understand the infinite number of relationships within this field that link the 1800s to the 1900s. To do so in the course of an internal tradition which reveals itself to be more than a merely useful abstraction but, instead, is a historical and cultural reality that is taken up and put into practice countless times.

Because the entire development of the argument tended to demonstrate, with reference to the facts, the provincial and conservative limits of the populist experience in Italy, it seemed opportune to end the book with a detailed analysis of two authors in whom the obvious crisis of anti-fascist progressivism most crudely sheds light on the contradictory, ambiguous, vague, fanciful and reactionary aspects that are *innate* to the populist position. The studies of Carlo Cassola and Pier Paolo Pasolini are 'exercises' through which we have wanted to demonstrate that our conclusions do not change, even when we apply the most specific and subtle instruments of literary criticism. Indeed, we wanted to use a certain wealth of analytical methods only in order to convince the reader that the 'question of method' is also one of those false ideological problems that our literary criticism has frequently mixed itself up with so as to hide a substantive uncertainty of outlook behind a position of principle. It seems to us today to make no difference whether we use the stylistic, the sociological, the historical or the so-called genetic-ideological method. In the game which, at this level, literary criticism represents, the one is equivalent to the other; indeed, it might be fun to use each in turn, one after the other.

Despite the fact that our analysis, especially in the first part, has as its fixed and fundamental object a series of ideological positions—we do not in any way feel we have provided yet another example of ideology critique. We have not in fact opposed a different type of ideology to the ideologies of populism. It will be apparent that the Marxism to which we refer does not imply as its necessary, logical consequence a world-view that can be imposed upon literature or on poetry. Our discourse is political, and fundamentally *political* is the sense of our *literary* argument. We do not know if the result matches our intentions, but we certainly forced ourselves to apply to an extremely important aspect of the nineteenth- and twentieth-century Italian literature that *partisan workers' critique*, which constitutes the ultimate aim of our investigation. We would not think it strictly necessary to make this point, which is always evident in the unfolding of the argument, if we were not aware that such observations would be made by many, whether in good or bad faith. Nonetheless, we are happy to clarify: we do not propose a 'workers' literature' as an alternative to bourgeois populist literature. This means that the theoretical reference to the working class serves in such matters, above all, to reveal the mystified nature of *all* these progressive bourgeois ideologies and to shed light on the substantial conformity or convergence of their perspectives (beyond contingent and superficial polemics).

Only through such a reference does the *constitutionally* petty-bourgeois character of Italian populism become as glaring as the light of the sun and only thus can it be completely and definitively condemned. Once this has taken place, we can confirm that the *political* conduct of the analysis does not exclude but instead facilitates and enormously clarifies the role played by populism *as a literary phenomenon* in the Italian literature of the last century. The conclusions of the investigation will probably surprise those who expect from such a standpoint fitting evidence of a crude workerism.

A final observation. The type of analysis that we engaged in naturally inclined us to develop a critical discourse where the singular personalities of writers ended up being diluted or stifled within the tableau of tendencies and movements. We have tried to resist this temptation. A scale of values is present in the book, relative (perhaps) to the capacity of each writer to express a more or less rigorous and profoundly populist position. It was right to do this, certainly not so that abstract aesthetic canons could be respected, but because only by identifying more effective singular contributions could one delineate a complex—rather than schematic—dynamic of actions and reactions, influences and developments. In this sense too, we do not use the term populism as the abstract object of our ideological fury but, rather, as the concrete and living expression of a political and literary myth, incarnated in figures, works, events.

PART I

Populism and Contemporary Italian Literature

Have you ever wondered why Italy has not had, in its whole history—from Rome to today—a single real revolution? The answer—the key that opens many doors—is perhaps the history of Italy in just a few lines.

Italians are not parricidal; they are fratricidal [. . .]. Italians are the only people (I think) who have, at the basis of their history (or of their legend), a fratricide.

And it is only with a parricide (the killing of the old) that a revolution begins . . .

Umberto Saba, *Scorciatoie*

The Beginnings
From Vincenzo Gioberti to Alfredo Oriani[*]

1

The use of the term populism is legitimate in literary discourse only when there is a *positive* evaluation of the people from the ideological, sociohistorical or ethical perspective. *In other words, for there to be populism, it is necessary that the people be presented as a model.* This is the reason why a poet such as Giuseppe Gioachino Belli[1] cannot, to my mind, be defined as a populist. For in his writings it never happens, not even as an aside, not for a fleeting moment, that 'the people' is, I will not say idealized but, at least, made the object of a progressive ideology. Between the poet and the material of his verse there is always a firm separation, or, better still, a marmoreal relationship of knowledge or representation. Affection, in the extremely rare moments when it shows itself, is never closeness—it is at most a mere liking: a non-programmatic sentiment that does not partake of an ideal outlook but ends on the purely human level. Remember Belli's theory of the 'monument'? 'Neither chaste nor even pious, but devoted and superstitious—thus appears the matter and the form. But the people are this, and this I reproduce: not so as to propose a model but to provide a faithful image of a thing already in existence and, moreover, one which has been abandoned without improvement . . . '. The fact is that Belli is a romantic realist for whom the preoccupations with the true noticeably prevail over those with the possible; whereas, as we shall see, in populist writers a large part of the inspiration is

---

* Vincenzo Gioberti (1801–52), Italian philosopher and politician. Influenced by Giuseppe Mazzini, he was committed to Italian unity and independence from foreign yoke, including freeing Italy from 'foreign' intellectual influences. Alfredo Oriani (1852–1909), Italian historian and writer. The Fascists claimed his works as precursors; they were published in 30 volumes edited by Benito Mussolini. [Trans.]

1 Giuseppe Gioachino Belli (1791–1863), Italian poet; particularly remembered for his popular sonnets in Roman dialect. [Trans.]

always occupied by the dream of what is not and might come to be, which is opposed to the motif—often secondary or, at least, represented in a second moment—of that which is and that which cannot be changed. One can make analogous observations about the Italian *veristi*[2] of the late 1800s, or, at least, about their earliest work. In Giovanni Verga, as in Belli, there is more truth than liking; for him too the cult of the real is more essential than the admiration for the people themselves.

For other writers, populism can be reduced to the celebration of a decadent myth, and thereby turned into an exclusively literary attitude whose cultural and ideological dimensions can, through a more careful analysis, be shown to be poor and limited. This is true, for example, of Gabriele d'Annunzio who, in *Novelle della Pescara*, despite escaping the severe strictures of Italian *verismo*, finds a positive value in the barbarism and ferality of the peasants and fishermen of Abruzzo. Likewise, all those who in the 1800s came to the people through the aestheticizing search for virginal sensuality and the celebration of the sensible. For these authors, populism remains circumscribed within a well-defined milieu, as a component of a fundamentally literary predisposition to life and human contact. When the ambitions are more extensive and the cultural 'frame' within which the populist element is located is widely influenced and directed by the decision to conceive the people positively, then the discussion cannot be simply literary but is necessarily historical and cultural, historical and political, or political *tout court*.

We will soon establish that populism, as a tendency, generally manifests itself among those writers and intellectual currents who work within the horizon of national literature and pose themselves the problem—from one standpoint or another—of political and ideological hegemony. The two terms, the people and the nation, reveal their reciprocal and indissoluble dependence, even when the reference to the people, to its presence and its prerogatives, takes on the character of a decisive social protest. Not wishing to sketch out, even in broad brushstrokes, the problem of populism in Europe, it seems

---

2 Representatives of *verismo*, a current in late-nineteenth- and early-twentieth-century Italian literature characterized, thematically, by a rigorous reflection on everyday life and situations (privileging local milieus and lives of the petty-bourgeoisie and popular classes). Linguistically and stylistically, it sought to reflect their ways of speaking and their environments. Among the principal figures of *verismo* are Giovanni Verga (1840–1922), Luigi Capuano (1839–1915) and Federico De Roberto (1861–1927). The term was then extended to painters and even composers of lyric operas that took for their subject-matter peasant and working-class life. [Trans.]

unquestionable that the birth of populist literature coincides with the birth or the rebirth of the nation, or, even more frequently, with the attempts to give birth or rebirth to it, to provide it with a new social content that would be more advanced and progressive. The objective need to organize a national culture within the political and social structures of a new or renewed nationality leads certain bourgeois strata—which do not always coincide with the groups that effectively rule the political and economic life of the country—to coalesce their ideological, literary and political interests towards the great popular masses. The different results that follow from this are strictly linked to the diverse factors from whence this relationship originates and by which it is determined: the greater or lesser presence of popular masses and peasants; the maturity of the ideological horizon of the dominant bourgeois stratum; the nature of the contrasts existing within the relationship between the groups from heterogeneous social and cultural formations; the capacity to develop literary solutions other than populist ones; etc. Yet some characteristics remain the same, particularly in the 1800s, partly because the various national populist experiences communicate and enter into exchanges to an extraordinary degree.

On the basis of the preceding arguments, no one will be surprised if we note that the great homeland of populism, in the purist's sense of the term, is Russia. On the one hand, we have a hundred million peasants whose silent presence has for centuries pressed upon the threshold of a History which has obstinately refused to consider or admit them; on the other, an extremely lively intellectual stratum unable to become a ruling *political* class and therefore throwing all its progressive energies into the organization, or, even more frequently, into the mythologization of the Russian peasant order—the historical and, at the same time, ideal form of a great Nation that bears *within it*, like the fertile seed under a blanket of snow, the principle of universal justice, of a non-materialist socialism that is as valid for spirits as it is for social conditions.

The vast amount of literature—often of an exceptionally high quality—that springs from these profound humanitarian aspirations as well as gives life and expression to them constitutes a formidable conduit for the peasant thematic across Europe. But no less important is the preaching of the theorists and the agitators, from Alexander Herzen to Mikhail Bakunin. It is worth recalling the influence, of the latter on the Italian literary milieu at the end of the nineteenth century. Even Carducci[3] would be affected by him.

---

3 Giosuè Carducci (1835–1907), poet and teacher; generally considered Italy's national poet and the first Italian to receive the Nobel Prize in literature. Explored the linguistic

France too gives its democratic, egalitarian, anarchic and, in some cases, socialist soul to European populism. The years 1815–60 are a veritable gold-mine of theories of the people. The inheritance of the Revolution, with its Jacobin and Montagnard spirit, is adopted by innumerable writers who—even prior to any classist vision of society—attempt to give an answer to the ills of capitalist development, to political oppression, to unemployment, to the hunger and increasing brutishness of existence. Some authors and works stand above the rest: Claude Henri de Saint-Simon's *Le Nouveau Christianisme* (1825); Jules Michelet's *Le peuple* (1846); Pierre-Joseph Proudhon's *Qu'est-ce que la propriété?* (1840) and *La philosophie de la misère* (1846). But although those are the true great fathers of French populism, Louis Blanc, Joseph Fourier, Hugues Felicité Robert de Lamennais, all provide numerous insights and footholds for investigations of a populist character. The tableau is obviously incredibly varied. The Saint-Simonian aspiration towards a fraternal organization of humanity—a motif that even made its way into Giacomo Leopardi's[4] 'La Ginestra' [The Broom]—is certainly not the same as Michelet's democratic programme which aimed to reconcile the popular and ruling classes in the sublime ideal of motherland, nation and progress; and this in turn does not coincide with the petty-bourgeois *ressentiment* that Proudhon expresses against the structures of a centralized State and the inexorable laws of massive capitalist economic development; nor is Fourier's utopianism the same as the strong moral and religious impetus to be found in the Christian-democratic appeal of Lamennais. But the spectrum of influences that stem from this group of thinkers and their direct political activity ends up falling on the national and foreign followers as an ensemble that is, if not homogeneous, at least indivisible. In Giuseppe Mazzini's *I doveri dell'uomo* [Man's Duties], one can find Saint-Simon, Lamennais and Proudhon. One can truly find a common element in these thinkers who, in every sense, come before Marx: there is an often profound, sincere and morally intense aversion towards some of the serious ills of contemporary society, despite the inability—due to

---

resources of Italian, revitalizing some of the less explored areas of the classical tradition, and interweaving them with the vernacular. [Trans.]

4 Giacomo Leopardi (1798–1937), Italian poet, essayist and writer whose works are known for their focus on the inescapability of human suffering; what elsewhere Asor Rosa has called his 'metaphysical synthesis of universal and personal pain [. . .] as a fundamental condition of human existence'. See Alberto Asor Rosa, *Sintesi di storia della letteratura italiana* (Florence: La Nuova Italia, 1986), p. 342. [Trans.]

analytical failings—to discover the structural roots of injustice and exploitation. Hence there is a failure to identify the working class as the force that can subvert this corrupt world and a related turn to the people as a tool of correction, improvement or education, *internal* to a given set of socioeconomic relations. Their maximal programme can be summarized with the following formula: against big capital (hence often also against the big bourgeoisie), in the name of the people, against *every autonomous* organization of the working class.

We will see that this attitude—like, in general, all aspects of the democratic and socially engaged culture of French origin—was widely disseminated throughout Italy.

Speaking of France, we cannot fail to mention the person or the works of Victor Hugo. *Toilers of the Sea* (1866) and, above all, *Les Misérables* (1862) convert into easily accessible (if overly ornate) novelistic form the bourgeois sentiment of indignation and disapproval for the egotism of the well-to-do classes and the sufferings of the popular ones. Without paying too much attention to the psychological depth of his characters, but taking particular care to create effects of humanitarian emotion, Hugo was able to produce unrivalled models of grandiose and striking populist rhetoric. Entire generations of both intellectuals and lay readers found Jean Valjean—rather than Platon Karataev— the ideal type for their vague yet fervid protest against social ills, the most outstanding example of a virtue that grows from below and even bases material well-being on the observance of certain essential moral laws. With these works, Hugo showed that this kind of populism did not shrink from an ethical and spiritual attitude founded on excessively rhetorical expedients, sentimental intrigues or sensational developments and twists. Aiming at an audience for this theme that would also include mediocre or uncultured readers, these were all extremely positive devices, thanks to the spontaneous encounter between petty-bourgeois and popular taste, to which we shall often have occasion to return. With *Les Châtiments* (1853), moreover, Hugo imposed across Europe a sort of rhetorical-civic poetry that uses the 'appeal to the people' as an essential instrument for a programme of democratic restoration against the tyranny of bureaucrats, high functionaries, extortionists, speculators, 'little men' of every stripe and status and so on. Carried by his voice, the bombastic spirit of Progress, *calme et fort, et toujours innocent* [calm and strong and always innocent], spread everywhere, and was met with the universal consent of those who—in the midst of the nineteenth century—still saw the world through the eternal struggle between the principles of Good and Evil, Liberty and Oppression. From his time onward, and long thereafter, *l'Art et le Peuple* would remain linked by the same chain of literary progressivism, swollen with words and endowed with a petty-bourgeois soul.

2

The phenomenon of populism was alive in Italy as well, although it did not reach the artistic and literary opulence of its Russian form, nor enjoy the ideal and political organicism of the French. The problem of the national revolution, which other nations had resolved in earlier times along more advanced and modern paths, also arose in Italy on more than one occasion. It is not by chance that, to use phrases dear to Italian critics on the Left, the 'first' and the 'second' *Risorgimento* are tied to phases of populist literary excitement. Neither should one underestimate the other element, the presence of an extremely pressing peasant question, not only in the Italian South but also to a certain extent across the country; so that, from the middle of the nineteenth century, it was possible for the most astute intellectuals to note that the consolidation of political unity could only come about through a radical reform of social relations in the countryside which would ally to the national impulse the faith and participation of enormous popular (peasant) masses—by and large indifferent or averse to it. We will not discuss this thesis which, beginning with the democrats of the nineteenth century, would then be transmitted to Gramsci's thought, and which is denied today by those who see in the sacrifice of the peasant problem the inevitable price paid for the need to industrialize the country.[5] It is, however, true that, through the nineteenth century, we can

---

5 See Rosario Romeo, *Risorgimento e capitalismo*, 2nd EDN (Bari: Laterza, 1962). In this selection of articles dating back to 1956–58, this historian aims to demonstrate 'the illegitimacy of the assumption of French historical development as an "exemplary" model of the development of a modern bourgeoisie and the capitalist state' (p. 44). Above all, he makes convincing arguments against the general view of the Risorgimento developed by Gramsci in which 'the agrarian revolution presented itself as a great instance resolving the profound contrasts of the history of the country; a powerful instrument unifying Italian society that would have created a deeper relationship between the State and the "national-popular" forces of culture and society' (p. 45). 'Such a revolution could not come about, in the nineteenth century, as a force standing against the expansion of modern capitalist relations, but only insofar as it would be able to advance them and, in a way, to identify with them (and certainly not by turning Italy into a country of peasants and artisans conforming to the ideals of petty bourgeois ideology of the early 1800s)' (p. 44). There are also some interesting hints for a critique of Gramsci in the first part of the brief article,

glimpse behind the work of writers and politicians the pressure of a subaltern social mass, more often than not undifferentiated and generic, which expresses itself in ideological forms that are diverse yet characterized by a common fact: they all revolve around the need to give a *bourgeois* (national) response to the problem of the historical presence and role of the political, social and cultural functions of the *people*. That this labour, despite being intense and continuous, did not give rise to a declaredly populist current can perhaps be explained by the characteristics of the Italian intellectual stratum over the course of the last two centuries of its history. The backwardness of Italian historical and social development does not permit that slow formation of a great bourgeoisie upon which, in the rest of Europe, the fate and fortune of a powerfully innovative and, at times, subversive modern culture is founded. In these conditions, the weight of the past shows itself to be heavier and more oppressive in Italy than elsewhere. In the absence of a rich, organic vitality of both culture and society, the phenomena of encrusted traditionalism and narrow provincialism continue to occupy a central position in the dialectic of Italian intellectual life; and our literature, caught between its age-old conservative vocation and its often weak and uncertain ambition for renewal, ends up oscillating between two possible extremes: an attachment to a closed spirit of *academic-aristocratic* origin, and the petulant, fastidious ostentation of *petty-bourgeois taste* and *morality*. Transported onto the populist terrain, these two attitudes have opposite effects, although they often appear within the same author or poet. One can probably attribute the responsibility for the condescending paternalism of which one finds so much in Italian populism to the aristocratic tradition in our literature, decanted into the new literary forms issuing from Romanticism. We owe instead the inability to free popular representation from the narrow confines of those chance occasions that had historically determined or suggested it to the widespread, indeed, prevailing petty-bourgeois climate of our culture in the period of the formation of Italian Unity, and which persisted in the fol- lowing decades, until today. In the first case, it is the excessive separation—in a properly spiritual and cultural sense—of the writer from the people that determines the ideologically artificial and voluntarist nature of the relationship established between them. In the second, it is the excessive 'contiguity' of

---

'Alcune ipotesi di ricerca marxista sulla storia contemporanea' by Umberto Caldogelli and Gaspare De Caro (in *Quaderni rossi* 3: 102–08), who attempt to bring to bear, for the first time on the historiographical plane, the *full* force of the analysis of the development of the working class within the development of the structures of capitalism, rather than on the methodological and political principle of the democratic 'national revolution'.

points of view and ways of life that reveals the weakness and limitation of the ideological position. This second possibility is not only the most widespread but also the most interesting, because it is perhaps within it that one must seek the most spontaneous and 'original' character of our populism. For when one is petty bourgeois—animated by guilt complexes as well as irritation towards one's class, which turns into the unsatisfied but indestructible aspiration to win a secure place among the ruling classes—the objective commonality of life with the people, the dense interweaving of one's respective social origins do not allow but, rather, stand in the way of a full identification of the intellectual with the people—a people he feels are too close to himself, in terms of the pettiness and wretchedness of everyday life, to be turned into *tout court* the *ideal* expression and image of a better world to come. In these cases, the ideal image of the people that the writer is able to compose is at most nothing but the projection of that complex of spiritual and moral values through which the petty bourgeois seeks to both distinguish himself from the bourgeoisie and draw ever-closer to it.[6] The most surprising cases of 'Italian populism' are those in which aristocratic cultural mentality and petty-bourgeois ethical spirit fuse and superimpose themselves in the same organism. To study Carducci from

---

6 The situation described here is certainly not only Italian. Writing on Proudhon, Marx gave this pointed and conclusive definition of the petty bourgeoisie:

> In an advanced society and because of his situation, a *petty bourgeois* becomes a socialist on the one hand, and economist on the other, that is, he is dazzled by the magnificence of the upper middle classes and feels compassion for the sufferings of the people. He is at one and the same time bourgeois and man of the people. In his heart of hearts, he prides himself on his impartiality, on having found the correct balance, allegedly distinct from the happy medium. A petty bourgeois of this kind deifies *contradiction,* for contradiction is the very basis of his being. He is nothing but social contradiction in action.—'Letter to Annenkov' (28 December 1846), in Karl Marx and Friedrich Engels, *Collected Works,* VOL. 38 (London: Lawrence & Wishart, 1982), p. 105.

Nevertheless, in Italy, the petty bourgeoisie is able to be, if possible, more mediocre and limited than its European (or, more correctly, French) model. At the same time, its influence on literature and on culture is wider, more tenacious and *enduring* than is the case in other western European nations from the middle of the nineteenth century *till today*. It is no coincidence that only in Italy, after the anti-fascist and anti-German resistance, was there an extremely widespread, diffuse democratic and progressivist revival, which testifies in this case as well to the *delay* with which experiences of every type (political, social and cultural) have manifested themselves compared to analogous foreign phenomena. It is evident that, alongside reasons of a historical and social form, specifically cultural reasons intervene to determine this attachment to a circumscribed and provincial 'indigenous' tradition.

this standpoint is to discover the way in which, in Italy, the concept of 'the people' was to remain closed within the confines of an old culture, even in the democratic camp. The bond within this poetry between Jacobin content and 'stylistic paternalism' is not so much contradictory *in itself* as it is coherent with a current that runs through Vincenzo Monti[7] and Giovanni Berchet,[8] before reaching Carducci and his followers. Within this framework, populism clearly loses much of its hypothetical value of protest and demand.

Despite the absence of a declared and ideologically coherent populism, if one were to look over the many testimonies of populist convictions in nineteenth-century Italian literature, one might well be surprised. While populism can be a vague philo-popular humanitarianism, which in turn descends from the now-clear consciousness of social differentiations, its origins must be sought in the Enlightenment. The first figures of commoners [*popolani*] that poetry embraced, not so as to turn them into material for folkloric or atmospheric depictions but to use them as positive terms of comparison in a social polemic, are the 'good yokel' and the 'smith' from the 'sounding forge' of Giuseppe Parini's *Mattino* [from his poem 'Giorno'].[9] These are still generic and moralistic (almost mythical) examples of frugality, hard work and meekness. Only the Romantics, following the example of comparable European theories, were able to frame a discourse on the people in a meaningful and explicit way. Brechet identified the people as the principal force of a modern and national literature; looked at more carefully, however, his concept of the people was at once too broad and too narrow: it implied a still-generic notion of 'modern culture' and referred to a sociological area that was anything but broad. For him, the people 'include all the other individuals who read or listen, not excepting those who, having studied and experienced as much as the others, nevertheless have a sentimental disposition'.[10] In other words, all the moderately cultured men; all those who one way or another had an experience of literature; concretely, the mass of the bourgeoisie who were well

---

7 Vincenzo Monti (1754–1828), Italian poet and dramatist. An exponent of Italian Neoclassicism, he is remembered for his translation of the *Iliad*. [Trans.]

8 Giovanni Berchet (1783–1851), Italian writer and poet, and a great champion of Romantic nationalism. [Trans.]

9 Giuseppe Parini (1729–1799), Italian poet and satirist. English quotations are from *The Day* (H.M. Bower trans.) (London: Routledge 1927), p. 34. [Trans.]

10 Giovanni Berchet, *Opere, Volume 2: Scritti critici e letterari* (E. Bellorini ed.) (Bari: Laterza, 1912), p. 17.

disposed towards literary innovation and reluctant to absorb the somewhat abstract refinement of quasi-classical style or traditionalist art. Berchet contrasts with this image of the 'substantial people' [*popolo grasso*][11] a lively and contemptuous description of the 'lower people' [*popolo basso*], to which he denies all possibility of being either the subject or object of literature.

> The dumb Hottentot, lying on the threshold of his hut, looks at the fields of sand that surround him and falls asleep [. . .] Perpetually enveloped in the smoke of his hovel and the fetid odour of his goats, there are no other objects that his memory can draw upon to depict, for which his heart beats with desire. The inertia of the fantasy and his heart is of necessity matched by that of his poetic tendency.[12]

Undoubtedly, throughout the Risorgimento, the concept of the 'people' oscillates between two poles, one of which Berchet describes here. The 'people' can mean either the national-bourgeoisie or the subaltern classes. It may even signify both at once for those writers who set themselves the task of uniting them into a single progressive organism as the motor of the national revolution. Even more often, the concept remains undefined or is used on the basis of an ideological convention that is deemed to be generally shared but which in reality vacillates according to circumstances or convenience. It would be useful, for example, to investigate the validity and extension of the term 'people' in the majority of writers and theorists of the Romantic period. One would be able to establish that the concept has, within it, a more precise political meaning but a less clear sociological one: it can be used in a polemical ideological manner, but it would be difficult to see it with reference to a *specific* social condition. These are the cases where the concept of the 'people' is *entirely* identified without remainder with that of 'Nation', and only makes sense in reference to it.

---

11 Literally 'fat people', but I use here the translation of this term in John Adams' *A Defence of the Constitutions of the Government of the United States of America* (1794). [Trans.]

12 Berchet, *Opere, Volume 2*, p. 15. It is interesting to bear in mind that Berchet places at the other end of cultural development the 'class of Parisians', that is, the refined aesthetes which he not only accuses of losing themselves in vacuous pleasures devoid of a healthy, modern popular spirit but also, drawing upon the judgements of foreign, principally French circles, of 'losing *all national character*'. Even though he makes reference to non-Italian models (the ballads of [Gottfried August] Bürger, for example), it would seem that his attitude is generally anti-cosmopolitical (and so in harmony with the most important expressions of romantic Italian populism—as we shall see when we look at Gioberti).

A slightly different point can be made with regard to Gioberti and Mazzini—they already perceive the real scale of the problem and, despite their too-great emphasis on national unity as a political priority, they feel that this cannot be changed or resolved without broad and active popular consent. This is not the place for a general discussion of their teachings. Rather, we wish to foreground those aspects of their thought that contributed, among later writers and into the twentieth century, to founding or strengthening the typical traits of Italian populism.

First, we must signal the spirit that animates Gioberti's conception of the *Moral and Civil Primacy of the Italians* (1843). The necessity of elaborating a programme able to coalesce the as-yet-disaggregated and shapeless forces around a fundamentally united drive pushes him to accentuate the element of ideal and cultural commonality already present in the furrow of a centuries-old national tradition. His discussion begins not from an objective evaluation of contemporary reality but from a rhapsodic re-evocation of a glorious past. The cultural and ideological reasons precede, in some sense, the political ones: *Primacy* comes before *The Civil Renewal of Italy* (1851). The concrete objective is to gather *all* possible forces within this attempt at 'Italian renewal'; the instrument used to achieve it is the *full* retrieval of the Guelph inheritance in which, according to Gioberti, consists the direction and meaning of Italian superiority over all other European peoples.[13]

Even if we neglect to explore further the extremely vigorous nationalist thrust of this position, we are struck by this aspect: that at the origin of our Risorgimento is a burning assertion of the positivity of all of Italy's history. *From the start of the process of unification, the concept of tradition is considered inseparable from that of renewal.* Gioberti finds words to express this opinion

---

13 According to Gioberti, Italy is 'the autonomous and eminent nation par excellence, because it gave to all cultured nations of the modern era the seeds of their civilization and, despite its decline, it contains these seeds alive and uncorrupted, whereas they are generally spoilt and altered among all other peoples. Hence it is only from her [Italy] that the human species can achieve the benefits of civilization. This means that Italy, as creator, conservator and saviour of European civilization, destined to occupy the entire world and to become universal, can be with merit greeted with the title of mother nation of human kind'—*Del primato morale e civile degli italiani* (Turin: UTET, 1920), pp. 41–2. It goes without saying that every nationalism involves a claim to primacy. It should be sufficient to recall Chapters 5 and 6 of Jules Michelet's *Le Peuple*, to which we owe the pompous affirmation *l'histoire de la France* is *celle de l'humanité* (*Le Peuple*, Paris, 1877, 5th EDN, p. 276).

that will remain true for all those positions which, despite changing ideological forms, will posit the prudent respect for the conditions *given* by the preceding historical development of the country as a precondition of all processes of transformation: 'a political doctrine that fails to graft itself on the customs, institutions, thought and traditions of a people will never be able to bring about lasting improvements in the people's destiny'.[14]

On the political plane, this means that national progress can only come about through the collaboration of all social strata with the fundamental political organisms. In *Primato*, where prophecy still takes priority over political forecasting, this conviction is concretized in an ideal embrace that encompasses the principal protagonists of the social and cultural life of the country, without excluding anyone. In 'Augurio all'Italia futura', which concludes the work, there is room for everyone: for governors and clerics, princes and writers, 'lovers of the mechanical arts' and 'men dedicated to industries and commerce'. In *Rinnovamento*, which followed the events and disappointments of 1848–49, the picture becomes clearer while retaining its original characteristics. In this new milieu, even the Giobertian view of democracy shows its face more plainly, revealing itself to be a seriously and intelligently paternalist reformism:

> A civic principality demands the friendship between the king and the people; and if the people are in internal discord, it is not to be hoped that they be in tune with their leaders. Hence [what is called for is] *a union between the bourgeoisie and the patricians, between the middle class and the populace, between the poor and the rich;* and since one cannot make the poor love the rich if the rich are not beseeched to think of the good of the poor, *it behoves one to improve the lot of the populace and civilize it through training.* So the principality, by advancing and leading that pious work, and linking together all the classes of citizens, must become conciliatory and democratic.[15]

The fundamental problem for Gioberti is the creation of a national 'historic bloc',[16] where the various elements that compose society come

---

14 Vincenzo Gioberti, *Del rinnovamento civile d'Italia*, VOL. 1 (F. Nicolini ed.) (Bari: Laterza, 1911), p. 26.

15 Gioberti, *Del rinnovamento*, VOL. 1, p. 31.

16 The Gramscian terminology is less arbitrary than might appear at first glance. See pp. 240–3 in this volume on the close relationship (at least on the cultural plane) between Gioberti and Gramsci. The motif of the union of the various social forces towards

together in agreement around common interests, leaving to the authority of the state the task of facilitating the development of an inter-class alliance and of mediating or alleviating any possible causes of conflict. The people is, from this perspective, *one* element in the bigger picture, participating with equal rights as other strata and finding in this participation its 'native recompense'. The nation and progress cannot do without the people; the people cannot do without the nation and progress: '[the populace] cannot be civilized if it is not national, that is, guided by intelligence and informed by kindness'.[17]

By contrast with these fundamental points, the form of government is 'a secondary and ancillary thing'; indeed, 'the democratic direction of society does not depend upon it but on reforms'; and the most important of these reforms are given 'by the transformation of the plebs into a people and by the transformation of artificial and arbitrary aristocracy into the aristocracy of merit and intelligence'.[18]

It is easy to understand how culture and literature become not just useful but also essential to such a programme. To a programme of alliance between classes there corresponds, on this plane, a problem of alliance between writers in light of the defined goals. In the chapters 'La dissunione dei Letterati' [The Disunion of the Literati] and 'Onde nasce la concordia degli scrittori' [The Origin of Consensus Among Writers] of *Primato*, Gioberti endeavours to understand why intellectual society in Italy appears so fragmented and what might be the means to recompose it into an effective unity. Now, we can ignore the fact that Gioberti discovered the cement of intellectual concord

---

democratic and progressive ends is, moreover, common to the majority of populist writers of this period. We should recall that Michelet had already affirmed, seven years before the publication of *Rinnovamento*: 'The world's divorce is above all to be found in the absurd opposition that is made today, in the age of machines, between instinct and reflection; it is the contempt of the latter for the instinctual faculties, which it thinks it can do without' (*Le Peuple*, p. 130). It is well known that with the metaphors of 'instinct' and 'reflection' the French historian sought to express, respectively, the healthy strength of the people and the intellectual capacity of the cultured bourgeoisie. Gramsci, in his assessment of Gioberti, uses an expression that is especially close in spirit to the judgement of Michelet: 'Gioberti, albeit vaguely, possesses the concept of the Jacobin "national-popular", of political hegemony, namely, the alliance between bourgeoisie-intellectuals and the people'—*Selections from Cultural Writings* (D. Forgacs and G. Nowell-Smith eds, W. Boelhower trans.) (London: Lawrence and Wishart, 1985), p. 248.

17 Gioberti, *Del rinnovamento*, VOL. 3, p. 127.
18 Gioberti, *Del rinnovamento*, VOL. 1, p. 45.

in adherence to the Catholic faith—this is the contingent aspect of his doctrine. But what remains valid and operational is the fundamental presupposition: 'the office of writer [. . .] is not a merely private literary responsibility [. . .] but a public and many-sided office; it is at the same time a dictatorship, a tribute, a priesthood and a prophetic ministry';[19] and: 'a literature cannot be national if it is not popular',[20] that is, if it is not intimately and profoundly tied to the feelings and ideals of the people. In Gioberti, this idea—that the ideologically qualified participation of literature is enormously beneficial for the peaceful progress of the country—is foundational, rearing its head in numerous places. If the future of Italy is to be democratic (and what Gioberti means by this expression is clear), its culture cannot retain the aristocratic characteristics with which it previously adorned itself. Put in the service of 'the people', it will be at once useful, modern and progressive.

All those who consciously set themselves the problem of creating a political and cultural hegemony able to function as an element of cohesion for a new ruling group, look to Gioberti, Gramsci included. But the links that Gioberti establishes when he ties the future to the past, renewal to tradition, reforms to respect for real situations, will continue to operate in the direction of a prudent gradualism even after his death. But his political and cultural teaching demonstrates that implementing any of the points of his programme necessarily entails all the others. If the objective is to channel all the national forces into a single direction, the national principle will prevail over all other concerns; if the national principle prevails, one must recognize that one is working on an inherited foundation within precise limits, and that any discourse of renewal will have to set off from there; if the discourse of renewal is tied to given conditions, it must end up with reforms, and the reforms will be the only instrument through which the people can hope to emancipate itself—and literature will endeavour to collaborate for its emancipation. Italian populism draws its moderate, gradualist, reformist soul from Gioberti.

For Mazzini too, the people is subordinated to the Nation, insofar as it can only be expressed within it. But his discourse, unlike that of Gioberti, is directed immediately to the people which for him is not *one* element in the picture but *the essential and irreplaceable force* of national development. Nevertheless, for Mazzini too, the people is an ethical concept even before it

---

19 Gioberti, *Del primato*, VOL. 3, p. 209.
20 Gioberti, *Del rinnovamento*, VOL. 3, p. 126.

is an object of sociological study. To associate the people with the process of national renewal does not mean attributing to it particular privileges but, at most, particular duties, because only by carrying out a duty does one derive the legitimate claim to a right. In the first place, we must underline the following aspect of the Mazzinian concept of the people: the disdain for material interest, for the egotism of individuals as much as that of the classes. Before any other consideration, Mazzini upholds the following thought: there is no social progress that is not at the same time progress of the spirit and of consciousness. Mazzini takes this aspect of his doctrine so much to heart that he does not hesitate to propose it heroically to his 'working-class' interlocutors:

> With the theory of happiness as the primary aim of existence, we shall only produce egoistic men who will carry the old passions and desires into the new order of things and corrupt it in a few months. We have therefore to find a principle of Education superior to any such theory, which shall guide men towards their own improvement with their fellow men without making them dependent either on the ideas of a single man or the force of the majority. And this principle is Duty.[21]

The fact is that *above the people* there are ideals that must be aimed at if the people are to become civilized and rise beyond their misfortunes. Their struggle to improve their material conditions of existence makes sense only if it is not an end in itself but, rather, is a means, an instrument to attain and realize within society those ethical and ideal principles of Unity and Progress:

---

21 Giuseppe Mazzini, *Doveri dell'Uomo* (Commisione editrice degli scritti di Giuseppe Mazzini ed.) (Rome, 1901), pp. 13–14 ['The Duties of Man' in *The Cosmopolitanism of Nations: Giuseppe Mazzini's Writings on Democracy, Nation Building and International Relations* (S. Recchia and N. Urbinati eds) (Princeton: Princeton University Press, 2009), pp. 82–3]. Consider also Pierre-Joseph Proudhon:

> Are you people for whom the existence of man has but one end: producing, acquiring and enjoying? [. . .] We must work because it is our law, because it is on that condition that we learn, we fortify, we discipline and assure our existence and those of our own. But that's not our end—I'm not saying our religious or supernatural transcendent end, but even our earthly end, our actual and entirely human end. To be human, to elevate ourselves beyond the destinies of our earthly condition, to reproduce in us the divine image, as the Bible says . . . that is our end . . . —*Textes choisis* (A. Marc ed.) (Paris: Egloff, 1945), p. 59.

In Michelet too, the theme of 'sacrifice', 'the thing that makes for true nobility', through which the people are able to raise themselves above all other social classes, is a constant.

[T]he law of Life is Progress; progress for the *individual*, progress for Humanity. Humanity accomplishes that law on earth; the individual on the earth and elsewhere. Only one God, only one law.[22]

Hence Mazzini does not suggest that the people should abdicate their concern for civic and social progress; rather, they should frame them in terms of ideal guidelines that allow them to benefit both individuals and the collective. In his writings there appears that concept of 'free producer' that will have such fortune in Italian populism between the end of the 1800s and the early years of the new century. Without trying to compare Mazzini's formulations with those of Sorel on this point,[23] there is no doubt that the memory of Mazzini contributed to the particular nationalist and patriotic accent given to the positions of Italian anarcho-syndicalism. There exists an extraordinary analogy between the way in which the Risorgimento theorist articulates the relationship between 'free production' and Homeland [*Patria*], and the one established by the revolutionary syndicalists between the particular interests of the producers and the general interest of the Nation. In this case, however, it is particularly important to underline the fact that the way out of working-class constraints is '*the union of capital and labour in the same hands*', which is to say, the '*[a]ssociation of labour, and division of the fruits of labour—or rather of the profits resulting from the sale of its products—among the producers, in proportion to the amount and value of the work done by each*'.[24] Working-class associationism is not a mere instrument for the defence of the subaltern classes against the exploitation of the bosses but also the way to escape from the unhappy condition of the waged by finally becoming producers and achieving civic and human dignity. For this to come about, it is necessary to gather sufficient capital to enable the establishment of this associative enterprise; but there can only be one path to gather capital from the wretched salaried workers: saving; but saving also requires sacrifice and the painful sense

---

22 Mazzini, *Doveri dell'Uomo*, p. 58. [This passage is missing in the abridged English translation.—Trans.]

23 More than of a real relationship one could speak here about a shared set of sources. The *trait-d'union* between the two positions is formed in this case almost certainly by the common Proudhonian inspiration which influences Italian anarcho-syndicalism through the mediation of Sorel. One cannot forget, moreover, that the free-market liberals also had a significant polemical influence on Italian anarcho-syndicalism, contributing to the formation of the latter's understanding of the relationship between general and particular interest (that is, of the single entrepreneur or worker-producer).

24 Mazzini, *Doveri dell'Uomo*, p. 84 / 'The Duties of Man', pp. 103–04.

of duty. With this we return to the starting point: once again, the aim set for the people has a fundamentally ethical and spiritual meaning, but with an additional element that Mazzini's programme is even more clearly characterized by: an attempt to valorize the reasons of the intermediate strata (more artisanal than working class) within the development of capitalism.[25] One might find it possible and even welcome the creation of a small-scale capitalism founded upon working-class saving as an instrument to resolve the inconveniences of large-scale capitalism, provided one sees the working class as potential members of the petty bourgeoisie to whom one could entirely attribute one's morality and vision of the world. The extremely powerful, even excessive ethical charge of Mazzini's teaching cements the foundation upon which is built the attempted reaction to the inexorable consequences of capitalist exploitation, without questioning its presuppositions or social conditions. The people, which realize the Homeland and are realized in Humanity, have the principal function of reabsorbing any *particularist* or *subversive* drives of the subaltern classes that might arise within the general development of a society in which all solidary classes must participate. Only by educating the affluent through the example of their own education can the wretched hope to better themselves, elevating themselves to the status of property owners. In fact: 'We should not seek to abolish property just because at present it is the possession of the *few*; rather, we must make it easier for the *many* to acquire it.'[26]

Mazzini bequeaths to the democratic current of Italian populism its unflagging moral charge: a tendency to look beyond the material interest and to yearn for the truth of spirit. More concretely, it seems to me that from Mazzini (or through him) there also flows the obstinate anti-worker attitude that is among the dominant motifs of our populist tradition. This aspect of his thinking stands out in *Doveri dell'Uomo* and other writings from the last decade of his life. *Doveri* is born precisely from the desire to express or check *working-class egotism* by contrasting it with the disinterest, generosity and idealism of the people. As evidenced by the intense tone of his polemic, Mazzini clearly felt that the working class, when it unites in socialist leagues

25 One might object that this was indeed the situation in Italy. But it is one thing to take cognizance of the objective backwardness of a situation in order to 'work' realistically upon it; it is quite another to *idealize* that backwardness and attempt to use it as a weapon against the general sociohistorical process of European development, 'holding back' Italy at its pre-capitalist level.

26 Mazzini, *Doveri dell'Uomo*, p. 84 / 'The Duties of Man', pp. 103 [emphasis added].

and trade-union organizations, places itself by definition outside the general interest of society, denying not only the principle of the Nation and the Homeland but that of the people itself. *To bring the working class back within the people* by inducing it to recognize the ethical law of universal Duty was therefore a task of fundamental importance: 'All the possible doctrines of *rights* and material *well-being* will only lead you to failure, if they remain isolated or solely supported by your own efforts; they will be only succeed in preparing the ground for the most serious of social crimes: a civil war between class and class.'[27]

All those who see the people as fundamentally the interpreter and symbol of a complex of ideas and values, for which it *must* struggle in the attempt to fully accomplish its spiritual mission on earth, follow this course.[28] This clearly intensifies the ethical and pedagogical qualities of populist literature, assigning it an extremely exalted function of protest, guide and educator, in the sense of cultivating in the people all the positive germs of their spontaneous generosity as well as preparing the dominant classes for a more careful consideration of the problems of the people. If one looks carefully, one always discovers some ancient Mazzinian incrustations in the moralism of the Italian populists of the nineteenth and twentieth centuries.

We can find certain analogies between Mazzini and Gioberti's positions, over and above the most obvious one, that for both the people leads back to and realizes itself in the cradle of the nation. Both expressed a civic and social conception of literature and culture.[29] The overall influence of the two on the

---

27 Mazzini, *Doveri dell'Uomo*, p. 16. [Passage missing in abridged English translation.]

28 No one better than Pietro Jahier has construed and expressed this element of of Mazzini's doctrine (see discussion at the start of Section 7). As in all those who will take up this position, in Jahier too the Mazzinian influences are inextricably interwoven with those of different origin, among which Proudhonian and Sorelian ones unquestionably prevail. [Pietro Jahier (1884–1966), Italian writer and poet. Strongly influenced by symbolist and hermeticist literary schools.—Trans.]

29 What's more, this position is typical of every form of democratism; in fact, the petty-bourgeois illusion of being able to exert effective pressure on reality through the 'battle of ideas, of culture and of art', etc., is ultimately founded on the politics–culture nexus. The idea that there exists a necessary and reciprocal relationship between the 'liberation of man' and the 'liberation of art' had already been expressed by Proudhon:

> The same solidarity that in modern societies engenders pauperism and raises
> up regicide and revolt against any form of power, also determines the decadence
> of literature and art; thus, the same solidarity that will cure our misery will make

Italian thought of the last hundred and fifty years has in no small part contributed to maintaining the predominance of the socially and politically
engaged current of Italian literature over the one we might call disinterested
or non-committal. They have contributed powerful and vague ideological and
religious baggage to this social commitment. In populist terms, it has meant
that the idealistic discourse on the people will often prevail over the direct or
mythologico-symbolic representation of the people itself. Supported by two
ideologues of such calibre, the Italian populists will be guided more by their
ideas of the people than by any affectionate respect and faithful love of the
people and their ideas. From here stems the highly ideological character of
Italian populism, more often than not incapable of turning the people into a
general idea—as was the case with Russian populism—and more frequently
prepared to dress the people in *one's own* general (political, cultural, spiritual,
religious, etc.) ideas.

While Gioberti and Mazzini created the foundations for the populism of
the future, in those same years, between the 1820s and 60s, liberal Catholics
were developing a vision of the people that was more limited and reactionary
but also more clear, solid and immediately realizable. Without question one
owes to Manzoni and his followers the first organic and extensive expression
of populist literature in Italy. In their work, we can already find a self-aware
and programmatic attitude with regard to both the ends and the contents of
a 'modern' Italian literature. Having become aware ultimately—following the
paramount example set by Manzoni—of the objective necessity of establishing
a positive contact between the intellectual stratum and the popular mass, they
develop this politico-cultural position coherently by occupying the entire

---

the ideal bloom once again. A new art is stirring, conceived in the entrails of
Revolution; I feel it, I divine it, though I am incapable of furnishing any example
of it whatsoever; a man of my century, wretched and poor, I remain beneath this
literature which no longer knows either myths or princes, nobles or serfs, which
speaks all languages, ennobles every toil, honours every condition with equal
health, and whose motto will always be JUSTICE AND FREEDOM—*De
la Justice dans la Révolution et dans l'Eglise,* VOL. 4 (Paris: Marcel Rivière, 1935),
p. 435.

Hugo had affirmed instead the principle of the fundamental political and ideological uses
of poetry through his own rhetorical forms: 'Art is human thought—see it break every
chain!—Art is the sweet conqueror!—To it belong the Rhine and the Tiber!—*Enslaved
people, it makes you free;—Free people, it makes you great!*'—see *L'Art et le Peuple* in *Les
Châtiments* (Paris: Libraire Ollendorff, 1910), p. 47.

field of literary instruments and forms, from fiction of high artistic quality to pedagogical and educational literature. All of this takes place in line with a precise ideological, religious and, in the final analysis, political decision.

At the heart of this position is the concept of 'humility'. It is pointless to linger at length on all of this. The fundamental features of this outlook are clear to whoever has read, for example, Manzoni's *I promessi sposi* [The Betrothed]. The evangelical words 'Blessed are the poor in spirit, for theirs is the kingdom of heaven' and 'It is easier for a camel to go through the eye of a needle, than for a rich man to enter the kingdom of God' form its essential premise. The commoner [*popolano*] can be considered the human being dearest to God because he is the most unfortunate. Far from demanding an improvement in his material condition, beyond the one that may be granted by Providence, he holds his 'humility' dear because he knows that it bears within it the infallible guarantee of a lofty prize, before which all the gifts in this world pale. Serene in the face of misfortune, cautious in his joy and happiness, meek, hardworking and peaceful, the Catholic commoner [*popolano*] finds the satisfaction of all his needs in his faith. When one rebels against this law, as in the case of Renzo Tramaglino, one suffers the consequences, learning at one's cost to pay more attention to written doctrine, avoiding rashness and futile bluster. When one conforms to the law without resistance, as does Lucia Mondella, the protective hand of God makes its presence felt: what is lost through pain is made up for in happiness, multiplied and made more precious by the memory of past misfortunes. 'Humility', in other words, is both a social condition and a spiritual state. In the nether regions of society is more ingenuity and faith than in the sublime heights. God's gaze willingly turns downward because it knows it will find there a ready, trusting reply.

Because of the complexity of the motifs that Manzoni mobilizes, it would certainly be difficult to call *I promessi sposi* a populist work. But the popular characters that appear in it are indeed populist because the writer represents them as positive values in the face of a corrupt world, repositories of that evangelical candour through which the kingdom of the heavens is more easily reached. The limits of Manzoni's type of populism are well known (essentially the same as that of the moderate Catholicism that inspires it): Gramsci has described them in terms that are entirely satisfactory from our point of view.[30]

---

30 'It is characteristic of Tolstoy that the naive and instinctive wisdom of the people, even when uttered casually, enlightens and brings about a crisis in the educated man. That is the most notable trait of Tolstoy's religion which interprets the gospel "democratically",

The principal limitation lies in Manzoni's stubborn conviction that popular positivity is unable to achieve complete autonomy from the rest of the world. Popular positivity requires a guide (in many cases, a brake): the Catholic religion and the Church. Platon Karataev (to follow Gramsci's argument) was a world unto himself; he was self-sufficient, complete, enclosed like a monad while giving off a warm, universal affection. Renzo Tramaglino, instead, cannot escape a judgement that rules him from above and closely accompanies him in each of his actions and gestures: the kingdom of heaven and the beneficence of God are his, but not without his primogeniture being contested by the aristocratic-Catholic Manzoni through the cataloguing of his terrestrial defects and weaknesses.

The conception of the humble remains almost identical among all the liberal Catholic writers of the 1800s. What changes, sometimes substantially, is how it is represented according to the different perspectives, whose origin is often strictly political. Indeed, it is one thing to describe humility as a spiritual good, as a privilege of the popular classes while deploring the material disadvantages which often weigh them down: hunger, poverty, oppression and so on. It is quite another to describe humility as a spiritual good in order to convince the popular classes to remain perpetually subaltern and oppressed, on the basis that through humility they will more easily find the path to eternal salvation. There are some differences between Manzoni and Cantù.[31] But it is also beyond doubt that 'humility' contains within it—in its intrinsically ideological and religious nature—every possible reactionary outcome. Renzo Tramaglino is not Omobono,[32] but he encompasses him; in the same way that

according to its initial and original spirit. Manzoni, by contrast, has undergone the Counter-Reformation. His Christianity wavers between a Jansenistic aristocratic stance and a populist Jesuitical paternalism'—Gramsci, *Selections from Cultural Writings*, p. 289. Gramsci's critique reveals itself to be less effective than it at first appears once we discover (unsurprisingly) that it sets out from the typical national-popular exigency. What Gramsci refuses in Manzoni is not populism but the particular form of populism that he represents. Indeed, according to Gramsci, Manzoni's 'attitude towards the people is not "national-popular" but aristocratic' (p. 292).

31 Cesare Cantù (1804–95), Italian historian and politician; moved from Romantic positions towards more clerical ones, taking up a neo-Guelph position according to which neither the Catholic Church nor the Enlightenment positions of the French Revolution alone could form the basis of Italian unification, which instead would have to develop its own national political philosophy. [Trans.]

32 Omobono delle Parabole is a character from Cantù's *Carlambrogio da Montevecchia* [Carlambrogio from Montevecchia]. [Trans.]

Omobono encompasses Renzo because, despite everything, the Catholic reactionary Cantù also reserves the kingdom of heaven for him.

The conservative or reactionary character of this liberal Catholic development is both evident and conscious. This is how the Christian feeling of popular humility can turn into the celebration of social subordination which is likewise a step towards the eternal prize. As Carlambrogio says to himself:

[S]top thinking of taking a step that is longer than your leg can carry you, you risk breaking your neck. Society is built like a pyramid: the rows are narrow and only make room for very few; these few are crammed together uncomfortably, repeatedly striking one another, and those who come up from below risk crashing to the ground. Down at the bottom instead there is room for everyone, with plenty of elbow room, and depending on one's build—some a little more others a little less—one can stretch out freely.[33]

And Omobono delle Parabole, the old peasant who embodies all the wisdom of the Christian people, answers those who ask if there is something new with the following words:

Yesterday as I was walking to the market, complaining that my broken shoes let in water and I could feel my feet getting wet, I bumped into poor Sandro, whose feet are bent and who walks with crutches; so I stopped complaining and thanked the Lord.[34]

And meditating on the ears of corn, he observes that some stand extremely high while others bend down to the earth:

Some are empty, the others full of wheat; do not therefore trust in appearances even among men: he who raises his head the most shows himself to have fewer qualities. Merit is modest.[35]

In the case of other authors, the same motif is coloured by naively popular [popolareschi] hues, as is the case with Pietro Paolo Parzanese,[36] who in the famous song 'Gli operai' [The Workers], reaches perhaps the summit of this

---

33 Cesare Cantú, *Carlambrogio da Montevecchia* (Milan: P. Carrara, 1899), p. 32.

34 Cesare Cantú, *Il giovanetto dirizzato alla bontà, al sapere, all'industria* [The Young Man on the Path to Goodness, Knowledge and Industry] (Milan: Carlo Colombi, 1897), p. 7.

35 Cantú, *Il giovanetto dirizzato alla bontà*, p. 8.

36 Pietro Paolo Parzanese (1809–52), translator and poet. Known for his translations of Victor Hugo and Alphonse de Lamartine, as well as of German Romantics. [Trans.]

exhortation to the humble classes to suffer, endure and persevere in the name of God and the Catholic religion:

> Let us suffer, brothers. When
> we were born, God said to us:
> You shall live working—
> and from the heavens he blessed us.
> Bread soaked in sweat
> and yet it is a gift of God.
> What He wants, we want;
> let us toil, toil [. . .]

And he ends with this pious encouragement:

> Let us toil! Nor let anyone say
> that we are the slaves of the rich;
> our fathers and forefathers were burdened
> more than us with toil.
> Guilty idleness, and nothing else,
> leads us to servitude.
> God made us who were are:
> Let us toil, toil [. . .][37]

In texts such as these, one finds that the religious attitude and the populist colour are a disguise for the more substantive ideological ploy which consists in creating effective instruments to pressure and direct the popular masses.

However, in the by-no-means-unworthy tales for the people by Pietro Thouar[38] or the Friulian stories of Caterina Percoto[39] (two authors who, incidentally, had a lively and lasting familiarity with the social strata they represented in their narratives), it can happen that the fundamental moderation of the writer is embellished by a sincere affection, a warm sympathy for the 'popular qualities' they bring into relief. Moreover, Manzoni's indications for how one should comport oneself towards the humble folk were best served by these two orientations: that of pedagogy and popular instruction on the one

---

37 Pietro Paolo Parzanese, 'Gli operai' in *Poeti minori dell'Ottocento*, VOL. 1 (L. Baldacci ed.) (Milan and Naples: Ricciardi, 1958), pp. 234–5.

38 Pietro Thouar (1809–61), writer principally known for his short stories. [Trans.]

39 Caterina Percoto (1812–87), writer and poet. In her writings she reflects the stagnant world of the poor Friulians under Austrian rule. [Trans.]

hand, and pre-*verismo* regionalism on the other. Both moved beyond the petty instrumentalization of Manzoni's programme carried out by the likes of Cantú.

The Catholic concept of 'humility', despite being widespread and successful in the first fifty years of the nineteenth century, would run out of steam on the literary plane before Unification, leaving the path clear for Giobertian and Mazzinian influences which, conversely, had first appeared to be on the losing side of contest. But, in exhausting itself and dying as a confessional and dogmatic attitude, it was to blossom into new forms and liberate its more generically Christian inspiration from its specific origins which here in Italy had been singularly Catholic. From this standpoint, the survival of this inspiring motif continues to this day: the evangelic feeling of popular humility will also touch writers who would like to think of themselves as secular to the bone, and whose fictional characters will instead cleave closely to the traits, hopes and aspirations of Catholic characters of that earlier period— albeit perhaps revised, as we said, in light of a vaster humanitarian and religious spirit. In other words, Italian populism will take from liberal Catholicism— whether directly or indirectly—the self-satisfied (or perhaps affectionate) representation of popular subordination and the tendency to consider as a (spiritual) good everything that relates to the people's earthly inferiority.

3

During the Risorgimento and until nearly the end of the 1800s, the distinction between the two contrasting populist conceptions remained sharp and lively. On the one hand, there was a radical and democratic populism, glorifying the avenging force of progress and often harking back to the mythic-rhetorical figures of the plebeian Sans-culottes of the French Revolution or the 'people' of the *comuni*,[40] or even of the ancient Roman proletariat. On the other, there

---

40 Between the thirteenth and fifteenth centuries, the *comuni* in Central and Northern Italy were the sites of some of the most 'original cultural developments in Italy'. As Asor Rosa writes in a later text:

> [I]n the narrow but lively confines of their walls emerges a veritable civilization, which reveals itself in the forms of architecture, urbanism, painting, sculpture, and literature. This civilization, and all the cultural and artistic expressions that are linked to it, should not be considered as a static fact, an offshoot of a quiet and tranquil industrious society. As we said, it is the product of an almost constant disturbance of the political and civic order, of which the struggles between internal segments of the *comune* and the battles between *comuni* are the most

THE BEGINNINGS • 53

was a Catholic and moderate populism which saw in the people the infant in need of education and—with lesser expenditure of rhetorical invention but with greater realistic sagacity—which specialized in the edifying tale, an even and relaxed narrative in a language that was perhaps not always modern, in the proper sense of the term, but generally simple and accessible to all. It is not out of place to observe, once again, that both discourses, although leading to contrasting conclusions, continue to turn on a common principle: the constitution of the Italian Nation. Differing on ends and means, liberals and democrats agree about the necessity, or at least the opportuneness, of popular assent for the founding of the nation. The disagreement re-emerges when the focus turns to the limits and forms of this participation, and this is also reflected in the different literary positions of the populists.

Some fundamentally political testimonies, behind which we can also glimpse possible literary solutions, show us how alive was the problem of establishing a relationship between bourgeois and subaltern classes towards the middle of the century. Particularly interesting is Ippolito Nievo's[41] *Frammento sulla rivoluzione nazionale* [Fragment on the National Revolution, 1859]. He identified, with clarity and a note of grave concern, the deep fracture between a cultured and intelligent minority, bearer of the values of the Risorgimento, and the large majority of the people ('the peasant masses') who were apathetic, indifferent and perhaps, in some regions, even tempted by paternalistic and reactionary governments, such as that of Austria. Having identified the faults of the liberals and politicians of the Risorgimento in general, who obstinately refused to lift the plebeian peasantry from its extraordinary poverty, he goes on to define the goals of the social task he demands, even at the cost of the sacrifice of the national economy as a whole. It is very clear that he feels the problem of the people to be tightly entwined with the overall framework of the foundation of the Italian nation, or even as pre-eminent and fundamental to it:

> Over this there towers the need to reconstruct national unity; to reconnect mind and hand (shoring up the political revolution that is on its way to fulfilment with the national revolution, which alone can

tangible signs.—*Breve storia della letteratura italiana: 1. L'Italia dei comuni e degli stati* [Brief History of Italian Literature 1. The Italy of the Comuni and States](Turin: Einaudi, 2013), p. 18. [Trans.]

41 Ippolito Nievo (1831–61), writer and patriot; inspired by Mazzini, he fought with Giuseppe Garibaldi's Expedition of the Thousand to conquer Italy, defeating the Bourbon army. The *Frammento* was published posthumously in 1929. [Trans.]

give it lasting support); that is, of inducing such a change in the opinions of the common rural people that they will link to those of the intelligent class, reuniting them forever in the love of liberty and independence; this is the meaning that can today be given in Italy to the phrase: national revolution.[42]

Within this democratic and Jacobin-influenced thinking, one can find inscribed (at least hypothetically) the problem of a populist-peasant literature. Nievo had confronted this, if somewhat at a remove, in some pages of *Varmo* and *Conte pecoraio*, or when he attempted a type of poetry that was both populist and appealing in works like *Amori garibaldini*. What we wish to emphasize here is not the literary aspect of these passages as much as the confirmation that we draw from them of the tight union between the concepts of 'the people' and 'national revolution' (distinguished from exclusively political revolution) that was already present in the work of the Risorgimento writers. We will rediscover this position to be alive and well right up to the present.

An analogous attitude finds expression in Carlo Pisacane's *Saggio su la Rivoluzione* [Essay on the Revolution, 1860], although he emphasizes the concept of equality more forthrightly (he is perhaps less clear in delineating a precise social problem): 'Nationality is the being of the nation [. . .]. In order for there to be nationality, no obstacles of any sort must stand in the way of the *collective will*, and no interest must be allowed to prevail over the general interest.'[43] Therefore, 'freedom without equality does not exist, and both are indispensable conditions for that nationality which in turn contains light and heat, as does the sun'.[44] In this case too, the quoted passages show how, in keeping with the most consistent democratic thought, the concepts of equality and revolution are tightly interwoven with that of nationality; that is, they ultimately demonstrate how the horizon within which this socialist-style populism operates remains that of the bourgeois drive for independence and unification of the Italian territory. This attitude too has a long history.[45]

---

42 Ippolito Nievo, *Opere* (S. Romagnoli ed.) (Milan: Ricciardi, 1952), pp. 1085–6.

43 Carlo Pisacane (1818–57), Italian patriot and early socialist. The quotation is from his *Saggio su la Rivoluzione* (Giaime Pintor ed.) (Turin: Einaudi, 1956), p. 76. [Trans.]

44 Pisacane, *Saggio su la Rivoluzione*, p. 99.

45 Like all the democrats of the 1800s, Pisacane gives rise to a twofold tradition. On the one hand, he gives sustenance to all those left-wing scholars who look to the Risorgimento for the indigenous origins of the Italian socialist and workers' movement. On the other, his social extremism, which is fully anchored in the principle of nationality, also legitimates

This mature understanding of the problem of the peasantry and the people—fated to eventually succumb before the plan of capitalist accumulation of the dominant bourgeoisie—was not, however, accompanied by immediately literary developments, except in a few instances. It is worth recalling at least one name in connection to Nievo's polemical pro-peasantry line: that of the priest from Calabria, Vincenzo Padula.[46] It is no coincidence that he, like Nievo and Pisacane, produced his best writings in the years straddling 1860, a year that throughout Italy seemed to rekindle the enthusiasm of 1848, even urging it on, on the waves of hope raised by Garibaldi's imminent adventure and later by its happy conclusion. We shall not examine the full span of his work, despite it being full of popularistic [*popolareggianti*] ideas but, focusing our attention on the set of articles dedicated to the *Stato delle persone in Calabria* [The Status of Persons in Calabria],[47] we will note that in the lengthy and

---

the national-popular interpretations of reactionaries and fascists. That this is not a merely polemical invention is confirmed by [the Fascist historian] Gioacchino Volpe, in his *Storia del movimento fascista* (Milan: Istituto per gli studi di politica internazionale, 1939). Volpe points to Pisacane's 'national [based] socialism' as one of the forms of political thought in which Fascism could discern its own distant origins. Less authoritatively, but in a manner more immediately significant for our investigation, Vasco Pratolini mentions Pisacane among the authors that were most important to his early development, alongside [Giuseppe] Ferrari and [Carlo] Cattaneo. See 'Continuità e sviluppo della dottrina', *Il Bargello* 9(1) (14 February 1937). [Vasco Pratolini (1913–91), Florentine novelist, scriptwriter and essayists, whose work is discussed at length in the second and third chapter of Part I of this book. See also Asor Rosa's earlier monograph, *Vasco Pratolini* (Roma: Edizioni Moderne, 1958).—Trans.]

46 Vincenzo Padula (1819-93), poet and patriot. Principally known for his important series of articles on social conditions in Calabria. [Trans.]

47 These can now be read in the impressive collection edited by Carlo Muscetta, *Persone in Calabria* (Milan: Milano Sera, 1950). [Carlo Muscetta (1912–2004), literary critic and poet; joined the PCI in the postwar period, leaving it in 1957; eEditor of Francesco de Sanctis' works for Einaudi.—Trans.] In writing about Padula's dramatic *Antonello, capo brigante calabrese*, Muscetta indicated the possibility of a populist-peasant literature, which he found implicit in Padula's work: 'Perhaps there flashed before Padula, alone in Italy, something akin to what Pushkin did for the Pugachev rebellion, demonstrating affection for this history of peasant rebellions which has yet to be written, and from which shine forth authentically epic episodes' (p. 207). Padula's story is mediocre from the literary standpoint, and far inferior to the descriptive and semi-sociological prose of his *Stato delle persone*, republished under Fausto Gullo's editorship (Milan: Universale Economica, 1952). In his short introduction, Gullo gives further evidence of the manner in which these nineteenth-century democratic texts were sympathetically appreciated by the workers' movement at the time, due to the commonality of ideas and political themes:

detailed analysis of the various social-popular conditions, Padula provides the first Italian example of sociological literature; he does so with a truly extraordinary wealth of data, including of an economic nature. But what interests us most is the mood, the politico-ideological vision, with which he artistically represents his peasants, sharecroppers, yokels, shepherds, goatherds, cattle herders, grocers, fishermen and watchmen. Padula lacks Pisacane's egalitarian concerns and Nievo's social awareness; his clear conviction that popular ferocity and coarseness is entirely to be attributed to the indifference or oppression of 'gentlemen' results in a fundamentally moderate and reformist attitude. But there is a profound sincerity and pity in how he looks at the centuries-old injuries of his people, a genuine love through which he is able to glimpse— in the stormy flashes of the savage human condition of these proletarian peasants—qualities of spirit and mind that have survived in their purest state: honesty, pride, force of spirit, sense of honour, the intelligence that remains awake and attentive under the burdensome weight of ignorance. The pages dedicated to the shepherds and goatherds are the forebears of what was later written on the topic. The title in Corrado Alvaro's *Gente in Aspromonte* [People in Aspromonte][48] loses much of its originality and freshness if it is read or reread after these impressions of Padula. The representation of the blind and ferocious peasant revolt, and of its inevitable corollary, brigandage, is a point of reference for those who want to understand the recurrent character of this theme in Calabrian or Southern Italian-inspired literature. Eighty years later, Carlo Levi, certainly knowing nothing of Padula, will explain and illustrate it in a surprisingly analogous way. Finally, we must remember that Padula initiates a polemic against the ills of state centralization that would recur as a fundamental motif of Southern Italian literature. In order to relieve the misfortunes of the Calabrian peasant, it is necessary to 'reclaim for the *comuni* the vast lands usurped by the large landowners' and entrust the indigenous population with care for the reform and the renewed social relationships, since the 'radical vice is centralization'. 'The question of freedom [. . .] is to be found in the

---

In highlighting the social content of the plot, we intend to bring to the attention of the reader what appears to us as the most significant aspect of the work, that which directly ties it to the tragic reality of the environment in which it came to light [. . .]. We must underline this social content all the more as it unfortunately has not lost its relevance almost a century later; this is a bitter remark that, although it leads to still sadder considerations, renders the reading of the drama without doubt more interesting and useful—which can do no harm.

48 Corrado Alvaro (1895–1956), Calabrian journalist and realist writer. [Trans.]

municipalities; and the state has placed itself in an odious position by usurping the powers of the municipalities and the provinces'.[49] We shall be reminded of these words when we come to Carlo Levi.

4

In the first decades following Unification, the populist inclinations of Italian writers were enriched by a wealth of different ideas and influences. In Giosuè Carducci's *Giambi ed Epodi* [Iambs and Epodes, 1867–79], the Jacobin and sans-culotte motif stood out in the forms of intense social polemic as well as a patriotic nostalgia for the Risorgimento. For Carducci, the people were the 'lowly plebs' who knew how to die for their freedom even when the patricians and the bourgeoisie hid under the heavy wings of ecclesiastical forgiveness;[50] they are the 'holy scoundrel', the 'martyr plebs'[51] who threw themselves 'fiercely' against the Austrians and fearlessly succumbed. It was a small step from the patriotic motif to the protest against inequality and social injustice: these heroic plebeians were without rights, nor did they have any after Italy's unification; still, they sacrificed themselves and their children for a motherland that was not *yet* their own:

> Your blood and the motherland today: to the law
> blood and bread tomorrow. And still
> you do not make laws, oh common people
> and, disinherited herd, you are without motherland.[52]

Later, the ardent inflections given to Carducci's writings by his imitation of Hugo would be mollified in the dreams of a genuinely popular democracy manifest in the medieval 'pictures' of 'Comune rustico' (1885) and 'Faida di comune' (1886). The no-longer Jacobin but bluntly populist end-point of

---

49 Muscetta, *Persone in Calabria*, p. 178

50 Giosue Carducci, 'Nel vigesimo anniversario dell'VIII agosto MDCCCXLVIII' [On the Twentieth Anniversary of the 8 August 1848] in *Giambi ed Epodi* (E. Palmieri ed.) (Bologna: Zanichelli, 1959), pp. 37–44. The ode was written to remember the insurrection of the populace of Bologna who, on 8 August 1849, attempted to prevent the Austrian troops who were rampaging across Italy after the battle of Custoza from entering their city.

51 Carducci, 'Nel vigesimo anniversario', pp. 56 and 67.

52 Carducci, 'Nel vigesimo anniversario , pp. 73–6. One should bear in mind that the poem was composed when the extremely harsh law on milling had been voted for by parliament. [This refers to the 1868 tax on milling, which raised the cost of bread, the staple food of the subaltern classes; this resulted in large-scale revolts that were often quelled only with extreme bloody violence.—Trans.]

Carducci's writing can be found in these poems as well as in the less poetic 'Parlamento' (1879). It was the primitive community of the peasant or paleo-communal type that the poet identified as the model for his idea of free government, at once strong and dignified. The relationship between authority and citizens was not mediated but direct; the relationship between the state and the people was more one of brotherly understanding and profound respect than of mere collaboration. Religious and patriotic sentiments were united. The religion of the motherland was no different from the religion of God. Between the world of work and that of civil society (see 'Il Comune rustico' in particular) there was a profound interpenetration: the commoner was at the same time a *natural* component of the 'little senate', a communal owner of the territory of the republic and an ever-vigilant soldier defending the borders of the motherland.

There were an infinite number of sources for this idea, covering the arc of French and Italian populist and democratic thought;[53] and Carducci's importance lies precisely in having bundled together all these tendencies, and, thanks in part to his prestige, placing them squarely within the lyric and civic

---

53 Many of our observations are drawn from an extremely meticulous analysis of Carducci's populist sources, which can be found in 'Testimonianze' [Testimonies] by G. B. Salinari that prefaced 'Parlamento' [Parliament], in the collection *Rime e Ritmi* [Rhymes and Rhythms] (Bologna: Zanichelli, 1935), with commentaries by M. Valgimigli and G. B. Salinari. In addition to the sources mentioned, we should add Heinrich Heine's *The Weavers* and *Germany*, to which Guerrini owes much, as is apparent from some of the citations of his work that we will provide below. But Michelet is also an enormous influence: take the framework of Carducci's 'Comune rustico' and compare it with that sublime and magniloquent epic of peasant greatness that forms the first chapter of *Le peuple* (*Servitudes du paysan*). We rediscover the same ideal qualities: sobriety, moral strength and health, the spirit of sacrifice and love of liberty; even the peasants' devotion to the military use of weapons, which Michelet notes is one of the most powerful aspects the French nation. Perhaps the very idea of the 'Comune rustico' can be derived from that passage of Michelet's work where the French historian laments the attempt to tear property and privileges from the poor *paysans de frontière* / 'border peasants', to whom France had for centuries owed the defence, conservation and productive cultivation of its natural borders.

Especially in all border countries, the rights of poor people are all the more sacred insofar as no one would have inhabited such dangerous marches without them; the land was deserted, there was neither people nor culture. And today, in a time of peace and security, you come to contest the land of those without whom the land would not exist! You demand their titles; they are buried; *they are the bones of their elders who kept your borders, and who still occupy its sacred line.*—Hugo, *L'Art et le peuple*, pp. 9–10.

traditions of Italian poetry. Thus, following the warm recollection of the Mazzinian and Garibaldian models, the lessons of the historians, theorists and poets of the French Revolution, from Blanc to Michelet to Hugo, and the rhetoric of Italian primacy from the Roman Republic to the medieval commune, Carducci forged a veritable *corpus* of populist themes and motifs from which his disciples would draw, as would many of those who later tried to conceal their debt so as to escape the charge of rhetorical magniloquence so often aimed at his work. If we add that, through the reading of Proudhon and the direct and indirect influence of Bakunin,[54] Carducci came to the threshold of a moderate and petty-bourgeois socialism—which yet again found its positive value and force in the theoretical and practical notion of 'the people'—it will be clear from now on how one can insert, by way of an easy contamination, a socialist or pseudo-socialist motif within a populist current. Better still, it will be clear how, *within this framework*, the one register flows into the other, so that the socialism is born *naturally* from the populism as its logical consequence, thus retaining all its qualities and limitations.

This is clearly visible in the work of Olindo Guerrini,[55] a poet of the Carduccian School. While he engages consistently and generously with the new socialist ideals, he knows not how to (he cannot) step outside a very

---

54 As G. B. Salinari reminds us in the note above, in the years following 1870, the then fervently Bakunian Andrea Costa—fellow disciple of Pascoli and of Severino Ferrari [(1856–1905), poet and literary critic, himself a friend of Pascoli and student of Carducci]—studied under Carducci. As we have mentioned, in those years Carducci must have been attracted by all those tendencies that posed the problem of 'direct democracy' or 'popular democracy'. To a poem such as 'Comune rustico', for which Michelet supplied the historical framework and the peasant 'spirit', others, such as Proudhon and Bakunin lent the strongly egalitarian and populist political and social solutions depicted within it. It is possible that Carducci had not read the passage of Proudhon cited below, but he certainly did not escape the influence of the position it expressed:

> [T]he people names, at one or two electoral levels, in keeping with the importance of charges, *all its functionaries*; and since, by the natural division of labour and the separation of industries, the ensemble of functions is nothing other than the social organism itself; since the totality of functionaries encompasses the totality of citizens, it follows that *the people as a whole enters into administration and into the state*; that every citizen fulfils a function, not servile or subaltern, but independent and responsible; that *all*, in brief, *are elected by one another*, and exercise their special portion of public authority . . . —*Mélanges, Articles de journaux 1848–1852,* VOL. 3 (Paris: Lacroix, 1871), p. 76.

55 Olindo Guerrini (1845–1916), poet and literary critic; wrote under several pseudonyms (especially 'Lorenzo Stecchetti'), and across genres, from realist to dialect poetry. [Trans.]

closely circumscribed cultural and social horizon. On the one hand, the Jacobin teachings of Carducci lead him to an ideological position saturated with a literary and intellectual form of rebellionism: for him too the people are 'cursed plebs'. On the other hand, *socialism is already in Guerrini*—as in many other writers of the 1800s and 1900s, right up to the present day—*a protest against hunger, a demand for the minimum necessary for life, a glorification of violent and desperate rebellion and a plebeian and peasant-type solidarity which is certainly not that of the industrial working class.* Hence, already in Guerrini, as later in many others, the 'scandal of poverty' takes up the entire space of poetic inspiration. It is clear that behind this literary decision lies a condition of social underdevelopment against which the author sincerely and indignantly protests. But this explanation cannot be used to justify the uniformity of themes and the monotony of polemical demands, unless one wishes to apply a reverse determinism, for which anything that can be explained by reference to a given social situation is positive. The backwardness of Italian society in the years straddling the turn of the twentieth-century produces, among other things, the following problem: writers are objectively presented with a limited set of poetic stimuli and real opportunities to fight this backward condition. *Wretchedness is without complexity.* So one should not be surprised if across several decades it is represented in such similar hues. One should also not be surprised if a manneristic atmosphere soon forms around it which is able to draw upon some of the most obvious tools of a classical- and traditional-type rhetoric (here the mention of Carducci is again fitting).

The common people of Guerrini are the 'wretched', who lack 'a piece of bread' and who, as they work, sweat 'blood, tears . . . '. Their revolts take on the character of ferocious slaughters, of desperate *jacqueries*:

From the cities, from the gloomy houses
    that the sun never embellishes,
down from the mountains, from the sea, from the rugged woods
    that the Northern winds whip,
come we damned plebs, innumerable
    fierce and desperate,
on you we descend
    armed with steel and vengeance [. . .][56]

56 Olindo Guerrini, 'Iustitia' (1878) in *Poeti minori dell'Ottocento*, p. 822.

The theme of solidarity among the wretched (*il volgo macilento*, 'the emaciated masses'), among those who recognize one another from the rough marks that labour has left on their bodies, is populism at its purest:

> They pass slowly. A febrile
>> tremor burns the brow of each.
> They pass solemnly and from the crowded
>> ranks not a whisper can be heard.
> Touching one another's hands,
>> each seeks out those near.
> If there are no calluses indicating labour,
>> that is the hand of a spy [. . .][57]

One should not believe that these attitudes are limited to a narrow circle of poets and writers. The paleo-socialist position is, in fact, common to many, revealing an extraordinary affinity of concepts and terms. We owe this 'Canto dei mietitori' [Song of the Harvesters] to Mario Rapisardi,[58] Carducci's rival; in it we encounter the familiar themes of hunger and servitude as well as blind and cruel popular rebellion:

> [. . .] We are poor plebs,
> noi siamo nati a viver come zebe,
> and to die so as to fatten the land.
> We will mow, mow the wheat for the lords.
> O good lords, O portly heroes,
> come to where we will mow.
> We will dance the Trescon, the Ridda
> and then . . . Then we shall mow down and scythe
> the heads of those lord [. . .][59]

It is quite likely that Guerrini found his characters among the day labourers of lower Emilia Romagna; Rapisardi discovered his among the peasants of the Sicilian latifundia. Yet their conclusions are very similar.

---

57 Guerrini, 'Primo maggio' in *Poeti minori dell'Ottocento*, p. 840.

58 Mario Rapisardi (1844–1912), poet, republican and participant in the bohemian, anticonformist literary movement *Scapigliatura*; and a devotee of Mazzini and Garibaldi. [Trans.]

59 Mario Rapisardi, 'Il canto dei mietitori' in *Poeti Minori dell'Ottocento*, p. 804. [The Trescon and the Ridda are names of popular dances.—Trans.]

The observation that the feats of the Risorgimento brought with them no substantial advantages for the popular and peasant masses was shared by both these writers and was a widespread theme throughout this period. The democratic Risorgimento idea of a necessary relation between 'nation' and 'people' is transformed into the socialist protest at the non-existence of such a relation in reality. The glories of Italian unification or of united Italy rest entirely upon the extreme poverty of large swathes of the population. Guerrini's violent and, at times, effective poems against Italian colonial expeditions—which relied on the unpaid sacrifice of poor commoners [*popolani*] destined to a terrible death, leaving their hunger at home and rediscovering it if and when ill or good luck returned them to their families—are well known. The sequence of lyric poems *Africa* by Mario Rapisardi, is marked by the same spirit; while in the poem 'Monumenti', the poet has left one of the most significant documents of this profound dissatisfaction for the non-popular conclusion of the Risorgimento, sarcastically describing the extraordinary flowering of commemorative statues in all the piazzas of Italy in memory of the loftiest of the nation's glories:

> Crown them! No matter that a weary scrawny
> crew of living larvae starve
> with their backs bent in foreign land,
> where they will sow their bones! No matter
> that there is no food or shelter,
> won't she [i.e. Death] be pleased enough with the war spoils
> through which Italian glory will take to the skies?[60]

In other words, we find here the Carduccian motif of the plebs who suffer, unable to lay down the law. The feeling for nationhood does not die in any of these writers linked to the extreme wing of the Risorgimento tradition, but it comes to be seen through the lens of acute social inequality. In short, Italy would only become a Nation once the popular strata could escape from their inhuman abjection and be summoned to assume real political responsibility; when they could make laws in which they would recognize themselves, working alongside other social strata. Analogously, the 'writers of the Resistance' would protest against the ruling bourgeoisie for its betrayal of the Resistance. Every Italian 'national revolution' will have its failures and its funeral orations. The ideals affirmed in the struggle will be far from any possible practical realization.

---

60 Rapisardi, 'Monumenti' in *Poeti minori dell'Ottocento*, p. 805.

In the end, it was fated that the vision of national harmony offered to the subaltern strata as their fulfilled redemption ended up being purely an instrument of the bourgeoisie. In it there was nothing that might challenge the dominant social relations with a total and subversive negation. In the post-Risorgimento period, as in the post-Resistance one, progressive writers, weeping, decrying and lamenting, did nothing but pick up the sad fruit of defeat and disappointment bequeathed by their preceding standpoint.

Not even anarchism escapes this climate of petty-bourgeois indignation. On the contrary. On a first reading, we are immediately struck by the poems of Pietro Gori,[61] because we discover in them the same themes as those of the properly democratic and First-Internationalist currents: sadness in the face of poverty and injustice; the celebration of man who, though weighed down by the shackles of tyranny, never gives up the yearning for the idea of a better world; but also sadness in the face of persecution and oppression. Then, on a closer look, we find some distinctive features too; strangely, not in the sense of a greater polemical ferocity or destructiveness but, rather, in the display of an even sweeter and softer sentimentalism than what is to be found in Carducci or Stecchetti.[62] The Italian anarchists reveal themselves as men of fine mettle— at least as far as literature is concerned: their humanitarianism is so genuine and heartfelt that it rids itself almost entirely of resentment or animosity.

Read the following poem, written in the Dominican prison of Livorno where the agitator was imprisoned for having organized a rally of workers in that city on 1 May 1890:

'La Cella'

Small and white is my little cell,
a nest of coenobites and pariahs;
from the world come the dulled
and pious echoes of light-hearted affections.

My heart is pricked with memories
of the bitter sayings of the melancholy countryside;
each hour ill-commanded ire
and damned dreams hum in my imagination.

---

61 Pietro Gori (1865–1911), anarchist poet. [Trans.]
62 Stecchetti is a pseudonym of Olindo Guerrini. [Trans.]

Two clay pots, a straw mattress, an iron grating . . .
before me the walls of a church,
and an oppressive melancholy air!

Across the ample starry night,
there descends onto the pain of the world
—made unripe by new offence—
perennial nostalgia [. . .][63]

We find ourselves a small step from *crepuscolarismo*.[64] Behind a spiritual attitude of this sort, instead of a violent and intense desire for revolt, we find a painful, sad, almost fatalistic reflection on the evils of the world. The cult of the family, the sacred feeling of love for the mother and the gentle memory of girls in the flower of youth are but the other side of the coin of this inclination towards suffering and mortification.[65] For Gori as well, the people are composed of 'pariahs', 'shipwrecked and continually battered by the waves / of a justice that knows no forgiveness', of 'famished peoples', that 'raise their suffering faces'; or, in the 'dream' of redemption, the 'hard-workers', 'not servants or parasites, not hatchet / men of thought', who have 'light in their minds / strength in their muscles, and in the depth of their hearts / poetry'.[66] Not even for him is there an alternative between the utopia of a kingdom of Man dominated by Work and the more concrete and immediate celebration of the daily 'small virtues'. In the successive series of poems entitled *Battaglie* [Battles], his voice certainly becomes more spirited, but it only serves to show how strongly the influence of Carducci's rhetoric was on all the civic poets of this period.

---

63 Pietro Gori, *Prigioni e battaglie, Volume 1: Prigioni* (Milan: Flaminio Fantuzzi, 1891), p. 72. The booklet bears the following dedication: 'To the people and for those who fight for humanism'.

64 *Crespuscolari* were early twentieth-century poets who opposed the dominant aestheticist, histrionic and heroic poetry of Gabriele D'Annunzio and his ilk, producing a demure prose poetry characterized by a 'flight from history' following the 'ruin of the ideals of the Risorgimento', and a certain impoverishment of poetic language. As Mengaldo argues, the '*crepuscolari* are always petty bourgeois, frustrated by a sense of failure, by a sense of defeat and social immobility—it matters little whether real or presumed' (see Pier Vincenzo Mengaldo, 'Intorno al linguaggio dei crepuscolari' in *La tradizione del novecento* (Turin: Bollati Boringhieri, 2000), pp. 16–17). [Trans.]

65 See poems 'Il parlatorio', 'Santa Giulia' and 'Nostalgia' in *La tradizione del novecento*.

66 Gori, *Prigioni e battaglie,* p. 102.

This attitude was much closer than it appears to the moderate, humanitarian socialism of other writers and intellectuals, among whom Edmondo De Amicis stands out as the best exemplar. *The protest against poverty did not imply a precise notion of social revolution. At the same time, the refusal of social revolution did not exclude the protest against poverty.* The connective tissue linking these two attitudes—beyond psychological or group differentiations—is to be found in a generic humanism, a rather widespread worship of justice, understood abstractly, and an evolutionary mentality sustained by petty-bourgeois positivism and moralism. On more than one occasion it has been pointed out that the book *Cuore* is a veritable *summa* of the positive ideals of the Italian bourgeoisie, in its phase of national organization. But one should add that the principal point of interest of the work lies in the intelligent way in which the author tries to graft a new evaluation of social relations onto the tradition of the Risorgimento. To do so, he is prepared to acknowledge the people as having all manner of qualities and importance: they stand foremost in sacrifices and effort; their contribution to the war of the Risorgimento was precious; and, overall, they are endowed with a noble and elevated nature. The class differentiations remain unchanged of course, although the humanity of individual relations might make them less harsh and more acceptable. In the famous letter of the protagonist's father, Enrico, on *Gli amici operai* [Our friends, the workers], he states:

> Look! *The men of the upper classes are the officers, and the workmen are the soldiers of labour*; but it is in society as in the army; the soldier is not only as noble as the officer, because nobility depends on the work and not on the gain,—on the valour, not on the grade; *but if there is a superiority of merit, it is on the part of the soldier, of the worker, who receive for their own work less profit.* Above all then, love and respect, among all your companions, the sons of the soldiers of labour, honour in them the labours and sacrifices of their relatives. Despise the difference of fortune and of class, which only the basest people use as measure for their feeling and courtesy; think that from the veins of field-labourers and artisans came nearly all the blessed blood that redeemed our country.[67]

---

67 Edmondo De Amicis (1846–1908), writer and journalist; his children's novel *Cuore* [Heart, 1886] met with enormous and lasting success in Italy and abroad; joined the Italian Socialist Party in 1896. The quotation is from: *Heart* (G. S. Godkin trans.) (London: Sampson Low, Marston, 1895), pp. 201–02.

5

Compared to these positions, which in one way or another are so clear, *verism* initially appears more cautious and sober in its representation of popular themes. What fundamentally characterizes populism? The conviction, expressed to different degrees, that the people are bearers of positive values that can in each and every case be contrasted to the corruption of society, to the injustice of destiny and men or to the brute violence of inequality. There is none of this in Verga. In Verga, the representation of the people is only one moment in a vaster picture, of which it represents a not particularly significant factor. Behind the proletarians of *I Malavoglia*[68] and of many of his Sicilian novellas, one finds a metaphysical vision rather than a historical one, a moral attitude more ontological than earthly, and an indignation and pessimism more universal than human.[69] Verga does not give the people a 'privileged' position in the great tale of suffering. What fascinates him is not the pain of the subaltern strata which he thought had laws and customs of their own as much as the inexorable, cyclical reaffirmation of a law common to all strata, to all men, to all living creatures, from the miserable donkey of the novella *Rosso malpelo*, to the fishermen of *I Malavoglia*, to the aspiring bourgeois Mastro-don Gesualdo, right up to the characters imagined but left unfinished in the final novels of the 'cycle of the defeated'. The refusal to make a direct judgement on the material represented and the stylistic-structural criterion of impersonality—fundamental canons of the naturalistic school— are applied by Verga with extraordinary facility, precisely because he has no

---

68 Literally 'the reluctant ones', was first translated into English as *The House by the Medlar-Tree* (Mary A. Craig trans.) (New York: Harper & Brother, 1890). It inspired Luchino Visconti's 1948 film *La terra trema*. [Trans.]

69 In an interpretation of the novella *Libertà*, Gaetano Trombatore has written:

> The fault of the yokel is precisely that of having believed that one could have justice in this world. And it is what one might call a metaphysical fault, since this criterion of judgement does not live in the real substance of the novella, but can be glimpsed only as the vague, indirect reflection of a feeling in the consciousness of the writer. He knows that the revenge of the rioters is a demand for justice; but he knows that this demand is abstract and unrealizable. He knows that the ignorance of the peasants is the ignorance of all men, who do not know just how useless is any action aiming to change the course of things; for the fundamental laws of humanity are the laws of nature itself, which one can violate, but which cannot be reformed.—'Verga e la libertà' in *Riflessi letterari del Risorgimento in Sicilia* (Palermo: U. Manfredi, 1960), p. 28.

progressive ideological position to defend. His ideology is his poetics, if we may put it that way. When the writer escapes the condition of being a stony and impassive witness, it is only in order to judge as mistaken—nay, as mad and desperate—every attempt to escape with violence, with organization, with a political programme from the condition of inferiority and pain that fate has assigned to us. Popular rebellion in Verga moves between the two poles of blind, animal violence, exemplified by the peasants in *Libertà*, and the easy class betrayal of the protagonist of the play *Dal tuo al mio*. There is no middle course: that is, there is no concrete hope of betterment, because the 'the struggle for existence, for well-being, for ambition' permits no deviation from its iron course and its awful egotism.

The paradox of Verga's work, which on closer inspection is merely apparent, lies here: it is *precisely* the refusal of populist hope and socialist ideas that leads him to the most convincing representation of popular life across the 1800s. The greatness of Verga, the poet of *I Malavoglia* is, therefore, not the work of chance. Were we to make an imaginative judgement, we would say that the bourgeois Verga refuses the cup of consolation which the bourgeoisie always has on hand when it approaches the so-called social problem. To protest and hope, these extremely dubious categories on the ideological as well as the literary plane, which invariably presuppose a subaltern position in those who voice them, he prefers knowledge and awareness. The refusal of a progressive ideology is the source, not the limit of Verga's success.

None of the *veristi* were able to maintain such a rigid and consistent position; perhaps only in Luigi Capuana and Federico De Roberto can we find a similar feeling for a universal law, one not applied to only one stratum or another, to one class of people or another. But for the others usually linked to this school, the tendency is to make a positive standpoint reappear in the representation of the popular subject matter, an indignation that alternates between the moralistic and social. From the Neapolitan Matilde Serao, who in the *Ventre di Napoli* [The Belly of Naples, 1884] provides a then much-imitated model of urban sociological investigation, charged with an explicitly polemical intent; to the Tuscan, Mario Pratesi, who hesitates between fully assuming a naturalist poetics and the enduring tendency towards a petty-bourgeois and provincial kind of moral judgement; from the other Tuscan, Renato Fucini, who in his stories so frequently creates popular types with whom he engages with deep human sympathy; to De Amicis himself, who, in his moderate and bourgeois *verismo* introduces, as we have seen, a whole set of openly progressive aspects.[70]

We are not interested in pursuing the developments and attitudes of individual writers who, in one way or another, can be linked to the problem of populism; not least because the names of many of them will be called upon below as witnesses to the ties to the past and to tradition that mark many of our contemporary writers. It is necessary, however, to underline that, precisely in the *verismo* period, particular tendencies of a regional or urban character began to be formed (or sometimes consolidated) which influence Italian literature even today. Even when *verismo* is not considered to have an immediately populist character, it contains factors that potentially are. One of these is the attention it lends to a geographically circumscribed reality of which the writer becomes what we might call a specialist, turning it into the almost unique object of his work. But regionalism is not always populist (consider, for example, the typically petty-bourgeois Lombard environment of Emilio De Marchi); however, it is often an easy, almost natural channel for a set of populist themes, as if the narrowing of the material horizon of inspiration represents a stimulus to observe more deeply the gradations of social strata. We allude to three large phenomena of regional-verist literature, each of which exhibits quite homogeneous characteristics, or at least strong affinities in terms of investigation, theme, language, and, most importantly to our mind, of sociological interests. The first is made up of the Neapolitan group: Matilde Serao, Ferdinando Russo, Giovanni Capurro, and, on a different and intensely literary level, Salvatore di Giacomo. The second is that of the Sicilians: Giovanni Verga, Luigi Capuana, Federico De Roberto, alongside whom it is possible to place, as exponents of a generically Southern Italian literature, the heirs of the Calabrian tradition of Mauro and Padula: Nicola Misasi and others. The third, finally, of the Tuscan writers: Mario Pratesi, Renato Fucini and Ferdinando

---

70 Luigi Capuana (1839–1915), writer and one of the central figures and theoreticians of *verismo*, along with Verga and Federico De Roberto. Matilde Serao (1856–1927), Greek-born Italian novelist and journalist; co-founder of the newspaper *Il Mattino* that was first published in Naples in 1892. Mario Pratesi (1842–1921), novelist and poet. Close to the traditions of the Risorgimento and Tuscan culture, he wrote extensively about peasant life in Italy. Renato Fucini (1843–1921), poet and writer (also known by the pseudonym Neri Tanfucio), and close associate of Giacomo Puccini who put some of Fucini's poems to music. [Trans.]

Martini, author of the novella *A Pieriposa.*[71] This list of writers is limited by mere chronological convenience, since in truth the discussion of these tendencies could easily continue beyond delimitations of time and school; we would then discover that each has its own, real autonomy, its own inner tradition that operates much more rigorously than a hypothetical national tradition. From the end of the nineteenth century onwards, this strong regional emphasis will be another characteristic of Italian populism. Does all this contrast with the initial observation about the national aspiration present in all populist attitudes? On the contrary, it confirms and restates it forcefully, at least as far as Italy is concerned. Regionalism is the expression of a bourgeois feeling of realism that seeks to escape, through the detailed analysis of concrete situations, from the palpable crisis of ideal horizons. To return to the *country*, to the *town*, to the *city*, to the customs and habits of the *region*, is in this framework to try and rediscover the drive to a more secure hegemony by means of the conscious awareness of new social tasks. Regionalism is not, therefore, the negation of the nation but the quickest and safest path to it. Populism constitutes one of its moments, certainly its most essential. To substitute a populism of facts and things, so to speak, for a populism of ideas is more effectively to carry out one's task of cultural and intellectual direction. A situation of the sort will present itself again in Italian progressive literature in the years following 1930.

I shall now present a few scattered thoughts on those minor writers who, though not raising themselves above the others from the aesthetic standpoint, reveal pertinent thematic and narrative aspects (particularly because they will influence the work of subsequent writers).

---

71 Emilio De Marchi (1851–1901), novelist, literary critic and translator; his narratives focussed on Lombard peasants and the Milanese petty bourgeoisie, and are marked by the influence of Manzoni. Ferdinando Russo (1866–1927), poet, journalist and songwriter; known mainly for his poems in Neapolitan dialect. Giovanni Capurro (1859–1920), poet, critic and songwriter; best known for his famous song 'O Sole Mio' (with Eduardo Di Capua). Salvatore Di Giacomo (1860–1934), poet, dramatist and Fascist intellectual; one of the signatories of the Manifesto of the Fascist Intellectuals; credited with reviving Neapolitan poetry in the vernacular. Domenico Mauro (1812–1873), patriot and man of letters; close associate of Vincenzo Padula, he participated in insurrections against Bourbon rule in the South in 1844 and 1848, joined Garibaldi's 'Thousand' in 1860 and was a left-wing member of parliament in 1865–70. Nicola Misasi (1850–1923), Calabrese short-story writer. Ferdinando Martini (1841–1928), writer and politician; governor of Eritrea between 1897 and 1907, and senator of the Kingdom of Italy in 1923. [Trans.]

First, Mastriani,[72] the tireless reporter of Neapolitan life over dozens and dozens of serialized novels published between 1860 and 1890; he was the forefather of that Neapolitan literature to which we have referred, as well as the acknowledged teacher of Matilde Serao. In Mastriani, as in few other Italian *appendicisti*[73] of the time, among whom for a short while we must even include Misasi, the populist themes are mediated by a linguistic form that also aims to be populist. In short, this is no longer a populism for the cultured classes but a populism for the people. On closer reflection, however, Mastriani's standpoint reveals itself to be not so far from that of the 'learned' populist writers of the period: the denunciation of poverty, moralistic indignation at the corruption of the popular strata of society by the exploitation and the vices of elites, paternalistic commiseration with the wretched in their suffering— in Mastriani too, these are the monotonously recurrent themes in the broad but shallow variety of the narrated episodes.[74] So how could Mastriani be so popular among the Neapolitan proletarian public? Perhaps because they were unable to detect the underlying meaning of the author's stance, and, like children, were caught up in the magic tricks of an inexhaustible if mechanical imagination? In reality Mastriani, precisely because of his cultural and intellectual limitations, reveals another important truth, the other face of Italian populism: yes, it is a bourgeois phenomenon, but it does not for all that stop being popular, at least potentially. 'The People', as we have said, is a theoretico-political invention of the bourgeoisie; but objectively as well it does nothing but reflect the behaviours, tastes, ethical and spiritual stirrings of the dominant class. In other words, 'the people' does not have ideologies or life

72 Francesco Mastriani (1819–91), dedicated numerous novels to the subaltern Neapolitan classes, inlcuding the so-called socialist trilogy; considered to have played an important role in establishing the foundations of *verismo* (also for the development of *Meridionalismo*, the study of socioeconomic and cultural problems of southern Italy that followed the unification). [Trans.]

73 Authors of serialized novels (or *romanzi d'appendice*). [Trans.]

74 An example among many possible ones: In the novel *I delitti di Napoli* (*Le ombre*) / The Crimes of Naples (The Shadows) (Milan: Soc. Ed. La Milano, 1907), p. 22, Mastriani puts these words—with their unequivocally democratic and moralistic flavour—into the mouth of a prostitute whom a young and honest commoner has told that he wishes to become rich in order to redeem and marry her:

> 'If you were rich,' she sneered, 'if you were rich, you would be ruthless like all the rich, and you would not have the heart that you do. I know well what the rich are . . . ! O! damn the rich, damn those thieves of the objects and the honour of others! And damn the gold with which they buy the flesh of the poor daughters of the people; damn the gold with which they burn honest marriage beds!'

opportunities beyond those suggested to it by the bourgeoisie. It is for this reason that it could recognize itself in the bourgeois morality of Francesco Mastriani—suitably simplified to the point of assuming the quality of an easy interpretive schema.

Ferdinando Russo, a poet who wrote in Neapolitan dialect, shows us that the people can become the mouthpiece of openly reactionary political and ideological values. Russo expresses a strictly verist poetics and taste: some of his descriptions of the Neapolitan lumpenproletariat are as solid and sober as anything written on the subject (see particularly the series of poems entitled '*E Scugnizze*[75]). The boundaries of his investigation are not ideologically delimited; he does not represent the people simply to titillate the moral sense of the bourgeoisie nor to encourage them to positively reconsider the entire social question; he also represents the people's attachment to the old values and the old political order. The protagonist in his short poem 'O Luciano d' 'o Rre' (1910) is an old oyster seller who, as a young man, was a cabin boy aboard a Bourbon ship, the *Fulminante*, and part of a group of guards loyal to Ferdinand II. His invective against the new order imposed on Naples by the 'Piedmontese', the Italians, stands out for its violence while his memory of the good old days—when sovereigns were the fathers of the people whose language they spoke and whose customs, superstitions and deeply-rooted beliefs they shared—is both bitter and touching. But behind Luciano's words there lies, as always, the fundamental theme of hunger and misery that justifies both the protests of the democratic and the Bourbon-friendly nostalgia of the Neapolitan plebs as well as the deep disdain for everything that ultimately belongs to the world of lords and intellectuals:

> Here we're all in the hospital!
> We all have the same illness!
> We've all been left half way up the stairs,
> outside the inn of Poverty!
> What do you want to tell me? That we're liberal?
> What's all your bluster about?
> When your son cries and wants to eat,
> look in your pocket . . . and give him liberty![76]

---

75 *Scugnizzo* is Neapolitan slang for street children. [Trans.]
76 Ferdinando Russo, *O' Luciano d''o Rre*, 2nd EDN (Naples: Cisterna dell'olio, 1918), p. 82.

Perhaps inadvertently, Russo had the brilliance to identify the reactionary temptation that is always present in the people. We shall see that this motif, while remaining secondary when compared to the myth of the progressive nature of the people, will also have subsequent developments.

At the other end of the geographical map of Italy, in Milan, Bertolazzi[77] turned his attention to the lowliest, to those fragmented, deprived and miserable people who were always on the edge of robbery, beggary and prostitution, if not already in the world of crime and vice. One owes to this author, writing in Milanese dialect, the invention (or rediscovery) of situations and figures who others would, fifty or sixty years later, pass off as the typical product of a polemic still deemed to be contemporary and effective. Think of Nina in *El nost Milan* [Our Milan, 1893], who knowingly chooses the path of prostitution as an angry and desperate way to compensate for the humiliation of misery and hunger; or Bianca in *Gibigianna* (1912), full of irrepressible sensuality and superstitious Catholicism (with that dramatic finale of moralistic, accommodating reparation); to Carloeu, known as '*el Togasso*', the violent one, the brute who wins women with the lure of physical and animal terror (and is finally murdered, which fits that melodramatic vision which is in no way in contrast to the colourfully folksy [*popolaresco*] spirit of the tale). Bertolazzi too is an artist of wretchedness. Like the Sicilians and the Neapolitans of the time, he too is interested in what we might call the naked and raw moment of survival; that stage of human existence that has yet to reach a truly social dimension and that flounders on the narrow margin between life and death; in permanent danger of material and moral disintegration. This is an Italy of common people, for whom progress and renewal end up blurring into a few, illusory myths that are also accidental and provisional in character.

Against this backdrop of rags and filthy homes, of vile commoners' [*popolari*] kitchens and hotels for the poor, is silhouetted the Fairy Godmother of the game of lotto, the fantastic resource as well as the great parasite of the Italian proletarian strata in the last decades of the nineteenth century.

---

77 Carlo Bertolazzi (1870–1916), journalist, dramatist and author who worked in the vein of *verismo* and the tradition of the national-popular. Many of his works were adapted for film in the post-Second World War period. Giorgio Strehler's production of Bertolazzi's play *El nost Milan* (1893) is the object of an important essay by Louis Althusser, 'The "Piccolo Teatro": Bertolazzi and Brecht' in *For Marx* (London: New Left Books, 1969). [Trans.]

Bertolazzi gives the second act of *El nost Milan* (first performed in 1893), the title *L'estrazione del lott* [The Lottery Draw]. A few years earlier, Matilde Serao opened *Il paese di Cuccagna* [The Land of Cockayne, 1890] with a chapter dedicated to *L'estrazione del lotto*; and earlier, that singular serialized novel that was *Il cappello del prete* [The Priest's Hat, 1888] by Emilio De Marchi, turned entirely around a case of prodigious prophesying around the same widespread popular game (and as further evidence for the universality of Italian poverty and the parallel spread of a blind trust in fate, that goddess of so many afflictions, one should recall that *Il cappello del prete* was published contemporaneously and, it seems, with equal success, in 'two very different newspapers', as De Marchi himself wrote, 'in two cities positioned almost at opposite extremes of Italy, in the *Italia* of Milan and the *Corriere* of Naples'). In this precarious and humiliating atmosphere, in this *Italy of the game of lotto*, even the persistent desire for life and happiness takes on a sarcastic and violent tone; as in the words of the commoner [*popolana*] Bigetta, who is well prepared to recognize the positive aspects of the lumpenproletarian condition:

> Ecstatic! After all, what am I missing? Of course, we're poor, that's true, we work to live, but here in the canteens one can eat without spending much; if we stay in the fresh air we have many night-time hideaways; when we're ill, there's the hospital; the government has even allowed me a beautiful lot of earth 'to keep the heart hoping'; what else can we desire? Some beatings? Hurrah for Milan, the number one place in the world [. . .][78]

Bertolazzi, discovering the Milanese lumpen proletariat under the influence of French naturalism, depicted the lowest level of a subaltern social condition that was also practically universal: indeed, even less than other sections of the Italian population, the northern Italian urban populace failed to offer material for a different account than the one which during this same period was offered by social-democratic, socialist or anarchist writers, by Tuscan regionalists (Pratesi, *L'eredità*), Neapolitans (Serao, *Il ventre di Napoli*) or Sicilians (Verga, *Libertà* and *Quelli del colera*). The thematic uniformity is once again the product of a point of view that is circumscribed within a sociologically defined milieu that was insurmountable by a cultured bourgeoisie which lacked the strength to overcome its moral and political scruples, to project itself into a European, extra-national and extra-popular dimension.

---

78 Carlo Bertolazzi, 'El nost Milan' in *Teatro milanese*, VOL. 2 (O. Vergani and F. Rosti eds) (Bologna: Guanda,1958), p. 44.

6

We have an ironic confirmation of this in those very writers who—in those same final years of the century—began to develop a sort of nationalist and authoritarian reaction towards the political and moral decadence of the country. What may be termed Italy's social immaturity does not allow for the assertion of a progressive or even populist literature at a high level of ideological and political commitment. In the same way, it does not provide occasion or material for a decisively and consciously bourgeois literature strong enough to form the direct and autonomous basis for its class hegemony—at least not without occasionally resorting to ambiguous compromises (grounded in rhetoric, paternalism or protest) with the subaltern strata. It is a fact that, in many of its most significant instances, the struggle against democracy and socialism is also conducted in the name of the people. It is a fact that the link with the most advanced ideological and political experiences of the Risorgimento constitutes a fundamental aspect even in the case of the nationalist writers, just as with the democratic and socialist writers of the post-unity period. It is a fact that the polemic around the formation of a strong and respectable national principle is carried out with tones and arguments not so different from those that the opposition on the Left employed when it demanded that the politically unified Nation should realize itself in keeping with social justice and the practical recognition of the function and the rights of the people. This can mean two things: that the reaction was able to conceal itself behind a populist screen, or that Italian populism and democratism were ideological and political attitudes that were open—*in themselves*—to a conservative and reactionary reading as well. The basic problem remains the creation of a dynamic and modern capitalism. Populism can be understood as the card played by the bourgeoisie on the different gaming tables set up for the experiment. In this interchange of positions, the thematic variants are much less relevant than it first appears; the many twists between the different phases of the discourse of populism are, as we shall see, extremely complicated (with one writer sitting at one or more tables); and yet the course we have outlined shows itself once again to be fundamentally one. It is certainly true that nationalist populism suffers, like its democratic counterpart, from provincialism, and that for bourgeois literature it represents an instrument that in twentieth-century Italy is used in an almost prehistoric manner and with uncommon crudeness. But this judgement simply confirms the persistently confused relationship in Italy between the intellectuals as a stratum and the process of historical development, in all but a few exceptional cases.

The defenders of the system, no less than its opponents, carry with them the inheritance of a centuries-old narrowness of horizons.

One should note that, even for these new orientations, the paradigmatic texts remain the same. Carducci is an essential source for nationalist and patriotic writers in the same way as he had been for the democratic and socialist ones. Over the course of his writings, he moves with ease (that is, without dramatic crises or serious second thoughts) from the Jacobin plebeian masses of *Ça ira* (1883)[79] to the commoners and peasants of the 'great' odes, 'Cadore, Alla città di Ferrara' [To the City of Ferrara], displayed like so many commemorative monuments and so on.[80] This was the same path travelled by many ex-Garibaldians and democrats, from populist deprecation of the bourgeois state to the praising of authority and of the strength of the patriotic and nationalist principle: from Garibaldi to, say, Crispi.[81]

However, the writer that we must recognize as the forefather of these attitudes is Alfredo Oriani. We find in his writings, this time seen from the standpoint of national and patriotic consciousness, that sense of revolt at the incompleteness of the Risorgimento. This is the motif through which he can be linked, on the one hand, to a number of the *left-wing* journalists of the 1800s and, on the other, to polemics by nationalists and fascists against the sins of the liberal, democratic and socialist political classes, pilloried precisely for their inability to satisfy the needs advanced but left unresolved by the movement for unification.[82] Perhaps the first to voice this sentiment in such

---

79 It is worth remembering Sonnet 6 of the series: 'Grave group of ancient statues / Beneath the messages that grow urgent / The people is there: all have but one thought / Let us die then, so the fatherland may live.'—Giosuè Carducci, *Rime nuove* [New Rhymes] (P. P. Trompeo and G. B. Salinari eds) (Bologna: Zanichelli, 1961), p. 391.

80 In 'Cadore' (1892), Verses 134–48: 'Your quarters blossom with blonde children, and from the rugged slopes the hay is scythed by proud singing virgins, their auburn hair twisted and swathed in black, their eyes sparkling with swift blue lightning; as the carter drives three horses down the steep tracks with his load of long-fragrant pine, and Perarolo bustles around its river lock, the hunt blasts out in the smoking hilltop mists: the chamois falls at the well-aimed shots, and the foe will fall when the homeland calls.'— Carducci, *Rime e ritmi*, pp. 212–13.

81 Francesco Crispi (1818–1901), patriot and statesman; one of the principal figures of the Italian Risorgimento, alongside Mazzini and Garibaldi. [Trans.]

82 One cannot ignore that this type of critique also influenced Gobetti's polemic on the Risorgimento, which was favourably received by Gramsci:

> [T]he line of demarcation between the reactionary and revolutionary spirit is, in writers like Oriani, extremely uncertain. We believe this uncertainty is directly derived from the element of national-popular that is present in these positions:

a drastic and pugnacious form, Oriani affirms that the bourgeoisie are those truly responsible for the disasters that followed unification; the anti-bourgeois spirit permeating numerous works of the period thus also derives from him. Clearly this is not the condemnation of a class but, rather (as already noted), a bitter attack on a certain type of political leader to which are attributed all the typical sins that characterize the bourgeoisie: slothfulness, sloppiness, embezzlement, clientelism, transformism, the defence of private interests, neglect of one's homeland and weakness on the diplomatic and military fronts. This repertoire would last up to the advent of fascism (and beyond). Having exhausted in *Fino a Dogali* [Until Dogali, 1889][83] and in *La lotta politica in Italia* [Political Struggle in Italy, 1892] the *pars destruens* of his programme, Oriani founded the *Primato morale e civile degli Italiani* [Moral and Civil Primacy of the Italians] in *La rivolta ideale* [The Revolt of Ideas, 1908]: the basis of the rebirth is, again, a certain concept of 'the people' bringing together the rhetoric of a glorious past, racial pride, pseudo-revolutionary moral energy and conservative political ambitions. For Oriani, the people is set to become the vehicle for the interventionist spirit that will flow into the First World War:

> The Italian people [. . .] was to be found entirely in the depths of the race which the barbarian infusions had rejuvenated, its ancient power and creativity continued even within servitude. Nothing was able to exhaust it; the genius of the people created the city communes, the *signorie*, the principalities, the great republics of land and sea, the new arts, modern legislation. A people that was great in individuals, which in the determination of its federalism perhaps surpassed that of Greece, but with the magnificent superiority given it by the universal idea of Rome and the Catholic idea of the papacy, which

the attempt to tie oneself in some way to the action of the popular masses always provokes, depending on the circumstance, the possibility of a *dual reading*. This explains why Oriani whose complete works were published between 1923 and 1933 under the supervision of Benito Mussolini, could be judged by Gramsci to be 'the most honest and enthusiastic proponent of Italy's national-popular greatness among the Italian intellectuals of the old generation.—*Selections from Cultural Writings* (D. Forgacs and G. Nowell-Smith eds) (London: Lawrence & Wishart, 1985), p. 251.

83 The Battle of Dogali, between Italian and Ethiopian troops, took place on 26 January 1887, on present-day Eritrean territory. The Ethiopians destroyed an Italian battalion, leading to desires for retribution that would eventually issue into the First Italo-Ethiopian War (1895–96) and the crucial defeat at the Battle of Adwa. [Trans.]

made it, through the tragedies and humiliation of all its defeats, a people of masters.

In this way, although Italy remained for long centuries an open field for the wars of Europe, because the major nations always fought one another in our greatest valley, none of them were able to conquer her. The jealousies of our conquerors cancelled each other out in conflict, but someone would finally have managed to prevail if the Italian people had not opposed to all of them the same invincible and enigmatic resistance.[84]

In relation to Oriani, it should be said that, like many other writers of the 1800s, the term 'the people' has in his literary and theoretical works a fairly precise political and ideological meaning while on the properly sociological level it appears more ambiguous and uncertain. Moreover, it is clear that Oriani does not intend to keep it circumscribed within the confines of the subaltern strata. For him, the people has, above all, an ethical and ideal value, not simply a social one. It is equally clear, however, that his concept of 'the people' does not exclude but, rather, implies an active participation of subaltern strata; in this, also he continues the line of certain political strata of the Risorgimento, although he develops it in a heightened patriotic and nationalist key (the people *within* the Nation and *for* the Nation).

The expansion of this new atmosphere is attested by the attitudes of the greatest of Carducci's disciples, Giovanni Pascoli,[85] in his passage from the socialist internationalism of his youth to the nationalism of his maturity. It is possible to see in Pascoli the channel for that ethical and spiritual mentality that was widespread among sections of the bourgeoisie between the end of the nineteenth and the start of the twentieth centuries, and which was destined to continue through to our days as the essential component of left-wing humanitarianism, as expressed by groups of intellectuals and politicians. One must, to begin with, recognize that for Pascoli the people have a better-defined

---

84 Alfredo Oriani, *La rivolta ideale* (Benito Mussolini ed.) (Bologna: L. Cappelli, 1924), pp. 139–40.

85 Giovanni Pascoli (1855–1912), poet and classical scholar. A socialist in his youth, he was mentored by Carducci at the University of Bologna. One of the foremost poets of late nineteenth-century Italy, his work straddles classicism and decadentism. For an English translation, see Giovanni Pascoli, *Last Voyage: Selected Poems* (Deborah Brown, Richard Jackson and Susan Thomas trans) (Los Angeles: Red Hen Press, 2010). [Trans.]

social physiognomy than is typical in those years: the people are for him specifically proletarian. We have not yet reached the point of crude terminological and ideological confusions observable a few years later in strictly nationalist writers. But the recognition of a social reality distinct from that of the bourgeoisie does not prevent the poet from denying all validity to the class struggle and, instead, to harking back to a law of the overcoming of economic and material conflict by the brotherhood of spirits and consciences: 'Here is the basis of my socialism: the certain and continuous increase of compassion in the heart of man. All the facts gathered by the materialists of history prove nothing but this: that man from being merely reasonable has become sentimental';[86] 'I believe [. . .] that the fact of love and charity has more scientific importance and substance, so to speak, than your economic and social theories'.[87] We will not linger on this point, which on more than one occasion has been the object of detailed and accurate investigation. We are interested instead in defining the conceptual horizon and historical judgement which grounds Pascoli's humanitarianism, and, consequently, his 'pietistic' conception of the people. While it has been observed that his humanitarian socialism *naturally* issues in interventionist and imperialist nationalism, what has not been noted is that the frame within which this evolution takes place is fundamentally characterized by deprecating the nascent industrial civilization and by nostalgic regret for the moribund agricultural and peasant civilization. *This is a point of fundamental importance for the development of our entire argument*: first, because it confirms that Italian writers of the nineteenth and twentieth centuries, when they write 'the people' they principally mean 'the peasantry'; and when they need to provide an image of labour, they turn almost exclusively to the forms of agricultural labour. Second, because it reveals that bourgeois and imperialist nationalism lacks the literary and ideological strength to explicitly recognize the assertion of large-scale industry and capital in Italy as a fundamentally *positive* historical datum; instead, this nationalism ambiguously champions returns to the past and anti-historical nostalgias whose fatuous, confused and rhetorical character should by now come as no surprise. There is no populist Italian writer who is able to show an understanding of any of this. Populism appears increasingly as a defence of traditional values that can purportedly be rediscovered beneath historical mutations (it is the path

86 Giovanni Pascoli, 'L'Avvento' (December 1901) in *Tutte le opere. Prose I: pensieri di varia umanità* (Milan: A. Mondadori, 1946), p. 230.
87 Pascoli, *Prose I*, p. 233.

followed by many writers, even those of the Resistance; Pratolini, for example). In Pascoli, the refusal, let us call it that, of capitalist inhumanity assumes the naive (but due to their obvious obtuseness also irritating) forms of a hankering for the old Virgilian Italy, 'saturnine earth, mother of fodder and mother of heroes'. Observe how a writer and the culture that lies behind him reveal themselves to be blind to the true nature of the historical and social phenomena unfolding around them:

> I may be deceived, but a struggle has emerged in the world in addition to those that already exist; a struggle compared to which those of the already ancient eastern empires, and those of Latinate Rome, and of what we might term those of Germanic Rome, were as nothing. Monstrous, enormous, infinite Ninevehs and Babylons, Carthages and Romes are being established. They will conquer, subjugate, wipe out everything around them, and then they will throw themselves against one another as though they were meteorites that had been thrown off course. What will become of us? Because this appears to me to be fatal and necessary, just as, in another order of things, another fate and another necessity reveal themselves to me. This: riches gravitate in such a way as to end up coming together in the same treasure. The little field is absorbed by the larger field, the larger field by the farm, the farm by the large estate, and so on. I am going to say that entire nations are expropriated of their landed property. Alas, who possesses the fields of the saturnine Earth, mother of fodder and heroes? The mortgage holder. And who is he? He is usually anonymous, a collective creditor. But bit by bit, this collectivity is reduced and simplified; the strong swallow the weak; there will be a time when it will be possible to name the sole owner of the whole world: a tyrant in whose service there will be a human species of slaves.[88]

In other words, capitalist development is represented as a giant and monstrous Moloch against which stands—as the last, desperate bastion of human values—the cult of the earth or, more concretely, the defence of small 'peasant holdings'. This political and ideological vision could produce nothing but a nationalism typical of underdeveloped counties, a typical 'imperialism of the poor'. We should not be surprised if the peasant, presently represented by Pascoli, will also make its way forcefully into nationalism and then Fascism—

---

88 Pascoli, 'Una Sagra' (June 1900) in *Prose I*, pp. 168–9.

to then escape the latter and become an integrating framework for a demo-cratic and anti-fascist attitude. Within this narrow conceptual frame, the 'humanitarian' and petty-bourgeois refusal of injustice and oppression can become so inflamed and insane as to transform itself without effort into the frenetic praise for that great, objective 'popular' massacre that is war. Pascoli himself shows how praise for agricultural work and the agricultural proletariat can turn into the theme of the people's war and colonial expansion. In his famous 1911 speech in Braga for the dead and injured of the Libyan war, 'La grande proletaria si è mossa' [The Great Proletarian Has Moved],[89] the link is clear between the compassionate representation of peasant poverty and the necessity and justness of the need for conquest. Pascoli focuses the entire first part of the speech on the subject of emigration which, as we shall see, was exploited enormously at this time by nationalist authors: war is born of the need to give the Italian people what they went wretchedly searching for beyond the borders of the motherland.

> [B]ut the great Proletarian [motherland] has found a place for them: a vast region washed by *our sea*, observed, like so many forward scouts, by our small islands; towards it our large island pushes out impa-tiently; a vast region that thanks to the work of our ancestors was already abundant in waters and crops, green trees and gardens; and now, due to the inertia of nomadic and indolent populations, has for some time largely been a desert. There the workers will not be tools, ill-paid ill-rewarded and ill-named, of foreigners, but in the highest and strongest sense of the word, agriculturalists *on their own* [land], on the earth of the motherland.[90]

The relationship with the democratic question of the Risorgimento is also clear where Pascoli affirms that the Libyan war represents the first overcoming of that separation between rulers and the people (that is, the peasant class), which characterized the entire merely political phase of the struggle for unity and independence:

> That people which resurgent Italy did not always find ready to answer its call, its invite, its command, is there. O fifty years of the miracle!

89 'Proletarian' could be either a noun or an adjective; it is feminine in this case, as would befit the expression *la nazione proletaria* (the proletarian nation), or *la patria proletaria* (the proletarian motherland). [Trans.]

90 Giovanni Pascoli, 'La grande proletaria si è mossa'. Speech delivered in Barga, 'Per i nostri morti e feriti' [For Our Dead and Injured] (Bologna: Zanichelli, 1911), pp. 9–10.

The peasants who were often reluctant and rejected it, those peasants who even far from Lombardy and Veneto called their emperor the emperor of Austria—when the *imperio* of Rome was in the hands of the last of its dictators—the peasants that Garibaldi could never find among his ranks . . . see them now![91]

Reading these lines, one would think that Pascoli had read Nievo's then-unpublished *Frammento sulla rivoluzione nazionale* [Fragment on the National Revolution], so close is the analogy between the concepts and examples (of course, Nievo was asking for land for his peasants while Pascoli gave them war; but it was nevertheless a war in order to give land to the peasants).

The war in Libya is thus viewed as the overcoming of classes in the common struggle against the common enemy: '[T]here are classes and categories there as well: but there is no struggle, or there is struggle for those who arrive first at the enemy's flag, over who first clutches it, over who dies first. Thus we see the people struggle alongside the nobility and the bourgeoisie [. . .] the artisan and the peasant dies next to the count, the marquis, the duke'. Reading these words, one has the feeling that Pascoli has before him the theoretico-militaristic conception of classes that De Amicis had theorized in his day, and that he is preparing to hand it over to the theorists of intervention and irredentism. In these outlooks too, the people is clearly the object of history; however, it was no less so in the writers of democratic and socialist indignation.

The motifs present in Pascoli's work are to be found scattered in the literature that preceded the First World War, forming one of its most essential aspects. With the birth of a real nationalist movement, the theme of the people is taken up in the light of this new ideological and political dimension—not without interesting, novel contributions when compared with the past. Enrico Corradini[92] is particularly significant as a writer who exhibits the spread of this theme across a vast amount of political and literary works of questionable value. A revolutionary syndicalist prior to becoming a standard bearer for nationalism, he introduces into the concept of the 'labouring people' that particularly rebellious and anti-bourgeois accent, of Sorelian origin, which

---

91 This and the following quotation: from Pascoli, 'La grande proletaria', p. 14 and 16, respectively.

92 Enrico Corradini (1865–1931), novelist, essayist and nationalist. A follower of Gabrielle D'Annunzio, he was active in the Fascist nationalist and militarist politics and culture, and became a member of Mussolini's government in 1928. [Trans.]

will underpin some of the early manifestations of fascism. The commoner is not for him the proletarian—the crude and wretched creature of socialist polemic—but the producer, proud of his capacity for work, of the dignity of his craft and his primordial strength, simply wishing to be recognized and used as the bedrock of the motherland. In the novel *La patria lontana* [The Distant Fatherland, 1910], Corradini also takes up the subject of Italian emigration (in this case, to South America). The narrative takes place around a clash of ideas and personalities brought to life by nationalist Piero Buondelmonti and socialist (more precisely: anarcho-syndicalist) Giacomo Rummo. After various episodes, the nationalist wins out and Rummo agrees with him, in an irrepressible burst of passion, that love of the nation comes above all. In the meantime, Buondelmonti has also matured in his challenging bond with the 'representative of the people', and markedly modifies the initial aristocratism of his position. The fact is that Buondelmonti and Rummo are able to begin discussing with one another because they find a common cause around on one thing, anti-bourgeois hatred: 'There was something to which they both assented as though they were one man: that the contemporary bourgeoisie should be put on trial, because it lacks all virtue'.[93] Moreover, it is no coincidence but a self-evident stratagem that it is precisely the socialist who shows the other that *love of the motherland is not incompatible with love of the people* but includes it as a necessary moment: ' "We must believe in the rise of the workers!" cries Rummo. "Believe, Piero, believe! They are our best brothers, the strongest and most generous among us. You yourself with your nationalist ideas, if you need strength, you'll find strength in them; if you need generosity, you'll find generosity in them!"' Beaten, Piero Buondelmonti confesses: ' "You open my eyes." '

Corradini's point is even clearer in his other novel, *La guerra lontana* [The Distant War, 1911]. The work's ideological hinge is a defence of colonial expansion as a vital necessity for economically-underdeveloped peoples (which is also the leitmotiv of the political speech 'La marcia dei produttori' [The March of the Producers],[94] delivered by him on 25 March 1916). The protagonist is the

---

93 Enrico Corradini, *La patria lontana* (Milan: Fratelli Treves, 1910), p. 186.

94 It can now be read in the collection that takes its title from this piece: *La marcia dei produttori* (Rome: L'Italiana, 1916). Corradini's fundamental idea, as it is of the other nationalists, is that imperialist war transfers the class struggle—until then carried out blindly by the proletariat—onto the plane of international relations: 'Just as socialism was a method of freeing the proletariat from the bourgeoisie, nationalism will be for us Italians a method of freeing ourselves from the French, the Germans, the British, the North and South Americans, who are our bourgeoisie.'—Cited by Lenin in 'Imperialism and

contradictory figure of a journalist, Ercole Gola, a corrupt womanizer who deep down is nevertheless not without genuine patriotic virtues. For various reasons he is enticed into battle against Francesco Crispi's African venture but instead, against his own interests, ends up supporting it to the very end. The pages that describe his disorientation and desperation at the defeat at Adwa, which he follows from Italy, are extremely interesting. Crispi is represented, at the moment of his disaster, as an old and noble oak beaten by the acrimony of parliamentary discord and pettiness: the mythologizing of this character, who will then be numbered by the fascist historians and theorists as one of those unlucky predecessors of the movement of national renewal, begins here. Still more significant is the presence, alongside Crispi, of other tutelary deities of populist Italian nationalism. When the news of Adwa begins to spread across Italy, two characters hasten to Gola's newspaper in Rome: one great, unnamed poet, in whom it is not difficult to glimpse Carducci, bitterly penitent at having once challenged Crispi's colonial ventures; and a furious provincial polemicist who, under the pseudonym of Lorenzo Orio, reveals the aggressive traits of Alfredo Oriani. It is no coincidence that while the journalists and correspondents fumed against the popular and socialist demonstrations that were then calling for the fall of Crispi's government and the winding up

---

Socialism in Italy' in *Collected Works*, VOL. 21 (Moscow: Progress Publishers, 1974), p. 359. Corradini's words are from 1910. Prior to this, democrat Gaetano Salvemini had provided a strikingly analogous justification for the Italian need to participate in the war that he then considered imminent:

> Due to past historical evolution, just as along with each state there are formed a set of dominant and dominated classes, so too in international relations there are stronger and weaker states: *bourgeois states* and *proletarian states* [. . . Therefore,] the proletarians of the privileged states, although they only benefit from the crumbs of the privileges won by the ethnic or political grouping of which they form a part, have an *immediate* interest in the maintenance of those privileges [. . . For this reason,] the proletarian classes of the proletarian states must keep their eyes wide open in the face of the internationalism of the more evolved and powerful proletarians; so as to avoid the fate of the savages of America, who believed in the internationalism of the friends of Christopher Columbus, who told them 'Long live liberty, we are brothers', and exchanged broken glass for gold.—'Irredentismo, Questione balcanica e Internazionalismo', *Critica Sociale* 19(3) (1 February 1909).

It is easy to understand on the basis of such statements how, on the threshold of the Great War, interventionism of a democratic type was destined to meet with the interventionism of a nationalist, pre-fascist type—practically merging with it over the course of the war. In a Salveminian writer like Pietro Jahier, we will find the precise echo of this bellicose populism which tries in every way to give a positive democratic character even to the terrifying onset of war. [On Salvemini, see note 1 of the next chapter].

of the African venture, Corradini was putting into the mouth of Orio a vehement defence of the fundamental innocence of the people and a sharp censure of the bourgeoisie, also considered responsible for the anti-patriotic behaviour of sections of the people:

> Wicked Italians! I have heard you scream against the foreigner, against those who in Turin throw mud against our flag! [. . .] [But] now I shall raise my voice and question you, so that remorse for the past may sink its roots deep into you and change your future. What have you done till now? What have you done? The people hated; what did you love? The people were made to hate something; what did you make them love? A new doctrine that was against the motherland and against you was preached to the people; but what have you done for the motherland and for yourselves? Yet you are all here and in the city where you live! You are members of parliament, local councillors, teachers, writers, journalists, and lawyers! You have the census, commerce, the laws, privileges, everything! You are, or should be the salt of the earth! You are the bourgeoisie! But you have done nothing! Everyone has lived for themselves and no one for all! Everyone has fed only his own egotism! No one has known, no one has wanted, no one has dared to see further ahead than the tip of their nose! And now you cry for the flag thrown in the mud! You lament the defeat of the motherland! O, is the motherland then something, you bourgeois? Is the defeat of the motherland something, you bourgeois? Is the flag also something you bad Italians? But, before now, when had you realised it? When? Answer![95]

Oriani's doctrine—once it passed through the flash in the pan of revolutionary syndicalism—prepared the ideological instruments for 'linking' the people to the great war that is about the begin. Literature inspired by the dreadful Great War will also be characterized by this tendency to highlight popular participation in the event: the last battle of the Risorgimento, but for the first time with the massive embroilment of the subaltern strata; a people's war, a peasants' war, where the queen of all battles, the infantry— the army of proletarians, producers and farmers—is the dominant force. On these points, democratic interventionists and nationalist interventionists will generally agree.

---

95 Enrico Corradini, *La guerra lontana* (Milan: Fratelli Treves, 1911), pp. 212–13.

From the First to the Second World War
Interventionism, Fascism, Anti-Fascism

7

Is it a coincidence that Italian literature has not produced any of those works that owe their universal renown to condemnation of the horrors of war and that accompanied the *worldwide* denunciation of the First World War? We shall attribute no greater importance than they deserve to Erich Maria Remarque's *All Quiet on the Western Front* or Henri Barbusse's *Under Fire*. Nevertheless, we must underline the fact that other cultures, other European literatures, have been capable of seeing war exclusively as an irrational and monstrous massacre; there have been authors outside our borders who, over and above the general motives for the conflict, have identified and condemned its pure and simple inhumanity. In these depictions, the goal of the battle lost its importance. What leapt out was the immediate, instinctive, truly 'popular' refusal of a *thing* that was as brutal as it was absurd. None of this takes place in Italy. The truth is that the *popular* denunciation of war does not find a literary expression there because the *populists* are all lined up for war; and aside from the elements of pure inhumanity that they register, they see only the general (ideological and political) reasons for the conflict. The entire democratic tradition of the Risorgimento flows into this new (supposed) occasion for historical and political revival. The Italian democrats demonstrate their love for the people, but not to the point of wishing them a tranquil and prosaic peace rather than a triumphant and glorious massacre. In such an ideological, and in many senses utopian, view, *the people is still conceived as the healthy power of the nation, placing itself in the service of the ideal and sublimating it through its self-sacrifice*. The political outlook of this discourse—or, better, the 'prize' promised to the survivors of the great slaughter—goes no further than a generic peasant reformism; but the idealistic perspective extends to embrace the role of the Italian mission in the world, which of course consists in opposing, with reassuring constancy, the rationale of spirit and consciousness to the purely material and economic one.

The Salveminian[1] component of this attitude is extremely powerful, and not just on the political plane, as one can see if one bears in mind that the writer most representative of it, Piero Jahier, explicitly reveals the influence of the historian of the Southern question. Jahier can be seen an *exemplum* of this aspect of the discourse, inasmuch as during the period of the war we discover in him both poetic and political ambitions. It is noteworthy that Jahier was the chief editor of two newspapers, *L'Astico*[2] and *Il nuovo contadino*[3]: the first, the 'newspaper of the trenches', was printed behind the frontlines between February and November 1918; the other, the 'newspaper of the peasant people', appeared in Florence between July and December 1918; these two organs of the press share the same themes. This continuity is also evident in his main poetic work, *Con me e con gli Alpini* [With Me and with the Alpini, 1919], which is completely unintelligible without an assessment of the 'democratic-peasant ideology' that underlies it, furnishing it with its essential framework. Jahier's decisive choice remains, in every occasion and every *forum*, the *popular justification* for war. The 'motherland of Garibaldi

1 Gaetano Salvemini (1873–1957), anti-fascist historian, member of the Italian Socialist Party and a *meridionalista*; deeply engaged in the question of Southern Italy. After his exile, he moved to the United States and taught at Harvard University. Several of his works, including *The Fascist Dictatorship in Italy* (1928) and *Under the Axe of Fascism* (1936), have been translated into English. [Trans.]

2 Named after the river Astico that flows between Trentino and Vicenza. [Trans.]

3 For an excellent selection of articles from the newspapers, see Piero Jahier, *1918. L'Astico, giornale della trincea. 1919. Il nuovo contadino* (Mario Isnenghi ed.) (Padua: Edizioni de Il rinoceronte, 1964). The introductory essay has a wealth of information, some of it previously unknown, on his spiritual and political development. However, it is perhaps a little too indulgent in its assessment of the writer's inner conflict between a sincere democratic spirit and the inadequacy of his chosen political instruments (which inevitably led him, even against his will, into the opposite camp to that of the popular bloc. Jahier did not know, for example, that *Il nuovo contadino* had been financed, through the mediation of Giuseppe Prezzolini, by the Agrarian Association of Tuscany, which brought together the agricultural and landowning proprietors of the time). This contradiction is nothing but another manifestation of the petty-bourgeois inability to take a rational and consequential position alongside the working class against the bourgeoisie and, in a sense, also against the people: the reference to Jahier's youthful reading of Proudhon and Sorel is illuminating, as it completes the picture of the his cultural and political sources, alongside the lessons of the Italian democratic tradition (Mazzini and Garibaldi). [Giuseppe Prezzolini (1882–1982), literary critic and journalist; founder of the cultural and literary journal *La Voce* in 1908. Emigrated to the US in 1929, and taught at Columbia University.—Trans.]

and Mazzini' could not fail to adopt as its own that war which, driven by reasons of justice and fraternity, was above all a 'revolution of the nations', a 'revolution of free peoples'. On the one hand, the war involves following through on a commitment, which is part of Italy's history and of its spirit, as the highest point of its national contribution to the supranational life of peoples—as stated with pride at the end of the war: 'Austria dies and dies of an Italian victory; because it is the Italian motherland that sows the *idea* that kills it. Garibaldi and Mazzini are the names of its victors'.[4] On the other hand, we find in Jahier the oft-stated acknowledgement that the war so horrifically fought out stands apart from the preceding ones because it bears within it that ideal charge which the poor nations and peoples have infused it with: 'for this reason [. . .] the world war has been called a revolution of peoples, in the same way that the French Revolution was the war of citizens'. As we have remarked, clearly behind Jahier stands Salvemini. We have first-hand documentation of this in Jahier's description of the historian's propaganda visit to the front, which was published in *L'Astico*: Salvemini is 'a real friend of the people'; 'coming up here to speak to the soldiers'; 'a true friend, of those who love in deeds and not just in words'. The summary of Salvemini's speech shows that even the most cultured and intelligent of the interventionists were unable to go beyond the most obvious of warmongering polemics. But we are not interested here in Salvemini's position; rather, we want to see how Jahier assesses Salvemini's personality because then we can grasp the logical and ideological link between the democratic spirit and the warrior spirit. Hence, for Jahier, Salvemini is someone who 'in peace helped the people to fight for social justice—and many soldiers, peasants in uniform, recognized him and stopped him to shake his hand'; 'in war he continued to help them, descending into the trenches with them to fight for justice amongst peoples—which is the foundation of social justice'.[5] According to Jahier, it is on this basis that one can justify the contribution of the Italian popular masses to the war, and to the Wilsonian dream of the Society of Nations, which aimed to unite all peoples in civilized coexistence, guaranteeing to each the objective possibility of progress and well-being.

---

4 This and the following quotation": from Isnenghi, *L'Astico, giornale della trincea*, p. 160 and 138, respectively.

5 Isnenghi, 'Perché vinceremo' [Why We Will Win, 9 May 1918] in *L'Astico, giornale della trincea*. p. 98.

But the argument would be incomplete if we ignore that, like Salvemini, when Jahier expresses an idea of the people, he inevitably associates it with that of the peasantry. His entire interventionist stance turns on this identification. When the virtues of the motherland, to which *L'Astico* makes persistent reference, concretize themselves in a precise judgement, in a direct allusion, it is easy to establish that they coincide with the traditional virtues of the peasantry—those same virtues that Pascoli in the *Grande proletaria* or Corradini in the *Patria lontana* had already highlighted:

No people has been stronger than the Italian one at enduring. Enduring the exile from the motherland to go abroad in search of work; enduring the harshest efforts that characterize the two daily jobs necessary to put something aside more speedily; enduring the pains of building one's home one floor per year, in instalments. 'To make virtue of necessity' is an Italian expression.[6]

With observations of this kind we are already in the atmosphere of *Con me e con gli Alpini*, perhaps the most noble and morally anguished work ever written on the subject of war, yet a work that is not without equivocations and ambiguities deriving precisely from Jahier's honest spirit of democratic participation in the event of war. The 'Declaration' that opens the work rings as follows:

Others will willingly die for the History of Italy
and perhaps some to sort out their lives in some way or other.
But I will so as to provide company for this hungry people
that knows not why it goes to its death,
a people who die because 'it cares for me',
among its sixty men under orders,
since it is the day to die [. . .][7]

The entire book sings the praises of the virtue of peasants and mountain dwellers, from which strength and human warmth without equal are said to spring; in the face of it, the writer's ability, for which soldiers love him, is to make himself entirely, even if secretly, humble before them. In this novel way, Jahier depicts the relationship between intellectual–officer and commoner–soldier, one of the typical forms by which a discourse of collaboration between

---

6 Isnenghi, 'Perché vinceremo', p. 98.
7 Piero Jahier, *Con me e con gli Alpini* (Turin: Einaudi, 1943), p. 7.

the subaltern strata and the bourgeoisie is established in Italy. But the process is not one-way: the intellectual becomes humble, because only thus can he conquer the popular soul and elevate it. The war is holy precisely because these peasants, despite ignoring the reasons for it, have accepted to fight it thanks to their own humanity's mysterious acquiescence.

For example, the soldier Somacal Luigi: a poor manual worker deformed by labour, he only becomes truly cognizant of the world through soldiering, because 'the air is good' among his comrades and alongside his lieutenant; he wants to 'remain in that fine air until the end'; and he enjoys being called a friend by his superior. In this figure we observe a paternalism of the kind found in the Risorgimento, which requires no further illustration. At the same time, we encounter the mystical attempt to meld with popular consciousness as the source of justice and the *justification of the bloody struggle* that is being waged. The poet will conclude: 'No doubt, Somacal, lame soldier, a laughing stock, you are my friend. By your side I have found Italy's honour. I say that Italy's honour is to be found low down, Somacal Luigi.'[8]

What strikes us in Jahier's attitude is precisely this religious desire to 'annex' to the massacre the ethical and subjective responsibility of the peasant-*alpini*[9] soldiers that make up his troop, from whom he learns a reserved and indirect but for this reason very profound way of loving and serving his motherland. One might say that the writer's protestant and democratic thinking, precisely because it obliges one to search for the causes that move the ignorant mass to endure the weight of the war with the greatest rigour, leads to an even deeper and more 'convincing' acceptance of the massacre. Jahier is indeed convinced that his *alpini* soldiers fight not only for their motherland but also, though unknowingly, for a universal goal of freedom and justice. The valence of the Catholic concept of 'humility' is reversed but it endures: everything exists in the people, even the reason they allow themselves to be massacred. Should we not finally admit that even this book is saturated in intellectualist rhetoric, in the same way as many other 'nationalist' books on the First World War?

Harbouring these convictions, Jahier emerges from the war even more persuaded of the need to construct an autonomous peasant politics which would respond to the needs emerging during the war from the great mass of Italian combatants and provide them with a central focus. But by virtue of

---

8 Jahier, *Con me e con gli Alpini*, p. 7.

9 *Alpini* are an elite corps of the Italian army specializing in mountain (i.e. alpine) warfare. [Trans.]

the positions it adopted and the fundamental choices it made, *Il nuovo contadino* demonstrated even more clearly the dead end to which a democratic populism of this sort leads. Peasant reformism *inevitably* bore within it a decisive anti-worker attitude. This motif was already present in *L'Astico*, in the guise of a resentment towards the workers who remained at home because they were considered 'irreplaceable and exempt'—while at the front the peasant-combatants sacrificed themselves for the good of all, that is, for the greatness of the Motherland.[10] But after the war, generic and moralistic accusations are abandoned in favour of directly political arguments: Jahier's cautious support for Lazzari's[11] reformism is also an indignant accusation against subversivism, Bolshevism, Red defeatism, strike mania, the narrow-minded economism of workers and the demand to overthrow the principle of property. To this climate of corruption and defeatism Jahier opposes, *like the nationalists*, an appeal to the ethical law of labour, which means joy in production, an almost religious acceptance of the sacrifice implicit in human labour, the capacity to reconcile and integrate the *economic* interest of various strata or individuals with the ideal interest of the collective. Peasant autonomy is therefore not the principal of social revolution. Every attempt to lead it onto this terrain finds a ready reply from Jahier:

---

10 In the article 'Nemici in casa. La corruzione', Jahier imagines an Austrian agent writing to a spy in Italy, listing the kind of moral and material damage that can be wreaked on the nation in struggle. 'I am pleased to see,' says the imaginary enemy,

> that those who have enriched themselves, *the irreplaceable and exempt male and female workers* spend and expand without measure, almost as much as the Austro-Hungarians (*todeschi*) [. . .]. And yet it is known to the Imperial government that their Italian counterpart alternates certain workers from the factories and workshops, substituting them with elderly soldiers, and that they no longer wish to treat a music teacher–doorman or a lawyer–lathe turner as irreplaceable [. . .]We must prevent this from happening. If combatants were to substitute these people, they would produce more, advancing from the worst to the best, and *with that greater awareness which comes from life in the trenches* [. . .]—Isnenghi, *L'Astico, giornale della trincea*. pp. 148–9.

11 Costantino Lazzari (1857–1927), socialist politician, co-founder of the Italian Workers' Party in 1882, which in 1885 merged with the Italian Socialist Party, where Lazzari served as national secretary from 1912 to 1919. At the outbreak of the war, he coined the slogan *Né aderire né sabotare* [Neither Participation nor Sabotage] to advance a position between the pacifist and interventionist wings of the workers' movement. [Trans.]

It is as though I heard someone answer: 'But we are peasants. We organize against the bosses to get a bigger share. Let the bosses think about that general interest.' To think only of the mess tin is to think like a slave. It is selfishness that has poisoned the workers' movement. We are all servants of society and society has no interest in those who do not know how to serve it well. The worker who approaches emancipation is the one who knows how to take on some risks and guarantee that service to society which is constituted by good production.[12]

It matters little, at least on the political and social plane, if an undeniable moral drive underpins statements of this type. On the contrary, when one looks into the Law to which Jahier subordinates his credo, one finds that, despite appearances, it is also incredibly rigid and uncomprehending: an 'ethics of poverty' is always the sign of a benighted mysticism which, behind an appearance of rigour, hides a timid and conservative soul ('Is there anyone that poverty has not improved? Poverty sharpens ingenuity and stimulates work: it is the poor peoples who progress; the wealthy ones go backwards. Poverty chases away privilege and honours work, it supports charity and keeps tyranny at bay'[13]). Much more important is the observation that the peasantry, according to Jahier, possesses *in itself* the inexorable source of its values and moral progress, and that is the source of its superiority over other strata and classes. 'It is the factory that must learn from the earth,' Jahier remarks, but only so as to then explain that to *productive partners*,[14] like the Tuscan tenant farmers, 'a politics of compromises governed through organizations' seems more suitable 'than a politics of violence such as the strike'.[15]

In this picture, the appeal to a government of the people remains a pure *petitio principii*, a statement of ethical and ideal values; while the revival in the name of the people of war-mongering resentments closely resembles the slogans wielded by nationalist writers of the time instigated for their specific anti-worker and anti-socialist ends: 'This people who has suffered for the

---

12 Isenghi, *L'Astico, giornale della trincea,* pp. 223–4.

13 Untitled editorial in *Il nuovo contadino* (31 July 1919) quoted by Isenghi in *L'Astico, giornale della trincea,* p. 207.

14 Jahier's expression (see Isenghi, Introduction in *L'Astico, giornale della trincea.* p. 232), We can trace the influence of Mazzini, Proudhon, Sorel, Corradini and perhaps contemporary free-market liberals.

15 Isenghi, *L'Astico, giornale della trincea.* p. 232

Italian motherland can lead it well. By insisting on Caporetto,[16] draft dodgers and defeatists want to bury our victory and take over the government [. . .]. But the combatants cry out: enough of that measly, cowardly, ignorant and corrupt Italy that stabbed us in the back while we fought'.[17] In the same issue of *Nuovo contadino* in which these words appeared, Fernando Agnoletti,[18] the Vocian[19] man of letters and war volunteer, would write an article of 'peasant' satire against the Bolsheviks; he would become one of the pillars of Florentine fascism and an assiduous collaborator of *Il Bargello*, the paper around which the young Vittorini,[20] Pratolini, and Bilenchi[21] would gather.[22]

8

We should not be surprised that the concept of 'the people'—upheld in the name of the motherland by the most different or even opposed political and intellectual tendencies—should emerge in an even more radically nationalistic

---

16 In the Battle of Caporetto (also known as the Twelfth Battle of the Isonzo or Battle of Karfreit, 24 October–19 November 1917), Austro-Hungarian forces alongwith German allies defeated the Italian Army. And for years thereafter, it became a rallying cry for nationalists and later Fascists, who presented themselves as redeemers of the national humiliation caused by 'liberal' politicians. [Trans.]

17 Isnenghi, 'Caporetto' in *L'Astico, giornale della trincea*, p. 217.

18 Fernando Agnoletti (1875–1933), writer and journalist; a volunteer in the First World War, he later joined the Fascist movement. [Trans.]

19 A reference to the journal *La Voce* founded in 1908 by Giuseppe Prezzolini, which took an anti-Positivist stance, displaying idealist, mystical and irrationalist tendencies. [Trans.]

20 Elio Vittorini (1908–66), novelist, translator and editor. Born in Sicily, he moved to Florence in the 1930s, where he collaborated with Malaparte, Pratolini and Bilenchi. Initially a 'left fascist', he was expelled from the Fascist Party for his articles in *Il Bargello* advocating Italian intervention in the Spanish Civil War on the *Republican* side. He later joined the clandestine Communist Party and fought in the Resistance. In the immediate postwar period, he published the novel *Uomini e no* [Men and Not Men], edited *Il Politecnico*, and co-founded *Il Menabò* with Italo Calvino. [Trans.]

21 Romano Bilenchi (1909–89), novelist, journalist and short-story writer. Having started on the left of the Fascist movement, he became chief editor of *La Stampa* under Curzio Malaparte in 1931, developing increasingly dissident views. He joined the resistance and the PCI in 1943, later becoming a director of *Nuovo corriere* and of the Marxist weekly *Il Contemporaneo*. [Trans.]

22 The article 'Il contadino e il bolcevicche' is signed by 'Agnoletti' like other pieces in *Il nuovo contadino,* but undoubtedly is an example of the Fernando to whom we refer for political, biographical and even stylistic reasons. This view is endorsed by Isnenghi to we have turned for advice on the question.

and anti-democratic form from the Great War. The war does not put an end to but, rather, facilitates the widespread affirmation and diffusion of Oriani's stance. Nationalist discontent with the territorial and political results of the victorious war comes together with the aggressive claim for popular rights: rights for that people who, having endured the material and moral weight of the struggle, is said to run the danger of being thrown back into a subaltern position by the incapacity or avaricious bad faith of the old ruling class. The significance of this attitude cannot be overstated in the study of the origins of fascism. It is far more common to emphasize the contribution of Gabriele D'Annunzio's 'superman' to the formation of certain ideological values of fascism: individualism, cult of heroism, aestheticism and so on. But, at least to begin with, during the formation of the fascist movement, the dominant discourse is the other one, which wagers on the anti-bourgeois resentment of the masses and on the capacity for agitation of a vaguely socialistic, republican and fierily revolutionary sloganeering. Out of this mixture of Orianism, Sorelianism and democratic nostalgias of the Risorgimento (the cult of Garibaldi and his more or less legitimate followers) is born Benito Mussolini's own position. A position that was certainly confused and adventurous yet effective precisely in its capacity to congeal, around the nascent movement, forces drawn from the old democracy, the nationalist tradition, and the young and very young mass of fighters who came out of the war filled with hatred, however indeterminate, towards the old liberal state. *The real anti-worker function of fascism could thus easily disguise itself in populist dress*: even more openly than on previous occasions, the notion of the people revealed itself to be an instrument of the bourgeoisie in its struggle against the autonomous organization of the working class. In a speech to the Dalmine metalworkers on 20 March 1919, Mussolini praised the ethical concept of labour, linking its consecration to the role of workers and peasants in the course of the patriotic war: 'It is work that speaks through you, not idiotic dogma or the intolerant church, even if it be red. It is work that, in the trenches, consecrated its right no longer to be effort, misery or desperation, since it must become joy, pride, creation, the conquest of free men in the free and great motherland, within and outside its borders'.[23] Corradian Sorelianism furnishes Mussolini

---

23 Benito Mussolini, *Discorso pronunciato il 20 marzo 1919 agli operai di Dalmine, S. A.* [Speech to the Workers of Dalmine on 20 March 1919] (Dalmine: Stabilimenti di Dalmine, n.d.). There are reasons to be doubtful about the real nature of the 'strike of a national type' praised by Mussolini, since the publication of the speech was overseen and printed, and

with the formula that serves from that point onwards to justify, with varying emphasis, the function of the 'worker' within society and the nature of his rights in relation to the state and the businessman: 'You are not the poor, the humble and the outcast, in keeping with the old rhetoric of literary socialism; you are the producers, and it is this quality to which you lay claim that also allows you to lay claim to the right to negotiate on equal terms with the industrialists'.[24] It is easy to move from this reappraisal of the 'dignity of work' to the polemic against the ruling bourgeois class which for Mussolini at this time comprised old-style liberals through to Catholics and socialists, all of whom were deemed guilty of having used the popular mass for a dirty game favouring individual interests: 'One day, I don't know whether sooner or later, you will be able to exercise important functions in modern society, but bourgeois or semi-bourgeois politicians should not be allowed to use your aspirations to play their own game.' Incidentally, at this time, Mussolini had few positive things to say about the *Confederazione Generale del Lavoro* (CGdL);[25] this is quite significant for an attitude that is presented to the masses as a popular-style choice that is *anti-subversive but revolutionary*. The judgement that Mussolini expresses here on the nature and function of the workers' strike is typical. Even if unintentionally humorous in form, the content of this part of the speech on the supposedly new (that is, *productive*) way of striking by the Dalmine workers is serious and probably intentional:

> The intrinsic meaning of your act is clear [. . .]. You have placed yourselves on the terrain of the class, but have not forgotten the Nation. *You have spoken of the Italian people, not only of your profession as metalworkers.* For the immediate interests of your profession you could have gone on strike in the old way, the negative and destructive

---

presumably paid for, by the boss. From our point of view, it is more important to emphasize how even fascist demagogy toyed with the populist motif according to the rule whereby every time the working class allows itself to become the people, it places itself in the hands of the most adventurist and unscrupulous bidder. What's more, the importance of the Dalmine episode was noted by the fascists themselves, if for no other reason than as a propagandist and political instrument. See Gioacchino Volpe, *Storia del movimento fascista* 1st EDN (Milan: ISPI, 1939) p. 28.

24 This and the following quotation: from Mussolini, *Discorso pronunciato.*

25 An Italian trade union founded by socialists in 1906. It operated clandestinely under fascism after 1927. After liberation, in 1945, it fused into the CGIL which is still the largest Italian trade union. [Trans.]

strike; but thinking of the interests of the people, you have inaugurated the creative strike, which does not interrupt production [. . .][26]

But we should not joke too much about these crude definitions by Mussolini, because on them will be built indisputably important things, such as the corporative theories and the Corporations. The relationship between class and Nation, profession and people, the ethics of the producer and of productivity, the subordination of the particular interest to the general (= 'popular'), constitute the cornerstones of that left-wing fascism that will play such an important part in the formation of intellectual and political cadres between 1924 and 1940. Those cadres will continue to refer to this Mussolini and to the fascism of the origins, sometimes opposing them to the consolidation of a more openly conservative and bourgeois fascism.

This intellectual climate helps us understand and assess positions such as those of Curzio Malaparte,[27] who also needs to be taken seriously, if for no other reason than that he contributes to the founding of essential elements of a particular tradition of literary fascism which, through the magazine *Il Selvaggio* and the *Strapaese* movement,[28] will influence numerous well-known writers of the fascist *ventennio*[29] and the Resistance. Malaparte is, at least initially, a typical distillation of all or nearly all the ideological components of

---

26 Volpe, *Storia del movimento fascista*, p. 28.

27 Curzio Malaparte, pseudonym of novelist and journalist Kurt Erich Suckert (1898–1957). An important literary and intellectual figure in the early period of Fascism, he was expelled from the Fascist Party in 1933 and internally exiled for his criticism of Mussolini and Hitler in *Technique du coup d'état* (1931). His experience as a journalist on the Eastern Russian front was the source for his novel *Kaputt* (1943). He joined the Italian Communist Party in 1947. [Trans.]

28 *Strapaese* and *Stracittà* were contrasting Fascist literary movements. The former aimed to affirm rigorously national qualities, and refused all cosmopolitan and foreign influences which it argued adulterated the purity of the Italian people. In contrast, the *Stracittà* wanted to 'deprovincialize' Italian culture by linking Fascism to the modern world or, more precisely, to European literature and culture. Asor Rosa noted that *Strapaese* insisted upon 'rural and peasant rootedness, appealing to original values of Italian identity, pulling faces [. . .] at one's enemies, at those left behind, at old-school "liberals"; on the other hand, *stracittà* beckons (clearly in post-*Futurist* manner) to modernity, innovation, to creative youthfulness, refusing old-fashioned ideas and the fearful remains of the old culture.'— *Storia europea della letteratura italiana*, VOL 3 (Turin: Einaudi, 2009), p. 312. [Trans.]

29 *Ventennio* refers to the two decades of Fascist rule, from 1922 to 1943. *Il Selvaggio* (1924–42) and *L'Italiano* (1926–42) were among the literary journals that promoted the *Strapaese* movement. [Trans.]

the nascent fascist movement. He is very young and a member of the Republican Party, which means he feels heir to the foremost elements of the Risorgimento. As an interventionist, he enrols in the Garibaldini, fighting on French soil, which realizes and legitimates his conviction that one must return to the *spirit* of the Risorgimento against the small-mindedness of the contemporary 'little-Italy' mentality. He is not only a revolutionary syndicalist and a follower of Corradini but also a fascist, a *squadrista*,[30] and a leader in the fascist unions. Malaparte's personal contribution to this rather coherent amalgam is not—as so often is claimed—his odd and adventurous Tuscan spirit, so much as a truculent conception of 'Tuscan-ness' that will give birth (and how!) to a multitude of imitators (and even some intelligent followers). Regionalism, then, above all, but not the bigoted and conservative kind—rather a violent, anti-philistine, crude and (in its own way) populist regionalism. Even the evocation of the past, which at times takes on the character of a purely reactionary appeal, must be seen essentially as an expression of animosity towards a gangrenous liberalism. In this picture, the people are the pure living force that is able to overcome the bourgeois attachment to power and corruption. Ultimately the truncheon is nothing but the rustic expression, healthy and virile, of a way of settling disputes. Against a decrepit and impotent Italy that looks to a putrefying European civilization, there stands an Italy that is useful in a fight and strong of heart; that is tied to the cult of traditions; and that is alive in the countryside and among the plebs, as well as in its daily struggles and its inexhaustible linguistic capacity.

It seems fundamental that this conception or attitude ground itself in the underlying experience of war, lived in a particular spirit. Among the variety of democratic voices singing the praises of war, it is interesting that the most audaciously discordant one—although within visible ideological limits—is precisely that of the interventionist and future fascist Malaparte. In his book *La rivolta dei santi maledetti* [The Revolt of the Damned Saints, 1921], he describes in sharply polemical terms the rout of Caporetto. He makes three main points: that the defeat was caused by the mutiny of a number of Italian regiments tired of the lengthy and terrifying massacre; that the responsibility

---

30 *Squadrismo* was the practice by Fascists of organizing armed bands to fight what they presented as the threat of socialism. It played a crucial role in the rise of Fascism before it took power, and was particularly frequently deployed by bosses and landowners to violently repress workers and peasants. These groups or *squadristi* are more commonly known in English as 'Blackshirts'. [Trans.]

for the episode fell on the shoulders of the ruling political circle and on the high command who were incapable, inept, and shockingly cynical; that one should heap praise on the human and military virtues of the great mass of fighters (especially the infantrymen), who bring to their revolt the spirit, exacerbated by injustice, of a great and unfortunate heroism, and of the same capacity to suffer and struggle that only a few weeks later would animate the defenders of the Piave, the Grappa and the Montello.[31] Let us not forget that the work was initially titled *Viva Caporetto!*[32] Malaparte is very clear about the subject of the work: 'I want to speak of that part of the nation in arms that wore neither feathers nor plumes and was not specially recruited or trained, *of that haphazard assembly of people from all regions of Italy,* without pockets in their jackets, without marks of distinction, unable to "scrounge" a uniform, etc.; *made up of artisans and workers, day labourers and labourers of all kinds, and above all of peasants'.*[33] Moreover, he weaves the tumultuous thread of his narrative, which is at once a protest and a demand for justice, around this people of workers and soldiers. Particularly effective are some of the final pages on the rout, where the soldiers jeer and insult the officers, bearing all resistance and discipline away as though in a muddy torrent—although Malaparte's debt to D'Annunzio is particularly evident in the description of the peasant character of the struggle (to the D'Annunzio, that is, of the barbaric-popular pilgrimage to the sanctuary of Casalbordino in *Trionfo della Morte* [The Triumph of Death, 1894]—yet another vehicle for the racist and nationalist discourse on the Italian people).

A few years later, commenting on the spirit of his work in *Ritratto delle cose d'Italia, degli eroi, del popolo, degli avvenimenti, delle speranze e inquietudini della nostra generazione* [A Portrait of Italian Matters, of the Heroes, People, Events, Hopes and Disquiets of Our Generation] which prefaces the second, revised (and tamed) edition of *La rivolta*, Malaparte states that he had wanted to find in Caporetto 'a kind of tumultuous and popular continuation of the Risorgimento, which would thus be anti-bourgeois, anti-philistine and

---

31 Refers to a river, a hill and a mountain respectively, in the province of Treviso (Veneto)—the sites of various battles in the First World War. [Trans.]

32 The book was repeatedly impounded by state censors for a title that appeared to celebrate the defeat of the Italian army. [Trans.]

33 Kurt Suckert, *La rivolta dei santi maledetti*, 2nd EDN (Rome: La Rassegna Internazionale, n.d.[1928]), p. 170.

anti-political'.[34] We see here how the relation he establishes between popular rebellion and the Risorgimento, between the people and the dominant bourgeoisie becomes evermore defined:

> The people of peasants and mountain dwellers, of the 'infantrymen', would have risen up against the so-called Italians, the false, corrupt, half-cultured rhetoricians, speechifiers and politicos, the historical 'left and right'—by which, let's be clear, we mean the liberals, democrats, socialists, the modern Italians, those men of the piazzas, the government, the cafes, the university, the academies, who ever since the 1870s have in a thousand ways, whenever they so wished, thrown discredit on the heroic, saintly, Christian Italy of 1812, with the excuse of patriotism or of rhetoric, of democracy or of social revolution. The people of the infantry should have implacably destroyed everything that was done from the breach in Porta Pia[35] till today—everything: taking men and their times back to the *soul* of the Risorgimento; to be the avengers of the true Italy, the Italy of the countryside and the simple folk [*popolaresca*], ancient, catholic, and anti-modern. Restoration. Counter-Reformation.[36]

We are already immersed in a 'savage'[37] milieu (the *Ritratto* was published in 1928). That this is not a case of a partial *a posteriori* interpretation or distortion is clear from Malaparte's previous works, such as the noteworthy *Italia barbara* [Barbarous Italy], which first appeared in 1925 for Piero Gobetti's publishing house; and the 'Ragguaglio sullo stato degli intellettuali rispetto al fascismo' [Report on the Situation of Intellectuals in Relation to Fascism], published as the preface to Ardengo Soffici's[38] *Battaglia fra due vittorie* in 1923. The dynamically anti-bourgeois, anti-proletarian *but popular* nature of Malaparte's fascism and that of his friends is confirmed here: 'The vile bourgeois and proletarian world against which we fought had few defenders among the people, but many among the intellectuals. One should note that our revolution was more against Benedetto Croce than against

---

34 Suckert, *La rivolta,* p. 58.

35 The Bersaglieri soldiers entered Rome on 20 September 1870 through Porta Pia, a gate in the Aurelian Walls, defeating papal forces and completing the unification of Italy. [Trans.]

36 Suckert, *La rivolta,* p. 58.

37 A wordplay on the *strapaese* publication *Il Selvaggio* [The Savage]. [Trans.]

38 Ardengo Soffici (1879–1964), Italian writer, poet, painter and sculptor. [Trans.]

Buozzi or Modigliani.'[39] And again: 'We should have filled Rome with the dead last October: how many people worthy of the noose in the great family of Crocians, Salveminians, of self-interested "patriots", and rhetoricians! The people would have kissed our hands.'[40]

The limit of this position is evidently not in being anti-liberal, anti-democratic, anti-bourgeois and, in relation to the socialism of the time, also anti-socialist. The limit of this position lies, as we have observed, in contrasting the cultural and ideological provincialism of a little liberal Italy with the cultural and ideological provincialism of a little Fascist Italy.[41] It might have been the responsibility of intellectual strata, on both sides; or it may have been the consequence of not-entirely-developed historico-social conditions. The fact is that, in contrast to the generically humanitarian and pietistic protest of democratic-populist poetry and literature, there stood—on the strictly literary terrain—a strongly regional protest, where the relationship to the tradition once again acts as a stylistic and thematic prison. There is, of course, the rallying to fascism of groups and movements, such as the Futurists and *Stracittà*, who at least in theory argued for the establishment of a correct relationship between the forces of Mussolini's social revolution and the literary trends of modernity. But, all in all, these are phenomena that make much less of an impact on the general characteristics of fascist art than does the vulgar populism of Malaparte and the other Tuscans.

Culturally, the fascist revolution, which is an aspect of the development and stabilization of Italian capitalism, reveals a simple but powerful recovery of localism.[42] There are two fundamental aspects to this literary position: the

---

39 Kurt Suckert, 'Ragguaglio sullo stato degli intellettuali rispetto al fascismo' [Report on the Condition of Intellectuals Attitudes to Fascism] in Ardengo Soffici, *Battaglia fra due vittorie* (Florence: La Voce, 1923), p. *xxiii*. To grasp Malaparte's ideologico-political standpoint, one should also bear in mind the following programmatic statement: 'I have always considered Marx to be *anti-revolutionary*. And I have always had faith in Sorel, who has certainly been the most *heroic* advocate of the individualist principle, the seed of which is to be found in revolutionary syndicalism'—Suckert, 'Risultati' in *La rivolta*, p. 275.

Bruno Buozzi (1881–1944), socialist trade-unionist and anti-fascist; clandestinely led the CGdL; Giuseppe Emanuele Modigliani (1872–1947), socialist politician and anti-fascist. [Trans.]

40 Suckert, 'Ragguaglio', p. *xxiv*.

41 Disparaging term for a 'weak' Italy, often used by nationalists and imperialists. [Trans.]

42 This facet of Fascism was, above all, true of custom, culture and art, and was known to many from the start. Gioacchino Volpe wrote: '[Fascism] soon accepted the traditional

celebration of the peasant and provincial character of Italian people; and the highlighting of regionalist tendencies on the thematic as well as the formal and linguistic levels, after the parenthetic first decades of the century, when the dominant orientations (*La Voce*, Futurism, etc.) were moving in the opposite direction. The phenomenon was visible particularly in Tuscany which, from this time onwards, until after the Resistance, has remained one of the centres most characterized by its provincialism.

What, for example, does Malaparte do when he brings his ideological and political convictions to the poetic and literary plane? Formally, he goes so far as to rediscover the tradition of burlesque and heroic-comic poetry that for many centuries was famously the breeding ground for the most antiquated yet innocuously crude linguistic play. Thematically, he invents (or reinvents) the figure of the Tuscan commoner, who is not only *straprovinciale* but also *stracittadino*, even restricted to his quarter or neighbourhood, and who will later provide the cue for all possible reprises and imitations of the fascist and anti-fascist Tuscan writers from the 1930s to the present. In the *Cantata di Strapaese* [Ballad of *Strapaese*][43] one finds, first, the geographical circumscription of this world: 'Between the rivers Bisenzio, Arno and Ombrone, and the Elsa valley is our kingdom'; and then its intellectual characteristics: 'From the bad to the good season there grows the grass of ingenuity'; and finally its moral grudges and hoped for forms of liberation: 'Alas nothing is sacred for us any longer, everyone is full of sin, but for our devotion we have a saint made of wood'. The anti-liberal attitude is reduced to a vulgar wisecrack: 'O you decrepit windbag, tell us who made Italy? Ah, this poor boot reduced to a slipper. Your liberal Italy was far more foolish than mad; had it ended up badly we'd not be all square. But whether it be cob or a peg, you'd have had it in the bud'. The figure of the *strapaesano* (in *Cantata dei cenciaioli pratesi* [Ballad of the Ragpickers of Prato] or in some pages of the *Avventure d'un Cavaliere di Sventura* [Adventures of a Knight of Misadventure]) becomes that of a thoughtless, thuggish, giggling, gluttonish, cuckolder of husbands:

---

values of the Italian nation; that is, it nourished itself with Italian substance; it was the necessary condition to be able to root itself within it, to have the collaboration or even simply the willing neutrality of Italian society *three quarters of which was an agricultural and peasant society* based on individualism'—*Storia del movimento fascista*, p. 210.

43 Curzio Malaparte, *L'Arcitaliano* (L. Longanesi ed.) (Florence and Rome: La Voce, 1928), pp. 25–7.

Like in the game of cards
which all line up behind the aces,
so all the ragpickers ride behind Malaparte,
making a great racket:
they know the art of fist-fighting,
O people of Prato, you're in a bad way,
they break heads wherever they go,
give sound beatings and make a racket.
Who can hold these ragers back?
The bad is far better than the good [. . .][44]

From the beginning, the rhetoric is that of *strapaesano*. A deceptively European Italy is fought with the myths of a truly provincial Italy. And the result is, once again, incredibly backward.

The taste for the tradition begins to take shape in these terms. We have said that regionalism, Tuscan-ness, constitutes its predominant aspect; but we can extend the observation to other elements of Malaparte's writing: a certain way of understanding life; politics as an 'adventure'; the mission of the intellectual; the characteristics of Italian 'civilization', and so on. We will see that the development of these ideas will be rich and by no means circumscribed by fascism. The 'populist-Tuscan' theme will outlive passing ideological and political convictions.

9

This position, had as its authoritative vehicle and interpreter the magazine *Il Selvaggio* edited by Mino Maccari.[45] At least in the first years of its life, it was characterized by a rigid profession of faith in the *strapaese*. In 1927, the Sienese writer and painter summarized the attitude of the *Strapaese* movement in these extremely clear terms:

Not only does love for traditions and country not create limits but it knocks them down, leading one to live a life that has roots in other

---

44 Malaparte, 'Cantata dei cenciaioli pratesi e delle loro mattane' [Song of the Ragmen of Prati and of Their Tantrums] in *L'Arcitaliano*, p. 82.

45 Mino Maccari (1898–1989), poet, painter and journalist; participated in the Fascist March on Rome in 1922; was associated with the cultural elaboration of an intransigent, anti-bourgeois 'left' Fascism, especially through *Il Selvaggio* which then took on a more localist and less *squadrista* stance. Gramsci derided Maccari's *strapaese* positions in *Prison Notebooks*. [Trans.]

lives, in a past that is evermore remote and that one can feel already alive in the future because of that love.

Strapaese has been made for this love.

Strapaese has been purposefully made so as to defend at the point of a sword the rural and rustic character of Italian people—over and above being the most genuine and straightforward expression of the race, the environment, the climate and the mentality in which the purest of our traditions are safeguarded, by instinct and love. *Strapaese* stands as the stronghold against the invasion of fashions, foreign thinking and the civilizations of modernity; insofar as such fashions, thinking and forms of civilization risk repressing, poisoning or destroying the characteristic qualities of Italians, which must form the essential element of that contemporary labour of formation of a unitary Italian State; in the same way as, if one thinks about it [those characteristic Italian qualities] have been the incomparable nutrients of genius, of art and of spirit.[46]

There is no need to recall the pages by Oriani cited above in order to understand that the basis of the discussion in this passage inheres to the way of thinking and acting of the provincial petty bourgeoisie rather than to a broader and braver nationalism.

In January that same year, Maccari had outlined his anti-modernist credo, in this case too relying on a concept of national tradition. On closer inspection, this tradition turns out to be regional, Tuscan:

It seems to us that were we to accept in its entirety, just as it is, the form that modernity is assuming—bastardized, international, exterior, mechanical, a concoction manipulated by Jewish bankers, pederasts, warmongering sharks and brothel keepers—it could tilt, corrupt and largely do away with the wealth of our race which has been conserved and transmitted from century to century by that *great friend and protector of peoples that is tradition*; against it, there stupidly rises the anger of our failed literati and of those unable to sell the meat roasted on the fire of tradition, and who therefore sell the grey smoke of *Novecentismo*.[47]

---

46 Mino Maccari, *Il Selvaggio* 4 (16 September 1927).

47 Mino Maccari, *Il Selvaggio* 4 (30 January 1927). [*Novecentismo* was a literary movement in the early years of the twentieth century, founded by Massimo Bontempelli (1870–1960)

This is confirmed by other contributions. For instance, that of Berto Ricci,[48] a figure far more significant than his current standing suggests; along with the other Florentine writer who died young, Dino Garrone,[49] he directly and indirectly influenced writers such as Bilenchi and Pratolini. It was Ricci who wrote in *Il Selvaggio* on 18 September 1927:

> Do me a favour! What sauce is there in this Italian-ness that is at home in neither Florence nor Rome, Trieste nor Naples, but that soars in the air above the peninsula as though it were a point and not a world, the greatest world of this world? It is not a question of regionalism; it is here precisely a question of Italy. And Italy did not deserve the misfortune of a twentieth-century-style express train of Italian-ness that, not dwelling in any city is also not the nation of any nation. In substance, all this Italian-ness without a country and without a backbone is reduced to a colourless and foolish European-ness; and so, if one knew nothing of our literature but Pirandello, Bontempelli or Lucio D'Ambra, one would despair of the motherland and would find refuge in Bourget or in De Vogüé, or in any Russian. Imagine an Italian who knew nothing of Tozzi and Cicognani.[50]

With this quotation we touch upon an extremely important element of the argument. Berto Ricci does not merely propose a generic, regional-populist outlook; he offers particular models. On top of the interweaving of ideological

---

with the title of 'magical realism'. It proposed imagination and adventure as the mythical forces of creativity against the naturalism and psychologism of late-nineteenth-century literature.—Trans.]

48 Berto Ricci (1905–41), writer, poet and Germanist, important Fascist intellectual; founded the magazine *L'Universale*, which was criticized by some for its 'left' leanings. He died fighting on the Libyan front. [Trans.]

49 Dino Garrone (1904–31), literary critic and author. Like many of his generation, he was influenced by the vitalism and voluntarism that accompanied much early Fascism. [Trans.]

50 Dino Garrone, *Il Selvaggio* 4 (18 September 1927). [Lucio D'Ambra (1880–1939), prolific novelist, critic, scriptwriter and director. Paul Bourget (1852–1935), French novelist and essayist. Eugène-Melchior de Vogüé (1848–1910), French writer and diplomat, wrote an influential book on the Russian novel. Federigo Tozzi (1883–1920) Sienese writer, whose work went largely unrecognized until the 1960s. Asor Rosa writes in a much later work: 'the fundamental *verismo* of (Tozzi's) work becomes corroded by an impetuous *decadent* current'—*Storia europea della letteratura italiana. III. La letteratura della nazione* (Turin: Einaudi, 2009), p. 207. Bruno Cicognani (1879–1971), writer and dramatist belonging to the current of *verismo*. Asor Rosa later saw him as displaying the 'hues of *crepuscolarismo* that was almost *decadente*' (p. 346).—Trans.]

and political motifs, one finds a specifically literary recommendation. The fascist, Ricci, loves Federigo Tozzi (to pick the most significant of the two examples). What does this preference mean? What value does it have in relation to the more general choice of perspective? Is it possible to establish an analogy between Ricci's attitude and that of other young writers such as Bilenchi and Pratolini? Very probably, the answer to this question lies in an analysis of that left-wing Florentine Fascism which provided the arena for debates over these and other problems concerning literary and ideological frameworks. We are not discovering anything new when we speak of the fascism of the youthful Bilenchi and Pratolini, or, in another way, of Vittorini. This is not a case of putting the past on trial, nor, obviously, is it a case of justifying the past on the basis of later ideological and political developments. The fascism of Bilenchi, Pratolini, Vittorini and others is of interest to us only because some of their permanent characteristics are formed within it: literary preferences, taste, ways of being. That is not to say that the relationship between these young literary men and official Fascism was peaceful; it was contradictory and contentious, as is often the case within parties, organizations and cultural movements between those in charge, the upper echelons and the young base. But the contradiction was for many years borne by the regime as an element of the system: in practice, from 1932 to 1937, Vittorini and Pratolini collaborated on page three of *Il Bargello* (not a literary magazine but a weekly, and then *foglio d'ordini*,[51] of the Florentine provincial Fascist federation). In other words, *the analysis of the fascism of these authors cannot only serve to affirm that they were already anti-fascists* in pectore; *it must also serve to demonstrate that their later anti-fascism was not disconnected from their earlier fascism.* Certain constants remain; they are essential to understanding their work and personalities.

It is not that people do not see how important the case of Tozzi is for the reconstruction of a Tuscan literary tradition, emerging after 1930 and continuing without interruption till today (which is to say, well beyond the Resistance). It is unnecessary to demonstrate Bilenchi's debts to Tozzi: open the volume of his *Racconti* [Stories] to any page and the closeness in theme, style as well as in the nature of the characters will be evident. Pratolini publishes some of his earliest short stories in *Il Bargello*, and they are discernibly

---

51 *Fogli d'ordini* were bulletins of the provincial federations of the National Fascist Party. [Trans.]

influenced by Tozzi.[52] Cassola, to pick a more recent name, declares that no writer counted as much to him as Tozzi. In which circumstances did the discovery of Tozzi take place? How did he influence these young men? The clearest answer comes to us, once again, from Ricci. Tozzi was great 'because he demonstrated with facts a centuries-old truth: that we Italians can be subtle, painfully ironic and in a certain grand manner sick and wicked while still remaining ourselves; with our countryside and walled cities, our rustic tone— without borrowing theatrical costumes and make-up from abroad'.[53] Here, then, is how one can fascistically praise an 'uncommitted' writer such as Tozzi. One must admit, that none of these young writers—Ricci, Garrone, Pratolini, Bilenchi, and Vittorini least of all—gives in to the temptation of proposing a directly 'propaganda' literature. But Fascism is recuperated through the equation 'nation = region'. That is to say, one is fascist if one grasps the 'true' sense of a determinate reality, remaining within the tradition and the country. As we can see, this is a position that is destined to endure. Pratolini describes his initiation to Tozzi in a passage that is striking from the autobiographical standpoint: to think that it was Rosai[54] who first introduced him to the Sienese writer (Tozzi and Rosai, against the backdrop of Via Toscanella;[55] and [Tozzi's novels] *Tre croci* and *Con gli occhi chiusi* read all in one night by the light of a candle stolen from his stepmother—once again we discover that in Florence every personal and biographical fact has had the extraordinary capacity, and the terrifying limit, of becoming a chapter of literary history). Then, more naively, Pratolini tries to demonstrate that Tozzi has his ideological and political papers in order:

> At one point in his little book, Cesarini, explaining exhaustively how Tozzi, having passed through youthful atheism returned to God, affirms that 'for politics it is almost useless to attempt to follow Tozzi's thought and so it is pointless to attend to its changes'. I think rather that one should attend to them because I feel that there are few changes in Tozzi's political convictions: after the indispensable

52 Vasco Pratolini, 'Racconto d'un Amore Vero' [Story of a True Love], *Il Bargello* 4(38) (23 September 1934); for a more bitter and skilled example, see Pratolini, 'Gesuina', *Il Bargello* 9(41) (8 August 1938).

53 Berto Ricci, 'Fortuna di Tozzi', *Il Bargello* 2(29) (20 July 1930).

54 Ottone Rosai (1895–1957), painter and contributor to *Il Selvaggio*; associated with Florentine Futurism, and to Ardengo Soffici, in particular.

55 Rosai's studio was located in Via Toscanella in Florence to which he devoted the eponymous work in 1922. [Trans.]

and inevitable (given his time and character) youthful experience of socialism, already in 1913—but even before that in his own mind—he and Domenico Giuliotti confess in the *Torre* to being imperialist and Catholic (that this last point is rather besides the point is another matter) and in 1919 he writes the chapter 'Le nostre ombre' [Our Shadows] in *Realtà di ieri e di oggi* [Realities of Yesterday and Today] that can be read as the spiritual testament of a fascist of the time.[56]

The illustration is somewhat laborious, but serves to reinforce the impression that Tozzi 'passes' into the living consciousness of these young authors for reasons that are not only of taste. The conclusion of the article is more interesting:

> We young authors should have a clear idea by now, and when it comes to the entry for 'novel'—line up alongside Palazzeschi and stop at Tozzi and Verga. With these peasants and these fishermen (*Il Podere* and *I Malavoglia*) clean air rushes into our lungs and nourishes our spirit.[57]

The name 'Verga' leaps from the page alongside those of Palazzeschi[58] and Tozzi. But isn't that simply in order to subject the Sicilian writer to an interpretation that is self-interestedly regionalist? Perhaps, we begin here to understand the reasons for the rather inadequate reprise of Verga's themes and suggestions in the realist and neorealist literature of the years straddling the Second World War. Although the reference to Verga here has equal weight to the ones to Tozzi and Palazzeschi, it is clear he is understood in a very particular manner: as a writer in all likelihood rich in local truths.

Even more significant in this light are Bilenchi's first narrative experiments, carried out in the shadow of *Il Selvaggio*, *Il Bargello* and the journal *L'Universale*, edited by Berto Ricci. On the political plane, Bilenchi expresses a far left position. But beware, 'far left' in this context means the demand for the application *in toto* of the principles of the fascist revolution and the glorification of the heroic period of the beatings and *squadrismo*. The *Cronaca dell'Italia meschina, ovvero Storia dei Socialisti di Colle* [Chronicle of a Petty

---

56 Vasco Pratolini, 'Vita di Tozzi' [Life of Tozzi], *Il Bargello* 7(13)(31 March 1935). [Domenico Giuliotti (1877–1956) co-founded the intransigent Catholic journal *La Torre* with Tozzi in 1913.—Trans.]

57 Pratolini, 'Vita di Tozzi'. [Federigo Tozzi's novel *Il podere* was published in 1921.]

58 Aldo Palazzeschi (1885–1974), pseudonym of novelist, poet and journalist Aldo Giurlani. [Trans.]

Italy, or, History of the Socialist of Colle],[59] published in 1933, but which appeared previously in installments in *Il Bargello*, adorns itself with this epigraph:'We do not believe in revolutions where there are no dead and that do not completely bury the past'; and opens with this warning:

> My peers, this is the story of the Italy of yesterday; we swear to hate every democracy.
>
> There are too many 'Fathers', even in our *Fascio*, who are either ready or rather anxious to begin to rule again, to clown about in the piazzas. And we know many young people who aspire to do as they do.
>
> How many little fascist magazines are like *Elsa* or *Marinella*.
>
> With all our strength we must oppose their aims and inclinations; one must be fascist in the real sense of the word, which for us must mean strength of renewal, destruction of all past ideas, all decadent civilizations, all useless religions.[60]

This little book is extremely interesting. First, because it convincingly describes the climate of a pre-fascist, dishevelled, blabbering, opportunistic, rustic socialism that was bound to arouse the resentment of the intelligentsia and good taste even before that of ideology and politics. Second, because it emphasizes the character of feud and family dispute that the struggle between fascists and anti-fascists assumes in the countryside and the town, marking out (even if not for the first time) a recurrent theme in the Tuscan writers who concerned themselves with this problem.

Still more interesting is *Vita di Pisto*, which appeared in 1931. In it, Bilenchi draws the figure of a boorish and belligerent commoner who exemplifies many of the essential human and political qualities of the perfect *strapaesano*, the *natural* precursor of fascism:

---

59 Colle di Val d'Elsa is a town in the Tuscan province of Siena. Impelled by the activism of local factory workers, it was later governed by a socialist. Maccari founded *Il Selvaggio* in Colle; and besides Bilenchi's *Cronaca*, it was the setting for Cassola's *La ragazza di Bube* (1960), Bilenchi's *Vita di Pisto* (1931) and *Conservatorio di Santa Teresa* (1940). [Trans.]

60 Romano Bilenchi, *Cronaca dell'Italia meschina, ovvero Storia dei Socialisti di Colle* [Chronicle of Petty Italy] (Florence: Vallecchi, 1933). This short work is dedicated to Ottone Rosai; Berto Ricci; Camillo Pelizzi [(1896–1979), Fascist intellectual and postwar sociologist]; Gioacchino Contri [(1900–1982), director of *Il Bargello*]; Giorgio Bertolini [signatory of Berto Ricci's 'Manifesto Realista' in 1933]; and Carlo Cordié (1910–2002), literary critic.

We should mention that our man was around nineteen years old, strong and handsome and, although young, very successful with women. He was intolerant of all discipline, impetuous, liked a scrap, was both intelligent and stubborn, the model of *strapaesani* of today, *strapaesano avant la lettre*, he was a headache and a problem to all those citizens who in every age are alas considered the flower of a city or town.[61]

It must be said that this sort of bold, likeable bully had featured in Garibaldi's campaigns, along with others of his ilk. He didn't have great memories of these campaigns but certainly had a high concept of himself and his own strength:

> Pisto inaugurated the season of beatings and fistfights, the foremost part of the life of the proud hill-dweller. He was a sort of apostle for 'capricious self-justification', and for an overly full and short-tempered life. Although he cared little for codes of conduct and regulations, he at least broke the unhappy spell cast by the hypocritical and vile habits of the time.

The debt owed to Malaparte and Maccari is clear. But more important is the definition of the human type which will survive its fascist embodiment. The *strapaese* mood of stories like 'La fabbrica' [The Factory], 'Il nonno di Marco' [Marco's Grandfather], 'Il capofabbrica' [The Factory Supervisor] and 'Un delitto' [A Crime], also composed between 1931–32, is not in contradiction with the *strapaese* character of *Vita di Pisto* but, rather, complementary to it. Bilenchi saw no conflict between these two aspects of his work: the style is surprisingly analogous in the political discourse as in the more 'intimate' narratives.[62] His peers and fascist comrades did not register any contrasts either. This is clear if we consider that Pratolini, in reviewing one of Bilenchi's books—the later famous collection of short stories *Il capofabbrica* [1935]—after having said that 'it is not necessary for the best of us to express ourselves by putting our "characters" in black shirts nor to procure the sacredness of the idea or the cult of heroes for our profane actions', ends up

---

61 This and the following quotation: from Romano Bilenchi, *Vita di Pisto* (Turin: Il Selvaggio, 1931), p. 15 and 25–6, respectively..

62 *Intimismo,* a literary tendency in mid- to late-nineteenth-century artists that focused upon intimate movements of the soul, displaying a sensitivity to inner states of consciousness and feeling. [Trans.]

concluding that Bilenchi's is a 'fascist art, which uses the men and contingencies of today to become civilization, and civilization has, like fascism, Mussolini, but as an expression of ingenuity it transcends the symbol and the generations so as to become a historical element. Bilenchi will achieve this in a novel that is popular and universal; terms that are united in the fascist ethic'.[63]

In these ways, an accommodation was considered possible between a relatively autonomous concept of literature and the revolutionary mission of the regime. That, in its official spheres, fascism was reluctant to adopt this position takes nothing away from the significance of the attempts by these young writers to impose it upon the regime. Above all, what is important is the development of a literary attitude, based on typically fascist motifs and themes, which led to results that were destined to live on in terms of style and experience. It is important to identify whether a 'character' is fascist or communist; but what is more important is the way in which one arrives at a stylistic definition of these characters. If, in the two cases presented, the path is analogous or even identical, we will experience the communist character as akin to the fascist one; we will experience them as being made of the same substance, the same nature, and then we *will have to consider them as equivalent from the literary standpoint*. It is precisely in the course of the 1930s that the regional and naturalistic signature that distinguishes the work of Bilenchi and Pratolini in their later years first manifests and then consolidates itself. At the age of twenty-one, Pratolini sketches this profile of a character:

> Donatello Becherini was not predestined for anything; he did not have a Brunetto Latini either by his cot nor in his youth; he was baptized like any other Christian; he was a young *strapaese*: cunning and hardworking; a passion for cycling, gambling and women, and also a little bit for politics.
>
> At exactly twenty years of age, he did his military service; he then married and then came kids: he counted up to three and stopped; it was time for war.
>
> Until then he had been a mechanic, going from garage to home and back; a quart of wine in the evening, some country walks and long trips to Florence on market days.

---

63 Vasco Pratolini, *Il Bargello* 8(23) (9 June 1935).

He was a stocky man, average height, dark eyes and hair; broad shoulders and strong arms. The clothes of an Etruscan or of Florentine artisan could have suited him [. . .].[64]

This character would become a cliché that Bilenchi will later adopt for the characters of the *Cronache*; it does not even matter to know that this one, Becherini, was a Fascist *squadrista* commoner from the local countryside and that the others were anti-fascist commoners from Santa Croce. The autonomy of literature from its ideological content is realized but in a paradoxical form: because ideology and politics do not fundamentally operate as elements that regenerate or revolutionize literary attitudes.[65]

Another element that should not be underestimated in the definition of the relationship of fascism to anti-fascism within the biographical and literary history of these writers is their tenacious and aggressive anti-bourgeois spirit. Yet before we look for its individual features in this or that writer, it is necessary to issue a warning: not only, as we know, was the anti-bourgeois tradition alive earlier in the works of nationalists and fascists—from Oriani to Corradini and from Mussolini and Malaparte—but it also continued to present itself as extremely combative and topical in the official attitudes of Florentine fascism. At least during the years leading to the war in Spain, *Il Bargello* exhibits a continual propensity to emphasize the popular aspect of the fascist revolution and to recall the bitter struggle against the old bourgeois, liberal and democratic ruling classes. In this setting, the anti-bourgeois sentiment of the young intellectuals appears much less scandalous than it may seem when looking over a welter of quotations isolated from their original context. *In this case too*, one should distinguish between the anti-bourgeois attitude of the ruling classes,

---

64 Vasco Pratolini, 'Omaggio a Becherini', *Il Bargello* 4(48). [Brunetto Latini (1210–94), was Dante Alighieri's guardian after the death of his parents.—Trans.]

65 In some extremely youthful and naive literary exercises, Pratolini reveals the already established tendency to create naturalistic and sensual characters. As is clear from the 'sketches' for Vent'anni di Uno *Il Bargello* 7(48)(1935), from which we draw that of a young girl which anticipates numerous characters from the *Cronache*, from the *Quartiere* and, above all, from *Amiche*:

The young girl was called Aura: she had dreamy black eyes that merged into grey; a great tangle of chestnut brown hair with reddish tinges; the oval mask of an angel for a face with the lineaments drawn by a young Michelangelo, and full lips ready to kiss the sun. In the following years, as the trunk became stronger, the rest of the plant remained beautiful, perhaps more beautiful—a daydreaming beauty, as though dipped in the sky [. . .].

which is probably a cover for more concrete conservative interests, and the naive and unconditional anti-bourgeois sentiment of the young 'base'. But *in this case too*, we are not interested in judging the good faith of these positions, or their relations to the real fascism of reaction and big capital, so much as in looking for and understanding whether this anti-bourgeois attitude, whose ideological origin is incontrovertible, continued to function as an active element even after the collapse of these writers' fascist political convictions.

As we have said, there is no question about the fascist origin of the phenomenon. Their cards are on the table—at least for some of these writers. Bilenchi, for instance, following Ricci on the road to a fascist universality goes so far as to condemn nationalism as a bourgeois expression, declaring: 'We do not even want a fascist International. The Empire is the one development of fascism, the empire darkly sensed, it's true, but it was sensed by Alfredo Oriani.'[66] And Pratolini, reviewing *Il capofabbrica* (it is no accident that he should entertain such ideas about Bilenchi): 'We young people have roots in reality, our spirit has been forged in [the writings of] Oriani and our flesh in fist-fights, military endeavours and on the warm bodies of Italian women'.[67] From these experiences and readings, to the declaration of a populism that is almost invariably extremely literary and intellectual, the step is but a short one. In some writers, it is evident that the anti-bourgeois *animus* is, above all, a matter of culture: the reproach against a way of life that is coarse, crude, uncivilized and the negation of life. This is without doubt Vittorini's fundamental standpoint; from the start he develops his own discourse which is strongly characterized by the defence of an intellectual and literary dignity that already operates with models and parameters of judgement that are quite assured. The contemporaneous collaboration with *Solaria*[68] and *Il Bargello*, while diminishing the idea that his relationship to the former journal was marked by a spirit of protest, projects onto the articles of literary and artistic criticism he contributed to the latter a meaning that would be difficult to misinterpret. The truth is that Vittorini developed a

---

66 Romano Bilenchi, '"Piede di casa" e Sviluppi Fascisti', *Il Bargello* 5(15)(9 April 1933). [The *politica del piede di casa* referred to a purely inner-directed politics, contrasted by Mussolini with Fascist expansionism.—Trans.]

67 Pratolini, 'Il capofabbrica', *Il Bargello* 8(23)(1935).

68 A literary review founded by Alberto Carocci in 1926. Its strong orientation towards European literatures and dissent towards Fascism lead to severe censorship and, therefore, ceased publication in 1936. [Trans.]

defence of the 'autonomy' of literature and poetry that continues to characterize his work even today. That said, the modernity of his taste will be justified—without merely bowing to the dominant diktats of the day—by a
political rationale we have noted in other left fascists. Vittorini's stance is
manifest, for example, in this judgement on Montale's poetry: 'those who
today deny the lyrical value of *Ossi di seppia*[69] [Cuttlefish Bones], do so with
a defeatist taste for denouncing the "spiritual discomfort of the time", the
taste of professors and philistines that the nostalgia for Gozzano, Angelo
dall'Oca and Giolitti bring together in art and politics'.[70] The explanation for
this attitude lies in the fact that the problem of populism is *one* among the
many that interests Vittorini. This interest takes a generically humanitarian
and universalistic form which is, for example, quite distinct from that of the
Tuscans. Nevertheless, in this period examples of anti-bourgeois sentiment—
especially in this combined political and cultural sense—are frequent in
Vittorini as well. *Il garofano rosso* [The Red Carnation], which came out
between 1933 and 1934 in *Solario*, is the story of an adolescent who in 1924,
the year of Matteotti's murder,[71] discovers life through his first complete erotic
experience and his first intense political clashes. A friend of the protagonist
describes the attempted revolt of the anti-fascist forces provoked by the news
of the assassination of the socialist deputy:

> All this confusion in which Communists, Masons and Liberals find
> themselves united under one banner like the Salvation Army reveals
> the petit-bourgeois mentality and complete lack of revolutionary aims
> in Italy's old political parties. As for Fascism, that's a good thing, I tell

---

69 Eugenio Montale (1896–1981), arguably the foremost Italian lyric poet of the twentieth
century; awarded the Nobel Prize for Literature in 1975; also produced literary criticism
and numerous translations of both prose and poetry (Shakespeare, Gerald Manley
Hopkins, James Joyce, T. S. Eliot, Jorgé Guillen, Dorothy Parker, etc.). His highly
acclaimed first poetry collection, *Ossi di seppia*, was published by the radical-liberal intellectual Piero Gobetti in 1925. [Trans.]

70 Elio Vittorini, 'Montale', *Il Bargello* 3(37) (September 1931). [Guido Gozzano (1883–
1916), decadent poet and writer. Angelo Dall'Oca Bianca (1858–1942), painter. Giovanni
Giolitti (1842–1928), liberal statesman, served as prime minister of Italy five times between
1892 and 1921.—Trans.]

71 Giacomo Matteotti (1885–1924), Italian Socialist politician who accused the Fascists of
electoral fraud; was killed a few days after his denunciation. His murder, and its celebration
by Mussolini, was a watershed in the consolidation of the Fascist regime. [Trans.]

you. Fascism, which you thought reactionary, will turn out to be really revolutionary and anti-bourgeois.[72]

That same protagonist, after the punitive raid by Fascist students against a crowd of demonstrators, reports:

> They all belonged to the newspaper-reading middle classes—from *commendatori*[73] to barbers. I got right in the middle of it, carried off my feet and hitting about me wildly. Suddenly I hear someone shout: 'Aren't you ashamed, doing this to old people!' And I see that my old man is a sturdy forty-year-old with black moustaches who could have broken my neck if he wanted to. Suddenly I felt that everything was spoilt, pointless . . . I would rather be with the crowd— but with a dangerous crowd, black with coal dust, fighting against machine-guns.[74]

The close of this second passage is interesting because it bears witness to the manner in which the sincere participation in the fascist 'revolutionary' experiment always carried with it—in what is perhaps an irrational or even mystical way—the temptation to widen this desire for renewal beyond the limits imposed by the regime. But more on this later.

In the work of others, the anti-bourgeois theme reveals itself in a more decisively political form. In the short story 'Visita al vecchio politicante' [Visit to the Old Politico],[75] Bilenchi provides a description of old liberals and freemasons, the faint-hearted, the opportunists and the ambitious who have joined or attempted to join the Fascist Party in order to bring to it their scheming spirit, not yet satiated with power. In other editions of *Il Bargello*, he polemicizes against De Amicis' *Cuore* (1886), deemed to be a typical example

---

72 Elio Vittorini, *Il garofano rosso* (Milan: Mondadori, 1948), p. 58 / *The Red Carnation* (A. Bower trans.) (London: Weidenfeld and Nicolson, 1953), p. 24. From a comparison between the first post-liberation edition of 1948 and the text that appeared in *Solaria*, we can see that the edits made to the latter were not particularly extensive. The only passages to stand—for the first time in the 'liberated' edition—are a conversation between the young protagonist and his father on the subject of socialism (see p. 114), and a long interior soliloquy of the protagonist on the subject 'Why are workers likeable?', which is marked by an irredeemably paternalist tone.

73 A title awarded for services to one's country; also colloquially used to address those of higher rank or social status. [Trans.]

74 Vittorini, *Il garofano rosso*, p. 78 / *The Red Carnation*, p. 50 [translation modified].

75 Romano Bilenchi, 'Visita al vecchio politicante', *Il Bargello* 5(2) (8 January 1933).

of the petty-bourgeois and pseudo-democratic mentality. Ricci repeatedly returns to the battle on all fronts against the bourgeoisie and bourgeois taste. In the article cited above, he even attributes the lack of recognition for Tozzi's work to bourgeois narrow-minded diffidence towards the hard reality of human existence to be found in Tozzi's writings. Pratolini, perhaps the most unswerving in underlining the popular origins of his viewpoint, goes so far as to define culture's general attitude towards the bourgeoisie:

> In this attempt to contribute to the polemical argument for a fascist culture we have wanted first, and above all, to clarify the political necessity and moral obligation that as fascists we have to advance and increase, to coordinate and facilitate, a popular culture that, by raising the intellectual level of the masses, reinforces the Idea in its social structure through a specific, conscious adherence to popular partici-pation in the doctrine and in its revolutionary developments.

> To conceive cultural speculation only as the property of the few is to reiterate the concept of bourgeois egotism that measures its own superiority against the enforced intellectual inferiority of others.[76]

Clearly these are largely moralistic positions. A few years later, having joined the anti-fascist current, Pratolini will justify it in the following terms:

> It must be noted that the bourgeois phenomenon is not only a men-tality but also, and above all, a circle of interests that determine that mentality. One must eliminate these interests in order to destroy that mentality. Were it not so, the French Revolution would not have taught us much and historical materialism would not have existed, even to later be disproven. The problem remains fixed in these terms and there is no point beating around the bush, issuing anathemas while avoiding the fundamental obstacle. One should state that the bourgeoisie is still a class and that to attempt a moral renewal of it from without is to lend oneself to its self-interested game.[77]

We must, however, make some observations. What takes the place of the moralistic anti-bourgeois sentiment of left-wing fascism? It would seem that, from this point of view, the undeniable maturation of a certain ideological

---

76 Vasco Pratolini, 'Tempo culturale della politica' [The Cultural Time of Politics], *Il Bargello* 9(14)(31 January 1937).
77 Vasco Pratolini, 'Calendario', *Campo di Marte* 1(3)(10 September 1938).

attitude leads to the denial of the problem. It is clear that to reproach the bourgeoisie for being a force standing against the (bourgeois) fascist revolution is
an example of youthful naivety. But in the subsequent work of these writers,
even of those who passionately identified with the Resistance, we can find no
more rigorous definition of the class function of the bourgeoisie. The anti-
bourgeois moralism falls away, but only to be replaced by anti-fascist moralism.
This too is a way to fight the bourgeoisie without questioning its underlying
economic and social motives. Moreover, Vittorini explicitly and consciously
becomes a bourgeois writer. Pratolini and the other populists, precisely insofar
as they follow a populist theme, are unable to go beyond generic definitions.
We also suspect that the anti-bourgeois theme is lost because the Resistance,
conceived as an emancipatory impulse that involves all ranks and classes, does
nothing to rigorously take it up and emphasize it. There is more anti-bourgeois
spirit in *Selvaggio* and on the third page of *Il Bargello* than there is in many of
the left-wing papers after the liberation.

Instead, another aspect of this anti-bourgeois sentiment which endures;
this helps us explain the reasons for certain shifts and conversions. It is undeniable that this anti-bourgeois animosity brings into touching distance the
'revolutionary' fascist and the communist. To be more precise: the communist
is the most total and distant adversary, but also the person who is recognized
as having the qualities of seriousness, conviction and heroism. It is not coin-
cidental that the bourgeois is his enemy as he is the enemy of the fascist. When
he is spoken of, it is with a certain respect (in the same way as they speak of
the Soviet Union), and often in a way as to shine a light on the almost analogical behaviour of the two extreme and inflexible factions. Bilenchi writes
in *Vita di Pisto*: 'Never has a gentleman of the Borgo[78] been in a punch-up in
the middle of the street, and never has he drunk in a tavern. He has always
remained conservative and bigoted and never sung either *Bandiera rossa* or
Giovinezza, other than at the last moment, opportunistically'.[79] At other times

---

78 Refers to the mediaeval quarters, in this case of Colle Val d'Elsa. [Trans.]

79 Bilenchi, *Vita di Pisto*, p. 61. This theme too is less scandalous and heretical than it
might appear at first sight. Volpe, in his *Storia del movimento fascista*, had shown the affinities alongside the profound and irresolvable conflicts between the two movements, socialist
and fascist; he goes on to argue that, soon after the war, both wagered on the revolutionary
overthrow of the existing system, to the point that 'in certain moments, a collaboration
and fusion between them could have arisen'. Indeed, both the movements 'wanted to take
up the legacy of the old regime and of the old ruling classes. Both were mass movements
or relied upon the masses. Both drew upon new or emerging social classes that wanted to

this awareness of contiguity rebounds on the fascist protagonist of events: for example, the student in *Il garofano rosso* later learns that, after the beatings and the occupations in which he had participated, they had called him 'a subversive [. . .], that is, a communist subverter of the Order Re-established by Fascism; a sort of little viper in the heart of the Local Motherland'.[80]

Not even this situation is completely new: think of the nationalist Buondelmonti and the trade-unionist Rummo in Corradini's *La patria lontana*, who end up finding themselves so close to each other precisely because they had been so far apart. But it is a fact that this feeling of family resemblance between left-fascism and communism (or what these intellectuals thought was communism) is the passageway through which many of them will travel from fascism to communism. Here too the *trait d'union* is constituted by that populist conviction that lies at the heart of their standpoint. Because these young intellectuals *love the people* that are hated by the bourgeoisie, or *hate the bourgeoisie* so as to love the people, their problem will be to experiment with different ways to apply their humanitarian ideology. Having attempted fascism, they then try communism and democracy. The fact that the second choice was, in the context of certain historical, political and social conditions, more correct than the first, does not mean that the first was simply an error or an illusion, as many protagonists of those events force themselves to believe. The survival of a theme and a set of tastes bear strong testimony to that.

Moreover, one should not imagine that these developing literary choices are not accompanied by a direct political and social commitment; quite the contrary, we must note that the properly political phase of these 'new' writers develops and peters out entirely within their fascist period. Later, after the Resistance, doing politics will essentially mean engaging in culture; Vittorini will fight his great *political* anti-fascist battle by defending the principle of the autonomy of culture and of literature from politics. But in these years Vittorini, Bilenchi and Pratolini lend directly political support to *Il Bargello* and other newspapers by holding positions that in no way can be considered opposite to or in contradiction with their later anti-fascist or socialist convictions—if those theoretically nebulous convictions can be

---

climb their way up. Both were anti-democratic, anti-liberal, etc.' (p. 209). [*Bandiera rossa* and *Giovinezza* are respectively communist (or socialist) and fascist songs.—Trans.]

80 Vittorini, *Il garofano rosso*, pp. 101–02. [This passage is missing in the English edition. It is possible the translation is based on the earlier edition that was subjected to fascist censorship. See Vittorini, *The Red Carnation*, p. 79—Trans.]

determined at all. In this area, too, we should acknowledge the consistency of intellectual and ideological development. But this consistency is required to underline the uncertain, generically intellectual and consistently bourgeois character of their populism.

It is significant that the highest and most intense point of their political commitment is marked by the war in Africa which *Il Bargello* unanimously welcomes as the recommencement as well as completion of the fascist revolution. In the conquest of Ethiopia and the foundation of the Empire, our young writers highlight, above all, the popular dimension and the goal of social justice. In a series of articles on 'Doveri della gioventù territoriale' [Duties of the Territorial Youth] (in *Il Bargello* 20, 22, 23, 25, 26, 28 and 34, 1936), Pratolini defines the nature of the war that had been launched: '[F]or the fascist, war is not materialism, it is a reason for the social revaluation of the Proletarian Nation. It is a people's war, and as such, not in mere words but in reality, because the people knows no diplomacy'. Its fundamental aim, its reflection on the soil of the motherland, is: 'To accompany the heroic actions with the conscious advancement of "social justice for the Italian people" is, perhaps, for us "territorials", the only way to render ourselves worthy of our fighting [fascist] comrades'. The fundamental problem is therefore that of securing, within the Empire, a privileged function for the proletarian soldier: 'I openly declare that I see work as occupying a place of honour at the heart of the operations in East Africa; and this is not a new discovery'.[81]

The echo of certain statements made by Jahier return to us with extraordinary force in the form of Pratolini's social-fascist progressivism: from the popular use of the war to the subject of the rights of labour won by the proletariat in the trenches, with blood and the sacrifice of life. Compared with the earlier democratic, nationalist or anarcho-syndicalist models, what is new is a heightened sense of the social dimension of the problems faced. This is most probably the fruit of a singular convergence of renewed Marxist interests and the dominant climate of the post-liberal and fascist period, where state intervention in questions of general economic importance was more easily admitted than before. 'Il Soldato torna contadino' [The Soldier Turns Back into a Peasant] is the title of some articles in the aforementioned series. It is impossible not to see how, behind the simple definition of the subject-matter,

---

81 Pratolini, 'Ragioni dell'azienda collettiva' [Rationale for the Collective Firm], *Il Bargello* 8(40) (1936).

one can discern the operation of the type of collectivist and anti-property social ideology that finds its first systematic form in the theorists of fascist corporatism. For the precise terms of this position, consider the following:

> Having become once again a day-labourer, the commoner who remains on conquered territory has only one absolute right: once the breathlessness of war is over, he has the right no longer to fall under the nagging weight of necessity or worse, indigence, and to have to believe he is still working under a 'master'. This is guaranteed to him by the State, the only master with any right to existence.
>
> [...]
>
> Property belongs always and absolutely to the State; only the State can raise the worker above the regime of private property which it controls and defends within the newly-defined national order. But within the imperial territory which was won through the force of arms by a people of day-labourers, this State cannot encourage (even through interference) phenomena of disguised profiteering or of embourgeoisement of the industrial workers, which depart from the hard everyday struggle of a fighting and working people.[82]

We can observe here how the socialism of numerous Italian writers and intellectuals, which is always extraordinarily ambiguous and vague, draws remotely on theoretical statements of this type where the concept of 'working people' forms a necessary and consistently generic corollary.

In this respect Vittorini is perhaps even more lucid and 'prophetic' than Pratolini. Parenthetically, we may note that we owe to him what is perhaps the most ingenious justification for the assault on 'Abyssinia'. Note that we say this without irony. For in the course of affirming a high concept of European and world civilization, Vittorini confers on the fascist endeavour the merit of having 'wiped from the earth the final "mystery of the blood", the final "independent civilization", the last "racial secret", which history must have been fed up with';[83] and perhaps more refined still from the theoretical and political point of view:

> I cannot see how any European ideology could fail to see the domination by Italy, a European nation, of Abyssinia as anything but good.

---

82 Pratolini, *Il Bargello* 8(47)(12 July–6 September 1936).

83 Elio Vittorini, 'Conti con la storia' [Settling Accounts with History], *Il Bargello* 8(30)(10 May 1936).

Even for the ideology of the Third International it must be a good. For it was clearly stated by its prophets that without passing through the stage of industrial exploitation of the people one couldn't achieve the ideal stage of socialism. If the men of the Third International really believed in their ideology, they would be happy to see Italy wipe from the face of the earth Ras and Negus. But that is not what the lawyerly quibblers of Geneva argue![84]

The historical outlook of the Italian presence in Africa is described in terms of this civilizing mission of progress. Here Vittorini develops one of those definitions that, barring minor details and terminological changes, could be penned by him today:

> This is the essence of capitalism: INDIVIDUAL SALVATION, for each to construct for himself a personal safety sign. The corporative idea only permits COLLECTIVE SAFETY; it is this idea of collective safety, safety for the whole people upon which [. . .] the economic possibilities of Ethiopia should be based.[85]

Consequently:

> The exclusion of private owners. But yes to *collective firms*. Corporative firms for agricultural colonization as well. How? In the same way as for industrial colonization. Work and technology. Specialist distribution of work. Organization of healthcare, culture, etc., from the centre of the firm. Property: of the State, or corporative or cooperative property (or union property, as we read in the journal *Lavoro Fascista* [Fascist Labour]); this needs to be resolved, but it is a formality.[86]

We have arrived at the utopia of the technologically-organized and self-sufficient society that will be one of the foundational elements of Vittorini's position in *Il Politecnico* and after.[87] Clearly the separation of these positions

---

84 Elio Vittorini, 'Atlantino universale' [Portable Universal Atlas], *Il Bargello* 8(20). ['Negus' and 'Ras' were hereditary or court titles of the Ethiopian (or Abyssinian) Empire of 1137–1975.—Trans.]

85 Vittorini, 'Ragioni dell'azienda collettiva'.

86 Vittorini, *Il Bargello* 8(41).

87 *Il Politecnico* was an extraordinarily influential cultural and political magazine established by Vittorini in 1945 in Milan, and published by Einaudi, with collaborators that

from those of fascist ownership and capitalism became ever stronger. But it is also clear that the collectivist theme of the 'labouring people', of 'social justice' and 'collective security', stemming from the *rigorous* interpretation of corporative prescriptions, tends to escape from the reality of the regime, only to then require other realities to take it up and satisfy it in the terms that first shaped it. The concluding product of this stage of the populist discourse is, as we have said, the overcoming of the individualist depiction of the social problem. Little by little, we can see a more broadly and genuinely democratic impetus being reprised, and gaining in shape and strength, within the ambit of the concept of the Ethical State and the Corporative State.[88] The bourgeois

included some of the most important cultural figures of the time, from poet and essayist Franco Fortini to philosopher Giulio Preti. Originally printed as a broadsheet that could be pasted up on the streets of Milan, it dealt with a stunning range of themes, publishing articles on themes from the FIAT factory to the Chinese revolution, translations of Brecht, Pasternak and Mayakovsky, drawings by Picasso and montages by John Hearfield. The journal began in the cultural ambit of the Italian Communist Party but in late 1946 Vittorini and PCI secretary Palmiro Togliatti had a public disagreement over the relation between the party and intellectuals. *Il Politecnico* stopped publication in late 1947. [Trans.]

88 However, one should not think that the ideas held by these young writers were the fruit of an individualist search for truth able, in any case, to break the fascist shell through their genuinely and openly heterodox positions. Behind these postures lies a *corpus* of fascist doctrines that inspires them. One cannot think otherwise after having read a passage such as the following, in which Giovanni Gentile affirms with great clarity the popular nature of the fascist state:

> This [Fascist] State—which is realized in the consciousness and will of the individual, and is not a force imposed from above—cannot have the same relationship with the mass of the people that was presumed by Nationalism. The latter, by making the State coincide with the Nation, and turning it into an already existing entity, which one need not create but only know, required a ruling class of a predominantly intellectual character which itself felt this entity that had first to be known, understood, appreciated and praised. Besides, the authority of the State was not the product but a presupposition. It could not depend upon the people; on the contrary, the people depended upon the State and on the authorities that it had to recognize as the condition of its life, outside of which sooner or later, it would realize it could not live. The nationalist State was therefore an aristocratic State, which needed to constitute itself in the force of its origin, in order to then assert itself over the masses. The Fascist State is instead a popular State and in that sense the democratic State *par excellence*.

See Giovanni Gentile, *Origini e dottrina del fascismo* (Rome: Libreria del Littorio, 1929), pp. 47–8. See also Francesco Ercole, 'Il Popolo nello Stato fascista e negli Stati democratici' in Guido Mancini and Francesco Ercole, *Stato e popolo nei secoli XIX e XX* [State of Peoples in the Nineteenth and Twentieth Centuries] (Rome: Istit. naz. di Cultura Fascista, 1938),

fascist position gives birth on the literary plane to the democratic bourgeois solution. Populism undergoes another turn. But the general ideological terms of the discussion remain practically the same, as does the popular request for the satisfaction—at the level of justice—of the basic needs of the propertyless or, at best, of the day labourer, the poor peasant, the generic commoner. As Pratolini writes: 'I see the "people" as linked to the "proletarian", and to be pedantic, it can be explained as follows: from the Latin *pòpulus*, "the lowest section of the inhabitants"; from the Latin *proletarius*, "the one who owns nothing" other than his soul and his right to life which he acquired the day of his birth: fascist mysticism'.[89] One will look to this concept of proletarian later as well, as the foundation for the anti-fascist popular revolt—not without some interesting broadening and deepening of the argument, as we shall see.

10

While these various aspects of a politically-engaged populist literature unfold in a clear and linear manner, other populist phenomena continue to reveal themselves in Italy in independent forms that will also flow into post-Resistance literature in different ways and to different degrees. It is not possible, however, to attempt an analysis of any of these as an organic group or tendency; they appear broadly as isolated experiments tied to the work of individual authors. The main interest that they hold for us lies, more often than not, in testifying to the fact that a certain nineteenth-century discourse is not yet dead in some strata of Italian intellectuals. On the contrary, it is pursued, albeit irregularly, according to a generic (if often only implied) democratism or socialism. The gallery of authors that follows serves, above all, to remind us of certain characteristics of Italian populism we have already mentioned.

Southern Italian literature continues to be the richest source of populist examples (of uneven quality) in the first 40 years of the century. The most elevated of those—and among the most important exemplars of twentieth-

---

p. 51, where one can find the statement taken up by many others in numerous different forms, that the nineteenth century 'was the century of *apparent* democracy in the democratic state; this is the century of *real* democracy in the fascist state'. For a (rather mediocre) review of the fascist positions, see Augusto Fantechi, *Trasformazione del concetto di democrazia e di popolo* [Transformation of the Concept of Democracy and the People] (Florence: Le Monnier, 1938).

89 Vasco Pratolini, 'Il soldato torna contadino' [The Soldier Turns Back into a Peasant], *Il Bargello* 8(42).

century Italian populist literature—can be found in the work of Raffaele Viviani. In few other writers is there such a lively and immediate sense of poverty, hunger and the harsh necessities of survival. Endowed with an uncertain literary and cultural understanding, Viviani oscillates between caricature, chronicle and realism. Yet, there is a clear direction to his discourse from '*O vico* [The Alley, 1917] to *Muratori* [Bricklayers, 1942], which is evident in the fidelity to a subject full of humanity and rich in documentary evidence. The most common protagonists of his comedies and poems are the plebeians of Naples, the lowest of the lumpenproletariat, those of the alleyways, represented without Salvatore Di Giacomo's complacency or petty-bourgeois sentiments *a là* Matilde Serao. Viviani is capable of a rare cruelty in his depictions (think of 'Gnastillo'[90] which, following the rhythm of a cheerful popular dance, represents the wretched life and death from exhaustion and hunger of an 'unlucky lad', an obvious Neapolitan type but represented here with freshness and immediacy). But the most characteristic of Viviani's traits, distinguishing him from the other populist writers of the 1900s (including those writing in dialect) is the attention he lavishes on the various sites and features of work. Here too we are confined to a generic world where the protagonists are fishermen, blacksmiths, builders, day-labourers and manual labourers of the lowliest kind. Work in this context never constitutes an autonomous and secure aspect of human life but is always closely related to misery and death, tied to it by a desperate and irreparable contiguity.

Viviani, in some of his songs, is able to bring to life this wretched condition of existence, highlighting the sense of material effort which is often raw and humiliating, and is the price of survival. This peasants' song from 1919 (drawn from the comedy *Campagna napolitana* [Neapolitan Countryside]) is beautiful:

> The sun and the air burn us;
> we're roasted in the middle of the fields;
> it's so hot that we can't breathe.
>
> This countryside is not ours,
> not like our toil.
> Peasant, you're an ant,
> but who gives you your provisions?

---

90 Raffaele Viviani (1888–1950), Neapolitan actor, writer, composer and poet. [Trans.] See his *Poesie* (Vasco Pratolini and Paolo Ricci eds) (Florence: Vallecchi, 1956), pp. 129–32.

And only by singing
can we lift this cross!
But who hears this here voice
that crosses the fields?

We are born in the middle of the fields,
we are big and we are here.
Were it not for the war,
we would not have seen the cities [. . .][91]

On other occasions, work runs directly into death, as in 'Favrecature' [Brickie],[92] about the fall of a bricklayer and the desperation of the family following the announcement of his death. The bit of Neapolitan melodrama the poet is unable to avoid is experienced and represented as an objective element of a determinate environmental reality. There is no trace of the complacent use of local 'colour' in the depiction of these scenes, although colour is used liberally. This is probably due to the great descriptive simplicity, which in turn is the reflection of the scrupulous honesty at its source. Note the immediacy with which Viviani narrates the facts, describes the reaction of the other builders to the events and, by way of conclusion, soberly introduces the element of populist compassion:

Under rain and the sun
works the bricklayer with a trowel in his hand
suspended from scaffolding,
outside, on the fifth floor.

Put a foot wrong,
a lopsided movement,
and like an angel he flies:
before he arrives, he's dead!

A cry and they come running:
people and builders.
'He still breathes . . . it's Ruoppolo!
He has two young children!'[93]

---

91 Viviani, 'Coce 'o sole e ll'aria coce' in *Poesie*, p. 144.

92 Viviani, 'Favrecature' in *Poesie*, pp. 157–61.

93 English translation available at: goo.gl/BrbdgC (last accessed on 18 March 2019). [Trans.]

Not even Viviani is able to get beyond this honest and moving conclusion. We can acknowledge that his populism is so intense and genuine precisely because it is barely ideologized; in this respect, whether consciously or otherwise, he absorbs the best lessons of *verismo*. But this elementary respect for the sufferings of the world exhausts the substance of his poetry. Viviani can teach nothing more; and this is already a lot within populism of the Italian type, whose weakness is to confuse a simple, progressive ideological schema with a popular reality.

The case of the other southerner is very different; Corrado Alvaro, who with *Gente in Aspromonte* [People in Aspromonte, 1930],[94] puts back into circulation in regionalist literature the themes and locations of the Calabria of his birth. The book is composed of 13 stories blending folklore, romanticism, regionalism of *Verist* origin as well as Pirandellian and even D'Annunzian influences. The vehicle for the depiction is the extremely literary posture through which the documentary material is filtered and re-filtered until it assumes the dreamlike forms of parables and archaic nostalgia. The majority of the tales ('Coronata', 'Teresita', 'Romantica', 'Vocesana' and 'Primante') appear vitiated by an improbable fantastical taste. One can clearly see that the author has aimed for a literary construction of the story and not truthfulness. The peasant or rural setting *serves* in these cases as a mere starting point for a discussion that is not at all confined to the narrow spiritual terms of the provincial problematic. The same could be said for the wider and more demanding short story, 'Gente in Aspromonte', that gives the title to the book. In this case too, the poetic investigation into an atmosphere that is archaic, mythical, outside of time counts for more than the documentary report on the social conditions and psychological characteristics of the protagonists. The last part of the story is decidedly fantastical, to the point of assuming the tones of popular drama (in this regard, we should see Vincenzo Padula or even Nicola Misasi on brigand mythology). Moreover, there is no doubt that the story 'Gente in Aspromonte' provides motifs that allow a partially different reading. For us, what is most important is that Alvaro was, for this work, considered one of the archetypes of post-Resistance populist literature ('one will discover the best of Alvaro when his Calabria ceases to be a romantic and decadent refuge, an oasis of original innocence and becomes the real Calabria

---

94 For an English translation, see Corrado Alvaro, *Revolt in Aspromonte* (Frances Frenaye trans.) (New York: New Directions, 1988). [Trans.]

with its shepherds and their lives full of struggle and misery'[95]). Despite this opinion being a little forced—since it establishes a tradition *a posteriori* against which to validate the final literary examples of it—we can say that Alvaro counts on the development of a populist theme simply to sustain, in extremely intellectual forms, a curiosity in the epitome of a peasant surrounding that had only partially been confronted and resolved in literary forms, and where each literary experiment occurred at some distance from the last one. We still believe that Alvaro sees the figures of the peasants, shepherds and Calabrian gentlemen in a fundamentally unrealistic light, where the generic humanism that the writer exhibits towards them is much diluted. But we recognize that, in the literature of the first three decades of the century, even this refined and aestheticizing attention could act as a populist stimulus. So the shepherds, who appear as motionless as terracotta statues against a background of fairytale forests and mountains, also became characters of a more general literary and political polemic, although their suffering and thirst for justice seem to the reader muffled, suffocated by an atmosphere of remoteness and suspension.

We can indicate another way that the populist and proletarian theme has been confronted, one that in the representation of a subaltern setting emphasizes a psychological investigation or even a characteristic of *intimismo*. In these cases, the sociological datum is principally based on the level of individual, personal relationships while the *milieu* is presupposed and hastily sketched out. The most obvious consequence of this attitude is the prevalence of soft and unrealistic hues in the finished literary works which reflect the literary standpoint of a crepuscular rather than properly decadent position.[96] A typical example is Carlo Bernari's *Tre operai* [Three Workers, 1934],[97] about a young worker Teodoro, who tries, in a series of personal and political episodes, to escape

---

95 Carlo Salinari, 'L'Italia di Alvaro' [Alvaro's Italy], *Il Contemporaneo* 3(25) (23 June 1956).

96 *Decadentismo*, or the decadent movement, was a late-nineteenth-century European literary and artistic phenomenon spanning authors and poets such as the *poètes maudit*, as well as diverse figures such as Marcel Proust, Thomas Mann and Luigi Pirandello. It is generally perceived to have focused on the unknown, the unconscious and the irrational, and championed a heightened, refined sensibility. The Italian variant of aestheticism is associated with the likes of Gabriele D'Annunzio, Giovanni Pascoli, Antonio Fogazzaro and, later, Luigi Pirandello and Italo Svevo. [Trans.]

97 Carlo Bernari is the pseudonym of anti-fascist writer and partisan Carlo Bernard (1909–92). [Trans.]

subjection to exhausting and degrading work and its milieu. Alongside we find Marco and Anna, friend and lover, also workers, also worn out by the same anxieties and dissatisfactions, but in a coarser and more confused way. The novel is not uninteresting in its description of important political facts of the early 1900s, such as the occupation of the factories in Naples, following the example of the analogous attempts in Turin. But the relationship between these events and the story of the individual characters is *deliberately* presented in ambiguous, uncertain, indeterminate form. Read in a certain way, *Tre operai* can be seen as the story of the workers' inability to act, to constitute autonomously on the political plane. But this interpretation is clearly forced and tendentious, because it presupposes a historical dimension and a dialectical force lacking in the novel. The element of *crepuscolarismo* and decadence in Bernari's populism derives precisely from this: the moral passivity, the developing torpor of consciousness, the dull-witted desperation of his workers are seen as the reflection of a nearly inescapable state of existence. *Teodoro is a drifter, a desperate man because he feels the condition of the worker to be a fate.* 'A son of a worker,' says his father, 'can only be a worker';[98] and once again in Anna's thoughts:

> Origin, family and class pigeonhole Teodoro's family, composing a social classification of all the people he has met until now. And at the end of this outburst she feels that she nevertheless has a right to a more comfortable life, that life which she has always had to sacrifice; and slowly a hatred creeps in for these people, the workers who force her into a life without hope.[99]

Having posed the conditions of the discussion in these terms, it follows easily that the real motif of the *Tre operai* is formed by the petty-bourgeois anxiety that snakes around the margins of the working class where it presents itself most adrift and fragmented. From this standpoint, those who affirmed that Bernari—from his first publications—represented precisely those aspects of a popular environment that aspire to become bourgeois were correct.[100] But

---

98 Carlo Bernari, *Tre operai* (Milan: Rizzoli, 1934), p. 50. [Trans.]

99 Bernari, *Tre operai*, p. 105.

100 The critic to whom we refer is none other than Elio Vittorini. His violent attack on Bernari, published in *Il Bargello*, exemplifies the annoyance and resentment that a revolutionary populist (fascist) feels towards an explicitly petty-bourgeois crepuscular populist (we do not know whether Bernari was already an anti-fascist, although he was certainly close to some models of the late-nineteenth-century moderate socialist protest, such as

this takes nothing away from the importance of *Tre operai*, precisely because it identifies and clarifies one of Italian populism's ways of being, revealing the widespread inability (or impossibility) to distinguish clearly the boundaries— psychological, sociological, moral—between the petty bourgeoisie and the proletariat.

Giovanni Cena[101] had already tested out something of the sort in the early years of the century in his *Gli ammonitori* (1904), the story of the printer Martino Stanga, of his encounters, his hopes and his friends. As Cena stated in his introductory note, the protagonist 'was one of the types that characterize our time, one of those creatures of pure sensibility and intelligence that the accident of birth leaves open to being inexorably crushed by the still rudimentary mechanism of our society'. In fact, Martino, abandoned by his companions in misfortune, either dead or imprisoned, is racked by the doubt that all his illusions of redemption and progress are destined to fail. Of course, part of Cena's aim was that of social polemic, which Bernari cannot ignore; but the affinities must be found in the pained, almost lachrymose, tones of a weak, non-virile pessimism used to describe the events surrounding these 'maladjusted' workers. This segment of working-class *intimismo* lies at the

---

that delineated by Giovanni Cena's *Gli ammonitori* [The Admonishers]). We will merely note the origin of several later positions, both democratic and anti-fascist, can be discovered in anti-bourgeoisism which Vittorini employs to condemn Bernari:

> Some have called for [*Tre operai*] to be subject to public vilification as a communist book or thereabouts; alas, some of these people see a national shame in everything published that does not ooze satisfaction. In fact, it is not even a book for the people who, thanks to a fortunate instinct, don't give a damn for their equals and their daily struggles for reality and the plausible, etc.; nor do they deign to show interest for anything less than the *One Thousand and One Nights* or *Puss in Boots*. Those deluded persons who think they are writing for the people by narrating the story of some unemployed people make me laugh. They are, of course, the very same who say, 'let us elevate the life of the people' and do not realize that what they mean to say is 'let's make the people bourgeois.' Are there not enough seamstresses and minor employees in this world? From Verona he sent seamstresses into ecstasy; but—God willing—neither Bernard nor [Hans] Fallada will be able to turn workers into minor employees. Nor will the *Domenica del Corriere* . . . —'Tre operai che non fanno popolo' [Three Workers Who Don't Make A People], *Il Bargello* 6(29)(22 July 1934).

[*Domenica del Corriere* was a weekly magazine that was also dispatched as a Sunday supplement to *Corriere della Sera* from 1899 to 1989.—Trans.]

101 Giovanni Cena (1870–1917), novelist and social reformer. [Trans.]

margins of populism, as an extreme manifestation of ideological and spiritual contiguity with the lower strata of the ruling classes. This current will remain particularly alive in Naples, where the dividing line between petty bourgeoisie and proletariat is continuously oscillating and unstable.

A case in point—on a much lower level—is that of *La ragazza di fabbrica* [The Factory Girl] by Tuscan author Armando Meoni,[102] the first draft of which appeared in 1931 as *Richiami* [Calls]. It is the story of a young girl who, having worked in a textile factory and consummated an unhappy love affair in a working-class environment, joins her mother, a woman of easy virtue, and becomes a prostitute. The working-class setting, which is soon left behind, serves only as a pretext for a marked psychological and *intimistic* depiction. The girl, corrupted but not to the point of wanting to abandon the child. she bears, is a figure quite independent of her working-class origins. On the sociological level she can be defined as working class, but she possesses a pronounced petty-bourgeois bearing. The presence of this sort of psychological investigation, the place given to the question of the senses, the rebirth of sensuality, natural maternal sentiment along with the unhappy and crepuscular atmosphere of existence, remind us of some of the highest exponents of Tuscan populism, in particular Pratolini; think of works such as *Via de' Magazzini* [Warehouse Road] and *Il quartiere* [The Neighbourhood]. Although the relationship is not direct, Meoni helps us understand this other face of the problem: the permanent petty-bourgeois vocation of certain strata of Italian populism which expresses itself in the murky form of tedium and dissatisfaction, in this vague aspiration for life to get better.

11

The more a populist conviction attributes positive and (relatively) autonomous values to the people, the more rigorous it is. It is clear that populism will never be able to achieve an entirely autonomous position since it is born as the expression of a bourgeois will for political, ideological and cultural hegemony. The boundaries of populism are therefore the same as those that the bourgeoisie determines at each moment of its history. Their extent is determined according to the level of pressure for popular participation within the stage of development and modernization of the national social structure; and they are limited to the extent that this participation is organized in authoritarian

---

102 Armando Meoni (1894–1984), writer and socialist. [Trans.]

fashion from above. There is no doubt, then, that a properly populist literary position corresponds more rigorously and directly to the political and ideological atmosphere of a democracy. Within left-wing fascism and during the *ventennio*, the writers we have frequently cited develop a lively interest in the social problem. The myth of social justice and the glorification of the labouring people, at times moralistically contrasted to bourgeois corruption, can be seen to develop logically in the passage from Oriani's nationalism to revolutionary fascism, absorbing bit by bit the residual contributions of socialist ways of thinking and of Sorelian ethics. The attitude of cultured men towards the people evolves further when they rediscover, after the 'parenthesis' of fascism, the democratic solution. In their eyes, communism presents itself as the correct application and practical realization of a set of cultural and social demands that no preceding movement had been able to satisfy, even though it had been able to articulate them. In their substance, these demands do not change; a real class standpoint never arises in the works of the Italian authors of this period. What shifts is the political angle from whence these demands originate. Populism continues to be the typical way in which writers and 'culture' are situated in relation to the society. But democracy and communism represent more organic and conscious channels of diffusion and affirmation of this attitude. Left-wing fascism, the attempt at an internal opposition, is overcome and denied when it becomes clear that only through the mutation of the bourgeois regime will it be possible to fully actualize, even on a political plane, the principle of 'popular revolution'.[103] The question of whether this 'popular revolution' too was a

---

103 From the political point of view, the beginning of the shift can be traced to the effect that the war in Spain had on the young generation of intellectuals, even those of fascist origin. In this case, too, the process is less straightforward than one might think. The passage from fascism to anti-fascism occurs through left-wing critique (on this issue and others) of official fascism which, in the eyes of these youths, seemed lacking in rigour and fidelity to the doctrine. The process can be summarized as follows: To start with, one should recall that, in the years after 1935, there was a lively debate in Italy concerning the nature of overseas movements that directly or indirectly harked back to fascism; the attitude of 'left-wing fascism' is on this issue extremely negative (see Ricci's *L'Universale* and the pages in Volpe's *Storia* devoted to the relations with European nationalist movements, on the 'fascist' character of which the author does not raise any doubts). This should be unsurprising if we bear in mind that the search for ideological and political purity—the fundamental revolutionary and populist element—is characteristic of this attitude, which could in no way imagine itself related to the overseas movements that were often openly and programmatically reactionary. A sincere social-popular fascism necessarily reacted to the anti-popular Sanfedismo [mobilized against the Parthenopean Republic in 1799] and

phenomenon of advancement and stabilization of the bourgeois system was not consciously posed then or even later. But it is certain that this myth forcefully served to align the youngest and most lively forces of Italian culture with the anti-fascist front. Moreover, the young intellectual recruits who in the passage from fascism to anti-fascism sought the chance to create a new and prestigious pedestal for culture—providing it with a new and more organic functional role—played a significant role in the creation of this myth. It is no coincidence that the left cultural front consisted principally of those intellectuals and writers who previously had maintained social-fascist ideals, whereas those bourgeois intellectuals and writers who for various reasons were anti-fascist during the *ventennio* and had always remained distant from the populist theme were estranged from it. We will reiterate that the populist attitude was

---

anti-collectivist Francoism with a surge of condemnation and rebellion. As Pratolini writes at the beginning of Franco's exploit:

> The Spanish Falangists are completely without a leader or an explicit proletarian base. Fascism is dictatorship plus a corporative proletariat, and the insurgents will have to be set aside for some time before they can be allowed to declare themselves Mussolinians. At this rate, we along with Sir Mosley and Rexism will end up accepting the burning crosses, *l'Action Française*, and hey! what a great party that would be! We can just hope that the Spanish people can rediscover themselves after this tragic *Vendée* of a new type. —'La politica estera . . . del piede di casa', *Il Bargello* 8(50).

These are unequivocal judgements but they cannot yet be considered completely heterodox if only a couple of issues later, addressing the question again in more general terms, Pratolini supports his argument with the position taken by *Regime fascista* (Roberto Farinacci's daily) which defined certain foreign 'fascisms' as:

> People who react with a single end in sight, whic is to say to not be disturbed while they go about their daily business which for the most part they conduct in *tabarins* and *maisons closes*. Of course, between them and the communists we prefer the latter who at least have a precise programme and are less hypocritical and demagogical'. Pratolini comments on this by stating: 'they too bear the original flaw: that is, [they believe] the light comes only from Rome.—See 'Vaspra', 'Precisazioni sui fascismi stranieri', *Il Bargello* 8(52).

This time, however, the criticism from within was no longer enough. The Roman legions supported the Falangist *Vendée*; the Duce proclaimed his solidarity with Franco, lining up his soldiers alongside those of Hitler, whose claim to equal standing with the original root of fascism, Italian fascism, was widely scorned by the youth. It was by now clear that fascism would no longer carry out its 'popular revolution'. Parting from it was the only possible solution. From this moment on, Vittorini and Pratolini's collaboration with *Il Bargello,* although uninterrupted—particularly as far as the latter was concerned—tends to become ever-more distant and neutral.

indeed the link between the two discourses: it is the typical form of bourgeois social commitment which is revealed in writers and intellectuals when they accord literature and culture the task of progressive intervention within the social reality of a particular country.

In the framework of this development, populism represents *one* moment of a veritable anti-fascist cultural ideology which varies in complexity depending on the case. In the years between 1937 and 1945, from the war in Spain to the end of the Resistance, a nascent left-wing culture, occasionally leaning on more advanced overseas events, quickly developed the fundamental presuppositions for a *modern democratic* discourse. From this moment onwards—much more so than before—it is impossible to isolate the populist position from the cultural and political context that encompasses and often justifies it. This will become all the more true after the Liberation. But the contrary is true as well: positions that often appear simply literary can be understood only with reference to the populist axis around which they end up coagulating and which they use to justify themselves. If one is to understand the development of the argument, it is necessary to turn one's gaze to this assortment of attitudes that naturally cannot always be in agreement with each other but that together form a sufficiently clear and homogeneous whole.

Particularly important for understanding the reasons that led some young writers to break away from fascism while still collaborating with fascist newspapers can be found in their attempt to elaborate a new concept of culture, one that was more dynamic, more modern, more *popular*. We have earlier cited a passage by Pratolini where he posed the need for the 'supportive, specific, conscious participation of the people in revolutionary doctrine and developments'. Moreover, in developing this line of thought, he went as far as to affirm that: 'In any case, one must inject into the worker (and into anyone) a higher possibility of social and revolutionary consciousness, one that is, so to speak, increasingly clear and defined.'[104] Convictions of this sort are at the root of a democratic cultural demand: the demand for popular participation in the revolution, which in any case is a feature of left-wing fascism, tends to become a conscious point of rupture with and protest against the conservative regime. Vittorini too enters into this argument, with a flexibility that shows he had read democratic texts (and perhaps Marxist ones as well). In 'Lavoro

---

104 Both quotations: from Pratolini, 'Tempo culturale della politica', *Il Bargello* 9(14).

manuale e lavoro intellettuale' [Manual and Intellectual Labour] and 'Unificazione della cultura' [Unification of Culture],[105] he advocates that everyone—
even workers and peasants—should be provided with the same cultural
foundations, so that 'manual labour' is not considered a punishment, and that
'intellectual labour' is not merely the result of social privilege. The concept of
culture as 'spiritual preparation', 'as an end, as a spiritual activity of Man', distinct from culture as 'professional preparation' takes this utopian form, which
is typical of Vittorini, and leads the Sicilian author to state: 'The worker who,
thanks to a need alien to his activity as a worker, read Shakespeare and Goethe,
represented the real urge towards culture. He evoked an ideal type that everyone
needed to take into account [. . .]. Were we wrong to conclude that popular
culture is the indispensable condition for every culture?'[106] In this way, Vittorini
too, while continuing—as can be seen from these passages—his evermore
'rigorous' argument on the autonomy of cultural principles, ties the fate of
the highest and most modern culture to the success of a people's culture—one
that is not mere information but spiritual elevation, and which is like the
necessary background and *liberatory* condition for every non-aristocratic intellectual enterprise. In a more concrete vein, Pratolini reprised, in a publication
that allowed a freer and more informed exchange of ideas, the problem of the
relationship between culture and society, civilization and the people:
'Civilization, over and above the fundamental condition of culture, comes to
mean the lived experience of social relations face-to-face with men whose
speculative capacities are inhibited by their real daily toils'.[107] And, he adds:

> Only by granting to society more broadly the privileges yielded by
> positive individual experiences can we reconcile culture and our fleet-
> ing destiny as writers with life; to the extent that in every effort we
> must recognize a craft, the product of which goes precisely beyond
> technique only on condition that it becomes an element of humanity,
> one that can be acquired and become subject of speculation.[108]

---

105 Elio Vittorini, 'Lavoro manuale e lavoro intellettuale', *Il Bargello* 8(43) (1937); and
'Unificazione della cultura', *Il Bargello* 8(53).

106 Elio Vittorini, *Diario in pubblico* (Milan: Bompiani, 1957), p. 75. (See also Vittorini,
'Diario in pubblico', *Il Bargello* 3 [1937]).

107 Vasco Pratolini, 'Civiltà in crisi?', *Campo di Marte* 1(4) (15 September 1938).

108 Pratolini, 'Civiltà in crisi?'

We can see here how certain terms return persistently: culture as the overcoming of technology; the culture–life relationship as social function and spiritual mission of the writer; the concept of civilization as the concept of human society. Left-wing democratic culture begins to articulate itself in all its elements, perhaps by using the scattered detritus and linguistic fragments of the preceding position. A point is missing from the complete definition of the new concept, and Pratolini hints at it in the close of this last passage.

The at-times rather narrow nationalism that distinguished many of the attitudes of earlier writers (but not Vittorini) now shows itself unable to bear the weight of this democratic turn; it seems necessary to replace it with a broader vision of the cultural problem. A new theme is born: that of Man, at once the stimulus behind and product of the intersection of literary and spiritual themes which were extremely free and rich at the time. It is not even necessary to underline the fundamental importance of this aspect, since it should appear evident that a large part of the populist polemic will orbit around it. In addition to the reprise of certain typical motifs of Italian nineteenth-century democratic thought—Mazzini's doctrine returns, even if indirectly, in many of these formulations—what this attitude signals is the attempt to tie Italian populism to a much broader theme, of European or global import, the fulcrum of which is once again the anti-fascist position. The validity of the people is no longer attested to (or not only, the oscillations are frequent in this regard by its politico-social function within a narrow national area); but draws its source from the evermore widespread conviction that the people is synonymous, at the highest level, with humanity; that the commoner is the absolutely pure image of man. We will see below the extent to which this conviction was generic and intellectual, produced by a vision that was also typical of bourgeois culture. It is enough here to signal and reiterate the tangle of reasons that solder the theme of 'Italian' populism on to the non-provincial outcomes of foreign democratic cultures and, to an extent, to Italy's pre-fascist culture, in its most European expressions.

In some authors, this process assumes the form—at least to start with—of a reflexive falling-back-on-oneself in search of new reasons to justify literary conduct outside immediately political and social commitments. In these cases, the passage from fascism to anti-fascism is characterized by the temporary predominance of literary investigations, even to the detriment of more general motivations that had encouraged the change of mind. This is in particular the attitude of the Tuscans, who now endeavour above all to clarify technical instruments and aspects of the poetic world that are relatively disconnected from the spirited earlier investigations. Opening up a new period of activity, Pratolini writes in *Campo di Marte*:

> We appear to be undergoing a period of revision of all our motivations, which are many, and not always orthodox. We will dedicate our work to documenting and specifying what faith has led us to believe; we will strain to clarify our judgement on the facts and ideas of our generation to which we will deny chauvinism and nationalism, slapdash and pedantic attitudes.[109]

The point of arrival of the cultural polemic within anti-fascism can, in these cases, be found in an attitude of prudent equilibrium between a realistic-nationalist theme and one mediated by the need to situate oneself in a European context. The refusal of a petty provincialism (= chauvinism) does not mean, even at this point, the acceptance *tout court* of the cosmopolitan (= internationalist) solution. Pratolini tries to lay the foundations for a literary investigation based on the *truth* of experience, and despite this (or perhaps precisely because of it), capable of escaping from a narrow circle of interests. The position becomes clearer still in a review of Bilenchi's *Anna e Bruno* [1938], a novel that also served as a response to similar apprehensions and needs:

> The *strapeasana* polemic, which revived strictly reactionary and conservative motifs, nevertheless had the merit of legitimating provincial values that cosmopolitan aestheticism threatened to render ridiculous. Despite the limits of an accurate interpretation able to balance chauvinism and the universal, one must recognize the merit of a reaction that put trust in potential individualities which time, a more careful preparation, and the value of talent would then support and justify. The judgement of history on those who considered *strapaese* as their alpha and omega will be that of a dead weight for (not just literary) civilization. Those who understood the *strapaesana* polemic in terms of an arbitrary starting point from which to explain their experience as men rather than writers, embracing its contribution in terms of revolutionary sensibilities, will instead be saved by history and will document an era in its social and cultural evolution.[110]

---

109 Vasco Pratolini, 'Calendario', *Campo di Marte* 1(1) (1 August 1938).
110 Pratolini, 'Calendario'.

From the literary standpoint, these choices could only take the path of a temporary drastic narrowing of the social and ideal horizons of research through which one could realize in depth what had not been given (and was still not given) in scope. Denuded of the patriotic and revolutionary ambitions of his early years, Bilenchi turned in the direction of a rigorous intimism: the truth of things was to be discovered through extremely sober and painstaking psychological investigation; in a revelation of reality that had the dry and fixed contours of a woodcut. The world within which his characters moved remained narrow and provincial, but through memory and phantasy it became possible to endow it with unexpected density and dimensionality. This is true particularly for *Anna e Bruno* and *Conservatorio di S. Teresa* [The Conservatory of St Therese, 1940], whereas in the two well-known short stories 'La siccità' [Drought] and 'La miseria' [Destitution, 1941], he went so far as to retrieve certain human characteristics of a clearly allusive character, set in an almost surreal atmosphere. The rather straightforward acknowledgment that behind the sobriety of style there hid a by-now rigidly anti-rhetorical and anti-fascist *animus*, helped considerably in consolidating the popularity of these stories, many of which today, seen in a historical perspective, reveal the provincial and experimental limits from which they had sought to escape. It is important to underline, however, that even in these oblique ways the subject of Man retrieved from history by the objective conditions of existence begins to establish itself throughout the young Italian literature. Think of the conclusion of 'La Siccità', when the very young protagonist is torn from his fatalistic sadness by the spectacle of a great fire bursting forth among the houses of his village: 'Having witnessed the disaster I made my peace with everyone. Nothing truly serious could happen to anyone when one had the help of so many people and when many others were ready to sacrifice themselves for us'.[111] From *solidarity* to *hope* the step is a short one: 'Suddenly I was struck by the hope that in the morning I would find the plants of the allotment, of the vast countryside, damp and green, as I had before'. Even the naked, bare Bilenchi has the notion of this *fundamental dyad* of anti-fascist humanitarianism, which henceforth we shall encounter on countless occasions.

Despite the difference in poetic worlds, Pratolini's investigation is very much analogous to the one we have been discussing. His intent, in the prose

---

111 This and the following quotation: Romano Bilenchi, *Racconti* (Florence: Vallecchi, 1958), p. 332 and 333, respectively.

of *Tappeto verde* [The Green Rug, 1941] and in *Via de' Magazzini* [Warehouse Road, 1942], is also to uncover simple human truth beneath the dullness of a humble and arduous everyday life. The autobiographical origin of the narrative gives a particular hue to the figures and places: the humble social origin of the characters tends, in this phase, to be presented as a spiritual humbleness; the awareness of suffering is tempered by a soft *crepuscolarismo*. The 'discretion' of the story does not prevent a new ideological or sentimental idea from introducing itself through these experiments of memory—the attempt to give the suffering of the protagonist an unprecedented dimension. Aside from the fact that the stylistic structure of the work already gives an anticipatory sign of the choral character of the *Cronache*, it is relevant that the story of the boy in *Via de' Magazzini* is conceived as the search for human contact, which at times bears fruit and at others remains unsatisfied. It opens with the child's first exploratory experience which is at the same time his attempt to place himself in relation to an already identifiable neighbour: 'I learnt to distinguish men one from another by looking through the gaps in a balustrade in a soldier's dormitory';[112] and it closes when his first love shows the youth the concrete possibility of being a man: 'Standing before her my turmoil was placated. At last, I could freely turn to another creature; with her I discovered the ability to talk and listen'.

The Tuscans, travelling along the same investigative path, were brought to an abrupt standstill because of their characteristic fidelity to the models, themes and places of their regional tradition. One must seek the fundamental points of the populist literary discourse elsewhere. At this time, Vittorini was the leading exponent of an exploratory anti-fascist literature. In some senses, *Conversations in Sicily*[113] can be said to represent the most typical book in this broad phenomenon of the formation of an ideology. It expresses more clearly than any other the *humanitarian credo* that will later inspire large parts of resistance and post-resistance literature. *Conversations in Sicily* is born of the awareness that a new period of self-consciousness and history has begun. The animosities and furies of the preceding experiences are conveyed without losing any of their original charge, which was always a little abstract and unrealistic:

---

112 This and the following quotation: Vasco Pratolini, *Via de' Magazzini* (Milan: Bompiani, 1949), p. 13, 91–2, respectively.

113 The novel *Conversazione in Sicilia* was serialized in the literary journal *Letteratura* between 1938 and 1939, and later published in book form by Bompiani in 1941.

'I think man is mature for something else [. . .]. I think he is mature for something else, for new, different duties. That's what we all feel [. . .] the absence of other duties, other tasks to carry out . . . Tasks that would satisfy our conscience, in a new sense'.[114] The voyage around Sicily is an exploration of one of the saddest and most wretched of human panoramas: among 'third class' Sicilians, who have only the oranges that they are paid with to eat, among the squalid ground-floor tenements of the villages of the interior, sinking as into wells in unlit blind alleys. But it is also and above all a fantastic, imaginative denunciation of the hardships of man *in general*, a protest against his deepest and most painful injuries. Here, for the first time, Vittorini advances the theory of the two 'human kinds', which will also be endorsed by many of the intellectuals rallying to the Resistance:

> [P]erhaps not every man is a man; and not all humanity is humanity. This is a doubt which arrives in the rain when you have holes in your shoes, and you no longer have anyone in particular dear to your heart, you no longer have your own particular life, you've done nothing and have nothing still to do, nothing even to fear, nothing more to lose, and you see, outside yourself, the world's massacres. One man laughs and another man cries. Both are men; even the laughing man has been sick, is sick; nevertheless he laughs *because* the other man cries. He is the one able to massacre, to persecute; the one who, in hopelessness, you see laughing over his news-papers and the ad posters for the newspapers; he doesn't belong with the one who laughs but also cries, in his calm, when someone else is crying. So not every man is a man. One persecutes and another is persecuted; and not all humanity is humanity, only those who are persecuted. You can kill a man and he will be all the more a man. And so a sick man, a starving man, is all the more a man; and humanity dying of hunger is humanity all the more.[115]

As Ezechiele, a 'popular' character tasked with voicing the idealistic facets of Vittorini's argument, says: 'The world has been badly wronged, very very badly, more than we ourselves know. The people in this picture is depicted as the reflection and image of the suffering of the world: in it there is more virtue,

114 Elio Vittorini, *Conversazione in Sicilia* (Milan: Bompiani, 1958), p. 35 / *Conversations in Sicily* (Alane Salierno Mason trans.) (Edinburgh: Canongate, 2003), p. 31 [translation modified].

115 Vittorini, *Conversazione*, pp. 124–5 / *Conversations*, pp. 110–11 [translation modified].

more love, more pity because it is the most offended against.' When the protagonist learns of the death of his brother in war, he moves through the lanes of the Sicilian town in tears, accompanied by symbolic figures of this universal suffering who, through their tears, are joined in unconscious solidarity: 'and they all became my followers: a cart driver, a dog, men of Sicily, women of Sicily, and even a Chinaman. "Why are you crying?" they asked.'[116]

The position of the writer no longer knows borders: from China to Sicily it is a long line of human beings waiting for the palingenesis to take place.

The lyrical language forces the protest and the appeal into stylistic forms whose intellectualism is evident today. But this is not the aspect that interests us most, although it can be easily grasped. It seems instead essential for us to underline a substantial limit in the ideological development of Vittorini's subject matter. If a scholar were to attempt to analyse more concretely the characteristics of this humanitarianism, I think they would find themselves embarrassed to go beyond the pure and simple proposition of the subject. A word does not reveal itself to be richer in meaning the more it is repeatedly bellowed in a poem or a novel. Quite the contrary, the *word* that is shouted out is less important than the *shout*, and the results of the artistic investigation are less well defined than the ideological intention that advances it. The same intellectualist forcing of the lyrical discourse ends up appearing as the consequence of an unachieved poetic and cultural maturity, of which the writer shows himself to be more or less conscious when he declares himself to be in the grip of 'abstract furies'. It may be objected that it is already important that there is a search for man. But an investigation is of value if it does not rest exclusively upon a peremptory act of will, upon a categorical imperative of moral conscience; if, that is, it is sustained by a lively sense of real conditions within which the discourse unfolds. Otherwise, the peremptory act of will, the categorical imperative of moral conscience, remains closed within an exclusively intellectual area, and the pretence of a 'revolution for man' is reduced to the more modest proportions of a 'revolution for culture' or, in even more limited fashion, of a 'revolution for literature'. Within this canvas, it turns out that the reference to the people is nothing but the tautological reference to the ideology of the writer: *humanitarianism does not serve the people, it serves humanitarianism*; the historico-social framing is but the convenient projection of a cultural position. Moreover, this is effectively

---

116 Vittorini, *Conversazione,* p. 163 and p. 211, respectively / *Conversations*, p. 147 and p. 127, respectively, translation modified.]

Vittorini's attitude from the time when, in *Il Bargello,* he theorized the need for a popular culture that would *free* Culture—the real one—from its historical obstacles, to the day when, in *Il Politecnico,* he would defend cultural autonomy from submission to politics. He always placed Culture at the centre of history, forcing Man to serve as its highest value. Here lies the severe limitation of Vittorini's populism, which manifests itself each time the writer focuses his attention on the social problem (as will occur later in the final draft of *Il garofano rosso* and in the *Le donne di Messina*). For Vittorini, the people is only a moment within a cultural discourse. The identification of humanity with the people only takes place insofar as the concept of the people subordinates itself to that of humanity. More correctly: the people is humanity; humanity can also not be the people. The later developments of Vittorini's thought demonstrate that between populism and humanism he chose 'humanism'; that is, he consciously and in a proper sense chose the path of bourgeois culture.

At this point we cannot silently overlook the fact that many of Vittorini's positions are derived from the important cultural operation of reading, studying and translating some of the most notable texts of Anglo-Saxon literature; and particularly the literature of the United States, when, in the years 1930–40, some young writers tried to widen the circle of possible cultural referents beyond that of an obvious and worn-out Italian tradition. We know that Vittorini was one of the principal protagonists of this endeavour. Today we can say that, more than anyone else, he learnt the lesson from writers such as Erskine Caldwell and William Saroyan, founders of the 'New Legend' as Vittorini calls them in his anthology of American literature.[117] But the reference is not only syntactical and stylistic. If we are able to understand what these young Italian writers were looking for in American literature, it will be possible also to understand the reasons for certain individual preferences. It appears quite clear that in American literature (or, more generally, foreign literature) they sought the satisfaction of certain needs and myths that, in embryo, were being formed in the cultural conversation of the preceding years. In this case as well, the cultural discourse pushed in two directions: *humanity* and the *people*. The United States appeared like the gigantic domain of democracy, in which the life of individuals was more often than not presented as a simple particle in the great, pulsating life of the masses. In the United States,

---

117 See Elio Vittorini (ed.), *Americana* (Emilio Cecchi introd.)(Milan: Bompiani, 1942).

crucible of races and destinies, to be a people meant—directly and almost sociologically, as we might say—to be humanity. The sense of this investigation
as a whole is clearly expressed by Cesare Pavese[118] in summarizing the reasons
for this youthful xenophilia:

> Our efforts to understand and to live were sustained by foreign voices;
> each of us frequented and lovingly loved the literature of a people, of
> a distant society, and spoke of it, translated it, made of it an ideal
> motherland [. . .]. Naturally [the fascists] could not admit that we
> were seeking in America, in Russia, in China and who knows where,
> a human warmth that was not given to us by official Italy. Less still
> could they admit that in it we sought ourselves.[119]

One can observe, as more than a mere curiosity, that in this period
America, Russia and China were the countries that most fascinated Italian
progressive intellectuals, for their enormous participation in the world of the
human 'whole'. Driven by analogous reasons as Pavese, Vittorini went as far
as to identify his favourite authors as those who, at least in appearance, seemed
to do the most to impose the flavour of a social theme (Caldwell, John Fante),
or one that was generically and generously humanitarian (Saroyan). It is clear
that in the same way as Pavese alludes to himself when speaking of this love
for distant peoples and societies, so Vittorini also defines his personal search
when he writes the following phrases concerning Saroyan:

> America is no longer America in this legend; it is a sort of fabulous
> new Orient; and man appears within it under the sign of an exquisite
> particularity, Filipino or Chinese or Slavic or Kurdish, in order ulti-
> mately to be always the same: the lyrical 'I', the protagonist of the work.
> What in the old legend was the son of the West, and was identified as
> the symbol of a new man, is now the son of the Earth [. . .].[120]

His gaze is turned to America, China, Russia; but then, in practice, the
young xenophile and anti-fascist writer is confronted with the problem of
making this apprenticeship in humanism and 'universalist' populism work concretely. The age-old question of the relationship between renewal and tradition

---

118 Cesare Pavese (1908–50), novelist, poet, translator, literary critic and editor. [Trans.]
119 The article first appeared in the Turin edition of *L'Unità* (20 May 1945. It has now
been published in the Pavese's anthology *La letteratura americana e altri saggi* (Turin:
Einaudi, 1953), pp. 217–19.
120 Pavese, *La letteratura americana*, p. 963.

presents itself again in this new form: as the need to link the abstract suggestion of a fundamentally literary culture with the recognition of the specific surrounding reality. Not even this progressive author with his new culture is able to leap over such a distorting impasse; indeed, his progressivism forces him (unlike the great bourgeois writers of the 1900s) not to neglect the social purpose and national setting of his work. A problem of tradition is reborn among apparently more unscrupulous cultural attitudes. In *Conversations in Sicily*, the most ambitious and abstract attempt in this genre, the latent anti-fascism operates as a negative element, betraying its contingent, fastidiously ideological character. Sicily like Alabama, Xinjiang, Turkestan or the Deccan Plateau; this is the aim of the work. But then everything is exhausted in the pure enunciation of the programme. From the literary standpoint, fascist moralism—because we do not escape the confines of moralism here—is equivalent to the fascist anti-bourgeois moralism of earlier years. At this point, one can already begin to think of how much this hurried and superficial way of reckoning with oneself and one's past weighed on the ideology and literature of the Resistance, of which Vittorini himself will offer, with *Uomini e no* [Men and Not Men], an unsurpassed archetype of moralistic wishful thinking. Pavese had already reflected on this problem that formed the subject of the first section of his essay on Sherwood Anderson, which he went so far as to title *Middle West e Piemonte*:

> Think of Italian literature's discovery of the regions in the period that ran from the late 1700s through the 1800s and which proceeded in parallel to the quest for national unity. From Alfieri onwards, all Italian writers struggle, often unconsciously, to achieve a profounder sense of national unity by penetrating evermore deeply into their regional character, their *real* nature, and thereby creating a human consciousness and language steeped in provincial blood and the full dignity of renewed life. Those who should especially reflect on it are my countrymen from Piedmont—where this simmering influence is felt most strongly the more distant is its realization, since we are distracted by too much dialectal specialization. We Piedmontese should reflect on the fact that though this rebirth historically began in our name, with Alfieri—and beginning with Alfieri, through D'Azeglio and Abba, on to Calandra and further down[121]—we have never

---

121 Vittorio Alfieri (1749–1803), tragedian and poet; Massimo D'Azeglio (1798–1866), statesman and novelist; Giuseppe Cesare Abba (1838–1910), writer and patriot; Davide Calandra (1856–1915), sculptor. [Trans.]

possessed the man and the work that, in addition to being very dear to us, was truly able to reach that universality and freshness that can be understood by all men and not only by our countrymen. This is our still unsatisfied need. Whereas, to the respective need, in their land and their province, the American novelists of which I speak sufficed. It is from them we must learn.

And so, the intelligent reader, when he hears speak of Ohio, Illinois, Michigan, Minnesota, Iowa, Indiana, Dakota, Nebraska, putting to one side—having savoured the rich harmony of Indian names—the exoticism, he should instead imagine in our colours those places that, eighty or so years ago, were prairies and forests that a first generation of Anglo-Saxons was endeavouring to breach, suffering austerity and hardship of biblical proportions, and that the second and third generation cultivated with no less hardship and with some cursing, or lost among a proliferating proletariat drawn from all the ports of Europe—Germans, Swedes, Bohemians and Italians—who also took from the pioneers of the Midwest the halo of the chosen people. The novels of Theodore Dreiser, Sinclair Lewis and, especially Sherwood Anderson, begin here.[122]

This is a passage of great lucidity and intelligence. But think of the grave misunderstanding that intends to 'read' the reality of Piedmont with mid-Western American literature as a guide. Despite the author's explicit warning, was this not the superimposition of a ready-made literary myth onto the concrete possibilities of understanding the world? What effectively worked in this position was ultimately its commitment to consider Piedmont *as Piedmont*, the specific object of a literary interest. Pavese (in 1931) rediscovers regionalism *tout court*, albeit vivified by experiences from across the ocean; he rediscovers the necessary relationship between region and nation; and he rediscovers the meaning and function of the province. With these interventions, he makes a powerful contribution to the establishment of a milieu that after the Resistance lends energy and motivation to the various local traditions which were, at times, smothered or mortified in the first four decades of the century. Of course, we cannot consider Pavese responsible for the facile popularization of his ideas by others. And yet it was he who wrote the incredible

---

122 'Middle West e Piemonte' was written in 1931; the passage cited can be found in *La letteratura americana*, pp. 33–4.

peasant novel, *Paesi tuoi* [Your Villages, 1941], which was welcomed at the time of its publication as a return to Verga. One might object that what is praiseworthy in this novel is not populist; that what is most genuine in Pavese does not take the direction of populism. But then it is even more significant that Pavese who was bourgeois to the core of his being, a cultured and intelligent man, also felt the need for populism. It is clear that he came under the influence of the surrounding culture and, in turn, reacting positively, contributed to creating and enriching it. Pavese too, when he felt the need to be a social writer, was populist; and he was so in an absurd and fantastical way that was permitted by his purely cultural and intellectual relationship to the people. We will see how he attempted to justify and theorize his position in relation to a more precisely political and social commitment.

The Resistance and Gramscianism
Apogee and Crisis of Populism

12

When the Resistance began, the ideology of anti-fascism endorsed it completely, becoming one of its cornerstones. There was no decisive split between the years prior to 1945 and those that followed, at least not at the level of culture. The development of a populist and progressive attitude finally found its desired outlet. Until then it had largely been a tendency among a small group of intellectuals; now it became and remained for a certain period the dominant position within the national ideological debate. At the time, one had the sensation, contested only by few, that a 'culture of the people' would impose itself on the various forms of elite culture, whether bourgeois or aristocratic. This was when the polemic against escapist and formalist, non-*engagée* literature reached its apogee. The old anti-bourgeois resentment expressed itself in this new form: everything that aimed to re-affirm the autonomy of art, its disinterestedness towards the social problem, was labelled bourgeois—the mission of art and literature was to win over the whole of society to a humanist horizon. In the same way as during the Risorgimento, the democratic period of the First International, the nationalist and social-fascist phase, and of the Resistance and the post-Resistance the urgent need to shake off the chain of obvious truths from culture, to bind it to a drive for national renewal, returned to inflame the social function and the popular content of artistic and literary activity. The proportions of the phenomenon, the objective impetus underpinning it, the set of ideological and cultural reasons that surround it are well wrought yet more varied, even more contradictory than in the past. Directly political and social forces outside of culture intervene to give it its character. The weight of certain literary and artistic traditions, not always in line with the socio-political intentions of the populist tendency, are forcefully evident. In other words, we discover that the populism of the Resistance and the post-Resistance is probably the most self-aware, most ideologically and politically 'organized' populism in our literary history. At the same time, it was unable to ever—or, rather, almost ever—exist in a *pure* state, to overcome internal contradictions in choice of style, theme, sentiment and taste. This is above all true in the field of literature and the figurative arts, whereas in the cinema the absence of a powerful national tradition allowed a freer and more daring inventiveness from the stylistic standpoint as well. This does not overcome the weakness of ideological and cultural frameworks, but in some ways transcends them in terms of the immediacy of the impressions, in the naked 'truth' of the story. In contrast, in narrative, poetry and painting, as well as literary and artistic criticism, the massive presence of extremely powerful confused and fanciful ideological ideas resulted in the inability to create a great, mature popular culture. In other words, the limits of the populist experiment of the Resistance must appear clear even to those who do not adopt an entirely different position. Not only can one judge that anti-fascist progressivism reflects what remains a traditional choice—one that, all in all, is scarcely able to break with the past—but also within the substantive limits of the cultural reformism, it is difficult to affirm that this was ultimately carried out with the adequate forces and instruments. We will see in each case how writers, poets and critics react, in an often rough and purely voluntaristic way, to an impulse that stems from social ambitions held in common.

There is no doubt that many cultural and literary attitudes remained generic and failed to assume an organically determined position, partly because the very historical drive of the Resistance remained generic and socially uncertain. It is not possible here to attempt an evaluation of the Resistance that could clearly identify the weight of the contributions of the various social groups that participated in it. But I think we can accept the most widespread interpretation of the Resistance, not only in its artistic representation but also in the political discourse of the left. *When it is affirmed that the Resistance is a great popular fact, one evidently means that it cannot be considered a model of class struggle.* Conversely, the element that characterizes it most is precisely the broad participation in the anti-fascist struggle of a vast socially diverse stratum of the Italian people who found, in that critical moment, a meeting place for a common set of intermediate objectives. The objectives were, roughly speaking, those of representative democracy, undergirded by strong social preoccupations: liberty, justice and the overcoming of the traditional blockages in the economic and political spheres. Clearly one cannot exclude the possibility that among the various forces in struggle at the level of the social, some were motivated by the greater or lesser spontaneous intention of using the anti-fascist 'occasion' in a class direction, that is, in a manner immediately anti-capitalist. But at the political level, the choice was unquestionably the alternative one, which tended to maintain the popular initiative within the limits demanded by the necessary alliance of the different social strata against the common number one enemy: Fascism and Nazism. Class movements such as the Communist Party adapted to and even became promoters of this alliance, advancing this strategy through a politics of national unity which would later lead to the notion of an Italian road to socialism as *necessarily* linked to the realization of the Constitution and bourgeois reforms.[1] In relation to these organizational issues there were

---

1 One should reread the speech by Togliatti to the cadres of the Neapolitan branch of the Communist Party on 11 April 1944, which was intended to explain and impose the *svolta di Salerno* that had occurred shortly earlier—see 'La Politica di Unità Nazionale' [The Politics of National Unity], *Critica marxista* 2(4–5) (1964): 13–46. [The 'new course of Salerno' was the shift in the PCI line decided by general secretary Togliatti along with Stalin, aiming at the formation of a government of national unity under General Pietro Badoglio. This involved setting aside the calls for the king to abdicate, in the interests of inter-class unity against Fascism.—Trans.] The fundamental preoccupation of Togliatti's reasoning was to impose on the party the thesis that it should represent a great *popular* force of unity and *national* renewal. All other tasks paled in the face of this one: the socialization of the means of production was set aside ('Of what have we communists not stood accused! They have accused us of being enemies of property. But those who accused us were themselves a gang of thieves who plundered all of Italy'—p. 17); past discords must be forgotten so that 'all *honest* Italians' can gather their common forces together in order to liberate the country from Nazi-Fascism ('today the *national duty* is not up for discussion and is the same for everyone: it forces us to *all unite* and struggle to chase the foreigner from the motherland'—p. 28). But what strikes us most forcefully is the disdain with which Togliatti refused the accusation against the communists of being anti-national ('They have accused us [. . .] of being anti-national [. . .]. Comrades, I challenge anyone, following the most rigorous historical and political examination, to find a single act of our party that has been in conflict with or has hurt the interests of our nation'—p. 18). Instead he attributed to the party and the popular Italian masses the merit of being leaders in the struggle to strengthen the nation, according to an autonomous line of development that significantly was tied to the Risorgimento:

> We are the party of the working class and we do not repudiate, and will never repudiate, this quality of ours. But the interests of the working class have never been alien to those of the Nation. Look to the past and remember how at the start of the national Risorgimento, when all that existed were small groups of workers separated from one another and still without a deep class consciousness, and of a rich political experience, these groups gave the most heroic fighters for the struggles of the masses, in the cities and the countryside, to liberate the country from foreign domination (p. 22).

very different pressures stemming from the tradition of struggle of left-wing parties and of qualified worker participation in the Resistance in the guise of initiatives that cannot be traced entirely to the class-neutral schema of anti-fascism (like the strikes in northern Italy of March 1943 and 1944). Yet it is significant that what the left-wing journalism of the time praised in the contribution of the working class were precisely those aspects that were 'less working class' (for example, the struggle to save the factories from the destruction at the hands of the Germans in April 1945 was portrayed as a way to participate in the defence and later reconstruction of the 'national economy'). From this political perspective, the working class came to be considered as a fraction—maybe even the most conscious and solid—of the Italian people; the 'national' role assigned to it finds its origin and justification in precisely this ideologico-reformist distortion of its nature and tasks. On the other hand, if we wish to remain at the politico-ideological and artistic-literary level, we see highlighted in numerous ways that the contribution of the workers passes into second place when compared to that of intellectuals and peasants. We could make a list of works, not just literary ones, which describe the labour of ideas and sentiments that led an entire intellectual stratum to the Resistance; many others could be given that narrate the vast and warm support of the great mass of peasants to the partisan formations in the plains and the mountains; but very few works are dedicated specifically to the problems of the workers' struggle against fascism (and none of these are literary, if we ignore a few hints in Vittorini's *Uomini e no*).

The direction of the 'class movement', which in the political as well as cultural arena affirms the absolute priority of a broad concentration of popular interests in as united a front as possible, is already present in 1945. To underline

---

Togliatti carried out the task entrusted by Stalinism to Western communists ever since the time of the French Popular Front. Some of his sentences seem literally Stalin's: 'The flag of national interests, that fascism has dragged through the mud and betrayed, we take up and make our own' (p. 23). But what is startling is the manner (and ability) with which Togliatti was able to insert this international recommendation into the furrow of the Italian tradition. Anyone who reads a text can grasp the way Togliattian and Gramscian communists so strongly feel the relationship with the democratic, Garibaldian, Mazzinian and Carduccian democratic Risorgimento. They were nothing but the belated exponents and prosecutors of that movement. Looking back to this Togliatti, it is also clear that there was nothing strange or exceptional about the attraction that the Communist Party exercised over intellectuals in the years immediately following the Resistance. Indeed, in that historical period, the party offered to culture and the intellectual stratum the same conditions, guarantees and prospects as any broad democratic movement. The democratism and populism of the petty bourgeoisie was gratified by it, as if from a sudden and unexpected revival of the 'more genuinely Italian tradition'. Adherents and allies flocked to it.

the decisive significance of the generically anti-fascist aspect of the struggle means relegating to second place—or at least to postponing *sine die*—the class character of the left. It was never so clear as in this moment that Stalinism and reformism work hand in hand. The sense of this attitude seems to be summarized in exemplary fashion in this quotation, drawn from an article by Ambrogio Donini, dedicated to 'Marxism in Italian Culture': 'Our task is not to fight an ideological battle between currents of thought operating on a consistently anti-fascist democratic terrain, but to establish among these various currents, which are the expression of particular social groups, a fraternal alliance tasked with destroying all residues of fascist ideology at the root'.[2] Like Minerva from the head of Jupiter, so, in the aftermath of the Liberation, the conception of the necessary relation between old and new culture, between the inheritance of the tradition and the transformative and regenerating drive of 'working-class ideology', emerges armed from the repertoire of Marxist commonplaces. Once the concept of the anti-fascist unity of culture is posited, it follows inevitably that cultural development is seen as an uninterrupted continuum of which the Marxist position is only the last, most developed addendum. Lucio Lombardo Radice writes in 'Eredità della Cultura Liberale':

> The world evolves, but the truths of the waning world are taken up by the new world, even if it is apparently spiritually distant from it. It is a serious error not to become a militant of working-class and anti-fascist unity in order to safeguard certain spiritual and cultural values, when it is precisely the working class that defends and promotes those values, when it is precisely socialism that invokes them.[3]

The textual echo of Stalinist statements is here fused with the particular attachment of the 'Italian intellectual' to his own ideological and cultural tradition. The entire idealist-Crocean legacy that characterizes the background of a large number of left-wing intellectuals after the Liberation is transmitted through such formulations.

---

2 Ambrogio Donini (1903–1991), Marxist historian and Communist senator. The quotation is from his 'Il marxismo nella cultura italiana', *L'Unità* (Rome edition) (5 January 1946). [Trans.]

3 Lucio Lombardo Radice (1916–1982), mathematician, educationist and Communist politician. See his 'Eredità della Cultura Liberale' [Inheritance of Liberal Culture], *L'Unità* (Rome edition) (19 September 1946). [Trans.]

Within this overarching vision, the progressive 'use' of culture essentially takes on, once again, the features of a protest and denunciation of the socio-economic backwardness of Italy. In the same way that the unity of anti-fascist forces is politically an instrument of struggle against the blockages and deficiencies of an underdeveloped capitalist system (according to the general principle that the construction of socialism cannot do without the initial implementation of bourgeois reforms), so the spirit of the Resistance exists within culture as a powerful moral indignation, as idealistic rebellion and sociological determination in the context of all that makes of our country after the Fascist *ventennio* a place of strong imbalances and violent contradictions. In correspondence to the initial, objectively rudimentary level of argumentation, the nature of these demands and cultural and social denunciations are also generally straightforward. The culture of the Resistance grounds its demand for renewal in the acknowledgement that, in Italy, the problem of survival itself is anything but resolved. Although the stylistic and thematic solutions of this attitude are not univocal, some elements are common to it and persistently recur. To use the terminology of the authors we are examining, we can note that the principal cause for scandal is the difficulty, here in Italy, of fully being men because one cannot be human until one has escaped the grip of life's fundamental necessities. Extreme poverty and hunger, oppression of social life and thought are, as they were fifty or a hundred years ago, the enemies to be identified and combatted. I do not think there is any doubt about this: from *Il quartiere* [The Neighbourhood] to *Le donne di Messina* [The Women of Messina], from *Sempione strizza l'occhio al Frejus* [Sempione Winks at Mount Frejus] to *Cristo si è fermato a Eboli* [Christ Stopped at Eboli], from *Pane duro* [Hard Bread] to *Cronache di poveri amanti* [Chronicles of Poor Lovers], from *Napoli milionaria* [Millionaire Naples] to *Speranzella*, a single sense of indignation is at work, a single *animus* which condemns the humiliation of a humanity that lacks the necessities of life. In this sense, the old democratic battle is taken up again.

At this point in our discussion, the relationship with the other elements of a pre-Resistance and pre-anti-Fascist cultural formation should be thoroughly clarified. On the one hand, a traditional theme whose origins can be found in the democratic and socialist currents of the 1800s flows into the literature of the years following 1945. It is no coincidence that the main organ for the publication of ideas in this period, the journal *Il Politecnico*, intentionally imitated Cattaneo's model. On the other hand, grafted onto these solidly and clearly democratic aspects is a store of twentieth-century ideas and motifs, among which mentality, taste, cultural debate—the genesis and character of which we identified in the period 1930–1945—play a large role. First, it should be noted that the populism of Resistance literature appears driven by a strong moralistic and ideological impulse rather than by a direct association with those popular strata of the population that have an interest in the process of renewal: the intellectual goes to the people but, *more often than not, before reaching it concretely and seriously, he turns it into a myth, into the reversal of his own image.* We can think in this regard of the position of Vittorini or Pavese, or of Levi, though the latter is on another plane and level. Often 'the scandal of poverty' which we spoke of previously turns out to be weak and ineffective because it is posed without resolving the problem of the relation between the concreteness of the denunciation and the generic nature of the intellectual symbols in which it is realized. The avant-garde experiment attempted by some fails because of an excessive respect for the conditions; conversely, the real conditions are not set out in a sufficiently robust manner so as to compensate for the failure of the stylistic attempt. The cry of protest for offended humanity flounders because of the inability of these intellectuals to be, if nothing else, seriously and profoundly populist. In relation to this, we must signal at least one aspect of this investigative weakness that is the source of so much confusion during this period. In the preceding chapter we said that, in the anti-fascist and Resistance standpoint, there was an attempt to extend traditional populism by identifying the People with the concept of Humanity. Very often the relationship between the two does not pass through channels that are politically or theoretically transparent but, instead, via subterranean and obscure analogical processes in which the mystical element prevails. In short, in some cases, it is very difficult to determine how much populism is the fruit of a conscious choice and how much of an irrational and obscure attraction, or even of an intellectual will to discover at all costs the link between the individual and the mass. Of course, in this case too, it is not possible to reduce the explanation of such a broad phenomenon to a widespread decadent climate; the root of populism, whatever hue it assumes, is nevertheless determined by the rallying of vast strata of intellectuals to the Resistance and to anti-fascism. But to note that the humanity spoken of in populist discourse at the time is frequently a sub-humanity, it is the Primitive, the irrationality of the world and history, to note this can be useful precisely to explain the political and ideological qualities of Resistance populism. Having outlined the genesis of the problem, no one will be surprised if on the ideological and political plane it presents itself in such an indeterminate and questionable form. Once again, the internal contradiction of the movement reveals itself anew: on the one hand, the powerful bourgeois drive is unable to reach full autonomy in relation to progressive preoccupations; on the other, the political and sociological concerns do not escape a typically decadent ambiguity. With regard to themes, it explains strong intellectualist and subjectivist residues that, taken individually, certainly do not constitute a negative element but become so when one tries to force them into the straightjacket of the social functionality of culture and art. With regard to protest, this explains the frequently generic character of indignation. With regard to the proposals, this explains the inevitable poverty of indications that once again do not elude the classical dichotomy of solidarity and hope. Even the positive aspects of the world are reduced to pure expressions of sentiments: the ethics of the good-hearted common people, an idea as old as the bourgeoisie, reappears even if dressed in more pretentious garb and with more generic justifications.

One of the most evident consequences of this ideological instability is the overcoming and annulling of that line of division that the 1800s had, in a quite rigid way, maintained between the democratic and Christian seams of Italian populism. Clearly, there is no explicit reprise of liberal Catholicism but, instead, a strong assumption of the general motifs of Christianity situated in the furrow of what can, at the level of political commitment, be defined as a democratic or progressive position. It is very often the case that, while on the level of practice, indignation and its demands belong entirely to the dimension of the old democratism, at the level of the general (statements of principle, declarations of hope, the definition of spiritual problems), a custom, a law, a vague religious spirit are set out which can be understood and justified only within the ambit of an evangelical-type Christianity. Sometimes this process of symbiosis comes about in a way we may call spontaneous and objective, through the discovery that the ethical laws of popular behaviour are *in themselves* Christian laws—even if the people are clearly unaware of it. For example, this is the case with Pratolini who identifies a *historical* core of populist-Christian ideas in the purity, sincerity, force of spirit and hope of his characters. Elsewhere, the process is subjectively self-aware, and the writer seeks a correspondence of the eternal truths of Christianity among the common people. This is the case with Pasolini, who thinks he finds the objectified image of salvation in the lumpenproletariat.

We shall not insist upon this presence of the Christian element in anti-fascist progressivism more than is necessary, so as to avoid the empty ideological formulas to which polemics of this sort are inevitably condemned. Having established that the secular-bourgeois cult of Man is not always without mystical and religious implications, we will not be surprised each time that such an identification shows itself to be possible. We will prefer to show that the set of *populist* notions and themes linked to this underlying framework remains closed within extremely limited confines and expresses a position that is destined to rapidly exhaust itself. The fact that we find ourselves confronted with a populism nourished by democratic programmes and Christian ideas will be only one of the elements in the picture, to be uncovered through direct textual analyses and concrete citations.

Within this framework, some authors will display fanciful and intellectualist qualities. This is true, once again, of Vittorini and Pavese, for whom it does not seem necessary to add much to our previous observations, at least as far as the validity of the results achieved is concerned. In their case, it is more interesting to examine the presence of this widespread mythology of the Resistance which, without ever becoming a serious and profoundly considered inspiration, circulates everywhere with the force characteristic of those general beliefs destined to become commonplaces within only a few years.

Vittorini's *Uomini e no* (1945) is perhaps the most glaring example of how some left-wing intellectuals' involvment in the Resistance was driven by the conviction that popular impulse could become the fundamental vehicle as well as the practical enactment of a renewed cultural position. With regard to the content and the animating spirit, there is no progress or development from *Conversations in Sicily* to *Men and Not Men*. The Resistance is presented as the mere occasion for a discourse whose rationale lies in culture and intellectual investigation. The historical, political and social motives remain secondary. What counts is the affirmation, within the historical, objective, popular revolt of a mythology of the spirit, which is constantly defended and supported against every attempt, even if misrepresented, to refer to certain concrete sociological and political reference points. At the centre of this position lies the ideological figure of Man, which absorbs all possible exigencies of renewal, mystifying them. A few years later, Vittorini will summarize the meaning of this attitude effectively:

> A writer who is able to posit through his work revolutionary demands
> 'different' from those that politics poses, is revolutionary. These are

demands [. . .] of man that only he is able to glimpse in man, that only he as a writer can catch sight of, that only he as a revolutionary writer can posit, and posit 'alongside' the demands that politics posits, positing 'more' than the demands that politics posits.[4]

We apologize if we are forced to repeat ourselves because of the monotonous refrain of themes and formulas, but we must say once again that Vittorini's position is questionable, not to the extent that he strenuously defends an 'autonomous revolutionizing' of literature and culture—a feature common to many twentieth-century avant-garde positions—but because he is unable to draw this autonomy away from the power of suggestion of progressive and Resistance commitments. *Men and Not Men* is a fundamentally wrongheaded work for this reason. Its linguistic and stylistic framework, a million miles from the dazzling inventiveness of twentieth-century European literature, is not enough to explain the irritation it elicits when we reread the book after some years. The irritation stems from the recognition that the work is nothing but a hybrid, a vague union between progressivism and avant-gardism, which exhibits an exclusive, closed and moralistic relation to the people. What cannot be accepted in *Men and Not Men* is precisely the presumption of imposing upon the world, as the solution to its problems, an intellectual attitude that smacks of tradition and caste. What cannot be accepted is precisely the old attempt—typical of the Italian intellectual—not only to make reality in his image but also that this image should be the salt of the earth, the prefiguration of a higher civilization, the key to the many evils of life. *Men and Not Men* makes one want to defend the Resistance in its genuinely popular form, which is betrayed here. Despite all this, despite our reaching a class judgement that strongly limits the scope of the Resistance, there is a big difference between it and the author. It is also true that the existence of a work like *Men and Not Men* justifies, once again, the doubts about the truly innovating qualities that such a historical phenomenon was able to imprint on the cultural and literary life of the country (beyond, of course, its social structuring). If an intellectual such as Vittorini was able to look at the Resistance with these eyes; if this vision of Italy was able to mark so much of the subsequent literature of the Resistance; if the criticisms directed at this work were merely of a politico-ideological character, while no one noted the contradiction between progressivism and literary avant-gardism, which was not incidental but substantive—this means that the Resistance was unable to break the link between renewal

---

4 Vittorini, *Diario in pubblico*, pp. 269–70. The article first appeared in January 1947.

and tradition. In other words, the same situation that marked the most auda-
cious experiences of Risorgimento populism now repeated itself in new terms.

The story of Enne 2, the bourgeois intellectual who brings to the anti-
fascist struggle all the anger of a disappointed and unhappy man is, from this
point of view, absolutely typical: the Resistance exists in relation to his personal
problem and not vice versa. This too would have been admissible if the reduction of an entire historical phenomenon to a case of petty-bourgeois intellectualism were not presented as part of a more general complementary process
of humanization of social reality seen through the prism of progressive ideology,
for which the personal case of the protagonist becomes, optimistically, a sort
of *necessary* and *positive* step towards the acquisition of higher human truths.
Moreover, the potential drama of the bourgeois individual who is tempted,
against his own nature, by populist aspirations is resolved in the easy affirmation
that everything which appears in the Resistance is positive as long as it is turned
towards the common and fundamental enemy. 'He did something like the
thing the Spaniard and Son-of-God did. He was lost but he fought alongside others. Did he not fight alongside them? It's not like it was just a case of
fighting and surviving. There was also fighting and losing oneself. And he did
this with many others who did the same'.[5] Is there not in this progressive *cupio
dissolvi* something reminiscent of Giuseppe Antonio Borgese's Rubè, his
anxieties and his end?[6] Besides, were we to be completely open, we would say
that Enne 2 behaves, from the ethico-spiritual point of view, like a typical left-
wing fascist who has passed over to the Resistance; not only because of the
strongly autobiographical elements that we can glean from it but also because
this relationship between social-fascism and progressivism lies behind the
irrational impulses of his actions, the desperate will to 'heal' through the link,
whatever it might be, with the world; the desire to affirm in the right field,
with the right men, lofty and *immutable* ideals. This impression can be confirmed in the most explicit way by looking at another work, *Le donne di Messina*
[The Women of Messina]. But already in *Uomini e No* [Men and Not Men]
other elements confirm it.

---

5 Elio Vittorini, *Uomini e No* (Milan: Bompiani, 1962), pp. 209–10 / *Men and Not Men*
(Sarah Henry trans.) (Marlboro, VT: The Marlboro Press, 1985). [All quotations have
been translated directly from the Italian edition.—Trans.]

6 *Cupio dissolvi* or 'I wish to be dissolved', from *Philippians* 1: 23–4. Giuseppe Antonio
Borgese (1882–1952), writer, journalist and literary critic, author of *Rubè* (1921). [Trans.]

Such is the distortion arrived at by this leftism that the problem of the relation between an individual case and a general one, already resolved in the ambiguous way mentioned above, remains drowned and distorted by a more general ideological affirmation that is even more ambitious in scope. It is the motif of all-encompassing Humanity that we have alluded to. *Uomini e No* suggests that all are men, the hunted and the hunter; and that only by virtue of common humanity can the hunted recognize themselves in the hunters and at the same time feel different from them:

As soon as someone has been offended against, we are with them and we say that they are man. Blood? There is man. Tears? There is man.

And the one who caused the offence?

Never do we think that he too is man. What else can he be? A wolf, really?

Today we say: it is fascism. Or rather: Nazi-fascism. But what does it mean to say that it is fascism? I'd like to see fascism outside of man. What would it be? What would it do? Could it do what it does were it not in man to be able to do it? I'd like to see if Hitler and his Germans would be able to do what they do if what they do was not in man. I'd like to see them try and do it. Take from them their human capacity to do it and then say to them: Go on, do it. What would they do?

Like hell, my grandmother would say.

Perhaps Hitler would still write what he wrote, and Rosenberg too; or perhaps write idiocies that are ten times worse. But I'd like to see, if men were unable to do what Clemm does, grabbing a man and stripping him, feeding him to the dogs; I'd like to see what would happen to the world because of their idiocies.[7]

This too is part of a certain humanitarian and Resistance mythology. The superiority of anti-fascism would then lie, above all, in the fact that anti-fascism recognizes that fascism too has human traits. The conclusion, on the plane of Man, is that such conversions are not impossible: Man is able to pass from democracy to fascism, and from fascism to democracy, remaining in essence the same—that is, Man.

---

7 Vittorini, *Uomini e no*, pp. 178–9

In subsequent works the decline of Vittorini becomes all the more evident. *Il sempione strizza l'occhio al Frejus* (1947) is an imaginative fairy tale in which, by way of symbols that are by turns too clear or too confused, the miserable situation of post-war Italy is described. But it is not enough to present the central family as eating bread and *cicoria* for months on end to convey ideas of hunger and pain. The atmosphere is instead that of a grotesque ballet, suggesting, where it is most accomplished, a vague aestheticism. *Le donne di Messina* (1949), on the other hand, is a more openly populist novel of Vittorini's. It narrates the affairs of a primitive community emerging from the moral and material destruction of war, finding shelter and organizing itself among the dilapidated ruins of a village in the Apennines between Tuscany and Emilia Romagna. All manner of individuals drifting out from the great storm of war find a place here: peasants from across the Italian peninsula, lorry drivers, ex-partisans, vagabonds and artisans. The atmosphere in which they move is that of the 'other duties' of *Conversations in Sicily*.[8] The overall effect is more than disappointing. These common people, made to sound like characters from Caldwell and Saroyan, end up as mere caricatures, not unlike the commoners from the naturalist novels of the same period. The hypothetical 'City of the Sun' that they create is similarly abstract and mystified, and corresponds to laws of humanity that are, as usual, ambiguous and intellectualistic. It is not by chance that here too the most relevant character is that of an ex-fascist or, rather, of a German. Known for having participated in round-ups and massacres, he joins the community and ends up becoming one of its main reference points. Vittorini affirms his humanitarian credo even towards this character. Before he is discovered, but while the police are already searching for him, one of the ex-partisans belonging to the group of drifters makes a declaration absolving him (though not devoid of contradictions and doubts):

> I do not know to what point you've pushed the man you're hunting. But wherever this man has been for a year and a half, he has lived with many who a year and a half ago he could have found himself killing; instead he has worked with them, made friends with them [. . .].
>
> Here we do not know which is the one and which the other. There could be some past enemies among us. And yet, after more than a year, we're just workmates.[9]

---

8 Vittorini, *Conversations in Sicily*, p. 31.
9 Elio Vittorini, *Le donne di Messina* (Milan: Bompiani, 1949), pp. 388–9.

The trajectory of Vittorini's work comes to a close with this moral—but it is always ready to be revitalized at the first opportunity (such as the struggle for democratic freedoms in Spain or the support for the uprisings of colonial peoples) that seems possible to rekindle its motivations and to call upon one of these holy men of the bourgeois religion of Man.

Cesare Pavese was certainly much more prudent and careful than Vittorini. When meditating on the difficulty of beginning the new popular art he was calling for, he wrote:

> What is not acceptable is to beat one's haunches to draw out a roar that instead sounds like a meow. The equivocal makings of the intellectual of yesterday do not change. In this world of individuals nothing changes, and words are not enough. Those who are obsessed with the dilemma 'Am I or am I not a socially-conscious writer?' and with the infinite variety of things, facts and souls—which turns into a kind of self-auscultation, as in the glorious times of *Frammentismo*[10] —should make their heroism coherent: they should force themselves to keep quiet.[11]

But this explicit polemic against the voluntarist attempt to create a social literature without a parallel and contemporary cultural maturation did not prevent Pavese from surrendering to the lures of the progressivist commitment which was all the more ambiguous since in his case it was justified by motifs of a personal and decadent order. Pavese sheds light on the mystical origin of a large swathe of resistance populism:

> [I]t can be said that the best of us, sullen and desperate as we were, had in the past often surprised ourselves thinking that only one thing might save us: a leap into the crowd, into the febrile burst of proletarian and peasant experiences and interests; thus the especially refined disease fascism infected us with would be overcome by the humble but tangible health of all.[12]

---

10 A literary tendency associated with the poets published in *La Voce*. Their poems were characterized by brevity and immediacy and lyrical flashes outside of any narrative structure or dramatic form. [Trans.]

11 Pavese, 'Di una nuova letteratura' [On a New Literature], *La letteratura americana*, pp. 243–4. The article was first published in *Rinascita* (May–June 1946).

12 Pavese, 'Di una nuova letteratura', p. 226. To better understand this 'leap into the crowd', see the quotation from *Il garofano rosso* [The Red Carnation] on p. 113 in this volume.

At the same time, he is intelligent and bourgeois enough to understand the sociopolitical limit of this impulse, refusing the ultimate consequences on the literary plane: 'in this attitude there is one latent danger: that of "going to the people". Especially in Italy. The fascists go to the people. Or the masters. And "to go there" is to dress them up, turn them into an object of our tastes and condescension'. But the need to discover the motive for his irrevocable vocation of being a socially engaged 'new writer'—a writer of *L'Unità* and *Rinascità*, a 'writer of the Resistance'—still leads him to reconcile, in a singular formulation, acknowledgement of an objective creative limit with the mystical-like irrational impulse of which he has spoken:

> One does not go 'towards the people'. One *is* the people. Even the intellectual and the 'master' who suffer and experience the fundamental labour of the passage from a civilization of obstacles and waste to one organized in the freedom of technology *are* the people and prepare a government of the people. Which is what communism wants. Democracy is this government.

In this way the problem can be circumvented but only to then encounter it anew with all its insoluble contradictions. One refuses the mysticism of 'going to the people' but replaces it with the mysticism of an apparently. spontaneous identification of the intellectual with the people which is founded, in turn, on the highly ideological conviction that the task of culture is already, *in itself*, a social function. One more step and we arrive at the decadent myth which resolves the contrast in a typically vitalist form: 'If ours is truly a proletarian and peasant reality, we need not brandish it as a problem or a distinction. *It will be enough to live it.*'[13] If we look into Pavese's credo more deeply, this conclusion is no surprise. For not just the conclusion but also the origin of the matter can be traced back to his strongly individualist and 'literary' set of interests. In other words, the writer's main concerns remain autobiographical, of an intimate nature, even when he appears to *transfer them* onto this external 'objective' entity, that is, the people. At the same time, in Pavese as in Vittorini, Levi and many of their followers, behind the apparent objectivity of the sociological determined referent, there resurfaces the same old myth of Man, this time in an even more rigorously cultural form. Schematizing the argument into a sort of diagram of forces, we can say that

---

13 Pavese, 'Di una nuova letteratura', p. 237, 238 and 227, respectively (from a previously unpublished piece, 'Il comunismo e gli intellettuali', 14–16 April 1946).

in Pavese (naturally, not only in his case), the 'people' is an ideological mediation, dressed up in the trappings of the social. It mediates between the pre-eminent subjectivity of the writer and the set of myths that constitute his culture. In other words, it is a hypothetical, *salutary or salvational* instrument destined to somehow fill the gap between individual and reality, tearing the one from the most inveterate and profound evils, handing to the other a sense a perspective. I believe that no other meaning can be given to statements such as the following:

> [T]he argument is this, that we shall not go to the people. *Because we already are the people and nothing else exists. If anything we shall go towards Man.* Because this is the obstacle, the shell that needs cracking: the solitude of Man—our own and that of others. The new legend,[14] the new style is all here. And, with it, our happiness too [. . .]. To propose that we go towards the people is to confess to a guilty conscience. Now, we have many regrets but not that of having forgotten what we're made of. We know in the social stratum that is customarily called the 'people', laughter is more frank, suffering more intense, one's word more sincere. And we take note of that. But what else does this mean than that when we're among the people we have already overcome solitude—or are on the way to overcoming it. In the same way, in the novels, poems and films that revealed us to ourselves in the recent past, Man was more straightforward, more lively and sincere than anything else here in Italy. But it is not for that reason that we confess our inferiority or difference from the men that make those novels and films. *In the same way as it was for them, the task is to discover and celebrate Man over and above solitude, over and above the solitude of pride and meaning.*[15]

It is not difficult to see that the best products of this position are to be found in those works by Pavese where he pulls back from the contradiction in which he's placed himself, that is, where ideology is overcome through a powerful and serious realization of the intimate nature of inspiration, outside of the myth of renewal and the intellectualistic strivings towards it. We refer

---

14 One should recall Vittorini's use of this expression which significantly serves as the title of the final section of his anthology *Americana*.

15 Pavese, *La letteratura americana*, p. 218. The article titled 'Ritorno all'uomo' [Return to Man] appeared in *L'Unità* (Turin edition) (20 May 1945)

in particular to the excellent example, *La Casa in collina* [The House on the Hill], written, perhaps not by chance, immediately after *Il compagno* [The Comrade]. It represents the clearest and bravest instance of a self-analysis of which few Italian writers were capable of in the post-Resistance period. It is a raw and ruthless confession, although betraying a morbid satisfaction in Pavese's own irredeemable impotence, in his egoism and—not by accident—his insurmountable solitude. When, conversely, Pavese enacts his pseudo-populist proposals, the deterioration of the result is very striking. *Il compagno*, for example, which appeared in 1947, is nothing more than a simple concession to the progressivist themes of the time. This is certainly not to say that it was written out of deference to some official directive, but simply because Pavese's subject matter is full of contradictions and ambiguities. The subject of *Il compagno* is in the same vein as his youthful poems 'Ozio', 'Crepuscolo di sabbiatori' and 'Esterno'.[16] But at least in these the popular characters or settings are purely and simply elements of that particular Pavesian world, made up of raw reality and a soft and murky atmosphere. In *Il compagno*, on the other hand, the tale assumes the form of a *Bildungsroman*: the protagonist, Pablo, a young misfit from Turin, comes via a variety of experiences to class-consciousness and joins the clandestine Communist Party. The most beautiful things in Pavese are also the most obvious: the atmosphere of the city, of the river and the hills, rendered with his usual taste and insight. But the educational process remains generic and forced, the figures of the conspirators superficial when not implausible. Despite this, the book's significance lies in the way that Pavese considers the mentality and origins of the communist militant. It is an approach which, in those years and the subsequent ones as well, will be widespread among progressive Italian intellectuals (or rather, among communist intellectuals themselves). When this Piedmontese author selects a notional popular figure to be subjected to this process of formation and transformation, he creates a character with typical anarchic qualities, which we are not sure whether to call petty bourgeois or proletarian; he locates him in a setting—among cafes, taverns, dance and variety shows, amid ballerinas, comics, fashionable tailors, builders, mechanics and lorry drivers—

---

16 The poems composed between 1932 and 1943 can be found in Cesare Pavese, *Poesie edite e inedite* (Turin: Einaudi, 1962), pp. 32–3, 56–7 and 105–106 respectively / 'Idleness', 'The Sand-Diggers' Twilight' and 'Outside' in Cesare Pavese, *Disaffections: Complete Poems 1930–1950* (C. Brock trans.) (Manchester: Carcanet, 2004), pp. 43–5, 189–91 and 117, respectively. [Trans.]

that resembles more a tumultuous and confused suburban milieu than a generic proletarian neighbourhood. In this atmosphere, with these characteristics, the protagonist is all the more real the more he resembles his creator: as the restless and uncertain guitarist who looks to his surroundings for something he knows not what. In short, Pablo is Pablo; and whether or not he becomes a communist is inessential to the formation of his character. Populism surrenders to nature; to be more precise, it is defeated by it. And on those rare occasions when the subject becomes more demanding and certain positions need to be confronted and dealt with, we discover that populism is justified only by a law of nature. It is the communist leader Scarpa who affirms it: 'One doesn't learn much from books. In Spain I saw intellectuals do foolish things like everyone else . . . What counts is one's class instinct.'[17]

While in practice the differences are extensive, it is surprising how close the endpoint of Pavese's work is to the beginning of Pratolini's. Pratolini too posits as a solid foundation of all his work the repeatedly affirmed conviction that instinct (or in Tuscan terms, *heart*) has much greater importance than any awareness or historical form of understanding. This priority of the human factor is already evidence of a straightforward populism. But the form with which Pratolini expresses this attitude is even more revealing of the naturalism at the basis of his image of the world. Even when it is a case of characters defined politically, the emphasis falls upon the material, even physical or corporeal source of certain choices and convictions. In the *Cronache*, it is this clear definition that summarizes the entire judgement on human and social reality: 'A communist is a man like any other, with excesses and depressions, showing impulsiveness and uncertainties, many litres of blood in his veins, five senses and a more or less developed intelligence.'[18] Consequently, the motor of history, that impetuous force of workers' struggles, will not be discoverable outside these elemental impulses of nature. When Maciste throws himself into the generous enterprise of saving as many anti-fascists as he can from the bloody fascist reprisal, the writer comments:

> The Party will chide you for committing the error of trusting in your *heart*; but if you never trusted your *heart* you'd not be in the Party.

---

17 Cesare Pavese, 'Il compagno' in *Romanzi I* (Turin: Einaudi, 1961), p. 451.

18 Vasco Pratolini, *Cronache di poveri amanti* (Florence: Vallecchi, 1953), p. 342. The two works by Pratolini to which we shall refer most frequently—*Il quartiere* and *Cronache di poveri amanti*—were originally published in 1945 and 1947, respectively.

Have you ever read a single line of that book called *Capital* which makes one yawn just to look at it? Did you become an *Ardito del popolo* because of the theory of surplus value or rather because your *heart* was offended?[19]

A whole gamut of emotions stem from the way the problem is articulated: solidarity, friendship, love, all those natural, immediate relationships that tie together the *humble*, the *oppressed*, the *disinherited* in a primordial and indissoluble bond. In *Il quartiere*, and even more so in *Cronache*, the thread of human relationships and so-called historical facts are interwoven with these elementary expressions of affective life: 'our feelings are simple and eternal like bread, like the water that runs from the drinking fountain and quenches our thirst without us being able to taste it'.[20] Naturalism merges spontaneously with populism. The conviction that the focus of the problem is in the nature of man—'it is here that the final knot of the question is undone by looking to the character, the temperament, the "nature" of the Florentines'[21]—ends up coinciding perfectly with the representation of a people that, even from a sociological standpoint, appears to behave in the way that Pratolini depicts. In this nexus, it is possible to discover how the choice of setting—which is, of course, a choice of inspiration or, if you prefer, of education—can influence the ideology of a specific writer as well as substantiate it. The Tuscan tradition, well known to Pratolini, leads him to adopt a specific literary position; his direct knowledge of the Florentine lumpenproletariat fosters a realist justification for this attitude; and, as we shall see, the progressivist ideology sanctions this bond without substantially modifying its characteristics, instead accepting them as they are and positively extoling them. The intimism of *Il tappeto verde* [The Green Rug] and *Via de' Magazzini* [Warehouse Road], arising from the experience of the Resistance, is converted into the collective chronicles of the subsequent works while retaining its basic sociological footholds. The world of the lesser Florence, caught between Santa Croce and Piazza della Signoria, poky and miserable, remains the permanent object of Pratolini's imagination.

---

19 Pratolini, *Cronache di poveri amanti*, p. 334. [Arditi del popolo was an armed antifascist group, founded in 1921, drawn largely from the First World War fighters and a number of leftist groups to resist the rise of Fascism.—Trans.]

20 Vasco Pratolini, *Il quartiere* (Florence: Vallecchi, 1954), p. 79 / *A Tale of Santa Croce* (Peter and Pamela Duncan trans) (London: Peter Owen Ltd., 1952).

21 From Pratolini's investigation on the people of Florence, 'Cronache fiorentine XX secolo' [Twentieth-Century Florentine Chronicles], *Il Politecnico* (December 1947).

In it he has finally found the long-searched-for path of a popular and 'revolutionary' literature.

However, it is extremely significant that this author—who is perhaps the most typical from the standpoint of populist symbols and sentiments—while glorifying the positivity of human innocence and proletarian freshness also, unknowingly, limits the meaning and import of this discovery in a drastic manner. On closer inspection, *Il quartiere* and *Cronache di poveri amanti* are works through which the traditional Tuscan theme (think of Tozzi or of Palazzeschi's *Stampe dell'ottocento* [Eighteenth-Century Prints], Cicognani's *Velia* or Meoni's *Ragazza di fabbrica* [Factory Girl]) undoubtedly finds an outlet *but,* because of the particular political and ideal judgement Pratolini envelops it in, *is not overcome.* For example, two of the exemplary qualities of a literary seam that is ultimately closed and *excessively* self-sufficient, that is to say, provincial, remain intact: isolation and atemporality, sentiments that are all too marked by the singularity of the setting and the weakness of the historical development of the specific situation or set of events. The quarter and Via del Corno are fragments of a popular reality that, by definition, is located at the margins of great social and historical processes, and is tied to these processes only in the form of defenceless victim or scapegoat. Within these boundaries, the characters represented end up undergoing their verdict with fatalistic resignation or even, particularly in *Il quartiere,* faint satisfaction: 'We liked our Quarter [. . .]. The streets and squares of the Quarter were our life.' From this point of view, even the 'positive characters' do not know, or are unable to look beyond, the blockages imposed upon them by the situation. When it is a case of issuing a rallying cry, it cannot be based on the acceptance of this elementary condition of existence. 'The long and short of it is,' says Giorgio, the young communist of *Il quartiere,* 'you've got to stick it out in your own home, in your own Quarter, help each other push ahead here among our own folk. I mean that if everybody stuck to their post here at home, and after all that's the place we know best, then everything would be a lot simpler.'[22] The natural consequence of this way of seeing—and of loving—a popular reality, means that at no point is the continuity between past and present overcome. Which means that not only does the present endure historically the weight of a centuries old condition but also, above all, it does not distinguish itself much

---

22 Pratolini, *Il quartiere*, pp. 1 and 4, and p. 90, respectively / *A Tale of Santa Croce,* pp. 5 and 9, and p. 122, respectively.

from the past, and constitutes nothing but the extreme prosecution of it. An extremely important element in Pratolini's populism is precisely this strong sense of an inheritance that has not yet been atoned for; that it, like the isolation of the quarter, can be experienced as a burden but often is savoured as an asset, as a mark of quality.

> The streets and squares of the Quarter were our life. Florentines of ancient lineage, of *ancient pelo*, as we put it jokingly. You might stand at the street corners, maybe under the very arch where Corso Donati was stabbed to death, without any suspicion of our heritage. For we are still, as we have always been, the *popolo minuto*, the lowly workers grown forgetful of our past. We were rebels, betrayed by our own stupidity . . .[23]
>
> [. . .]
>
> We are a people worn out in servitude and struggle. We pay the penalty for wrongs done centuries ago. Our own wrongs, just as the faces that look down from Masaccio's frescoes in the Church of the Carmine are our own faces.[24]

In this case too, naturalism and populism walk hand in hand. On the one hand, there is the deep and typically Tuscan conviction that certain characteristics of the people are transmitted and conserved generation after generation, through a variety of historical events, as a sort of self-defence against arrogance and oppression. On the other hand, progressivist protest is founded on the realization that a specific social state remains the same from century to century, that change will not be the fruit of an abstract political remedy but only of extensive popular participation. Only an act of love will be able to restore justice, in the same way as only love can save one from the effects of the corruption and moral decadence that accompanies economic misery. Pratolini will write in the presentation of his book, *Cronache*:

> They were poor people, good and bad, simple and corrupt—the same as you encounter everywhere. They had limited the world to a single

---

23 Pratolini, *Il quartiere*, p. 4 / *A Tale of Santa Croce*, p. 9. [The useful notes to this translation explain that *antico pelo* comes from Dante's *Inferno III*, and means 'white-haired with old age'. Corso Donati was a leader of a faction of nobles who was assassinated in 1308.—Trans.]

24 Pratolini, *Il quartiere*, p. 79 / *A Tale of Santa Croce*, p. 107.

road, their own, and in it they found their completion. *Those able to save themselves from confusion owed it to their own capacity for love . . .*[25]

Here Pratolini's progressivism reveals its elementary underlying vitalism, which is even more important than any evangelical colouring such an attitude might suggest. The great protagonist of his *Cronache* is life itself, with its relentless and immutable flow. Good characters and bad are reabsorbed into that existential flow and included and absolved. From Life, this deep current that carries and overwhelms everything, gush the elemental Forces: Good, Evil, Love; Maciste, the Lady, the Youths of Via del Corno. These are the symbols of reality, 'capitalized' symbols that the author, like his characters, needs in order to 'achieve thought'.[26] This is the meaning and limit of Pratolini's optimism. Life has within itself the capacity to be rescued. It renews itself without changing. Every season and every generation are the same as the ones preceding. But that is also because no offence or oppression can completely smother hope's yearning—the hope for improvement. And hope is life itself which cannot come to a halt; it is love which is always reborn and flowers anew. It is a guarantee that one goes on, come what may. If not Providence (although sometimes we must think it is), it is the very course of things and feelings. In the popular solidarity that emerges, there is a force that overcomes centuries because its characteristics are fixed in blood and flesh.

Here all the elements of rebellion and redemption arise from the deepest stratum of consciousness, the one that is a small step away from instinct and is often identified with it. At the origin is nothing but a confused protest, an insufficiently clear but already anguished sense of being the victim of injustice that one has been unable to resist. The youths of *Il quartiere* have reached this point: they recognize the physical closeness, the intimacy of bodies, a first way of feeling united against the laws that they have not given themselves:

> And with each day that passes we draw closer and closer to each other. Giorgio is right: it becomes evermore clear that our world is bounded by the Arch of San Piero and Porta alla Croce. By our confused attempts to deny the very existence of any street and square that does not belong to our Quarter, we are unconsciously preparing a defence for ourselves against something in the outer world, something that

---

25 Vasco Pratolini, 'Presento il mio libro: *Cronache di poveri amanti*', *L'Italia che scrive* (April 1947) in *L'Italia che scrive* (April 1947). *L'Italia che scrive* was a book review founded in Rome in 1918 [Trans].

26 Pratolini, *Cronache di poveri amanti*, p. 537.

has betrayed us. It has always betrayed us, for the memory we have of our father's father is someone who died poor and worn out in a hospital bed, or in the workhouse, or struck down at work, from the last nut on the frame of the loom that needed tightening. Our own father is a picture of exhaustion, dragging himself along; and our mothers have a shawl on their shoulders, and sigh as they empty their purse on a Saturday morning. But we draw our young bodies closer to one another. We link arms and make a long line, and the street is all ours at midnight.[27]

Then, in the *Cronache*, comes the anti-fascist struggle, the Party and the awareness of injustice. But, as we have mentioned, the communists are like everyone else and 'the Party is like the winter hot water bottle'.[28]

In 'Cronache fiorentine XX secolo', as he carries out an enquiry into the city and the people of Florence, Pratolini repeatedly returns to the myth of the innate difference that distinguishes their political and human attitudes, their ideal choices and their passionate outbursts. As he writes: 'To understand a people, and specifically the Florentine, one must confront the man in his natural environment, cut him open and see what's inside'. When this operation is completed, he rediscovers—on both sides—an affinity of passions, a capacity for faith, a youthful impetuosity all characteristic of the political struggle in Florence between the establishment of Fascism and period of the Resistance: 'After centuries of certitude and of well-meaning revolutions, the Florentines had rediscovered their ancient blood. From one end to the other the ideological postulates were soon discounted, and each person manned the side of the barricade on which he found himself when the first shots were fired.'[29] The fascists are themselves in some sense ennobled by their fanatical attachment to the idea: 'The Fascist Social Republic only saved face in Florence. A face that poked out from behind the chimney stacks and the skylights with a machine-gun. Only in Florence was there a real civil war between patriots and fascists.' In his depiction, Pratolini reveals a sort of residual youthful sympathy. In a way, he is confessing that he once liked them for that uncompromising violence, which could seem synonymous with revolutionary spirit, and will

---

27 Pratolini, *Il quartiere*, p. 80 / *A Tale of Santa Croce*, p. 108.

28 Pratolini, *Cronache di Poveri Amanti*, p. 296 (the definition is given by an old worker from the Berta Plants; his comrades call him 'the Poet').

29 Both quotations: Pratolini, 'Cronache fiorentine XX secolo', p. 177.

later be rediscovered in the correct sense in the Partisan actions and those of the Gruppi d'Azione Patriotica (GAP):'The cruelty of Florentine fascists was legendary, in the same way as some of the most resolute actions of the resistance are owed to the Florentine GAP'.[30] And in the *Cronache di poveri amanti* one discovers in places this distant indulgence, when the fascists are represented in their rough but lively natural brutality: 'Cheerful people, with a strong stomach, with a ready laugh, the youth of the Revolution'; 'The happiness of the fascist comrades, as violent as a quarrel, their blood-coloured nostalgia, their infantile smugness, their drunken habits revealed to him a world of bravery and abandon from which he felt excluded'.[31] But if 'the Party is like the winter hot water bottle', if the heart counts much more than consciousness, if the Fascist is an enemy of instinct more than of reason, if solidarity is a fact of nature and hope a feeling that grows along with blood, it is logical that the sort of political struggle incarnated in these protagonists is translated into symbols as elemental as they are vague. The result is that in Florence even the struggle of ideas has centuries-old, natural roots:

> [B]etween the years of 1919 and 1925, the political battle pitting fascism against anti-fascism directly took on the appearance of a 'partisan struggle'; right away, the street became its stage, in ambushes, murders, destruction and derision: the barbaric spirit that explodes dumbly in peoples consumed by extreme civility. Fascism imposed itself in Florence in the same way that the Guelfs imposed themselves: through the physical annihilation of their rivals, through terror.

And he continues:

> Guelfs and Ghibellini, Blacks and Whites disembowelled one another over the course of four hundred years; they picked a fight with their neighbours over prestige even more so than for markets or florins. They are a people become expert through age-old sacrifices and betrayals. They do no believe in revealed Truths. Their chronicles record personal disputes, quarrels over women, or between districts and factions, that were expanded into Universal commitments: the

---

30 The GAP were small bands of partisans formed by the Italian Communist Party in 1943 modelled on the French Resistance. The Partito d'Azione, a liberal-socialist, social-democratic and republican party had its own GAP. [Trans.]

31 Pratolini, *Cronache di poveri amanti*, p. 177 and 182, respectively.

Divine Comedy is a private invective of an exiled man against a dominant faction.[32]

This was not an entirely new view of the struggle between fascism and anti-fascism. Malaparte had already written: 'In some regions we see the behaviour of the Whites and the Blacks returning.'[33] Gherardo Casini, who also speaks of a continuity between past and present, will view the phenomenon of *squadrismo* as a political struggle also circumscribed by the district, the *rione* and the piazza:

> The blood of the fallen will regenerate Florence. In the name of Mussolini, the Florentine people will take to its piazzas, which for centuries have been defined by history and glory, and then languished in the shadows of a silence broken only by the murmured gossip of the daily events of the city. From Piazza Ottaviani to Piazza Mentana, from *rione* to *rione* the *squadristi* of the 'Desperate', of the 'Red Lilly', of the 'Red Dante' lay claim to the masculine spirit of ancient Florence.[34]

This is the spirit of Cerchi and Donati, Savonarola and Ferrucci. It is inevitable that Pratolini's acceptance of this sort of discourse, like his appeal to a folk [*popolaresco*] mythology, is the only way to give meaning, credibility and passion to the struggle between the two. It has been insufficiently noted that, if in the course of the 'Night of the Apocalypse' on the one side stands Maciste, 'the popular avenger who is known as Samson, the Angel of the Annunciation',[35] on the other we find Pisano, 'the Archangel with raised sword'—and the contest takes place between the two composed and proud brave men, among the ravings and fears of the supporting cast, as though between horses of an ancient lineage or protagonists of the ancient popular saga.

With these observations we return to our starting point. The great success of *Cronache* lies in the effective correspondence between an elemental conception of the class struggle, which is extremely diffuse at all levels within the post-Resistance workers' movement, and its naive, sincere and partly authentic reflection in Pratolini's *oeuvre*. The hasty mythologizing and symbolism came together with the revolutionary romanticism of the readers, with their basic class inexperience, with the near general acceptance of a certain 'human' way of confronting history, political conflicts and the struggle of social strata.

---

32 Pratolini, *Cronache di poveri amanti*, p. 182.
33 Suckert, *La rivolta*, p. 14.
34 Gherardo Casini, 'Firenze e lo squadrismo', *Il Bargello* 8(51) (4 October 1936).
35 Pratolini, *Cronache di poveri amanti*, p. 323.

Sinking to the level of a certain mentality of the 'lesser people' [*popolo minuto*], Pratolini in some sense skipped centuries of economic and social development in order to grasp the heart of a human condition still depressed by the weight of poverty. That the readers of those years understood themselves in the light of this denunciation shows that this tradition of the 'heart' and of 'nature', of anarchic 'rebellion' and of 'hope' was by no means dead. Pratolini rediscovered a full expression of the democratic attitude in the story of the *cornacchiai*,[36] but wagering upon the driving force of feelings more than on the sociological evidence of the protest. Definable as the 'poet of hope', he found in this area his greatest and most definitive limitation. It is too easy to condemn as reactionary this elementary and closed way of breaking down history into its primitive elements and of tying them to the chronicle of the heart and of nature. It would be more correct to conclude that Pratolini, at the highest point of his trajectory—towards which he persistently aimed during the years of *Il Bargello*—was able to reinterpret and express with fervid sincerity that humanitarian need that the intellectual movement of the Resistance bore as its distinctive and fundamental characteristic. The backwardness of his standpoint was linked to the general backwardness of the movement.

Perhaps the most accomplished work of this period is *Cristo si è fermato a Eboli* [Christ Stopped at Eboli, 1945] by Carlo Levi. This is not because it is devoid of the shortcomings of ideology and taste that we have registered in the authors we have examined; or because it is unquestionably novel from the formal-artistic standpoint and capable of opening an original chapter within contemporary Italian literature. The limitations of Levi's sensibility, as it opens itself to the archaic Lucanian peasant civilization, are perhaps all too obvious. It has been noted that this relationship contains a powerful aestheticizing and irrational charge, so we will not insist on it any further. Equally evident are Levi's borrowings from the tradition of southern Italian democratic thought, from Salvemini to Fortunato,[37] 'one of the best and most humane thinkers of the region',[38] but also Tommaso Fiore[39] who wrote in Piero Gobetti's

---

36 *via del Corno*, literally 'crow's way', is the street on which *Cronache di poveri amanti* is based on; its inhabitants are known as *cornacchiai*. [Trans.]

37 Giustino Fortunato (1848–1932), historian and politician; one of the founders of *meridionalismo*. [Trans.]

38 Carlo Levi, *Cristo si è fermato a Eboli* (Turin: Einaudi, 1960), p. 165 / *Christ Stopped at Eboli* (F. Frenaye trans.) (London: Penguin, 1982), p. 178.

Rivoluzione liberale, under the title of 'Lettere pugliesi' [Apulian Letters], a large part of a work that would reappear some years later as *Un popolo di formiche* [A People of Ants, 1952], having become timely due to the climate of anti-fascist resistance. It remains true to say that these, like other elements— the irrational view of the world and the democratic-peasant outlook—are elaborated anew by Levi with a power of depiction and a cultural gravity that are missing from the majority of contemporary progressive writers and, specifically, from those of a populist bent. I would like to note, first, that of all the works linked to the people and sharing its ideals and hopes in those years, *Cristo* is uniquely grounded in a pronounced sociological outlook. Neither Vittorini nor Pavese, nor perhaps Pratolini, can aspire to that praise. And neither, and this is especially true for Pratolini, can they be said to have made such room for an objective, historical survey of the context without ceding to the 'literary' desire to invent the beautiful love story, the 'interesting' familial or personal tale. From a certain point of view, one can definitely assert that a good fifty per cent of the representation of the peasant world in *Cristo* is the self-representation of Levi's vision of the peasant world, with all the dangers of intellectual complacency that this entails. But, in contrast to other works that could be said to be sociologically significant, such as *Cronache di poveri amanti,* the subjectivism of the standpoint hardly ever entirely betrays the historico-sociological structure of the subject matter in favour of a page of beautiful description, local colour or folklore pure and simple. However questionable, the domineering authorial presence within the work operates as a filter for the complicated reality of the milieu. Even when this produces a distortion, more often than not it reveals the coherence of his general conception of the problem. We can and must refuse the interpretation and solution that Levi gives of the peasant problem; but it is necessary to recognize that his way of elaborating a populist position has a cultural and ideological maturity that is lacking in other writers of the period.

This is confirmed by the fundamental motif of the work, in which it is not difficult to detect the presence of a point of view analogous to that of the anti-fascist humanitarianism that permeates the entirety of Resistance literature, but that Levi is able—from the first page of *Cristo,* where its theme is set out—to situate within an extremely concrete sociological perspective:

---

39 Tommaso Fiore (1884–1973), writer and politician; also concerned with the Southern Italian question. [Trans.]

'We're not Christians,' they say. 'Christ stopped short of here, at Eboli.' 'Christian', in their way of speaking, means 'human being', and this almost proverbial phrase that I have so often heard them repeat may be no more than the expression of a hopeless feeling of inferiority. We're not Christians, we're not human beings; we're not thought of as men but simply as beasts, beasts of burden, or even less than beasts, more creatures of the wild. They at least live for better or for worse, like angels or demons in a world of their own, while we have to submit to the world of Christians, beyond the horizon, to carry its weight and to stand comparison with it. But the phrase has a much deeper meaning and, as is the way of symbols, this is the literal one. Christ did stop at Eboli, where the road and the railway leave the coast of Salerno and turn into the desolate reaches of Lucania. Christ never came this far, nor did time, nor the individual soul, nor hope, not the relation of cause to effect, nor reason, nor history.[40]

It is clear that Levi too judges reality according to the semi-mythical schemas of Man and History; Levi too has, as constant points of reference and criteria of judgement, general opinions formed in a straightforwardly bourgeois intellectual tradition. But Man, to whom he looks and History, according to which he judges, do not remain general opinions, voluntarist statements of truth. Levi does not escape the space of myth; on the contrary, the reality he describes tends for him always to become myth as well—the symbol of a permanent condition of Man. But, as sometimes occurs, myth is embodied by him in a concrete *figure* and the dispute unfolds in a context of painful earthiness: Man descends in the form of the wretched southern Italian peasant and adopts his primitive existence, outside of history, outside the uninterrupted but ultimately superficial flow of conquests and wars. The struggle for a *better world* which constitutes the naive basis of the progressive position, is touched upon and put into crisis by the myriad doubts that arise for the intelligent observer when he contemplates the injuries and cancers of this millennial backwardness.

This more serious way of posing the relationship between ideal and real— we are intentionally adopting democratic terminology so as to make more evident certain values that exist within the same anti-fascist experience—allows Levi, despite his egocentrism and aestheticism, to find himself closer to the

---

40 Levi, *Cristo si è fermato a Eboli*, pp. 9–10 / *Christ Stopped at Eboli*, pp. 11–12.

popular 'world' that he represents in his work. This does not mean that he is any less bourgeois than the other anti-fascist authors; on the contrary, we think he is so in a more knowing and profound way. But precisely through *bourgeois maturity* he is able to realize a less futile and transient adherence to 'peasant reasoning'. There is no petty-bourgeois arrogance in him, the narrow-minded caste mentality of so many of his contemporaries. At a certain point, his natural tendency to a broad and cordial humanitarian feeling in which one can recognize a decadent form of superman-ism serves to *open him up to* contact with external reality, with the world of the poor. The fact that he presents himself in the novel as a sort of good and serene Jove, an affectionate and sweet Sovereign in exile surrounded by these new, exotic subjects, can lend the narrative an indisputably paternalistic tone. But it is also why an attempt at mutual understanding is established between this sophisticated intellectual from the North and this archaic civilization ten thousand years behind him, a spontaneous struggle to understand and appreciate each other. In this way we arrive at a very important point. In *Cristo*, Levi does not engage in a progressivist argument in the common sense of the term. He does not need to call for civil and political rights for his peasants; he does not believe that they can become men merely by turning into citizens. Levi stands out in this as well: more intensely and profoundly than anyone else, he identifies a *completely positive set of values* in peasant civilization which need not be disintegrated or destroyed but, rather, recognized and conserved. It is clear that this conviction harbours the gravest political and ideological error. But here the political and ideological error, the formation of an indubitably anti-historical myth, operates as a drive to accept this peasant population as a real, great model of humanity. From this vantage, Levi's populism is absolutely unconditional. It is the only one that recalls the intensity and force of some of the models of Russian populism.

In this framework, even the extensive space given over to the magical and irrational aspects of the primitive world being portrayed is presented as a form of understanding, a moving closer—like a key that is necessary to penetrate its heart. Doubtless there is a profound difference between Pavese's way of using the instruments of ethnology and those that typify Levi's approach. In the case of the former, there is a tendency to reduce the whole of reality to a series of ancestral symbols which thereby come to have a meaning and validity in themselves, pregnant as they are with autobiographical and intellectual content. In the latter, we witness an attempt to insistently use myth as an interpretative instrument—albeit an imaginative and analogical one—in relation to an environment that *by definition* cannot fall under logical and historical criteria. In the case of Levi then, ethnology is only a phase of a richer and more complex process which can in no way be confined to a mere cultural position. From History to Pre-history, and from Pre-history to History, there is, regardless, a solid form of communication; and the fact that the author's culture is distinguished by irrational implications in no way constitutes a break but, rather, a dynamic impulse to knowledge.

This is proven by the way in which, alongside the solid appreciation of peasant civilization, Levi deepens his analysis of the reasons why the local petty bourgeoisie is unable to be more than a parasitic social stratum, equally blame-worthy as the large landowners and provincial bureaucrats for the general socio-economic backwardness of the country. Among Levi's positive features, I would include this acute hatred for the rural petty bourgeoisie, from which only very few individuals are exempt. On this point, we must grasp the personal distance of the Piedmontese author from the democratic southern Italian tradition which he blames for being unable to resolve the fundamental problems of these lands, for failing to overcome the prejudice of the inferiority of peasant civilization and, therefore, leaving an unbridgeable separation between sincere reformist intentions and their practical realization.[41] Conversely, one can find a concrete indication of struggle at the political level too, only in the refusal of the *dirigiste* and petty-bourgeois solution. What counts most in *Cristo* is that only by accepting certain 'historical' characteristics of this prehistoric world can one find the impulse that enables the age-old and mortifying inferiority complex to be oversome. Only when this path has been travelled does it also become possible to define and appreciate the fundamental laws that govern peasant civilization, and to rediscover in them, in a still-germinal state, the connotations of a common humanity, the virginal and profound qualities of an existence that is unlimited with respect to its awareness, reason and history. Pity, compassion, resignation, natural goodness,

---

41 See Levi, *Cristo si è fermato a Eboli*, p. 165 / *Christ Stopped at Eboli*, p. 178:

'Orlando's despair', widespread among those men of the Italian South who give serious thought to the problems of their country, which stems from a deep-seated sense of inferiority, and therefore they can never fully understand their own coun-try and its problems. The point of departure is, quite unconsciously, a comparison that should never be made, or at least should not be made, until the problems have found a solution. Because they consider the peasant world inferior to the world outside, they are bogged down by a feeling of either their impotence or revenge. And impotence and revenge have never created anything living.

the inalienable sense of justice, the obstinate diffidence towards authority and the messianic expectation of transformation make this isolated corner of earth a great crucible of forces, an inexhaustible reservoir of energies that wait only to be recognized and liberated.

The limits of this conception are, as we have said, political and ideological. His sincere and profound love for the peasants leads Levi to hypothesize a new order, in which this archaic civilization could survive alongside other more advanced ones without being oppressed or exploited by them. Levi goes so far as to associate his general vision of transformation of Italian society with this respect for peasant reality. That transformation is possible in his eyes if one replaces the principle of an authoritarian, centralizing state with the principle of a state as a 'group of autonomies, an organic federation'.[42] Here, certain fundamental principles of Italian democratic thought merge with more or less vague reminiscences of the Russian populist reflections of Alexander Herzen and Nicolay Dobrolyubov.[43] One cannot say on the basis of the text of *Cristo* whether or not there is a direct relation between Levi and these precedents. Certainly for him the principle of general regeneration is strictly linked to the solution of the peasant problem. This is another aspect that underlines his straightforwardly populist attitude: 'Unless we have a peasant revolution we shall never have a true Italian revolution, for the two are identical.' And the solution of the peasant problem can only be found within peasant civilization itself: 'The unit or cell through which the peasants can take part in the complex life of the nation must be the autonomous or self-governing community.'[44] We have even rediscovered the Russian *obscina* here, the myth of the typically peasant structuring of society, which self-organizes itself through its own laws of coexistence and justice.

What strikes us negatively in Levi's point of view is not so much the utopian element, which is a permanent feature of genuine populism, so much as the presumption, already present in *Cristo* and increasingly clear in his public stance, to turn that vision into a component of a political programme and of the action that follows from it. Failing to understand that the only way to resolve the peasant problem was to shatter and destroy the peasant social

---

42 Levi, *Cristo si è Fermato a Eboli*, p. 223 / *Christ Stopped at Eboli*, p. 240.

43 Nicolay Dobrolyubov (1836–61), Russian journalist, poet and revolutionary democrat. [Trans.]

44 Both quotations from: Levi, *Cristo si è fermato a Eboli*, p. 222 and 223, respectively / *Christ Stopped at Eboli*, p. 239 and 240, respectively.

order via the capitalist development of the country, allowed Levi to honestly and passionately mythologize this primitive reality. But he thereby opened the doors to an artificial enlargement of the Southern Question in Italian literature. This opened a breach for the ranks of those who, identifying the centre of gravity in the great peasant masses of the South, once again boldly resuscitated petty-bourgeois regionalism and democratism. 'Levi-ism' is much worse than the Levi of *Cristo si è fermato a Eboli*, because in Levi's followers, and in Levi himself in the following years, what had been an effective (if partial) depiction of a plebeian [*popolare*] world is taken up again as the general strategy of an extremely retarded and ambivalent class movement. The strategy was ambivalent and retarded precisely because it was linked to the principle of the autonomy of the peasant problem, which concealed within it the subordination of the class struggle to a process of simple adaptation and *normal* transformation of the political and economic structures of the bourgeois state.

Levi's error coincided with the one underpinning anti-fascism and Resistance populism. The presumption to assist the *general progress of the nation* would, within only a few years, show itself to be a mere factor in the bourgeois attempt to transform an underdeveloped nation into a modern capitalist one. Only a rigorous class standpoint could identify the limits of this attitude and advance towards a far more radical and profound critique. But this assessment was lacking. The populism of the Resistance became, with its limits and its a-classist vices, the ideology of the workers' movement in the field of arts and letters. And the workers' movement itself ensured that, on this front, a fundamentally reformist politics was matched by an analogous attitude of 'democratic and constitutional protest'.

13

The analysis of the vast field of Resistance and partisan literature will lead us to surprisingly similar conclusions. Going beyond the merely autobiographical and documentary testimonies, which are often very lively and honest, we will try to grasp the embryonic ideological core and inventory the somewhat limited political intentions to be found in the depiction of human attitudes and instinctive choices. Only then does one notice two or three recurring themes infuenced by the great figures of the time. In particular, I would say, the most influential figures are Vittorini and Pavese, who—compared with Pratolini and Levi—exhibit the lure of an already acknowledged and affirmed intellectual and cultural leadership.[45] The entirety of the 'literature of the Resistance' converges on these themes: freedom, justice, national solidarity against the oppressor and a confused but fiery feeling of hope and expectation. Studying its character cannot add much to our analyses, precisely because it is borne on the back of those intellectual positions that anti-fascism had previously developed. But we can register the widespread diffusion that the theme would achieve in the years after 1945. That populist-Resistance literature did not produce any masterpieces, either then or later, is something widely known and lamented. It is not so easy to identify the reason why no works emerged from the large mass produced that could be said to manifest maturity and force of unquestionable achievement. *We would like to advance one hypothesis for this that follows from the overall direction of our argument. The literature of the Resistance fails to achieve any surprising literary or ideological discovery because it limits itself to previously made discoveries.* It is not a phenomenon of revolution or invention but, rather, despite appearances, the epigonic manifestation of a culture whose myths had already been formed, which possessed its own limited symbolism and a series of easily imitable models. Works that came later, namely, *Conversations in Sicily* and *Paesi tuoi* [Your Villages], which intersected in a very different way with the mature works of Levi and Pratolini, and fully absorbed the meaning of the 'progressive' cultural development that took place between 1930 and 1945, showed that the literature of the Resistance could not so much innovate and transform the past as 'bear witness', through the naked evidence of the action, to what until that point had fundamentally been a theoretical and cultural orientation. The result of this bearing witness is frequently not the perfect symbiosis between the moment of culture and life. More often than not one finds in the partisan experience of one apprentice writer or other that the voluntarist adherence to action unreasonably transcends the justification with which the historical intellect furnishes it. Alternatively, the truth of the account overwhelms the ideological and political reasons that lie behind it (this is probably the one that produces the best results). But the overall impression is, nevertheless, that these young writers who have come through the partisan experience repeat a lesson derived from others.

The text that perhaps is most typical of this standpoint is Italo Calvino's *Il sentiero dei nidi di ragno* [*The Path to the Nest of Spiders*, 1947]. Written when

---

45 In English in the original. [Trans.]

he was only twenty-three, it already displayed the awareness—despite the carefree and innocent atmosphere that pervades the narrative—that it could be considered a *summula* of the experience of left-wing Resistance. At the same time, it exhibits a repertory of commonplaces drawn from Vittorini, Pavese, American literature, as well as communist pamphlets.[46] First, it is emblematic that Calvino's protagonist is a mouthy and precocious child, brother of a prostitute and little lumpenproletarian genius from a wretched Ligurian alley. What's more, Calvino locates the action of the story among a badly broken partisan band, the worst imaginable, made up of southern Italian drifters, *carabinieri* in hiding, waiters, petty thieves, black marketers, strange characters of all sorts. Calvino perhaps intended this choice polemically, wanting to demonstrate, even if indirectly, that the partisan struggle had its reasons and its heroism even where the human material that sustained it came from the darkest and most unwholesome sections of society. In reality, he took a path that was less scandalous than it must have appeared to him at the time. It was the one of Pratolini's *Cronache di poveri amanti* and Pavese's *Il compagno*, as well as the one later taken by Pasolini in *Ragazzi di vita* (1955). Even in the hyper-rational Calvino, the progressivist orientation took a one-way route, from history to sub-history, from consciousness to sub-consciousness. For him too, the anti-fascist struggle was essentially an 'elementary, anonymous urge to vindicate all *human* humiliations; the worker from his exploitation, the peasant from his ignorance, the petty bourgeois from his inhibitions, the outcast from his corruption.'[47] Having sunk to these depths, does one return from the dark caves of instinct to the clarity of rational decisions? There is no doubt that there is such an attempt in this work—as there is in Pratolini, Levi and Pavese—but it is conditioned by the starting point, by the profound conviction that there cannot be redemption for anyone if there remains a single corrupt individual, a single pariah. The demonstration, therefore, swings

---

46 This tendency to encapsulate the typical attitudes of the anti-fascist and Marxist intellectual group to which he belongs is characteristic of Calvino. In his synthesis, he displays the undeniable ability to rationally elucidate what in many others is merely intuited or felt. This constitutes a virtue but also, in many ways, a limit, above all, on the plane of invention and creativity. *La giornata di uno scrutatore* [The Day of A Scrutineer] (Turin, 1963) is from this angle close to *Il sentiero nei nidi di ragno*, despite the fact that many of its ideological and thematic attitudes have changed. For a detailed discussion, see our review 'La Giornata', *Mondo nuovo* 5 (1963): 7.

47 Italo Calvino, *Il sentiero dei nidi di ragno* (Turin: Einaudi, 1954), p. 146 / *The Path to the Nest of Spiders* (Archibald Colquhoun trans.) (London: Collins, 1956), p. 138 [translation modified; emphasis added.—Trans.]

between these poles like a pendulum: on the one hand we find, once again, Man (as the political commissioner Kim states: 'This is what I believe our political work is, to use human misery against itself, for our own redemption, as the Fascists use misery to perpetuate misery and man fighting man'). On the other, we encounter the most elementary of hopes, a primitive cluster of expectations that can only belong to the confused lumpenproletariat—or to the intellectual without a class consciousness (Pietromagro, the drunken cobbler, the master of Pin the street urchin, affirms: 'But commit a political crime and one goes inside just the same, it's at least with a hope of a *better world*, without prisons, one day'[48]).

But what is it that can weld the intellectual's abstract orienatation that has been *lent* to the people—a preoccupation with culture and ideas, the Humanity of the bourgeois tradition—to a hatred that is 'anonymous, aimless, dumb',[49] which is the brutal way for the amoral lumpenproletariat to participate in the partisan experience? Here, with the introduction into progressivism of the motif of History, Calvino expressed the most original element of his argument, which would then recur frequently in his work and that of many others. The soldering of ideal and real, of the highest aims of the Resistance with the coarsest and most unreflective elements of the population is assured by History itself:

> That age-old resentment which weighs down on Dritto's men, on all of us, including you and me, and which finds expression in shooting and killing enemies, the Fascists have that too. But with us nothing is lost, not a gesture, not a shot, though each may be the same as theirs—d'you see what I mean?—they will all serve if not to free us then to free our children, to create a world that is serene, without resentment, a world in which no one has to be bad. The others are on the side of lost gestures, of useless resentment, which are lost and useless even if they win, because they are not making positive history, they are not helping to free themselves but to repeat and perpetuate resentment and hatred in our eyes, though always, perhaps without knowing it, *we* shall be fighting for redemption, *they* to remain

---

48 Calvino, *Il sentiero dei nidi di ragno*, p. 146 and 56, respectively / *Nest of Spiders*, p. 138 and 51, respectively [emphasis added—Trans.].

49 Calvino, *Il sentiero dei nidi*, p. 145 / *Nest of Spiders*, p. 137.

slaves. That is the real meaning of the struggle now, the real, absolute meaning, beyond the various official meanings.[50]

It is rare to encounter a more tautological operation than this. From this point onwards, one will need to add to Calvino's literary biography this typical way of delegating to the justificatory flow of external events what he is unable to resolve at the level of rationality. This reveals a much less 'historicist' bent than might at first appear (if one were then to be struck by the sudden urge to substitute the perhaps less vacuous words of 'Destiny' or 'Providence' for that of 'History', who knows what involuntary existential and mystical urges might be provoked; after fifteen years, *La giornata di uno scrutatore* demonstrated that by dint of attempting to explain everything with the philosophy of history, one could no longer explain anything). It is worth underlining how the appearance of this theme, never before presented with such decisiveness, furnishes a strikingly new ideological element to progressive literature: *the conviction that History is with us, that History is with the people and, therefore, it will not be able to abandon us.* From here we encounter new bases for the mystifications of hope which—as Calvino states—offers shelter to workers and peasants, petty bourgeois and lumpenproletarians, all of whom are carried by the miraculous 'wave of [national] redemption'.

In this riverbed bubbling with illusions, communism is—as it is for the Florentine commoners of the *Cronache*—a dream of serenity and peace, the elegiac nostalgia of simple souls as yet untouched by capitalist civilization:

> 'Lads,' he begins in a resigned voice as if he does not want to put any-one out, even Mancino, 'each of us knows why he's a partisan. I was a tinker and used to go round the country and my cry would be heard a long way off and the women would come and bring their broken cooking pots for me to mend. I used to go into their houses and joke with the servants and was sometimes given eggs and a glass of wine. Now I can't go round the country any more because I'd be arrested; and then the bombing has messed everything up too. That's why we're partisans; so we can be tinkers again and so eggs and wine can be cheap, and so we can't be arrested any more and there'll be no more air raids. And then we want communism too. Communism means there won't be any more houses where the door's banged in one's face,

---

50 Calvino, *Il sentiero dei nidi*, pp. 145–6 / *Nest of Spiders*, pp. 137–8 [emphasis added—Trans.].

so one's forced to enter by the chicken run at night. Communism means going into a house and being given soup even if one is a tinker; and if there's pudding at Christmas then they'll give one pudding. That's what communism means. For example: here we all are so full of lice that they almost drag us about in our sleep. Now I've just been to brigade headquarters and seen they have insect powder there. Then I said: fine communists you are, you don't send this to our detachment. So they said they'd send some. That's what communism means.'

The men have listened to him attentively and with approval; these are things anyone can understand. One of them who is smoking passes his cigarette to a comrade, and another who has to go on guard promises not to cut his time short and to stay the whole hour before calling for his relief. They all began discussing the insect powder which is to be sent to them, if it will kill the eggs as well as the lice or if it will only stun the insects so that an hour later they'll be biting more than ever.[51]

By situating this legend within a popular and rustic atmosphere, the ideology is in some senses legitimated, but only because the limits of this discussion remain extremely narrow and provincial.

Il sentiero del nido di ragni is, as we can see, a book full of ideas and big ambitions. Even works that are ideologically more modest display similar qualities and are extraordinarily attuned to fundamental questions. A significant example of this is *L'Agnese va a morire* [Agnese Goes to Die, 1949] by Renata Viganò,[52] an honest and at-times-intense evocation of the Resistance in Emilia Romagna. Even in *L'Agnese* one can detect typical aspects of anti-fascist ideology, although less visible behind the objective, almost documentary development of the narrative. First, this is true of the entirely peasant environment, where the partisan struggle becomes an almost natural rebellion against the Germans and the boss, influenced as it is by family ties, the deep voices of instinct and a spontaneous and concrete demand for justice. Second, there is the character of the protagonist who is chosen—according to a mechanism that

51 Calvino, *Il sentiero dei nidi*, pp. 129–30 / *Nest of Spiders*, pp. 122–3. [The words are spoken by Giacinto, the ex-tinker who acts as the 'political commissar' in Dritto's detachment.—Trans.]

52 Renata Viganò (1900–76), writer and partisan. [Trans.]

should by now be clear to everyone—from the lowest level of political consciousness, where it is difficult to distinguish, as we have repeatedly stated, between instinct and consciousness. Indeed, Agnese is nothing but an elderly peasant, humble, plump, ignorant, silent and yet determined and inwardly proud to carry out her work to the very end, to the extreme sacrifice. Viganò's work expresses a direct and indubitably genuine populism, and it is to her credit that she does not spend too much time outlining Agnese's underlying 'motives', leaving them to emerge from some of her choices and actions. However, by excavating her character and exploring the world in which she operates, it is possible to detail the political and ideological context of this populist attitude. In Agnese's thoughts, in her words, in her instinctive sympathies and her hatreds, we will discover a morality that is not dissimilar to Calvino's Ligurian protagonist, Giacinto. However, it is outlined in the simpler, less intellectual forms that will mark certain typical characters of the communism of Emilia Romagna. Almost at the end of her life in the Resistance, Agnese comes to a flicker of awareness of the reasons guiding the struggle, which Viganò describes as follows:

> She now knew, she understood. The rich want to be ever richer and make the poor ever poorer, more ignorant and humiliated. The rich earn during wartime, it costs the poor their lives [. . .]. There were some, however, who had something to say about this: the party, the comrades, many men and many women who had no fear. They said that things could not go on like this, that the world would need to change, that it was time to have done away with war, that everyone needed bread, and not only bread but the rest as well—to enjoy oneself, to be happy and satisfy some wants. And they threw themselves against them, despite prison and death, although fascists didn't want that [. . .]. This was the party and it was worth being killed for it.[53]

Viganò brilliantly organizes the peasant participation in the Resistance around this programme of basic needs in which the crude economic factor is raised to a vision of essential human well-being. The most successful passages are probably those that describe in anonymous, objective manner how family by family, farmstead by farmstead, village by village, spreads the secret, the elusive network of local partisans, constituted by artisans, sharecroppers, day labourers, boatmen, fishermen and numerous obscure Agneses.

---

53 Renata Viganò, *L'Agnese va a morire* (Turin: Einaudi, 1949), pp. 173–4.

Were we absolutely rigorous, we would have to say that Viganò is so objective as to be able to adopt a standpoint typical of the peasant mentality, always inclined to concede the leadership of struggle to a class or group of individuals outside its own sociological circle (due to that traditional absence of autonomy that marks every attempt of the peasant class to participate in the historical process). Indeed, in *L'Agnese*, while the bulk of combatants are overwhelmingly drawn from peasant stock, the commander is an intellectual who comes from outside and is charged by the party with organizing and *leading* the struggle. The peasants openly recognize the legitimacy of this investiture, and the superiority of the man to whom they owe obedience. One of the partisans says of the commander: 'He speaks like us. While he speaks you understand everything, you think you can remember it, and then—yes—you know what he said, it remains forever in your head as if you'd thought it yourself. But not with the same words.' And Agnese comments: 'He knows what we do not know. That's why he's the commander.'[54] Even this shows how *L'Agnese* is close to numerous other works of the Italian Resistance, where the *leader*[55] is, nine times out of ten, an intellectual—in keeping with a process of knowing–unknowing autobiographical and ideological *transfert* which results in mod-elling history on the hopes and programmes of restricted groups of cultural representatives.[56] Nevertheless, the basic urge for redemption that animated the Italian Resistance is both reflected and confirmed in these works. The people plays a decisive role here precisely because it is represented as at once the protagonist and instrument of a process of liberation from despondency and poverty. No one was able to move beyond this primary objective of protest and humanitarian redemption. The historical model these writers aspired to, that of the anti-fascist Resistance, probably did not permit anything more. While the essential was aimed at, only the first steps were taken. *The unitary quality of the struggle meant that the limits imposed upon it by the*

---

54 Viganò, *L'Agnese va a morire*, p. 239.

55 In English in the original. [Trans.]

56 In almost the same words, Pratolini describes the attitude of communist Ugo, who reflects on a leader's speech during the last few party meetings before the unleashing of the fascist reaction: 'What Comrade Sgorgio said *he would be unable to repeat word for word, but it was convincing*'—*Cronache*, p. 58. But the attitude is certainly older and sinks its roots (perhaps unconsciously, it's true) in the enduring subaltern vision of the popular classes. Despite every effort, the popular 'autonomous' hero of the Italian Resistance is not born. The only figure of hero *deemed possible* is once again that of the 'tormented and ide-alist' intellectual.

bourgeois allies were not crossed; and the popular uprising, the uprising of peasants, lumpenproletarians and intellectuals, was knowingly forced along this channel.

14

The set of myths and values developed by anti-fascist thinking undergoes its trial by fire in the years of the Resistance and in the immediate postwar period. The blazing light of this experience is akin to being dazzled—striking but superficial. Only a short while passes before the period of reflux begins and a great number of those forces that had focused on the revolution and renewal retreat into conservative positions. We have already said that the reasons for this premature withering are to be sought in the impetuous and erratic atmosphere that pervades Italian anti-fascism and its political appendage, the united Resistance. We should not leave it unsaid, however, that some positive elements can be found in the very inorganic and indeterminate character of the initial drive, elements that even today allow us to have a sympathetic approach towards the efforts of the period: their freshness and in many cases authenticity, an uncalculating love of risk and of the unexpected, a desire to break— even if prudently—with pre-established canons and authorities. There is another factor to be considered: although still caught within substantively national themes and concerns, the major populist authors of the Resistance never ceased to anchor their work, in one way or other, in the great contemporary currents of European and world literature (we have supplied evidence of this where it has arisen). Moreover, in some cases the very discovery (or rediscovery) of provincial realities appeared as or became the discovery or rediscovery of single elements of the more general modern humanist problematic. *Cristo si è fermato a Eboli*—just to cite the most significant example from this perspective as well—owes its vast success to the author's ability to mediate the specific historical case of Lucanian peasant poverty in a dream of universal palingenesis. But analogous phenomena could be found in the cinematographic field where this reference to a justice without borders is constant and intense.

But what was probably the most fecund and generous aspect of the anti-fascist position—which many considered to have begun in 1945, at the time of the liberation—was in truth already at an end or about to end. The populism to which *Uomini e no, Cristo si è fermato a Eboli* and *Cronache di poveri amanti* bear diverse witness, represents the product of ten to fifteen years of development and, with these works, it reached its culmination. From this moment a new chapter begins that, while using all the preceding instruments and achievements, inserts them into a very different framework where powerful new ideological and political factors come into play. From a populism of a fundamentally intellectual origin, characterized by approximation to an ideal and an impetus derived from feelings, by the abstract palingenesis of the will and humanitarian mythology, we move to a populism that is ideologically evermore rigid and always more directly committed to a progressive standpoint. Alongside the reflux of certain intellectual strata towards disengaged positions, we should also point out that from this moment the left-wing political forces exerted a more decisive role in the direction taken by cultural life. The analysis necessarily moves from the creative plane to that of critique and 'direction'. What counts now in the formation of the populist current is not so much the initiative of individual artists as the entire texture of the politico-ideological relations in which that initiative operates. The function of the Italian Communist Party becomes fundamental.

By this we do not mean that the conjuncture involves a real ideological turn. We have already provided testimony, with citations, that a certain politico-cultural attitude is present within the Communist Party, at the time it comes out of hiding, in perfect parallel with the national-reformist position that Togliatti clearly theorized on his return from the Soviet Union in 1944. But around the years 1947–48, an array of facts converge to create a climate in which the party's claim to cultural leadership becomes more intense and exacting. The influence of Zhdanovism, which we today tend to minimize too hastily, has a considerable weight in the genesis of this orientation, but another factor is the progressive political isolation into which the party is forced by the collapse of the pact of national unity.[57] The beginning of the struggle for

---

57 See articles by Roderigo [pseudonym of Palmiro Togliatti] in *Rinascita* from this period. In particular, 'Orientamento dell'arte' [The Orientation of Art] (October 1949), which contains a violent attack on Massimo Mila in relation to a discussion on music that had taken place in the Soviet Union in 1948, and 'Direzione ideologica' [Ideological Direction] (1949); and the commemoration for Zhdanov (August 1948). The highest example of this tendency is the article by Felice Platone on 'La politica comunista e i problemi della cultura' [Communist Politics and the Problems of Culture], *Rinascita* (July 1947), where he affirms:

It seems to me that these decisions commit the intellectuals who follow our Party, or gravitate more or less around it, to two things in their specific fields: first, to work *honestly* and *sincerely* according to *their vocation and talent* for the progress of culture; second, *not to come to terms with, not to yield to the more reactionary ideologies, those hostile to the new culture,* nor to their cultural and pseudo-cultural

realism—which Zhdanovism also encouraged, but in Italy was particularly impelled by the existence of an earlier democratic-realist current—constitutes another aspect of this more marked ideological aggressiveness.

What do these phenomena—Zhdanovism, internal and external Cold War, *programmatic* choice for realism—have to do with populism, which is what we are concerned with? It seems to me that the relation between the two sets of elements of communist cultural politics is extremely clear. Populism and reformism continue to be the cornerstones of the official decisions of the Communist Party in this period. The populist legacy—feeling, heart, hope, constitutional protest, humanitarian indignation, democratic denunciation— remains substantially without variation. But Zhdanovism strips away the European ambitions of Italian populism, exalts its national-provincial characteristics, cuts the ties of taste and form of the homegrown experiments from that of foreign ones, rigidly subordinates research to a utilitarian end, one that is more propagandistic than political, substituting the sometimes generous reformism of the intellectuals with the mean and sectarian reformism of the bureaucrats. The Cold War destroys the possibility of realizing, in Italy, a bourgeois culture of broad European sweep—closing populism within renewed borders of cultural provincialism. It makes the external aspects of political and cultural behaviour fundamental—the struggle for peace, for freedom of press, against censorship, against clerical obscurantism. Finally, the argument for realism—based on the 'high-minded' illusion of being able to anchor the progressive ideological choice in a determinate aesthetic form—ends up confirming and restating the naturalistic characteristics that Italian populism already bore with it, whether by tradition or by choice. Far from promoting the cultural maturity of Italian literature, it accentuates its conservatism and 'indigenous' nature. Once again the historical opportunity to break the link between a present rich with agitation and a past viewed as too closed and limited was used to illuminate and deepen the contingent and particular traits of the 'Italian situation'. Zhdanovism, this retrograde international phenomenon, the expression of an extremely feeble moment for the workers'

---

manifestations of any kind; not to come to terms with, not to compromise with fascism and Trotskyism, with the most pernicious enemies of democracy and of all progressive culture.

We see here that Zhdanovism is nothing but a symbiosis between an extraordinary carelessness on the theoretical and scientific plane with a closed bureaucratic spirit on the ideological and cultural plane.

movement and its ideological elaboration, welded itself perfectly with certain aspects of our democratic progressivism—in particular, with the vocation, which never completely died off, to give pride of place in literature and art to the problems of the country, of the locality, of a single political or social situation. If here in Italy we did not have 'socialist realism' in the strict sense of the term, this was only because our 'socialist realism' was precisely this: founded on the acquisition in a provincial guise of the ideological orientation promoted by the reformist and bureaucratic non-working-class theorists of the Soviet Union, and by their epigones and vulgarizers across the world and in Italy.

Our picture would be incomplete were we not to add to the factors considered above the powerful influence on literature, the arts and ideology of the writings of Antonio Gramsci, which were published over this period.[58] The great importance that this Marxist theorist attributes to the problem of intellectuals in Italy is widely known. Literature, the arts and culture likewise represent examples of this fundamentally politico-ideological interest. The evaluation of the role that intellectuals must play in this process of national renewal is solicited and determined by the fact that the intellectual stratum in Italy has, at least since the fifteenth century (barring a few parentheses), behaved like a caste completely autonomous from the country's need for political and social development. It has been incapable of going beyond aristocratic refinement, rootless cosmopolitanism or a pedantic and even reactionary academicism. According to Gramsci, in Italy, the very term 'national' has a different cultural meaning to elsewhere. It cannot be considered to obtain that powerful popular and democratic charge that the Nation requires to escape a purely State-centred or political form, so as to become a vital organism functioning at the level of the social as well as of culture.[59] How to create a profound and organic

---

58 Between 1949 and 1951, the volumes *Gli intellettuali e l'organizzazione della cultura* [Intellectuals and the Organization of Culture], *Il Risorgimento, Letteratura e vita nazionale* [Literature and National Life] and *Passato e presente* [Past and Present] were published. The first two were published in 1949 and, therefore, are most significant to our enquiry; the others came out in 1950 and 1951, respectively. [*The Writer and the People* was written before Valentino Gerratana's critical edition of the *Quaderni del carcere* (*Prison Notebooks*), first published in 1975.—Trans.]

59 Gramsci observes that in many languages (such as, German and Russian) 'national' and 'popular' coincide; in French they are closely connected and 'national sovereignty and popular sovereignty have, or had, the same value':

relation between intellectual enquiry and vast popular needs has been the dominant question for all those thinkers and movements that have sought a serious strategy for various uprisings for independence or national renewal. How to create such a relation today, after past bourgeois failures, is the dominant question of a workers' movement that aspires to escape from the narrow horizons where reformist leaders have forced it for decades. The problem of the intellectuals–people relation is therefore only one aspect of the much greater vision of class struggle, which Gramsci develops in the *Prison Notebooks*, where he outlines a task of national hegemony for the Communist Party. This hegemonic task encompasses specifically working-class interests alongside those of the masses who are pressured to accept the necessity for revolution by the persistence, in Italy, of extremely precarious living conditions. After the experience of *Ordine nuovo* and the factory councils, Gramsci's reflection of the party and the Italian national revolution, lead ever further away from the attempt to theorize and found genuine workers' institutions for a classist State, and ever closer to a prudently realistic vision of Italian history past and present, where the elements of the objective situation—the level of economic and social development, the function of the political organization, the needs for ideological education and the historical tasks of the bourgeoisie and other non-bourgeois strata—play a decisive role. Literature and culture, in general, occupy such a large place in his thought during these years precisely because Gramsci now conceives the revolution to be a great popular fact borne along by extremely diverse energies and supported (and necessarily so) by all possible instruments, even the most obvious and traditional ones of the bourgeois progressivist polemic with which the ideological and cultural choices of the Communist Party tend to be identified in the final analysis. This identification is not so much in relation to the substance of the demands, which often remain unchanged, so much as with the *nature* of the arguments that support and

---

In Italy, the term 'national' has an ideologically very restricted meaning, and does not in any case coincide with 'popular' because in Italy the intellectuals are distant from the people, i.e. from the 'nation'. They are tied instead to a caste tradition that has never been broken by a strong popular or national political movement from below. This tradition is abstract and 'bookish', and the typical modern intellectual feels closer to Annibal Caro or to Ippolito Pindemonte than to an Apulian or Sicilian peasant . . .—*Letteratura e vita nazionale* (Turin: Einaudi, 1952), p. 105.

[See *Selections from Cultural Writings* (David A. Forgacs and Geoffrey Nowell-Smith eds, William Boelhower trans.) (London: Lawrence and Wishart, 1985), p. 208.—Trans.]

advance them.[60] It is clear that Gramsci's notes have a substance and rigour that the cultural politics of the Togliatti period tend to persistently degrade through the conciliatory confusion of the objectives and demands of the democratic tradition with those of the new partisan polemic of the working class. However, it is also clear that there is a link between the national conception of the party, which the politicians of the Communist Party had already put in place in 1944–45, and these aspects of Gramsci's thought. Above all, his notes on the 'cultural battle' of the democrats and the progressivist supporters of the Communist Party carried much weight.

On this subject, Gramsci's thought is clearly tied to the nineteenth-century current of democratic thought. I don't think it necessary to demonstrate again the relations between this phase of Gramsci's work and some essential elements of revolutionary French Jacobinism— although it is interesting to note that even in this respect Gramsci retraces the steps of the Italian democrats (from Carducci to De Sanctis to the early socialists) who found the source of many of their positions in French culture and history. It is more important to see how he identified certain Italian precursors and thereby, more or less consciously, revealed origins of his thought. Moreover, Gramsci is aware that in positing the problem of the relations between intellectuals and national life, he simply returns to a fundamental thorny issue already confronted by others. I think it is important that, in the drafting of his notes, Gramsci bestows at least part of his sympathies on *all* those who, independently of their ideological starting points, understood that the renewal of culture and literature is impossible without the resolution of that vexed issue. This can be confirmed via some quotations that clearly express this demand:

> We have said that the word 'democracy' must not be used only in the 'lay' or 'secularist' sense but can also be used in its 'Catholic' and, if you like, reactionary sense. What matters is that a bond is being sought with the people, the nation, and that one considers necessary

---

60 It has been rightly noted that the concept of the 'national-popular', that is so important for Gramsci, draws its origin from Russian revolutionary thought and should be linked closely to the existence of a vast peasant question, as well as to the pressing need for a not-yet-realized democratic-bourgeois revolution (Romeo, *Risorgimento e capitalismo*, p. 25n12). This is confirmed by the analyses that we have dedicated to the politico-cultural line of the PCI after the liberation, which was entirely informed by the need to overcome the traditional lacunae of bourgeois intellectual development, before one could move on to a (hypothetical) successive phase that would be immediately socialist and grounded in the working class.

not a servile unity resulting from passive obedience, but an active unity, a living-unity, irrespective of content . . .[61]

It can also be confirmed by highlighting certain preferences or acknowledgments of intellectuals and writers who at first sight appear to be far from Gramsci's ethical and ideological milieu but who struck him deeply because of their broad, non-provincial ambitions. This is the case, for example, of Alfredo Oriani, about whom it is said in a note that he 'needs to be studied as the most honest and passionate advocate of Italy's national-popular greatness among the Italian intellectuals of the old generation'.[62] The close attention Gramsci dedicates to this aspect of the problem leads him, if not to share, certainly to take up again some of the formulations of the moderate Ruggero Bonghi, even in the curious interrogative form in which they became famous.[63] And the question of language, as it had been outlined by Alessandro Manzoni, becomes for Gramsci another aspect of the broad task of creating an effective national unification, operating not only at the political level.[64]

We also owe to Gramsci his recognition of the powerful populist charge contained in Francesco De Sanctis'[65] positions, both on the political plane and, even more, on the artistic and literary ones. Gramsci credited the Neapolitan critic with attempting to express 'a new attitude towards the popular classes and a new concept of what is "national" ',[66] while his tastes also

---

61 Gramsci, *Letteratura e vita nazionale*, p. 63 / *Selections from Cultural Writings*, p. 206 [translation modified].

62 Gramsci, *Letteratura e vita nazionale*, p. 17 / *Prison Notebooks*, Vol. 3 (Joseph A. Buttigieg ed. and trans.) (New York: Columbia University Press, 2011), p. 328.

63 'Here is the "catalogue" of the most important questions to be examined and analysed: (1) "why is literature not popular in Italy?" (to use a phrase of Ruggero Bonghi)'—Gramsci, *Letteratura e vita nazionale*, p. 58 / *Selections from Cultural Writings*, p. 200 [translation modified]. Ruggero Bonghi (1826–1895), scholar, writer and politician. [Trans.]

64 We must not forget that Gramsci was—even if indirectly—driven to reflect on these problems by the debate on the 'national' tasks of Italian literature that had begun in the years around 1930 in even fascist Italian newspapers and magazines. See, for instance, the comment on Ercole Reggio's article, 'Perché la letteratura italiana non è popolare in Europa' [Why Italian Literature is Not Popular in Europe], which appeared in *Nuova Antologia* (1 October 1930). See Gramsci, *Letteratura e vita nazionale*, p. 67 / *Prison Notebooks*, Vol. 3, pp. 113–14.

65 Francesco De Sanctis (1817–83), foremost Italian nineteenth-century critic and historian of literature. Garibaldi appointed him as the Minister of Public Instruction, he also served as Minister of Education in four Italian governments from 1861 to 1881. [Trans.]

66 Gramsci, *Letteratura e vita nazionale*, p. 6 / *Selections from Cultural Writings*, p. 92.

lent inspiration to this broad and generous programme of regeneration of the people–nation relationship. All this allows us to situate and explain Gramsci's support for the naturalist and verist novel. As he wrote, in 'Western Europe this form of the novel was the "intellectualist" expression of a more general movement of "going to the people". It was a populist expression of several groups of intellectuals towards the end of the last century, after the democracy of 1848 had disappeared and after large masses of workers had emerged with the development large urban industry'.[67] Having already revealed its power thanks to the idealist, Crocean and democratic traditions, the majesty of De Sanctis' thought would emerge further reinforced among progressive critics thanks to these shrewd notes of Gramsci's.

If we analyse the preference Gramsci showed towards the legacy of the Italian cultural and ideological tradition, it will be clear that, with regard to this as with other problems, he tended to draw on those authors who had called for a serious, non-idealist, non-utopian need to unify the intellectual stratum for the purpose of the realization of certain political tasks. His positive judgement on Vincenzo Gioberti, for example, stems from this. He argued that Gioberti was able to couple the concrete national sense of the function of intellectuals with a fundamentally Jacobin spirit and equally with an active antipathy for Mazzini who 'provided only aphorisms and philosophical allusions which must have seemed empty talk to many intellectuals, especially Neapolitans'.[68] From here stems Gramsci's partial sympathy for (or comprehension or re-evaluation of) the moderate-enlightenment current present throughout the history of the Risorgimento, which to his eyes at least had the merit of never forgetting the real conditions of the issues at stake. By contrast, the democratic-extremist current had all too often opposed pure idealist statements to the scientific understanding of the world. In the cultural camp, this means simply that where, so to speak, consistent democrats had harked back to an ideal concept of the Italian people that bore no actual relationship to it as a historically and socially determined mass, the moderates—from the left-wing represented by Gioberti all the way to the liberal Catholics, and every gradation in between—had based themselves on certain real characteristics of the Italian nation, even if only to glorify and conserve them in their secular

---

67 Gramsci, *Letteratura e vita nazionale*, p. 5 / *Selections from Cultural Writings*, p. 92.
68 Gramsci, *Il Risorgimento*, p. 104 / *Prison Notebooks, Vol. 1*, p. 152 [translation modified: Gramsci here speaks specifically of 'Neapolitans' whereas Buttigieg unaccountably replaces this with 'Southerners'.—Trans.]

immobility. From this perspective, Gramsci's attitude towards Gioberti has a very particular importance, for Gioberti can legitimately be considered the source of many Gramscian positions on culture, intellectuals and the national-popular. There can be no doubt as to the existence of such a relationship. It is confirmed, first, by Gramsci's explicit declarations which are not only general but also specific to those problems that particularly interest us.

Gioberti, albeit vaguely, has the concept of the Jacobin 'national-popular', of political hegemony, namely, the alliance between bourgeois intellectuals (or *ingegno*[69]) and the people. This holds for economics (Gioberti's ideas in economics are vague but interesting) and for literature (culture), where his ideas are clearer and more concrete since not so much hangs in the balance.[70]

More important is that Gramsci cites in his notes on the Risorgimento a passage from Gioberti which, quoted more extensively, reveals itself as a precious guide to understand the basic ideas of the communist thinker:

A literature cannot be national unless it is popular; for, although its creation is the work of a few, its use and enjoyment must be universal. In addition, since it must express common ideas and feelings and bring to the surface those senses which lie hidden and confused in the heart of the multitudes, its practitioners must not only aim for the good of the people but must also depict their spirit, such that this becomes not only the end but in a way also the beginning of civil literature. And this can be seen from the fact that this literature does not rise to the height of its perfection and efficacy unless it is incorporated and becomes in a sense one with the nation. Neither do I believe that ancient Greek literature towers above all in excellence, other than because it was able to relate to the people that possessed the literature more effectively than all other peoples, so that where it was truly public, literature today is in comparison 'private'. If ours was once 'the highest in Europe, today it is more or less the last as far as words and things go'. This is because it has withdrawn from public and civic life and become a matter of academic intercourse or the pastime of the idle.

---

69 Literally brain, intelligence, wit, ingenuity, talent, etc. Implied here as a synecdoche for intellectuals. [Trans.]

70 Gramsci, *Il Risorgimento*, p. 145 / *Selections from Cultural Writings*, p. 248.

Since Italian renewal needs to be democratic, even literature must participate in it and concern itself with the good of the people. This is not to say that it should take place in diaries or popular books, because, as we have already repeatedly warned, the democratic idea changes if it is separated from its companions. *Intelligence and the nation are the originary re-composition of the common people, which cannot be civic if it is not national, that is, united with the other classes; and progressive, that is, guided by intelligence and informed by courteousness.* Equally, literature cannot be truly democratic if it does not have as a foundation that superior science and erudition which is the privilege of the few, but is still necessary in order to nourish and develop popular letters. Such a literature cannot be democratic if even the writings that praise the humble social orders lack the goodness and excellence of the motherland's genius, of its selection of ideas and subject matter, or the simple elegance of its formulations. Those who believe that pages or books thrown hurriedly together, helter-skelter, with a lack of judgement and taste in images, feelings and words, can be useful to educate the people, deceive themselves. The same goes for those who consider these compositions expeditiously, through a vulgar and cosmopolitan philosophy that seeks neither intelligent refinement in the authors, nor the proper stamp of one's nation. It happens to be harder to write good books for the people than for the learned, because in addition to the intrinsic value of what is spoken about one must add care in the choice of material and mastery in rendering it fitting for the common folk. Hence no modern nation is rich in such writing, and us least of all.[71]

---

71 The passage from *Il Risorgimento*, p. 145 [Gramsci, *Selections from Cultural Writings*, p. 248], starts at the beginning of our quotation until the phrase: 'this can be seen from the fact that this literature does not rise to the height of its perfection and efficacy unless it is incorporated and becomes in a sense one with the nation'. It might be interesting to note that Gioberti, continuing his discussion in 'Del rinnovamento civile d'Italia' (*Il Rinnovamento* 3: 126–7) goes on to cite names of authors that count as models and guides for this modern, popular style. So it is extremely significant that, when it comes to providing concrete examples, among the few classics he cites as those that merit the adjective 'popular' are Gaspare Gozzi, Giambattista Gelli and Carlo Goldoni; among the very few modernists to be imitated, he lists Alessandro Manzoni, Niccolò Tommaseo and Cesare Cantù (the last two, according to Gioberti, 'attended to various types of popular instruction in indefatigable fashion, and deserve to find emulators and imitators in Italy', *Il Rinnovamento* 3: 128).

While it might be unfair to retrace one by one the passages of Gioberti's text, comparing them with appropriate citations from Gramsci, it is clear that there are certain striking analogies. The starting point for the two theorists' arguments, that is to say, their fundamental axiom, is more or less identical. 'The premise of the new literature cannot but be historical, political and popular,'[72] writes Gramsci, and: 'To conclude: a work of art is more "artistically" popular when its moral, cultural and sentimental content is in greater accord with national morality, culture, and sentiments—and these should not be understood as something static but as a continually developing activity.'[73] Identical (or, at least, extremely close) to Gramsci is Gioberti's deprecating attitude towards the traditional faults of the Italian intellectual stratum and Italian culture (where even the aversion to cosmopolitanism returns) to which he opposes the idea of a lively and concrete national-popular literature. Gramsci's deeply felt need to not bow to utopian solutions, to remain among things, in touch with an empirically accepted reality, ended up drawing him into an indigenous tradition whose daring for the cause of renewal had always appeared bland and limited. The attempt to theorize and realize a new 'Renewal of Italy'—bearing in mind the likes of Gioberti in the cultural field—could not be possible without shedding light, once again, on the objectively conservative function represented by the popular element within this framework. Moreover, the typically bourgeois attempt to weld together people and nation in order to realize a profound and *general* democratic process, posed itself for Gramsci—precisely because it was adopted with a spirit sympathetic to the destiny of the popular masses—in a form that was anything but explosive and revolutionary: *the moment of consensus ended up getting the better of the moment of rupture and polemic.* Gramsci penned ambiguously paternalistic statements:

> Every intellectual movement becomes or returns to being national if a 'going to the people' has taken place, if there has been a phase of 'Reformation' and not just a 'Renaissance' phase, and if the 'Reformation–Renaissance' phases follow one another organically and do not coincide with distinct historical phases (as was the case in Italy, where, from the viewpoint of popular participation in public life, there was a historical hiatus between the movement of the communes [Reformation] and the Renaissance movement).

---

72 Gramsci, *Letteratura e vita nazionale*, p. 14 / *Selections from Cultural Writings*, p. 102.
73 Gramsci, *Letteratura e vita nazionale*, p. 24 / *Prison Notebooks, Vol. 3*, p. 46.

Even if one has to begin by writing 'serial novels' and operatic lyrics, without a period of going to the people there can be no 'Renaissance' and no national literature.[74]

We should not be surprised if, starting from such firm opinions, Gramsci always puts the historical, objective fact of existing reality in the front line, going so far as to soften the edges of a possible transformation in order to insistently underline that, above all, and at whatever cost, it is necessary to make contact with the people, as they are, as they live and feel. To the words already cited: 'The premiss of the new literature cannot but be historical, political and popular,' Gramsci adds (with a clarity that is useful if we wish to understand what 'historical', 'political' and 'popular' mean for him), it 'must aim at elaborating that which already is, whether polemically or in some other way does not matter. What does matter, though, is that it sinks its roots in the human popular culture as it is, with its tastes and tendencies and with its moral and intellectual world, even if it is backward and conventional.'[75] Gramsci goes so far as to exhibit a broad interest in that lowest form of popular literature, that is, the feuilleton or fourth-rate melodrama. Only through genres that are *naturally* popular can one establish contact with the great mass of readers, even if in a distorted and mystified way:

It is this question that represents the major part of the problem of new literature as the expression of moral and intellectual renewal, for only from the readers of serial literature can one select a sufficient and necessary public for creating the cultural base of the new literature. It appears to me that the problem is this: How to create a body of writers who are, artistically, to serial literature what Dostoyevsky was to Sue and Soulié or, with respect to the detective story, what Chesterton was to Conan Doyle and Wallace.[76]

When one then moves from the level of theoretical statements to that of concrete proposals, Gramsci does not think it absurd to suggest veritable formal disguises or regenerations of these subspecies of popular literature that enable one to project into a much wider circle of readers a spectrum of emotions and ideas that is no longer conformist or reactionary as it had been in the past. Speaking of Raffaello Giovagnoli's *Spartaco*, Gramsci writes: 'As

---

74 Gramsci, *Letteratura e vita nazionale*, p. 67 / *Prison Notebooks, Vol. 3*, p. 319.
75 Gramsci, *Letteratura e vita nazionale*, p. 14 / *Cultural Writings*, p. 102.
76 Gramsci, *Letteratura e vita nazionale*, p. 14 / *Cultural Writings*, p. 102.

far as I recall it, it seems that *Spartaco* would lend itself particularly well to an attempt that, within certain limits, could become a method. One could "translate it" into modern language: purge it as a language of rhetorical and baroque forms, cleanse it of a few stylistic and technical idiosyncrasies, making it "current" '.[77] One could object at this point that Gramsci's observations on the feuilleton, and more generally on that particular sector of literature that is traditionally referred to as 'popular', relate more to the sphere of the pedagogical-political than to the artistic in the proper sense of the word. It is indeed difficult to distinguish what in his work is intended to be educational and instructional, and what an explicitly aesthetic concern. However, one cannot forget that Gramsci's thoughts on the national-popular lead to two fundamental conclusions the importance of which is not merely polemical, random or contingent. The first concerns the absolute pre-eminence he attributes to problems 'internal' to culture, from which follows the generally implicit and yet obvious refusal of any cosmopolitan or even simply xenophilic solution. The second concerns Gramsci's firm conviction, restated on numerous occasions, that there can be no cultural or literary development without passing though a 'national', autochthonous phase. To better understand these points, it is instructive to read a note he devoted to an article by a certain Argo (published in an issue of the periodical *Educazione fascista* in 1933), which was forcefully critical of Paul Nizan's position on the 'new literature'.[78] Here Gramsci outlines the ideas we have cited on the 'historical, political and popular' character of the new literature and on the necessity of capturing the public of the feuilletons, so as to turn it into the 'cultural base' for these more advanced literary experiments. Here we see him restating his aversion to thinking that the potential birth of a modern culture could be exclusively developed along the lines of 'an artistic school of intellectual origins'. But we are even more interested in the fact that in this text he reveals a historicist credo upon which his entire argument is constructed and from which stems the prudent moderatism that animates and inspires it; a prudent moderatism and realist historicism that will so often serve as alibis for those who would have refused *in principle* any political or cultural solution of a 'revolutionary' type. 'It is a serious error to adopt a "single" progressive strategy according to which each new gain accumulates and becomes the premiss of future gains. Not only are the strategies

---

77 Gramsci, *Letteratura e vita nazionale*, p. 134 / *Cultural Writings*, p. 352.

78 Gramsci, *Letteratura e vita nazionale*, pp. 12–14 / *Cultural Writings*, pp. 99–102.

multiple, but even in the "most progressive" one there are retrogressive movements'; Gramsci's refusal to accept the 'leap' from one cultural situation to another as possible and positive has its origin, and is developed, based on this theoretical foundation. Gramsci is in agreement with Argo on only one point of his dispute with Nizan, but it is a point that includes all the others, the real *point of the matter*:

> Argo's only valid objection is this: the *impossibility of going beyond a national and autochthonous stage of the new literature and the 'cosmopolitan' dangers of Nizan's conception.* From this point of view, many of Nizan's criticism of groups of French intellectuals should be reconsidered: the *Nouvelle Revue Française,* 'populism' and so on, including the *le Monde* group; not because his criticism is politically off-target, but because *the new literature must necessarily manifest itself 'nationally', in relatively hybrid and different combinations and alloys.*

In this way, Gramsci's national-popular ends up becoming the iron cage of tradition and of the *status quo* of Italian society coercing all the attempts at renewal. On the one hand, there is an acknowledged need to not lose contact with the formal, linguistic and stylistic experiments of *our* past; on the other, it is firmly reaffirmed that the starting point of the new literature must be the real level of popular consciousness, however backward that might be. From this perspective, there is a decline in importance in the intense critique that Gramsci advances in various places (for instance, against Manzoni) against the concept of the 'humble', as the typical expression of the aristocratic and paternalistic relationship between the Italian intellectual and the people. What matters more is that Gramsci's concrete recommendations converge towards an idea of literature where the pedagogical-local element dominates all others, thanks to the profound conviction that a 'modern humanism' must show itself able to 'reach right to the simplest and most uneducated classes' of the people if it wishes to achieve a 'national point of view'. It is not by chance if, among the very few positive examples that Gramsci is able to cite as Italian representatives of this 'modern humanism', he names 'Guerrazzi, Mastriani and our few other popular writers'.[79]

The gravest consequences that follow from this attitude are, to our mind, the yet again deferred reference to a fecund, critical relationship between our culture and the great culture of the European twentieth century, in particular

---

79 Gramsci, *Letteratura e vita nazionale,* p. 107 / *Selections from Cultural Writings,* p. 211.

with the revolutionary experiences of the avant-gardes; and the foregrounding within the progressivist movement of an infinite series of local and provincial particularisms. Gramsci's national-popular gave to Italian populism that ideological unity it did not previously possess; at the same time, it removed the only vital chance it had, which—as we have repeatedly stated—consisted in the often vague but generous attempt to tie particular socio-political demands to a general climate of humanitarian protest. Gramsci's repeated assertions, following the Croce–De Sanctis line, of the preliminary need for a profound regeneration of moral life was not enough to guarantee the success of his recommendations. It soon had to be acknowledged that this typically idealist operation was at the very best able to lead to a show of generic dignity. Gramscians, so much worse than Gramsci, would finish the job, quickly enclosing the old populist polemic within democratic-provincial limits. This is a moment—between 1948 and 1965—where progressive literary production reached very low levels.

15

The first and most conspicuous consequence produced by this climate was the rebirth of truly regionalist tendencies. Regionalism, as we know, had never died in twentieth-century Italian literature, and anti-fascism had already contributed to its revaluation—think of Pavese's attitude towards Piedmont, Pratolini's towards Florence or Vittorini's towards Sicily. But from this moment onwards, the reference to a determinate local reality is adopted with a much narrower and more provincial spirit of invention. The partial and particular insistence is no longer a sufficient pretext for an ethical and ideal polemic that ranges beyond the occasioning instance; the writer's discourse remains enclosed within precise historical and environmental determinants, draws nourishment from it and indulges as a heritage within it, which—while it may sometimes prove bitter and difficult—is always precious. An exaggerated accentuation of the properly local elements follows from this. Sociological diligence is never too far from pure and simple folklore, and the love for the specific character of a particular section of the Italian people becomes the involuntary but very evident adherence to a set of archaic, pre-historical values which the people cultivates. There is a lament for the poverty, the backwardness and the material suffering of the people; but very often the representation of poverty, backwardness and material suffering is shown to be only an indirect way to glorify the people's capacity for resistance and revival in the face of the accumulation of adverse circumstances. At a certain point the relationship between pain and hope, suffering and solidarity, becomes so tight and indivisible as to suggest to the reader the impression that, all told, such a world is altogether positive. *Anti-fascist regionalism distinguishes itself from verist nineteenth-century regionalism in this way as well: by appearing in the shape of a vacuous and superficial optimism.* The root of this attitude is partly politico-ideological and partly purely aesthetic. Many, despite their apparently documentary commitment, highlight the exclusively intellectual aspect of the 'going to the people', which in turn rests on the irrational basis of a confident admiration for everything that is genuine, pure, instinctive and uncorrupted in the lower strata of society. In this period, we can find numerous supporters for the myth of the Italian 'noble savage' able to get by in all situations, without having to sacrifice feeling or good-heartedness. Meanwhile, others will highlight the positive outlook that the ongoing political struggle gives to popular hopes going back centuries. In such cases, *the 'noble savage' becomes the Communist Party, the Workers' Movement, which are also distinguished by their sensitivity and good-heartedness, that is, they are made in the image of the people that they must redeem and save.* The populism of these years, too often developed and supported—even if only through a complicit silence and suitably softened judgements—by Marxist and left-wing critics, turns out to be shaped by this folkloric mixture of democratic commitment, communal spirit, intellectualized hankerings for evasion and progressive political perspectives.

Pratolini's personal development offers a typical example of how in this period one can move rapidly from the vague but sincere enthusiasms born of the Resistance to a phase of determination and 'fixation' of populist ideology in paradigmatic formulae lacking any revitalizing charge. In this regard too, we find that he is one of the authors who have contributed most to forming the qualities of our national populism. *Le Ragazze di San Frediano* [The Girls of San Frediano], published in 1949, is an exemplar of the 'popular tale', where the obvious descriptive abilities of the author, no longer redeemed by a breath of epic enthusiasm, now serve merely folkloric needs. The description of the environment manifests a near-documentary precision. The titles of some of the most significant chapters confirm this: 'Il rione dei beceri modello' [The District of the Model Boors]; 'I ferri del mestiere' [The Tools of the Trade]; 'C'è sempre un gobbo in Sanfrediano' [There's Always a Hunchback in Sanfrediano]; 'Una partita, un pugno, e una digressione sull'uso e sugli effetti del frontino' [A Match, a Punch and a Digression on the Use of the Effects of the *Frontino*[80] . . . Behind this repertory of minutiae, the populist *animus* is conserved in immutable form, but it tends to reveal its artistic weakness evermore openly as the instinctive charge that sustains it is gradually lost, becoming a mannerism, repetitively monotonous and irritating. For example, the motif of the atemporality of the district returns, such that the inhabitants of Sanfrediano:

> [D]ressed their myths and flags in more modern ideals, but their intransigence, animosity and devil-may-care attitude remain the same. And if between piazza Signoria and the sepulchres of Santa Croce the shadows of the Great wander tirelessly to light the icy spirits of modernity with sacred fire, in the alleys of Sanfrediano the people who were coeval with those Fathers move around in the flesh, entirely at home in the surroundings.[81]

The motif of poverty and of its inseparable partner, hope; the vitalist motif of everyday reality in which one delights and finds satisfaction:

> The people of Sanfrediano are at once sentimental and ruthless, their idea of justice is represented in the spoils of the enemy hung from a lamppost; and their image of paradise, illustrated in a proverb, is poetic and vulgar: a utopian place where there is an abundance of millet and a dearth of birds. They believe in God, as they say, because they believe 'in the eyes and hands of the one who made us', and logically reality ends up appearing as the best possible dream. *Their hope is to be found in what day by day they are able to gain, and which is not enough for them.*[82]

But *everything is now outlined with didactic clarity, from which ideology emerges stronger but the poetry is completely absent.* The same vulgar story that Pratolini tells in *Ragazze* reveals how un-modern one can be despite the uninhibitedness and inventiveness of the language. Florentine boorishness is a commonplace that has been feasted upon by five centuries of novels about the period of the communes. To rediscover this in 1949 was also to rediscover the

---

80 Literally, a slap on the opponent's forehead or *fronte*. [Trans.]

81 Vasco Pratolini, *Le ragazze di Sanfrediano*, Florence, 1954, pp. 7–8. The novel appeared for the first time in *Botteghe oscure, Notebook 3* (Autumn 1949). [The last sentence uses an untranslatable Florentine expression, *di uscio e bottega*, literally 'of the doorstep and the shop'.—Trans.]

82 Pratolini, *Le ragazze di Sanfrediano*, p. 7.

narrative tradition which had expressed it through the inseparable union of contents and stylistic choices. The form of the 'chronicle' was an original invention, inspired in various ways by twentieth-century literary forms (*frammentismo*, the poetics of memory, the feeling of time, etc.); the form of the 'popular tale' (or novella) involves a congenital conservatism. One should not forget that *Le ragazze* comes after *Le cronache* but immediately precedes *Metello* (1955). Besides, even if boorishness becomes a positive popular value, as it does in Pratolini's stories, one is forced to ask if we are attracted to them because of their unseasoned display of instinct or as a reflection of a vitality that has not been restrained but is already *historically* positive. In either case we are led to the conclusions already stated at the start of this chapter.

Pratolini's name is also important because a series of imitators converge around it, going beyond the characteristic Florentine and Tuscan setting. Before *Le ragazze*, *Cronache di poveri amanti* acts as a central model. This latter work reveals a type of milieu and characters that would be adopted especially where the historical and social conditions appeared to suggest objective affinities. The Neapolitan writers, in particular Bernari and Rea, provide characteristic examples of this in the way they interweave reportage and history, family events and collective events, the life of the district with that of the street, that of the street with the life of the city. Alongside the very strong tradition of Neapolitan literature—from Ferdinando Russo to Salvatore di Giacomo, from Raffaele Viviani to Eduardo De Filippo[83]—one should also signal this relationship of a new kind between different regionalisms. It helps to identify a line of continuity in the development of a lumpenproletarian experience that will gradually extend to the entire national territory, with incredibly irrational results. But before we come to more painstaking analyses of these elements, we must specify more general aspects of the literary movement of the time.

Without question the polemical debate around the southern question [*meridionalistica*] gave a powerful contribution to the development of regionalist populism. We will not investigate the political and historico-ideological shortcomings of this attitude, which for many years meant that the predominant action of left-wing parties was to protest against the traditional bottlenecks of the Southern economy and society, and to attempt to resolve them. It is enough to say that, on this point, the Italian workers' movement showed

---

83 Eduardo De Filippo (1900–84), Neapolitan actor, playwright, screenwriter and poet. [Trans.]

its fateful dependence on the democratic tradition which contributed to the growth and exacerbation of its separation from the real problems of capitalist and workers' development matured and intensified. The entire weight of this culture, which was not only that of a purely tactical and political choice, came to influence the climate in which functionaries of the party and intellectuals, writers and theorists operated. *Before being a political choice, the study of the southern question is an ethical and spiritual attitude, a mentality and a custom.* At the origin of this phenomenon one can again find De Sanctis and the other democratic populists of the South. Some of them are today being rediscovered by other democratic populists who support the workers' movement, importing the entire weight of their political and cultural preferences into it. We then find Gramsci's judgement on the failure of the Risorgimento (the peasant question was in large part focused on the South, which is why Gramsci ended up advocating a commitment to reflection on the specificity of Southern Italy at all levels, including the cultural). There is also the extremely strong and fascinating tradition of 'classic' *meridionalismo*, from Fortunato to Salvemini, to Dorso and on to Fiore, which in these years, directly or indirectly, exerted a great influence (in 1949 the complete works of Dorso were being published; Salvemini, who returned to Italy in 1947, was involved in intense political and polemical activity; and Fiore's *Popolo di formiche* won the Viareggio Prize in 1952). Finally, we find widespread participation in the left-wing cultural movement by southern intellectuals who seek, through this political and ideological contact, to preserve and strengthen what was their 'best asset: the secular and humanist tradition of a great thought of liberation'.[84] *It is difficult to measure how much damage the tradition of meridionalismo did to the workers' movement as a whole.* On the literary plane, it meant, nine times out of ten, a retreat of the critical line, further strengthening of the folkloric and localist tendencies and the intensification—as far as questions of taste are concerned—of fully provincial and dialectal linguistic and stylistic elements. It is true that a nation and a literature unfortunately bear with them the inheritance of their own backwardness; but it is also true that the genius of an intellectual stratum often shows itself in its ability to leap over the objective limits to which some would like to confine it, inventing for itself the conditions of a profoundly innovative discourse, *an avant-garde discourse*. This, moreover, is a lesson that no democrat will ever learn, because for him the step-by-step transformation

---

84 Here *meridionalismo* refers to the specific approach to issues concerning the Italian South and its insertion into the new Italian state, including the so-called Southern Question that is so memorably discussed by Gramsci. [Trans.]

of existence is the *conditio sine qua non* to each next step. The result is that nothing seriously changes.

The Neapolitan area forms the backdrop to most southern Italian literature. For obvious reasons, Naples provides a broad repertoire of populist themes. This can be explained by the history of the city itself. Having become a metropolis even before the formation of Italy, it never found in the support of the central government or the shrewdness of its administrators the strength to realize an effective healing of its ancient wounds. Hence, some of its basic conditions of existence remained unchanged over the years and decades, even tending to worsen and putrefy. At the heart of this was the absence of a solid, modern economic structure. The extreme precariousness of the sources of livelihood produced sociological precariousness, instability of individual and collective destinies, difficulties in the function of moral and social laws, and finally the predominance of poverty, corruption and defeat.

In the bowels of this great city, a vast popular mass survived misfortunes, catastrophes and wars—it is unclear how. Even more miraculously, it survived its own everyday sorrows. As we have said, the persistence of a certain social and economic state produces the persistence of objective and subjective characteristics in the population. In other words, if a commoner of Masaniello's time lives in conditions no different from a commoner in 1945, logic and fate dictates that the latter will act and conduct himself according to a code of rules, sentiments and affects analogous to those that guided the commoner of Masaniello's era. And if in different historical moments a literature is formed that is directly inspired by the representation or the denunciation of these conditions of the common people, logic and fate dictates that it will reflect the persistent immobility of this condition, and will, consequently, be forced ceaselessly to pursue the paths of the same polemic, the same moral and sentimental legacy, the same human and social wretchedness. One can therefore determine a first characteristic of populist Neapolitan literature: *a sociologically static situation results in the constant return of a determinate theme.* The differences in connotations are minimal between the commoners of *Micco Passaro* (1619) by Giulio Cesare Cortese or of Giambattista Basile's *Muse napolitane* (1635) and those of the most recent works by Domenico Rea,[85] Bernari and De

---

85 Pseudonym of Tommaso Asaniello (1622–47), Neapolitan fisherman and leader of a popular revolt against Habsburg Spain in 1647. Giulio Cesare Cortese (1570–1640), poet and significant figure for dialectal and baroque literature. Giambattista Basile (1566–1632), poet

Filippo. Differences of a historico-literary order, which can without question be established between them, are often far less significant than this immutable ground of things, and hence of feelings, morality and lifestyle. And yet the ideological acquisitions that do exist and modify the physiognomy of the popular characters and their naive perspectives are not always the most successful novelties. All this can be explained by the weight of the populist mythology in the strongest Neapolitan writers as well as in the others—they must *be accountable* to a literary tradition that was formed over the course of centuries, and to a social condition that over centuries has remained unchanged. Here too the name of Pratolini seems to dictate the line; but his naive symbolism of feelings is dilated in an obvious and superficial way by the Neapolitans. In *L'oro di Napoli* (1947), Giuseppe Marotta offers an already complete repertory of 'Neapolitanism'. As if exhibited in a gallery of greater or lesser paintings, rich in anecdotes and characters, the myth of this good and unfortunate Neapolitan people—to be precise, the more unfortunate it is the more good it is—fully unfolds. In a city where 'all the trades lead to poverty and pain, because whoever today is a gas worker tomorrow will be a cabinet-maker or a baker, and so the commoner of the Stella district turns and turns again between trades as though lying on a bed of nails',[86] it is the figures of the misfits and drifters that come into the foreground: the nutter, the braggart, the raffle organizer, the shyster [*paglietta*],[87] the 'wheeler-dealer'. Behind these one finds the protagonists of the humblest and most despised trades: water-carriers, cobblers, barbers, drivers; and further back still those that, like the don Raffaele Caserta of the story 'C'è mestiere e mestiere' [There's Trade and Trade], have done a bit of everything: the dog and bird trainer, the guitar teacher, the tool sharpener, the fishmonger, the investigator, the mender of watches and umbrellas, the photographer of the dead, the driver, the painter of *ex votos*. It is very easy to conclude that the writer's attitude to this material is reactionary, because he lavishes an indiscriminate sympathy and facile optimism on the cases narrated. Marotta synthesizes the precious and eternal spirit of the popular Naples, the 'gold of Naples', as follows:

---

and courtier, remembered for his collection of Neapolitan fairy tales, including the two earliest versions of *Rapunzel* and *Cinderella*. Domenico Rea (1921–94), writer and journalist, whose novels focused on the difficulties of postwar reconstruction in Naples. [Trans.]

86 Giuseppe Marotta (1902–63), author and successful screenwriter. The quotation is from his *L'Oro di Napoli* (Milan: Bompiani, 1947), p. 185. [Trans.]

87 *Paglietta* is Southern Italian slang for the hat worn by third-rate Neapolitan lawyers and, by extension, a synecdoche for lawyers themselves. [Trans.]

The ability to get back up after every fall; a remote, inherited, intelligent and superior patience. Let us roll up through centuries, the millennia and perhaps we will find their origin in the convulsions of the earth, in the puffs of deadly vapours that erupted suddenly, in the waves that climbed over the hills, in all the dangers that threatened human life; this patience is the gold of Naples.[88]

It is obvious that a morality founded upon endurance is a quietist and 'anti-popular' morality. But how can one forget that the progressivist Pratolini set out from a concept of the people analogous to this when he developed his humanitarian ideology?

Get a bellyful of the poverty that grinds us down, day and night, that burns us like a slow fire, like consumption. For centuries we've been fighting back, unharmed, aloof. Then a man gives way, a woman falls—but they had been fighting back for centuries, for an eternity they kept themselves on their feet, propped up by a despairing hope. And suddenly this hope had gone from their hearts.[89]

Although the relationship between Pratolini and Marotta is indirect, this just demonstrates—as we have stated numerous times—that the populist theme is *in itself* lacking in strong arguments and can easily, with minimal modifications, make way for reactionary attitudes as well as progressive thought. We should not be surprised then if, over and above the differences in narrative quality and stature, we feel Marotta to be close to other Neapolitan writers of his age, despite what we may initially be led to think by the ideological and political differences between them.

Carlo Bernari, for example, in *Vesuvio e pane* [Vesuvius and Bread, 1952] openly polemicizes against the corruption of his city's ruling class. But from the strictly narrative standpoint, he does not add anything of importance to the definition of the Neapolitan people; for him too, patience, underlying goodness, a fundamental (if confused) thirst for justice are all basic characteristics on which to dwell; for him too, the entire sense of a human attitude can be enclosed within the face of a mask, the eternal mask of Naples, Pulcinella, who is even capable of defeating Death with the inexhaustible strength of a mysterious attachment to life: '"I, however, am alive!" cries out Pulcinella; and to demonstrate that he is truly alive, he brandishes the coffin he'd used to

---

88 Marotta, *L'Oro di Napoli*, p. 18.
89 Pratolini, *Il quartiere*, pp. 31–2 / *A Tale of Santa Croce*, p. 45.

sit on, to hide, to take refuge and often to hammer on Death's head until Death truly died'.[90] In truth, the most valuable document here—one not discredited by vain folkloric or moralizing ambitions—is Bernari's novel *Speranzella* (1949). It clearly takes its cue Ferdinando Russo's insight about the *naturally* reactionary character of the Neapolitan people and develops it with a degree of invention. However, in *Speranzella* too we do not rise above a level that is anecdotal and sketchy, where in an entirely obvious way, *as in a piece of political reportage*, the writer illustrates the contrast between generations by pitting the communist son against the monarchist mother.

Drier, harder and 'angrier' is Domenico Rea, not so much in the images of Neapolitan life to be found in *Spaccanapoli* (1947) and *Gesù, fate luce!* [Jesus, Bring Light!, 1950], but in the representation of that zone of peasant poverty that surrounds Naples and which truly represents the author's original populist discovery. In *Ritratto di Maggio* [Portrait of May, 1953] and in *Quel che vide Cummeo* [What Cummeo Saw, 1955], Rea is able effectively to capture the characteristics of this coarse and basic life where the odours of the stable and the potent scent of poorly washed bodies seem to materialize in an almost oppressive atmosphere. The contrast between 'gentlemen' and the wretched has become enormous: on the one hand, there is all the happiness in the world, on the other, all the pain. Rea is particularly brilliant when he reduces the terms of the question to the more evident physical aspects: being well and being happy means eating enough, smoking when one wishes and living in a comfortable home. To be unhappy is to not eat, to want everything and have nothing, to smoke when one finds a cigarette butt on the street, to dress in rags, to drink nothing but water and *to be certain that none of this will ever change*. The absence of a precise progressive intent renders his images firmer; but, naturally, it does not prevent the moral of the fable, even in his better works, from being the patient acceptance of a reality from which one had vainly attempted to escape. The story of Cummeo is that of a destitute man who finds the spark of hope only when he returns to the fold, giving up trying to escape his fate. Rea's commoner from Campania is more bitter and desperate than the Neapolitan lumpenproletarians of Bernari and De Filippo, but not even he can stop being what he is, namely, an individual for whom the horizon of consciousness is that of nature and for whom life is

---

90 Carlo Bernari, *Vesuvio e pane* (Florence: Vallecchi, 1953), p. 483.

indistinguishable from survival. Therefore, not even in Rea is evil or woe so strong as to entirely stifle its stolid and superficial 'opposite'—hope.

The observations made so far (that could be repeated for those other authors in which political commitment is even more evident, such as Incoronato and De Jaco[91]), lead us to identify another characteristics of Neapolitan populism: its marked petty-bourgeois spirit. Even Pratolini can, no doubt, be accused of being petty bourgeois; his cult of feelings is from this standpoint exemplary. But in him there is often a vigorous plebeian tone that redeems some of the laxness and ambiguity. What remains very alive is the sensation that, in Rea's works and even more in those of Bernari, the distance between the intellectual personality of the writer and the objective representation of the people is resolved more often than not by making the scales tip towards a petty-bourgeois morality. This aspect of Neapolitan populism can be explained, once again, in two ways. First, one can say that the extreme proximity between the lowest rungs of the bourgeois social ladder and the true people can be found in the sociological configuration of Naples itself; where the economic situation is persistently precarious, the osmosis between the petty bourgeoisie and the proletariat is also continuous. Second, the Neapolitan literary tradition has willingly confused the sociological and moral terms of the relationship. Think, for example, of Matilde Serao: even when she provides depictions of reality that are immediately popular, she maintains an evidently superior viewpoint, of the kind that could only be expressed by a petty-bourgeois intellectual whose interests and way of life are very close to the people or even to the lumpenproletariat but who is always ready to distinguish herself from them through her aspirations and moral convictions. Moreover, it is evident that the distance between the petty bourgeoisie and the people is not seen or experienced by the author as a form of conscious and historical opposition; the petty-bourgeois author feels herself to be different from the people, but this difference serves only to attribute to the people her own moral and ideal convictions, and her worldview—as though they were its own objective properties. This is what the specific paternalism of populist Neapolitan literature consists in; it is undoubtedly

---

91 Luigi Incoronato (1920–1957), short-story writer and novelist, born in Montreal to a family of Italian migrants, his novel *Scala a San Potito* [The San Potito Steps, 1950] focused on the miseries of wartime Naples. Aldo De Jaco (1923–2003), writer, journalist and member of the PCI, author of *La città insorge: le quattro giornate di Napoli* [The City Rises Up: The Four Days of Naples, 1956], on the popular revolt against German occupation in late September 1943. [Trans.]

facilitated by the natural petty-bourgeois propensity that always exists in the people, and in the Neapolitan people perhaps more than elsewhere, for reasons of which we have spoken. With an eye to this characteristic, one can also explain the type of relationship that doubtlessly exists between democratic Neapolitan populists and a typically petty-bourgeois writer such as Eduardo de Filippo. The moral which brings to a close *Napoli milionaria* [Millionaire Naples, 1945]—the work of De Filippo from which many ideas and intuitions of 'Neapolitanism' are drawn—expresses, unquestionably with great wisdom, a profound sense of reality. But its morality is also that of patient waiting, the petty-bourgeois morality of those who realize that, once the storm has passed, they should retreat back into their home like prudent snails, because storms pass and life must continue as before: '"We got to wait Ama," says Gennaro to his wife. "We got to get through the night."' And in the background, behind the pain, the dim light of hope begins to glow once more.

A judgement that is perhaps even more negative must be made in relation to that southern Italian literature which takes its inspiration—more or less directly—from Levi's work. In *Le parole sono pietre* [Words are Stones, 1955], Levi is working at an incomparably lower level than in *Cristo si è fermato a Eboli*; and not only because of the journalistic tone of the text and its marked episodic form. The truth is that by this point the flow of discoveries has dried up; what the writer had found to be original and authentic in the peasant world is not enriched by a single important observation. The basic concept remains that of 'self-government, peasant autonomy',[92] but it is now denuded of ambiguity and of its extremely vital prophetic charge. The discussion now proceeds from a transparent political and ideological perspective and, *precisely for this* reason, shows itself to be completely unacceptable *as a political and ideological proposition*. The conclusions we already reached regarding *Cristo* are still valid: Levi the messiah and rhapsodist of peasant civilization is politically insignificant but poetically and 'populistically' extremely original and important; Levi the political theorist of peasant self-government is poetically insignificant and politically a dangerous anachronism.

But this is not the preferred path taken by Levi's many imitators who instead choose, among the many ideas suggested by their teacher, those that are more forcefully characterized by irrationalism and decadentism. Rocco

---

92 Carlo Levi, *Le parole sono pietre* (Turin: Einaudi, 1955), p. 21 / *Words Are Stones: Impressions of Sicily* (Angus Davidson trans.) (New York: Farrar, Straus and Cudahy, 1958), p. 14.

Scotellaro's works,[93] from *È fatto giorno* [Day Has Come, 1954] to *L'Uva puttanella* [The Puttanella Grape, 1955], amply demonstrates the kind of artificial intellectualistic charge that can be contained in a 'naive' position. Let us set aside for a moment consideration of Rocco's personal experience—so rich in heroic and pathetic elements that are anything but alien to an involuntarily vitalist standpoint—and reread his poems and prose without compassion, attentive only to how the ideas of the people and of human redemption appear in them. One will note that, where the poet does not succumb to pure protest or propaganda, his discussion retraces—if anything with greater stylistic and ideological uncertainty—classical models of populist-democratic aestheticism whose origin is to be found not just in Levi but perhaps even more so in late-nineteenth-century Italian poetry. It is not by chance that we find in Scotellaro, who was born and lived among Lucanian peasants, a greater detachment from them than we find between the best Levi and the characters of *Cristo*. Indeed, in Levi, the bourgeois point of view is so developed as to enable him, without effort or fear of confusion, to draw closer to the standpoint of the people, concluding with a magnanimous embrace, in a generous if paternalistic palingenesis of feelings. In Scotellaro there is no effort of will and reason able to overcome the hurdle of everyday familiarity, of a mistrust inevitably born from eating the same bread and suffering in the same prison. Once the real face of the people is uncovered, which all in all is less pleasant than how it is usually portrayed,[94] Scotellaro is unable to repair this precarious relationship between himself and the peasants, except through a celebration of a sensuous and aesthetic kind, or through a seemingly pure documenting of the peasants, in which the protagonist speaks of himself as if through a tape recorder (as in *Contadini del Sud* [Southern Peasants]).

What Levi judged as the 'Marseillaise of the peasants', the poem 'Sempre nuova è l'alba' [Dawn Is Ever New], perfectly exemplifies the stylistic and linguistic forms as well as the expressive tones through which Scotellaro

---

93 Rocco Scotellaro (1923–53), writer, poet and socialist politician; his writings are rooted in the peasant class to which he had been born. [Trans.]

94 Scotellaro always represents the peasants with strange characteristics that make them look like grotesque beings that are not completely human and even animal-like. In his unfinished novel, *L'uva puttanella* (Bari: Laterza, 1964), the peasants who participated in the occupation of the lands from prison are described as follows: 'the second one came down to the courtyard after us. The movements were the same as those of a herd of rabbits, chickens, turkeys, of pigs first enclosed then released from the farm' (p. 113).

renders the celebration, and through which he attempts to realize a certain type of contact with the world of the peasants.

Stop shouting inside me,
stop blowing on my heart
your warm peasant breath.

Let us drink instead a cup full of wine!
So that our cheerful evening
might quieten the desperate wind.

Still the brigands' heads
on pikes appear, and the cave,
the green oasis of sad hope
keeps a clean stone as a pillow.

But you cannot turn back on the paths.
Other wings will flee
from the reeds of the nest,
because as time passes
the dawn is new, it is new.[95]

But in these lines we can hear Carducci and d'Annunzio—perhaps even Hermeticism.[96] In other words, we find here an accumulation of extremely old stylistic forms that come together to compose (or assume) a type of relationship that is also extremely old and predictable. That said, how was a new type of relationship possible if all the work on the Southern Question was dominated by historical ambiguity? Once again, it was proposed that southern Italian democratic intellectuals should reprise their traditional democratic function; that they should therefore lead, consider, love and celebrate the peasants and the people, as had other democratic intellectuals. The most visible consequence on the literary-political plane was that while the Lucanian peasants existed, with their suffering and their hopes, the 'new southern Italian

---

95 Rocco Scotellaro, 'Sempre nuova è l'alba' in *E' fatto giorno* [Day Has Come] (Milan: Mondadori, 1954), p. 96.

96 *Ermetismo* was a literary movement of the 1920s and 1930s, whose chief proponents were the poets Eugenio Montale and Giuseppe Ungaretti. The term alludes to the 'closed, not easily communicable character of the poetry [. . .] and hence to expressive and stylistic models that tend towards the mystical and are intended for an elect group of the initiated. Mallarmé and Valéry were its principal inspirers; later Eliot and the other [sic] Englishman, Wystan Auden (1907–73)'—Asor Rosa, *Storia europea*, p. 336. [Trans.]

peasant culture' that Levi had hoped for did not.[97] It was simply illusory to appeal to it to begin a populist discourse of a new type. The path and its outcomes were decided in advance.

The sociological and pseudo-literary writings of Danilo Dolci[98] (*Racconti siciliani* [Sicilian Tales, 1963] belong to an even more corrupt and decadent Levi-ism. In his case, one cannot separate the judgement on his work as a writer from that on his direct political intervention and participation. Dolci has often been criticized for the typically individualistic character of his efforts which always only partly reckoned with the existence of organized forces such as unions and parties, to which, conversely, a more mature political judgement would have assigned the direction of struggles and their use in the formation of a superior popular consciousness. But what has not been noted is that Dolci's individualist choice is derived from a certain concept of the people and a certain way of understanding the relationship—once again—between the intellectual and the people. When one understands the people—as Dolci did and does—as a shapeless mass, teeming with basic instincts, endowed with an infantile psychology and adult appetites, it is not possible to relate to it except pedagogically—that is, in final analysis, individually. From this stems the importance of the example and the necessity of a true secular mission. But one cannot have a missionary conception without mystical and religious content. Indeed, underlying Dolci's discourse is a set of Christian morals and hopes: Levian humanitarianism is blunted in a pliant atmosphere where the reference to goodness, fraternity and solidarity towards the poor takes on uniquely confessional tones. The peasants, fishermen, artisans and southern proletarians are changed back into the humble people of the Christian tradition.

---

97 'With these poems he not only established himself as a poet but also as the *true exponent of the new southern Italian peasant culture*, the expression and value of which can only be poetic (in the same way that another youth, Piero Gobetti, had played that role after the war for the workers and intellectuals of the north, but on a rational plane)'—Carlo Levi, Introduction to *È fatto giorno*. The singular juxtaposition of Scotellaro and Gobetti is also repeated in Levi's introduction to the new edition of *L'uva puttanella*, where he explains more clearly that 'both, by different routes and with a different character, demonstrate in exemplary fashion, how one can educate oneself by educating others, how one can win one's freedom and autonomy by recognizing and winning freedom and autonomy outside oneself, *in others, in the people*'; and that 'only in this formative revolution can the *values of history* be saved'.

98 Danilo Dolci (1924–97), sociologist, activist and poet; extremely active in southern Italy and Sicily, especially, for his fight against underdevelopment and the power of the Mafia. He was nominated for the Nobel Peace Prize on a number of occasions. [Trans.]

What is new in Dolci is that, having accepted popular humility as necessary and indispensable, he also attempts to become humble and renounce intellectual paternalism. But every regressive operation contains its opposite— the bad conscience of superiority, the subterranean anguish at being different and the voluntarist impulse to identity. Among other things, this explains why the stylistic and narrative solutions of the *Racconti siciliani* are ambiguous and imperfect: the attempt to perfectly mimic environment and psychology ends up as an extremely irritating faux naif attitude from which it emerges that, appearances notwithstanding, the author is an aesthete.

The *Terre del sacramento* [Lands of the Sacrament, 1950] by Francesco Jovine[99] does not exhibit the most obvious defects of Mediterranean literature, and so he appears to be a separate and solitary author, not of great stature but dignified and sometimes effective in developing his theme. We can reaffirm a judgement we made in 1961 about this Molisean writer ('Each rereading of *Terre del sacramento* takes something away from the enthusiasm with which we first read the book'[100]), with an even more negative inflection, which testifies to the inexorable flow of time. Some qualities survive this deterioration: his remarkable moral commitment, his robust narrative ability and the sobriety of his ideological framework. In contrast to Levian writers, Jovine gives little space to aestheticizing and decadent temptations; he goes only so far as to create around his characters a somewhat remote atmosphere, reminiscent of a peasant or rustic legend. Contrary to the Neapolitan authors, he does not submit to obvious folkloric tinges—he merely makes some references to the superstitious and naive world of peasant psychology. Conversely, his greatest limit is the acceptance and full application of a narrative–stylistic–ideological model that appears not to have grasped all the psychological, sentimental and ideal revolutions of twentieth-century art. In other words, the apparent paradox of Jovine lies in this: he is a more accomplished and mature writer than many of his contemporaries only because he seems deeply and seriously tied to the narrative tradition of the nineteenth century and hence is, at least structurally, older and more behind the times than them. The success of *Terre del sacramento*—within the narrow parameters permitted by the experiment— lies in the happy spontaneity with which peasant ideology expresses itself in

---

99 Francesco Jovine (1902–50), writer, journalist and essayist. [Trans.]
100 From a profile of Francesco Jovine published in *Nuova generazione* 4 (1961): 14.

the naive forms of the popular-rustic tale. There is no doubt that Gramsci, who detected '*in* Guerrazzi, *in* Mastriani, and *in our* few other *popular* writers' the only Italian exemplars of a 'modern humanism', of a 'sui generis modern secularism', would have liked this novel.[101] Jovine registers a rich and direct experience of the flow of provincial life in *Terre del sacramento*. This is note-worthy, especially if compared with the evident artificiality of so many other southern Italian works. The types of the various classes that he depicts—the gentlemen of the village, the lazy and parasitical landowners, the intelligent professionals saddened by a life without opportunity, the poor students, the wretched but tenacious yokels, hard workers but devoid of any awareness—have a flavour of truth and an undeniable sociological consistency. Around this human material Jovine weaves a historico-ideological design, in which Gramsci's reflections on the southern question play a large part. The protag-onist of *Terre del sacramento* is Luca Marano, a poor student, the son of yokels, who takes on the task of defending his maternal kin and refuses to betray them. This is unlike the usual behaviour of all those who, having struggled to escape the lower social strata, accept to live in that subordinate or almost servile condition typical of the minor southern Italian intellectual who, more often than not, is the tool of the bosses and the large landowners. It may be inter-esting to note two fundamental themes of Jovine's narratives come together in Luca which had previously been kept separate: the history of the minor southern Italian intellectual with his anxieties and his limitations, and the story of the peasantry oppressed not only by hunger and poverty but also by ignorance and superstition. Luca, however, is a new character; he is decisively marked by the birth of political consciousness and by the profound feeling of a necessary relation with the popular masses. In short, Luca is a Gramscian intellectual who refuses the task of intermediary to which he is consigned by the dominant social strata (the entire sub-plot concerning the relations with Laura Cannavale clearly alludes to this potentially regressive solution to the problem); he establishes a lively, working connection with the peasants which remains (necessarily at the start) on an affective plane but already begins to anticipate the possibility of a different, more profound and organic contact, inspired by a clear progressive politico-ideological vision. The ideological anal-ysis of Luca's character cannot correctly evaluate his true proportions and his real character unless we add that nearly the entire story of *Terre del sacramento*

---

101 Gramsci, *Letteratura e vita nazionale*, p. 107 / *Selections from Cultural Writings*, p. 211. [Asor Rosa inserted and italicized the preposition *in* replacing the article *il*.—Trans.]

takes place within a *mythological atmosphere*. Here, the Gramscianism of the author becomes fused with (at the same time as it contradicts) a conception of the popular that is a little older and more provincial. At a glance, Luca is a Gramscian intellectual; if we consider his figure in a more comprehensive manner, he is a peasant hero, a figure from a saga. Here Jovine takes up again some of the most typical themes of Italian populism (our thoughts turn once again to Pratolini: think of Maciste from *Cronache*, of Metello). Luca Marano is very handsome, tough, lucky in love, soberly dressed, rich in ingenuity and intuition. Even physically he stands above his yokel relatives. In contrast to them, he escaped without much effort from the shadows of superstition and clerical obscurantism, almost as if by a natural reaction. From this perspective, Jovine is prepared to force the typological verisimilitude of the character so as to accentuate his exemplary nature and almost epic strength. Even before he dies, the yokels speak of him as if he were outside of time and, accepting his great superiority, contribute to confining him to a legendary dimension:

> The peasants went around convincing themselves that Luca knew everything that could be known about their interests, their individual story as well as that of their families. They didn't say: 'Luca knows' but 'Luca remembers'. It was as if the exact age of the young man had disappeared for them and Luca was the same age as all the yokels of Morutri.[102]

Killed by the fascists and the *carabinieri* who had formed a coalition for the protection of property, Luca enters the realm of peasant myth through the collective grief of the women of Morutri, like Saint Michael the archangel, temporarily defeated but in fact immortal. All this can be moving and full of pathos within well-defined sentimental limits, but it merely confirms Jovine's rustic orientation—his interpretation of Gramscianism is correct, but for that very reason demonstrably disappointing. Pratolini had been much more successful in mixing populist epic, legend and celebration. Jovine had a stronger sense of the human drama than the Florentine writer, and a laudable vein of melancholy and pessimism, but not enough to save his talent from the constitutive limitations of his orientation and ideology.

With the establishment—over a short period of time—of these regional, provincial and rustic tendencies, the populist ideology of anti-fascism unwittingly enters its crisis phase. We say, 'unwittingly', because in these years the

---

102 Francesco Jovine, *Le terre del sacremento* (Turin: Einaudi, 1950), p. 381.

democratic and populist euphoria was still very widespread. But it is clear today that, in the writers and works examined in this chapter, the process of emptying out and repetition is already very advanced; we are no longer on the crest of a wave but close to capsizing. Before turning to the crisis of populism and the final attempt to save it by the explicit summoning up of the lumpen-proletariat, we must examine some of the ways in which the populist literature of the period was tackled by Marxist critics. It is easy to conclude that the absence of clear alternative proposals not only helped to spread the stalest and most provincial forms of populism but also that this absence stood in the way of the positive crisis of certain historical and literary standpoints; that is to say, it prevented new proposals alien to the democratic equivocation of the preceding years from emerging. The result was that the evident death on the creative plane of anti-fascist ideology was only accepted with great difficulty on the critical and theoretical one. This favoured the perpetuation—beyond all expectations—of positions that had by now simply crystallized and, hence, were sterile.

16

Many of the constitutive elements of critical Marxist positions had already been elaborated in Antonio Gramsci's *Prison Notebooks*. If the following pages seem to move rather too quickly, it is because we are trying to avoid repetitions and will therefore refer back to earlier judgements about Gramsci's concept of the national-popular and its theoretical and interpretative consequences. From the start, however, it must be said that the literary criticism of the intellectuals tied to the Communist Party, when it does not simply reprise democratic positions, can be more correctly defined as Gramscian rather than Marxist. This distinction means—at least as far as cultural and literary problems are concerned—that Gramsci's teaching leads militant-intellectuals of the workers' movement away from the pure vein of Marx's thought; and that it funda-mentally serves as a vehicle for the spread of generically progressive and anti-fascist positions without any serious class content. Proof of this is that when theoretical reflection seeks to return to a more serious and profound reading of Marx's texts at all levels, the Gramscian line (which runs from Gramsci to his followers) will be decisively overcome or refuted. In substance, Gramscianism in literature and literary criticism is characterized by pure and simple conser-vation; it is the expression of a heightened and sectarian predominance of ideology over the scientific and class analysis of historico-social and historico-cultural phenomena. The framework within which this mentality and method is inscribed is still that of the general conviction (an aspect of a veritable world picture) according to which the workers' movement and Marxist thought are inheritors of the best part of the bourgeois cultural tradition. This conviction is very much alive on the political as well as the historical plane.[103] On the historico-cultural and the historico-political plane it means that the Gramscian critic does not consider anything that concerns his humanist-democratic formation as alien. The boldness of these recoveries knows no limit—once the mechanism of a gradualist and reformist vision of culture is activated, one can go, to give some concrete examples, from Mazzini to Spaventa,[104] passing via

---

103 Ottavio Pastore has written: 'We are the liberals of the twentieth century because we fight to give greater freedom to the greatest number of people'—'I liberali del secolo XX' [Liberals of the Twentieth Century], *L'Unità* (31 August 1948). Radice and Salinari insist strongly in their interventions—see 'Dibattito sulla cultura marxista' [Debate on Marxist culture], endorsed by *Il contemporaneo* 3(15–20)—on the concept of communism as 'true liberty' and as the supreme expression and embodiment of all authentic liberal demands. In turn, Manacorda testifies to the Risorgimento-style nationalism that would be the crystallized form of Gramsci's reflections: 'On 20 September, Rome continues to celebrate, as it celebrated yesterday, its festival, the birthday of the Italian capital. And the entire Italian nation will continue celebrating the day when the greatest obstacle to Italian unity was removed'—'L'eredità del XX settembre' [The Legacy of September 20], *L'Unità* (21 September 1949). [20 September is celebrated as the day of the liberation of Rome and national unification. The public holiday was abolished during the period of Fascism.— Trans.]

104 As Manacorda stated in *L'Unità* (2 June 1949):

> Perhaps not a single page of Mazzini would survive our criticism today, perhaps not an entire period of his political action, but a thousand fragments and a thousand acts of his thought and his action *continue to form a legacy that can be taken up today* by the class and the party that lead the Italian people beyond the point that Mazzini had reached. Being aware of the historical limits of his work means not just recognising *his true greatness*, it means also and, above all, that *if the ends set by Mazzini*—national unity and the secular democratic republic—are today proposed to the Italian people with much greater hope of success, this is due to the fact that the working class forces *to which Mazzini looked with confidence*, have directly taken on, through their party, the responsibility of leading the political struggle and *have at the same time recognized the truth of this part of his teaching* [. . .]

Also the following of Manacorda's judgement on Spaventa, where through the obvious contraposition of classical liberalism and 'clerical liberalism', one even ends up reprising the 'topicality' of the thought of a 'man of the right', as the Neapolitan thinker had unequivocally been:

De Sanctis, Croce and the endless ranks of those *meridionalisti* intellectuals—but always with a pronounced preference for thinkers of the idealist and democratic (or even liberal) current. Gramsci is himself assimilated to this outlook and ends up being at once its proponent and victim. It is no coincidence that in reviewing his *Passato e presente*, Salinari comes out with this statement which, although not new, is expressed with originality, because it ties into a consistent bundle of choices the political line of the party, a progressive cultural attitude and the necessary presence of a political culture:

> [F]rom here stems the conviction that, in the same way as in the fields of economic structures and political institutions it falls to the working class to take up the reins of the democratic-bourgeois revolution, which had been interrupted at birth, and to carry on by putting a break on the process of involution that pushes the bourgeoisie to renege on its own achievements, so in the field of culture it falls to the intellectuals tied to the progressive movement to take up and carry forward the revolutionary demands of that bourgeois culture strangled by the narrowness of our ruling class and threatened with death by clerical obscurantism.[105]

In turn, Muscetta, returned to the theme of the need for Marxism to put to work the progressive bastions of great bourgeois thought:

> We must discuss seriously with the neo-Enlightenment thinkers, the neo-positivists and neo-Aristotelians; but with all respect for their

---

From the liberalism of Silvio Spaventa, who *at least* aspired to identify with the state and with the country as a whole, we have arrived today at clerical liberalism, which goes no further than the narrow defence of immediate class interests and subordinates the state and its apparatuses entirely to it, *without even attempting any more* to maintaining action in a higher sphere of general national interests—'Silvio Spaventa e lo stato liberale' [Silvio Spaventa and the Liberal State], *L'Unità* (20 July 1949).

105 From Carlo Salinari's review of Gramsci's *Passato e presente*, *L'Unità* (15 January 1952). This reading is further confirmed by Mario Alicata:

I may be wrong but I think that *the construction of Marxist culture in our country must go through the struggle for the construction of the great movement of a free, modern, national culture* of which Marxism should represent the axis, the sinews, the soul, a soul that is not scholastic, not made up of quotations and expectations and illuminations from above of course, but a living soul which, in order to be living, must be securely anchored in praxis . . .—'Troppo poco Gramsciano' [Not Gramscian Enough], *Il contemporaneo* 3(26) (30 June 1956).

authoritativeness, I do not believe that we need to set aside Diderot and Pietro Verri, Helvétius and the abbot [Ferdinando] Galiani, nor barter Bertrando Spaventa for [Carlo] Cattaneo, Antonio Labriola with [Filippo] Turati, Hegel for Aristotle, or vice versa, with the futile pretence that the questions of our time are new.[106]

He thus ended up giving a somewhat restricted bourgeois sense—including in the fanciful use of certain images—to the revolutionary process of the working class, to which the sincere spirit of revolt alone could not make credible a non-credible 'historical appeal'.

In order to build socialism the proletariat cannot retrace the path of the passive revolution that the Italian bourgeoisie—lacking Jacobin militants—pursued under the leadership of liberal Catholicism. Today it cannot do this because it does have a leader and this leader, for as long as they make use of it, belongs by historical right to the *Jacobins of our proletariat*, to the Communist Party and to all the other socialists who have been able to and will be able to remain *modern Jacobins*.[107]

Such positions could have given birth to a profoundly and originally populist criticism. But we can't say that this took place. The truth is that progressive, activist and political concerns overwhelmed any attempt to give a more precise definition to the theme of this new, popular and national art. On better inspection, none of the Gramscian critics show any serious commitment to going beyond mere general statements. For all of them, the national-popular remains a vague, indistinct aspiration instead of a properly thrashed out and profound problematic. Consider how generic Salinari's description of a phenomenon such as post-Resistance neorealist literature is—not to speak of the prospective for its future he provides:

---

106 Pietro Verri (1728–97), philosopher, economist and historian. Ferdinando Galiani (1728–87), economist and leading figure of the Italian Enlightenment. Bertrando Spaventa (1817–83), Neapolitan philosopher; helped spread the influence of Hegel into Italy; served three times as a member of parliament; supported universal suffrage. Carlo Cattaneo (1801–69), philosopher, patriot and writer; played an important role in liberating Milan from Austrian rule in the insurrection of 1848; had profound faith in reason and its capacity to transform society which he thought needed to be carried out collectively. Filippo Turati (1857–1932), sociologist and one of the most important leaders of Italian socialism.

107 Carlo Muscetta, 'I poveri fatti' [The Poor Facts], *Il contemporaneo* 3(16) (21 April 1956).

It presented itself [. . .] as a *committed* art against the sort of art that tended to avoid the real problems of our nation; it polemically opposed new contents (partisans, workers, strikes, bombardments, firing squads, land occupations, shackdwellers, shoeshines, street-walkers) to the art of pure form and soft memories [. . .]; it attempted a radical change in expressive forms that underlined the break with the preceding art and could express the new feelings more effectively.[108]

Without disputing the last claim, which appears false *in re*,[109] this way of bundling up contents, themes, motifs, without even attempting to rediscover in them the presence of various sociological levels and hence of different literary and documentary commitments, seems very significant. Salinari offers a sort of *summa* of progressivism, animated by a fundamentally moralistic and ideological impulse ('Neorealism was nourished [. . .] first of all by a new way of looking at the world, by a new morality and ideology that characterized the *anti-fascist revolution*'[110]); but he says nothing precise about the properly sociological dimension of the problem. Were we to follow this critique to its conclusion, we could say that Gramscian culture is weak as a whole because it lacks an objective and historical idea of the Italian people to which it must, however, continuously refer because of the its general framework. Within it we can find progressivism, democratism, the ideology of populism, but it lacks populism itself as a lively and original take on reality, as the consciousness of a profound relationship with a determinate social reality. The aristocratic tradition and paternalism of the typical Italian bourgeois intellectual reverberate even in Gramscian-Marxist culture and criticism.

However paradoxical it may seem, the reasons why these Marxist critics cannot be said to be working class are the same for which they are not populist. At base, we have a banal terminological confusion which reveals a profound

---

108 Carlo Salinari, *La questione del realismo* [The Question of Realism] (Florence: Parenti, 1960), p. 41.

109 Salinari clearly alludes to neorealism's break with the 'formalist' art of twentieth-century Italy; but remains silent about this little detail: such a break is promoted in the spirit of a general return to the expressive forms that were typical of the nineteenth century (as will become clearer below). From this perspective, the phenomenon is without any real innovative capabilities, unless we consider what is modern to be that which is closest to the day before yesterday than to yesterday.

110 Salinari, *La questione del realismo,* p. 41.

theoretical uncertainty. The absence of a deep reflection on the concept of class leads, almost as a direct consequence, to the lack of a deeper reflection on the concept of the people. *The people and the industrial working class are, in common parlance, synonymous*; discussion slides from one term to the other, from one concept to the other, almost without the critic realizing that between them lies an abyss. Speaking of Pasolini's 'ideal world', Salinari writes that it exhibits 'a relationship between him and the people, that is, between the modern intellectual who is aware of the crisis of capitalism but is nourished by history and the working class'.[111] And there is a general spread of terms such as 'popular classes', 'popular strata', 'popular bloc of workers and peasants' to signify that undifferentiated compound of subaltern social forces in which real entities such as the working class and the people are enveloped and submerged without distinction. It follows that the sociological reference is, in both cases, extremely ambiguous: not only does the working class lose its vital qualities in this sea of democratism, but the indications and perspectives of criticism are not even able to provide the people with a definite physiognomy. On the plane of individual judgements, the dominant trait is that of a vague empiricism: populism is at once solicited and fought, misunderstood and favoured. The most original and advanced forms of populism of this period pay the price for this attitude whereas the more sporadic and inconsistent manifestations draw succour from it, directly or indirectly.

It is no coincidence that Gramscian criticism has shown little understanding and even less of a liking for the most typical examples of Resistance and anti-fascist populism, such as Pratolini's *Cronache* and Levi's *Cristo*. Works such as these reveal two faults: the evident attachment to some of the great sources of twentieth-century inspiration, and the inadequate rigour of the ideological framework. The critical discourse was unable to enrich the concept of the people that those writers had advanced, even if only ambiguously and sometimes confusedly; at best, following the classical forms of ideology, they had opposed to it the concept of the people that the party promoted as the material basis of its political action in a no less ambiguous and confused manner. The truth is that, on the descriptive-sociological plane, the writers knew more about the people than the critics. Overlooking this fundamental point of anti-fascist literary production, which is fundamental not just because of the sociological verisimilitude of the documents but also for the felicitousness and

---

111 Salinari, *La questione del realismo*, p. 143.

the novelty of the artistic invention, the entire effort of the Gramscians was dedicated to channelling the spontaneous ferments of progressivism into more ideologically correct frameworks. This means, first of all, the refusal of all the experiences of Decadentism and avant-gardism, the explicit demand to return to the nineteenth century and the desire—even when it comes to the artwork—to make a democratic and humanitarian conception of the world coincide with the forms of a clear, rational realism. Salinari lamented the difficulties of giving birth to a serious neorealist narrative movement, attributing them to the fact that 'our writers have not had the courage to break with the decadent tradition, to overcome the great examples of Proust and Joyce and return to the lessons of nineteenth-century Russian and French realism'.[112] Second, the Gramscian tendency of considering the artwork from a politico-pedagogical perspective served to bolster those elements of programmatic realism and sententious moralism that democratic-Marxist criticism drew from its own development and tradition. The *ideal* result of these positions—never explicitly and deeply theorized but often subordinated to oscillations and uncertainties even of a tactical sort—could have been *a type* of artwork in which the realistic robustness of the formal framework was an appropriate bearer of progressive ideological and political values. Even in this case, however, on the literary plane, we never get further than simple statements of principle. For a direct theoretical grasp of this critical attitude, we will have to rest content with some brief comments in which Salinari summarizes the sense of his argument in 'La sorte del romanzo contemporaneo' [The Fate of the Contemporary Novel]:

> [I]t seems evident that today one cannot write a novel as one did in the nineteenth century; but it seems no less evident that today—in the same way as yesterday—we cannot write without two fundamental elements that lie at the basis of all narrative, that is to say, a *narrative axis* that supports the work, and the development of *character* around which the events unfold.[113]

With this quotation, we return to the starting point. One could only establish a necessary relationship between 'ideological awareness' and 'artistic success' by wholly condemning the most vigorous and modern elements of

---

112 Carlo Salinari, 'Tre errori a Viareggio' [Three Errors in Viareggio], *Il contemporaneo* 1(22) (28 August 1954).

113 Salinari, *La questione del realismo*, p. 179.

twentieth-century art, in which this link is more often than not absent and frequently denied or even *criticized*. One could only put 'character' at the centre of artistic creation if one gave up the examination of the nature of capitalist society, ignoring some classical Marxist analyses of the alienation of the person in such a society, and substituting for the perhaps partial effort to understand reality the cliché of a humanity that can be disassembled and reassembled at will, according to the laws of an apparently sectarian moralism which is actually reformist and petty bourgeois.

We should not be surprised that, since it was subjected to such critical pressure (with equivalents in the visual arts and cinema), progressive and anti-fascist literature tended to produce results that were increasingly less lively and instinctive and ever-colder and schematic. One must recognize today that Pratolini, in going from *Cronache* to *Le ragazze di Sanfrediano* and on to *Metello*, was obeying specific ideological indications as well as betraying a loss of inspiration. In *Metello* (1955), narrative replaced chronicle; a human being leapt out from the anonymous crowd of caricatures; the passage from nature to consciousness prevailed over the pure and simple celebration of nature; a rooted socialist conviction issued from the necessary historico-social-individual passage away from the vague populist and anarchic hopes of the past; the realistic narrative form took the place of the earlier lyricism which was itself rich in results but no longer applicable to the new experiences. What more could have been hoped for from an author if not this honest adherence to the fundamental principles of the Italian route to socialist realism? The discussion surrounding *Metello* revealed, in the tangle of often contradictory judgements, the splits among the group of Gramscian critics as well as the general inability to overcome the terms of the problem as they had been posed by the very protagonists of that tendency. The populism of Gramscian origin proved to be a dead end precisely when it appeared to be welcomed and put into practice by one of the greatest of contemporary writers. But just like in 1945, when the fundamental examples of anti-fascist literature were taken as the starting points for a forward-looking cultural perspective, whereas they were only the culmination of the earlier labours, so ten years later it was not understood that—in its limitations—*Metello* was the final, supreme effort to make the form of a genuine populism coincide with the dictates of Gramscian poetics. This was erroneously considered to be the occasion for a debate that, one way or another, was intended to be *positive*, that is, to count as a *further* deepening or a new and more serious application of the *same* ideological principles from which Pratolini had set out. The truth is that it was not the work or its author that needed to be questioned but, rather, the ideological climate and the political reasons that inspired them. Failure to realize this meant, for many, restricting the debate within narrow limits and thereby renewing the general risk of misunderstanding and error; and doing so at the very same time as specific instances of the debate were being bitterly criticized.

We can say today that Salinari was right when he identified *Metello* with the Gramscian ideological position, even if he was obviously wrong to accord it artistic success. *Metello* exemplified the cultural policy of the Communist Party, faithfully reproducing many of its characteristics. In this sense, it can reasonably be thought to be the positive result of a decade of ideological and political influence. As Salinari wrote, it 'captures the moment of expansion of the postwar Italian populist movement, the fusion of popular experiences (the struggle for survival, poverty, solidarity and friendship) with the anti-fascist one, and with the change in social consciousness.'[114] Muscetta was equally correct in denouncing the artistic imperfections and frequent concessions to the idyll, to *bozzettismo*[115] and *Sanfredianismo* in *Metello*; and yet he was wrong to find the reason for these deficiencies in the weakness of the 'historico-ideal framework', in the inability of the writer to elaborate a robust and convincing historical structure, in the absence 'of a deepening of the ideal motifs that must lead the popular movement towards socialism and which have become so fervent ever since the victory of the Chinese revolution until the present day'.[116] *Metello* suffered from an overabundance of ideology, not from its absence. It was an ideological novel *par excellence*; its limits—beyond the author's personal ones—were the limits of an ideology and of a determinate form of populism.

Only Franco Fortini[117] took this line when he argued that 'the debate on *Metello*, is less concerned with the truths to be found in that novel, [it] is a

114 Salinari, *La questione del realismo*, p. 48.

115 The tendency of an author to use a sketch or draft [*bozetto*] as a narrative technique. This is often used in a somewhat derogatory sense, to imply a certain superficiality in the representations this technique provides. [Trans.]

116 Carlo Muscetta, *Realismo e controrealismo* [Realism and Counter-Realism] (Milan: Cino del Duca, 1958), p. 103.

117 Franco Fortini (1917–94), essayist, translator, cultural commentator and one of the foremost Italian poets of the twentieth century. Over the course of many decades, Asor Rosa engaged in debate with Fortini, although he also recognized the latter's great abilities and the cultural and political affinity that linked them. Summarizing a crucial bone of contention in a textbook on Italian literature, Asor Rosa writes:

conflict about the evaluation of historico-political reality and about the type of "choice" that the critic-reader and, even more, the critic-leader must make'.[118] Therefore, the question did not concern *Metello* so much as the historico-politico-ideological framework. This was what Fortini defined with the felicitous expression 'Metellism':

> *Metello* is a book in which the problematic of that sector of Italian society of which we have spoken, and which we might call the Italy of neo-bourgeois pseudo-sociality (accentuating the decorative, confirmatory character of the book, its lack of moral decisiveness, and so its lack of 'interest'), is in no way absent from the structure, language, subject, historical 'time' and *ethos* of the narrator. *Metellismo* is the (historico-political more than literary critical) attitude that explicitly *denies* the primacy of that sector. And denies it also *to the extent* that the politics of the Italian left are in fact the politics of social reforms, a politics 'of transition'. Proof of this is the social-democratic

---

His conviction that every type of [literary/cultural political] engagement can be absorbed, commodified and distorted by the capitalist society in which we live [. . .] does not cause him simply to abandon poetry but, rather, to rigorously purify it of all political immediacy, entrusting to its *formative* and *ordering* capacity the function of alluding to a human and social dimension that is different and opposite to that in which we live. In this we can see—in addition to the intelligent overcoming of the contradictions contained in the more vulgar forms of contemporary literary [political] engagement—the reprise of a *utopian tradition* that is well established in European poetry, from the German Romantics to French surrealists. The one objection that could be levied against this argument is that one might well poison the wells and hide one's tracks (which is to say one might continue today to write poetry, writes Fortini, 'only if it accepts to circulate without hope of returns or of echo', while being able to count on the fact that 'the literary use of language is homologous to that formal use of life that is the aim and the end of communism'), but we are then justified in asking what distinguishes Fortini's progressive utopia (who through form wishes to indicate a *future*) from Montale's conservative utopia (who through form wishes to freeze a *past*). Probably nothing, and that is probably how it should be (since for both it is a case of 'poetry'). But what sense is there then in relating poetry to communism, if not for the somewhat obvious one that everything we do is related to that which others do—which is to say with *History*—independently of the greater or lesser quantity of *ideology* that we inoculate it with?—*Sintesi di storia della letteratura italiana* (Florence: La Nuova Italia, 1972), pp. 459–60. For further reflections on the polemics between Fortini and Asor Rosa, see Alberto Toscano, 'Translator's Introduction: The Labour of Division' in Fortini, *A Test of Powers*, pp. 29–35. [Trans.]

118 Franco Fortini, *Dieci inverni* (Milan: Feltrinelli, 1957), p. 100.

conception of the function of literature and the novel: its edifying, emotive, enthusiastic and confirmatory function, which is the opposite of the critical-educational one of revolutionary literature. Proof of this is the illusion that in the current phase of Italian political economy, novels and films can play a 'progressive' and 'popular' function that is not retrograde; this illusion is born of the improper transposition, in our time, of the progressive function exerted by national-popular literature in a now waning phase of the bourgeoisie (Gramsci's error) and of the progressive function exerted by socialist literature in contemporary socialist countries.[119]

Stated in this way, this argument could be usefully developed through to its final consequences. The populism that we might term 'classical'—the populism of the nineteenth-century democratic tradition, anti-fascism and the Resistance—ossified and died within the structures of ideological discourse. Superimposed upon and aggravating the exhaustion of classical populism's problematic was an evermore decisive shift in contemporary socio-historical reality. The populist-Gramscian ideology and the class reality advance, from this moment on, through a typical scissor movement: the movement of crisis and difficult conjunctures. Little by little, as the 'rules' of the subject matter solidify and become clearer, enabling writers such as Pratolini to escape from 'ideological confusion' and move towards completely lucid informative concepts, the 'game' that inspires these rules finds itself evermore distant from the real conditions of the historical process. Ideology and reality no longer correspond, not even in a moralistic or propagandist tension. Speaking of the people, representing the people, celebrating the people becomes *ever-easier* at the political and civic level; and always more *useless* and *unproductive* at the artistic and literary level. Neo-capitalism and the working class construct *new rules of the game* for themselves. On a daily basis, the 'people' is a concept that democracy accepts and applies as one of the most mystified instruments of its stability. The populist polemic is reabsorbed by the very development of things. The populist polemic dies—once again without realizing it—when Italy goes from being a backward country to an economically and socially developed nation. The real mass existence of the working class emerges, in its naked and striking autonomy, from the broken links of populist ambiguities. Between the ideologists of the workers' movement and the class itself there is

---

119 Fortini, *Dieci inverni*, p. 101.

no longer any relation. It is increasingly less possible to pass off the literature of the 'working people' (nostalgic, backward looking, conservative, reactionary) as working-class literature. It is not by chance that the 'objective' crisis of Gramscian populism shows that the true addressees of this art are the contemporary petty bourgeoisie, who can be easily steered and influenced by a discourse that makes sentimental appeal to themes such as 'the struggle for existence, poverty, solidarity and friendship'. The working class remains *beyond* all this. Populism does not touch it, because it experiences a daily refusal of the small hopes and prudent objectives that typify popular reformism across history. *Progressive* discourse is broken down by reality's concrete development no less than by its own internal contradictions.

The attempt to re-establish a new equilibrium for progressivism and lead it towards new positions turns out to be extremely difficult and, finally, impossible. The crisis of *Metello* not only puts an end to all hope of practically realizing the Gramscian national-popular but also discovers that two souls coexist within it which are destined to become separated from this point onwards. Muscetta's national-popular exists on a very solid trunk composed of a democratic and an enlightenment tradition. At a closer glance, perhaps only in him do we find the will to clarify the terms in which a concept of tradition is revealed and how it operates. Among Muscetta's literary preferences there are, notoriously, people like Boiardo[120] and Belli, both of whom he appreciates for their powerful populist charge. This lively inclination to distinguish, within the historical furrow of our literature, the 'true' from the *false popular* leads him—even if only implicitly—to sketch a line of continuity between the experiences that are genuinely closer to the aspirations and sorrows of the common people. His love for Padula and Viviani bears witness to and exemplifies the type of internal discussion to which the critic refers when he is placed before the concrete artistic expressions of contemporary populism. To the follower of a perhaps rustic but serious and genuine populism, lacking in intellectual morbidity and complacency, the aesthetic and literary limits of Pratolini, Levi or Scotellaro's populism will have appeared evident. But Muscetta's populism also failed to overcome a fundamental choice: having

---

120 It is not by chance that on two occasions, while writing his review of Alcide Cervi's books, Muscetta is reminded of Boiardo's *Orlando innamorato*: the first time as an expedient to create the appropriate atmosphere with regard to the narration of Cervi, the father; the second, as a direct reference to style (see Muscetta, *Realismo e controrealismo*, p. 117 and p. 123).

exhausted all that Pratolini could offer, his attention fixes upon, is aroused by and consumed in a discussion of *I miei sette figli* [My Seven Sons, 1955] by Alcide Cervi who, we regret to admit, represents the *summa* of the well-to-do peasant communism that for so long marked the humanitarian bourgeois ideology of the left-intellectual movement. The painful recollections of the father of the seven heroes of the Resistance are closely interwoven with the productivist cult of the earth (that is, the pride in carrying out one's trade well), the benevolent understanding of human solidarity, the fundamental idea that Christianity and socialism, if not one and the same, are at least dependent upon one another, and the respect for the motherland, of progress, of liberty and of democracy. Politically we are presented with nothing more than the programme of solidarity of the Reggio Emilia socialist tradition that goes from Camillo Prampolini[121] to municipal and administrative communism.[122] This is a picture of society and political struggle from which the class struggle and class hatred are absent even in the guise of an instinctive feeling (conflicts with the bosses are fundamentally questions of method: how one manages the land, technological innovations, etc.). At best there is the conviction that the clash between rival factions could be resolved through an act of goodwill, with the fraternal union of all the good people against injustice and evil. Popular wisdom expresses its most solid and durable credo: If something is good, why not do it? If someone or something is bad, what prevents everyone, united, from fighting and beating them in the name of hope in the good?[123] Muscetta admires Cervi's book for the sincerity of the feelings

---

121 Camillo Prampolini (1859–1930), socialist politician. [Trans.]

122 Alcide Cervi, *I miei sette figli* (Rome: Editori Riuniti, 1955), p. 33:

> Let us help bring up the kids without difficulties and illnesses; let us help disabled workers; let us build nurseries and schools; let us provide work, us, the organizers of the exploited and the unemployed. It is because we want to look after our neighbours through the building of cooperatives, mutuals and political organizations—the symbols of the proletariat. This religion is all the more powerful if they are not repudiated by the better off peasants, the land managers of which there are quite a few in our province. With us, the further one goes the more one gives.

123 Cervi, *I miei sette figli*, p. 167:

> [E]very paterfamilias wants his children to be safe. There is only one means for this safety, *that Italians recognize themselves as brothers*, that they do not allow themselves to be divided by lies and hatreds, *that the unity of Italy is finally realized*, but as a unity of souls, the unity of patriotic hearts. I do not say this now

expressed in it. But it seems obvious to me that one can in no way agree with the critic's judgement, singling this story out as one of the works that 'marks the beginning of a new literature'.[124] In other words, the concept of the national-popular resulted in the utopia of a populism that was instinctive, immediate and avoided the mystifications of cultured literature, something that no critical hypothesis could reasonably consider as realizable in the objective historical conditions of the time.

With respect to the Gramscian criticism most directly inspired by the cultural politics of the party, the crisis of Resistance populism does not simply lead to the abandonment of the fundamental criteria of ideology. But, just as it was no longer possible to support the theoretical rationale of a calmly progressive populism, in a totalizing and schematic way, so it became necessary to recognize the validity of those populist forms that signalled the crisis in practice of traditional populism. Following the logic of their argument, the communist critics went so far as to include, within the uncertain arc of their commitment, increasingly ambiguous and heterodox understandings of the concept of the people, to the point that they found themselves judging and even celebrating the presence, in literature and poetry, no longer of the people but the lumpenproletariat. At this point, the merest appearance of Marxism vanished from their standpoint, and what remained was ideology in its most voluntarist and abstract form: mere question begging, contradicted at each instant by the painful and desperate reality of the works themselves. We must add that, at the endpoint of this trajectory, the extreme fidelity to certain principles had an adverse effect on criticism and its outlook. Pasolini, who had been viewed with considerable suspicion at the start when he manifested a respectable need for crisis and irrational revolt, was increasingly appreciated as his work gradually adapted to the forms and themes of the official ideology of the movement—that is, as he gradually fitted into pre-established frameworks

---

for political reasons, I have always thought so and if you've read the book you know it is the story of my whole family. Because if it were true that Catholics, communists and socialists cannot agree, then the history of my family would be destroyed—my family, which if it did anything positive, it was thanks to the strength of two faiths. If you say that one cannot agree, then the mother, who remained Catholic until her death, disagreed with her children, and I too will have been against her, repudiating the faith of my children's youth, which had been Christian—and *of this they took the best seed and united it with the great communist idea.*

124 Muscetta, *Realismo e controrealismo*, p. 124.

that were more political than aesthetic, more propagandist than exhortatory. And the judgement about Pasolini, which has always been conditional or, at least, hesitant ended up melting away only with the publication of the work that represented his highest moment of schematicism and didacticism. We refer, of course, to *Una vita violenta* [*A Violent Life*], a book that Salinari judges to be very important precisely because in it 'there is the character' and 'the unequivocal proposal of an ideological axis that supports the structures of the novel and of an ideological axis directed towards socialism'. The story of *Metello* was repeating itself. Tommasino Puzzilli, the Pasolinian Metello, was liked because one found in him the 'reintroduction of character, that is, the attempt to give to a person that organic form that had been destroyed by decadent literature'.[125] *Una vita violenta* was liked because it responded to a criterion of ideological caging of the poetic inspiration that even managed to wrap the party straitjacket of the prudent spirit of edification around the lumpenproletariat. Beyond the acceptance of the lumpenproletarian motif and the proven capacity to subordinate it to the old democratic and anti-fascist discourse, there is nothing else remarkable in this field today.

17

The final manifestations of Italian populism are born in a cultural and political atmosphere of crisis and opposition vis-à-vis the one described in preceding chapters.

With *Il taglio del bosco* [Woodcutting, 1953], *I vecchi compagni* [The Old Comrades, 1953] and *Un matrimonio del dopoguerra* [A Postwar Marriage, 1957], Carlo Cassola is already outside the Gramscian perspective of the national-popular. In his work, the myths of progressivism appear reversed: the people are represented as victims and not as protagonists of history. From his point of view, the refusal of political commitment is the singular demonstration of a much broader attitude. Behind his anti-communism is a radical lack of faith in human achievement, in the real possibility of world transformation. In his work, the Resistance—the linchpin of an entire cultural attitude or even vision of the world—is represented simply as a lost opportunity, or as the historical pretext for a new betrayal of the naive hopes of the people. *In this picture, populism can survive only as the enquiry into the elementary truths of humanity* which historico-social factors tend to conceal or suffocate. Whereas

---

125 Salinari, *La questione del realismo*, p. 183 and 180, respectively.

that collective intellect of History, which is the 'body of [communist] intellectuals' reveals, behind the more ambitious ideological formulations, a substantive ambiguity and dishonesty, the people, even in their spontaneous sectarianism, continue to give succour to an extreme, almost desperate survival of human values—'for me, as a non-communist, it has always been easier to talk to a worker than to a communist intellectual. The real barrier was not set by the worker who began by telling you: "You're a bourgeois, so I don't trust you"; this dotting of 'i's was proof of fidelity and frankness [. . .]. The real barrier was posed by the intellectual with his appeal to "what unites us not what divides us", which ultimately sounded like an appeal to muddle-headedness.'[126] The political dimension of the discussion is reduced to a vague liberalism or to an even vaguer democratism. Cassola's people has only a contradictory and desultory relationship with this political dimension which fails to make any impact on its true nature.

In Pasolini, the literary and ideological criticism is even more precise. The communist position is accused of 'tactical prospectivism', in other words, of having imposed a prefiguration of the real on literature, forcing it into a purely schematic approach or a merely edifying moralism. What failed in the communist position was the naive conviction that introducing a strong element of moral and political tension into the artwork would allow given conditions to be overcome or the future to be optimistically anticipated. In practice, the crisis of Resistance ideals (a crisis of realization stemming from an unanticipated strong conservative reaction) reveals that, even on the literary plane, it is necessary to go deeper if one wishes somehow to reconstruct a concrete and realistic need for overcoming and renewal. In other words, one must know, and know firmly and even cruelly, before one begins believing again in new myths and new values. 'The masses of the nation,' writes Pasolini in 1957, 'did not match up to the hopes placed in them by the minority leaders and workers—especially of the North. Italy was what it was; hope was more tautological than justified. The establishment of a new broadly national-popular style was presented as a utopia, as a verbal prolepsis.'[127]

The people remains both the end and the source of all aspiration to the good, to purity, to innocence. But it was necessary to arrive at a less politically

---

126 Carlo Cassola, 'Reazioni sentimentali' [Sentimental Relations], *Il contemporaneo* 3(19) (12 May 1956).

127 Pier Paolo Pasolini, *Passione e ideologia* [Passion and Ideology] (Milan: Garzanti, 1960), p. 342.

and ideologically mystified image of it. The concept of the 'working people' was now too compromised by its daily propagandist use and, furthermore, too contaminated by its natural propensity to act as a dynamic element of History. Beneath their commitment to labour, the people incubated far more determinate and precious living values; to rediscover these values was to corroborate a certainty in the world that was not bequeathed by History and the practical tasks of men. *Beyond or beneath the working people is the lumpenproletariat, the people in a pure state, denuded of History.* It is to them that Pasolini, the poet who critically observed the failure of all attempts to turn the ideological commitment of progressive historicism into the material of poetry, addresses himself.

Cassola and Pasolini come from the same crisis, they write in the same years, and are much more similar than they appear at first sight. The difference between their poetics and their works leap clearly to the eye: Pasolini's descent into the Underworld is not the same as Cassola's ascent to Limbo. The one pursues truth through the celebration of the elementary forces of existence, and ultimately conquers a grain of certainty having traversed the visceral and the sexual; the other moves towards a pale consolation by staking everything on the sentimental. The one gathers full-bodied, full-blooded, scintillating linguistic and stylistic instruments from all corners to express the dimensions of a reality that is materially and physically extremely dense; the other goes so far as to enervate his narrative discourse with stylistic elements so simple as to appear abstract, in order to glean from the world a highly reduced vital essence. Despite this, Cassola and Pasolini belong to the same historico-literary dimension; they are rivals and brothers of the process of dissolution of an Italian populism in crisis. Indeed, both *fundamentally* betray a refusal of History, a drastic abandonment of the progressive conception. *The one and the other effect a typically regressive operation: beyond becoming, to the sources of being.* The people once again becomes nature and, as such, fundamentally foreign to the changes brought about by time and contingency. Think only of the role that the motif of atemporality and naturalness plays in a writer such as Pratolini, to whom both Cassola and Pasolini owe something. Even in *Il quartiere* there is the attempt to see the objective immobility of the world of the people as a factor of protest; as an element, even if a contradictory one, of the inexorable flow of history. In this sense, Pratolini is a typical writer of the Resistance and anti-fascism. For the others, who really come after the Resistance and anti-fascism, the fundamental problem is not that of transformation and not even,

I would say, of living but, rather, that of surviving—better still, of existing. After progressive populism, we find the existential populism of Cassola and Pasolini: that is, populism transformed into a category of existence, into a metaphysical category, an abstraction of spirit. The subjective, lyrical and irrational element becomes predominant again. In the writers of the Resistance—for example, in the case of Pratolini or Levi—the path of *commitment* moves from the creator to objective reality. The deformation or lyrical interpretation of the real should never predominate—at least not in theory—over the respect for certain socioeconomic and historical qualities of the popular world being represented. In Cassola and in Pasolini, the creative process goes from the object to the subject, from reality as stimulus for sensations or sentiments to the spirit, the originary source—the only truly essential one—of those sensations and sentiments. The people, over and above being a category of existence, becomes the autobiographical image of the writer. The sociological datum is violated by the literary invention, to the point of being completely absorbed by it. The process of knowledge is turned back on itself: Cassola and Pasolini simply recognize their own image, *their own inner world* in that of the people or the lumpenproletariat.

In this sense too, an essential moment of the culture of anti-fascism and the Resistance is left behind. In Levi, Pratolini, Vittorini or Jovine, as in the ranks of the *meridionalisti*, there was an attempt to transfer literature entirely into life. Everything that went in the opposite direction was considered to be formalist and 'bourgeois'. The ideal would have been to create a work of art that moved in the world like an instrument of war, performing a directly social task without specifically literary residues. Cassola and Pasolini restore the predominance of literature, the former consciously and explicitly, the latter not without contradictions and compromises, but he too in quite a clear way. For Cassola, the only surviving value is precisely literature; we will see, however, that for him reality itself has no meaning until the writer recomposes it in the work of art through the patient work of style. For Pasolini, literature comes to establish a dialectical relationship with reality but remains the preeminent term of a discourse to which aestheticism and philology furnish the foundation and meaning. The historical cycle of the populist experience is closed with this return to the past. Having cultivated for some time the illusion of using the theme of the people as an instrument of rupture with an entire artistic culture, it becomes possible to recognize that it is not even sufficient to break the limits of a literary conception of the world. On the whole, Cassola and

Pasolini are closer to the Italian literature of the *Novecento*[128] than writers such as Levi, Pratolini, Pavese and so on. Do not be deceived by the novelty of the themes, which in Pasolini seem scandalously outside the tradition. What counts in him, as in Cassola, is the propensity to see the world through the filter of a cultural and literary ideology, where even the force of sentiments and passions is subordinated to a fundamentally stylistic enquiry.

Noting a final analogy between these two enables us to give an even more pointed meaning to their parallelism, the value of which indubitably is more historical than critical, more political than interpretive. Cassola and Pasolini begin to develop their decadent popular symbology at a time when the themes of Resistance and progressivism were still vital. Their first works are interwoven with others exemplifying national-popular ideology (*Metello* was not published until 1955). It is difficult to deny that they too come under the influence of the dominant climate of this period. This is demonstrated in their decision to focus on matters of popular concern. But they already labour under the substantial weight of their prior education, which for both falls outside the remit of committed politics. In the same way that Levi, Pratolini, Vittorini and Bilenchi had, since their youth or adolescence, nursed concerns of a political and social nature, so Cassola and Pasolini inaugurate their literary apprenticeship under the sign of a refined aestheticizing spirit. When their attention turns to representing the people, they will not forget the flesh and blood that had informed their previous years. But we have said this already. It is necessary now to take cognizance of the fact that populism does not become for Cassola and Pasolini something won or achieved once and forever, which is then held to with fixed determination and faithfulness. In effect, the Resistance writers show that they do believe their progressive choice is valid across the entire arc of Italian history and literary history. Cassola and Pasolini's populism bears within it the causes of its own dissolution. The search for ultimate existential truths inexorably corrodes the fabric of practical, concrete and historico-social truths to which it had briefly been led. At a certain point it becomes inevitable that it should re-emerge, naked and desperate, from the realist envelope that had contained and expressed it. Populism was insufficient (Cassola) or powerless (Pasolini) to convey that set of total values that the two bore within them, and which they mistakenly thought they could represent more concretely and

---

128 Literally, 'twentieth century', the term refers to a trend in Italian letters. For a discussion of the 1960s debate on the 'literary ontology of the *Novecento*', see Fortini, 'Clarifications' in *A Test of Powers*, pp. 115–24. [Trans.]

effectively through populism. In this situation, returning to the past becomes not only a historico-literary necessity but also an intimate, private one. The reprise of a nineteenth-century literary mythology is not only the involuntary homage to a climate that becomes prevalent again after the populist 'infatuation' but is also, and above all, the writer's positive recognition of the initial reasons for his vocation. It has not been noted enough that Pasolini and Cassola's work, by now sufficiently rich and mature to be judged in the round and perhaps even definitively, is perfectly circular in form. *Un cuore arido* [A Barren Heart] is closer to the stories *Alla periferia* [On the Outskirts] and *La visita* [The Visit] than it is to *La ragazza di Bube* [Bebo's Girl] or to a *Matrimonio del Dopoguerra* [A Postwar Marriage]. *La religione del mio tempo* [The Religion of My Time] and *Poesia in forma di rosa* [Poem in the Form of a Rose] return to the poetic experiences that preceded *Le ceneri di Gramsci* [Gramsci's Ashes], bypassing, denying and criticizing what Pasolini considers today the mortifying and disappointing experience of civic commitment and politico-ideological 'dedication'. Cassola *programmatically* reissues his juvenilia in *La visita*. Pasolini rediscovers his Christianity and launches it anew, decisively tipping in its favour the balance of the precarious equilibrium reached between religious spirit and Marxist convictions. The confession of populism's inadequacy could not be any more final. The two writers contribute with their work to the crisis of traditional populism. They gather the fruits of this crisis, attempting to establish a non-classical variant of the populist theme. But the way in which they posit the overcoming of a determinate literary and ideological attitude is already a crisis of the crisis—that is, a crisis without a functional antithesis. The history of the two authors now separates, as it had been separate at its distant formative origins. Cassola moves past the destruction of the populist myth, issuing in a renewed but always naive and provincial Arcadia of good sentiments. Pasolini enters the path of a tearful desperation, of self-pity, where the individualistic motifs become prevalent or, rather, exclusive. The one and the other, united once again, show the same complete blindness to the reality of the contemporary world. In this final phase, their egotism reaches extreme levels, exhausting itself as a fact that is no longer literary but personal.

In the field of populist literary experiences, before Cassola and Pasolini, there is a void. And it is clear why. Cassola has now repudiated populism's appeal: he can no longer serve as an authoritative model. Pasolini, on the other hand, inspires a series of lumpenroletarian imitations in literature and cinema. But it was inevitable that his indications, which were always informed by a powerful cultural awareness, would—among the imitators—dissolve into a mass of vulgarities. Attempts to follow his path were all the more ridiculous and painful to observe when a residue of vainly ambitious theorizations were overlaid on the often crude and summary representation of a squalid subject matter. In the case of Giovanni Testori[129]—this second-rate Carlo Bertolazzi— we may even be scandalized because 'today some still believe that a worker cannot commit a crime, without hurrying to track down the social, environmental and political causes'.[130] Indeed, 'tying that crime to the complexity of all the causes (that are not only social, environmental and political *but are also those that sink their roots into the bowels of existence*) appears to involve discrediting a class'. Testori is instead convinced that 'the real disgrace, the literal scandal is to act as if that class was deprived of the ability, strength, richness and autonomy to support such a gesture'. 'The truth lies in the opposite and History is there to prove it: when a class achieves the height of its consciousness it is ready to rediscover in itself *the sacred and undeniable institutions of its existence*'. In this way, the lumpenproletarian and pseudo-working class formation that the writer represents ends up as the materialized image of the higher world of truth. Like in Pasolini, after a fashion—but when it comes down to it without Pasolini's capacity to precisely identify this set of eternal values that underlie that materiality. Consequently, what comes to the forefront and camps out there uncontested is the other pole of the subject, the crudely physical and material one. The theme of sex, the whole range of its degenerations and pathologies, is at the centre of this particular dimension of proletarian life. Pimps, prostitutes, pederasts are the most typical interpreters and heroes of these roles. At this point, one clearly and definitively escapes populism. In full neo-capitalism, the development of society removes from the populist thematic both the space for manoeuvre and the meaning of the task of opposition and contestation. Yet the marginal social strata remain outside, or are indeed expelled from this process of absorption into the broad and welcoming structures of the system, like the detritus of a gluttonous mastication; notwithstanding the objective insignificance of these strata, left-wing writers throw themselves upon them, in a final burst of humanitarianism and

---

129 Giovanni Testori (1923–1993), playwright, writer and critic. [Trans.]

130 Giovanni Testori, Interview in *Mondo nuovo* 2 (1960), p. 45. The following quotations are drawn from this interview.

progressivism. Defeated at the level of historical commitment and conscious existence, the people sinks into its own viscera and dissolves. Once this operation is concluded, there is no longer a people, only shapeless sludge.

18

The overarching meaning of our analysis is that populism is responsible for much of Italian literary moderatism across the nineteenth and twentieth centuries. If the argument so far has been persuasive, this conclusion should not come as a surprise. Let us track down and fix this latest truth: the social commitment of the writer is insufficient to determine the substantive (literary, poetic) novelty of his work. The Italian experience (even if we want to abstain from overly general formulations) tends to demonstrate the opposite: the writer's social commitment is often at the expense of his inventive boldness; all the more so if, as happens in Italy, the content of the commitment shows itself to be retarded and limited. We do not want to repeat ourselves but we must reaffirm that the attention dedicated to a condition of sociohistorical underdevelopment for more than a century and a half has given rise to a literature fundamentally characterized by a monotony of themes and a dearth of discoveries. Obviously this does not mean that Italy remained actually immobile and devoid of an internal dynamic for so long; it means, rather, something much more serious—that it is the writers who remain closed, as in a prison, within a situation of historical, objective backwardness that suffocates their own ambitions of renewal or even revolution. To anchor one's research in this objective *level* meant, in practice, not having the strength to overcome it through a more decisive negation or a bolder, more mythical anticipation. The truth is that all the more staggering inventions and surprising paths of twentieth-century literature appear to be denied to Italian populism. There is nothing more alien to our populists than that avant-garde spirit from which spring all the actual literary 'revolutions' of the twentieth century. By persisting in gazing upon and commiserating with misery, hunger, the misfortunes of the subaltern classes, they remained enslaved to a climate of pedestrian humanitarianism and sterile protest. To listen to the populists, literature should serve only to console the afflicted and elevate the oppressed. For this reason, all too often they resort to the weapons of *sentiment* and the *heart*. Within the scope of their sensibility there is still place for a *positive* conception of the modern world where honesty, purity, goodness, naivety and sacrifice can be considered essential forces of human coexistence. In this way, the socioeconomic backwardness of Italy found its perfect equivalent (which should never have been the case) in the ideal categories invoked to support a certain transformative polemic. That was what Italy was like, so that is how its committed literature had to be. Naturalistic fidelity to the represented object served as a limit even on the plane of artistic enquiry. So it is not as arbitrary as it may at first appear to place alongside one another populists of democratic, nationalist, fascist, social-fascist, anti-fascist, Resistance and Gramscian origin. Populism follows the ideological path laid out by the bourgeoisie, gradually changing its attitudes, figures and myths. But what does not change is precisely the way of considering the function of literature to which is attributed a task that is directly social. Once it is assumed that, in his writings, the 'modern' writer cannot be disinterested in the problems of national development, the people become for him the projection, myth or material force in which his literary mission is embodied. It therefore appears logical—as well as historically proven—that the fascist social commitment is born out of the democratic social commitment; and that the anti-fascist social commitment should build upon the premises, ideas and postulates of fascist social commitment, and that there is an overall line of continuity rather than opposition that can be traced between these different experiences, from the end of the Risorgimento till today. While the literary horizon coincides with that of the nation, one can never exclude a process of development (or of contamination) of this sort. The literary moderatism of populism is also produced by the conviction that committed writers in practice accept—even when they explicitly deny that social commitment is at the same time national commitment—that there is no class progress in absence of national progress; that the progress of classes signifies the progress of the nation, and vice versa. To this principle, which is not refused either by democrats, fascists or anti-fascists, there corresponds on the literary plane an analogous inclination to consider as absolutely paramount all those problems—not just of content—which are rooted and exhaust themselves in the narrow world of Italy. One might say that the credo to which the Italian writers of commitment obey, whatever their political or ideological allegiance, is this: Let us first create an Italian literature that contributes to raising the entire country to the level of the most advanced situations; only then will we establish an Italian literature that is also European. Nationalists in the literary field, even when internationalists in politics, the populists could not escape from this well-trodden furrow.

Within the framework of this national tendency, the reference to the people, the very concept of the people, take on their full meaning as an 'obstacle' to a modern literary discourse. The notion of 'people' is the mythical receptacle of those pre-capitalist values that the writer opposes to the inevitable development of a certain sort of society. To represent the people is more often than not to embrace its tendency to immobility, the heterogeneous social factors that compose it, the nostalgia for the past that it always harbours against a backdrop of ambiguous sympathies, sometimes progressive and sometimes reactionary. Only very rarely is the creative effort of the writer able to turn this human and sociological material into a simple pretext for a much more general topic, the literary and ideological presuppositions of which can be found outside the tradition. More often than not it happens that the topic remains circumscribed by the local and provincial limits within which the people is historically manifested. In such cases, we end up learning about the Sardinians, the Sicilians, the Romans, the Florentines or the Piedmontese, but nothing about the conditions in which modern man finds himself living, acting and suffering. The widespread regionalism that marks Italian literature from the nineteenth century till today is ultimately based on the false assumption that an accumulation of particular truths is able to form a general truth. In practice, particular truths remain as they are and truth in general is not even touched upon; indeed, it hides behind the screen of a world that the populist does not even set himself the problem of discovering.

A series of strictly literary facts follow as a necessary consequence from what we have said. Respect for tradition leads to setting off on new and unused paths. The populist writer generally possesses a very lively sense of a stylistic, literary and formal inheritance that is already an integral part of his way of seeing and of resolving the problem of 'modern' Italian literature. The concept of 'nation' implies the reprise and conservation of an indigenous heritage that is valid not only on the ideological plane but also on the formal one. One cannot constitute *the* national literature by making the most of a cosmopolitan culture. If that is the objective, one needs suitable instruments. And so here too we see the predominance of continuity over innovation, of conservation over rupture. Post-Resistance regionalist literature is, as a whole, closer to the verist regionalism of the nineteenth century than to any of the literary forms of the European twentieth century. Pratolini is cognizant of all the Tuscans of the nineteenth and twentieth centuries, up to that Tuscan by election, Alessandro Manzoni—more than any other European writer his contemporary. Pasolini, despite his broad poetic culture, *as a civic poet* closely imitates models such as Carducci and Pascoli, while as an *intimist poet* he shows a broader capacity for reception and assimilation. In short, if we can say that the same poet, in the presence of options other than populism, behaves in a freer and more modern way, it is the populist commitment itself that calls for a more obvious and traditional set of linguistic decisions. Moreover, it is evident that one cannot perform the task of direct social and civic penetration without adopting linguistic forms that can be broadly appreciated; at the very moment that one sets oneself the problem of communicating and convincing, it is (generally speaking) necessary to descend to the expressive levels (as well as to the ideal level) of those to whom one's message is directed. In this case as well, the reference to populism shows itself to be an alibi (for the sometimes inventive laziness of the writers) and a brake (against possible attempts at renewal). The sociological representation of poverty—already weak as a theme and an idea—is given linguistically poor and commonplace forms because it is presented as a *means* the *end* of which is the progress of national society. Moreover, considering the work of poetry as the mere instrument of a broader and more essential sociopolitical discourse prevents the starting point, which is constituted by a determinate analysis, from giving way to a process of complete artistic transfiguration. More often than not, the determinate analysis also remains the most disappointing from the literary standpoint. Hence, there is an insufficient *interval* between the observation of reality and the linguistic result. What is typically sacrificed in this sort of literary procedure is precisely the task of metaphorical mediation assigned to poetry. Vulgar sociology and naturalism— forms that are so frequent in Italian populism—are the fruit of this mistaken inclination to draw something that is immediately socially useful from art.

These last observations should not, however, lead us to attribute Italian populism a greater documentary quality than it has. On the contrary, all our analyses have demonstrated that the sociological aspect of populism never prevails over the generically ideological or ideal one. The presence of objective data, even if powerful, can rarely be translated into a complex framework that has properly scientific validity. In our writers there is undoubtedly the cult of particular situations, the most striking effects of which are regionalism and municipal spirit. But just as it is difficult to find in their works a sufficient degree of linguistic and stylistic development (or revolution) to mediate between the occasional pretext and the general truth, so it happens that a certain hiatus establishes itself between the objective, documentary datum and the ideal proposition that stands opposed to it. The former often remains a coarse, shapeless or deformed observation point. The latter takes up all the space that twentieth-century literature reserves for theoretical discoveries and linguistic inventions. The lack of a serious scientific and positive spirit, from which stems this incapacity to create a truly great and properly sociological literary practice, is but the other face of a very powerful ideological charge, which is also common to populists of all tendencies. Whatever one says, even this widespread inclination to ideological reasoning is the reflection of a situation of social and cultural underdevelopment, the residue of a nineteenth-century mentality. The great experiences of the European avant-garde all set out from the critique of the very concept of ideology as it had traditionally been understood, each time repudiating, dissolving or producing a deliberate parody of it. Where the bourgeoisie had completed its process of maturation and crisis earlier and more profoundly, the world of values upon which it had supported itself in the period of growth and apogee underwent a precocious and prophetic rupture in the intuitions of artists and writers. In situations such as these, when one does not merely—as happens more often than not—take cognizance of the current disintegrated state of things and instead attempts to turn to the future, the prediction always ends up affirming that the crisis will widen and become sharper. Italian populism comes before all this; the choices it made till today were made as if the experiences of the great avant-gardes had not even been broached; as if an extremely high level of consciousness and self-awareness had not been reached by the evolutionary process of European culture. Consequently, for Italian populism, forecasting the future is *always* an optimistic faith in the progressive (or progressivist) re-composition of the crisis which can be achieved through the conquest or miraculous reappearance of imperishable human values that pass unscathed throughout the storm of the modern world. Ideological 'prefiguration' and ideal 'outlook' are permanent elements of populism, because they translate the naive hope that constitutes the secret of its soul.

The most significant part of Italian populism is formed by the knot linking the theme of the people to that of hope. It is hope that sustains the soldier-peasants of Jahier in the mud of the trenches and the snows of the Alpine peaks; hope that nourishes Pratolini's commoners in their secular daily struggle against misery and corruption; hope that makes Levi's archaic proletarians believe, despite everything, in the dream of a just renewal; hope that inspires the heroism and audacity of the people in arms in the tales of the

Resistance partisans; hope that shines in the clouded consciousness of Pasolini's lumpenproletariat like a desperate spark of life. If the people are the receptacle for perennial human values, hope is precisely the pivot on which the system turns. It is the chief virtue for progressivism. It substitutes for the people's inability to rationally judge the world and for its impotence to act in a revolutionary sense. It is a *naturally* compromising and gradualist sentiment; it is the projection of an objective sociohistorical immobility on a strictly ideological plane. The idealizing charge of populism ends up fully embodying itself in hope; in turn, hope confirms and deepens populism's purely ideological vocation, its rarefied dream in a beautiful world that perhaps will be. The invitation to hope is always an invitation to ignore. He who knows does not hope.

That at a certain point the spontaneous virtues of populism and the cultural politics of the workers' movement should be soldered together is no longer surprising. The reasons for it have been traced to the formative and ideological traits of left-wing intellectual groups. This decision did not appear mistaken on the literary plane only because it was based on the recovery of a tradition that was itself extremely poor and provincial. Rather, its fundamental limit was historico-cultural, because it assumed that Italy would necessarily undergo the same process of social development that had been characteristic of other, more advanced European nations (many decades prior). This perspective (which is obviously not only cultural but also and, above all, political) can be summarized as follows: Italy has not yet traversed a full, mature phase of bourgeois democracy because for more advanced processes to be established one must first pass through this phase and fully exhaust it; constructing a populist-progressive literature can be an important contribution to the development of this intermediate step; the acceptance of the 'natural' factors of populism and tradition is a necessary condition for a certain progressive drive existing in the literary and artistic world to be taken up and channelled within the ideological structures of this basic choice. But this project, the fundamental outlines of which can already been found in Gramsci's thought, did not take into account the fact that the Italian situation could have developed differently and hence could have required a very different level of maturity and boldness in its cultural and literary perspectives. Today we can say that Italy, in the passage from underdeveloped nation to developed capitalist country, has raced through the stages of its adolescence and social maturity. The classic model according to which bourgeois democracy necessarily had to precede the achievement of the dominance of social capital did not take place here.[131] Or, more precisely, it was compressed into a very brief period and into historical situations which meant that it did not lead to the cultural and social phenomena that traditionally followed from it. In other words, the twenty years since the Resistance did not give birth to that national and progressive bourgeoisie upon which one counted to give direction and practical effectiveness to the perspective of national-popular literature. The capitalist stratum replaced it as leaders of the country, even before the progressive bourgeoisie could form and impose themselves on the crest of the wave of anti-fascist progressivism. At the same time, the people, instead of solidifying into a real and autonomous socio-political entity has—in the course of capitalist development—gradually lost its original characteristics, until it made way for new forms of social presence and new concepts—such as those of the 'masses'—which are very different from the traditional democratic postulate of the 'working people'. The national-popular position was defeated by the prevalence of conditions alien to the ideological hypotheses upon which it was founded, even before it was defeated by its inner contradictions. The formidable development of the working class and capitalism, the further confirmation of the definitive absence in Italy of a strong bourgeois class, the progressive socio-conceptual dissolution of the people into more generic historical formations, these are all factors that converge to defeat the populist tendency with all its corollaries and its premises. It has been noted that when confronted with the ultimate consequences of the sociohistorical process, the populist tendency openly reveals the irresolvable nature of the dilemma that undermines it: either it acts as a mere support for the process of expansion and affirmation of capitalism or it resigns itself to singing the praises of an eternal, ahistoric natural happiness. Therefore, progressivism's only choice is between Arcadia and Reformism.

---

131 Asor Rosa is referring to the claim that bourgeois class relations need to precede the existence of capitalist production because of the latter's specific class relations. The Marxian notion of 'social capital' refers to the cycle not simply of individual capitals—passing through productive and circulating phases—but the interaction between all capitals necessary for the reproduction of capital *as a whole*, which 'thus includes the reproduction (that is, maintenance) of the capitalist class and the working class, and hence the reproduction of the capitalist character of the whole process'—Karl Marx, *Capital, Volume 2* (London: Penguin, 1992), p. 468. See also Tronti, 'Il piano del capitale' [The Plan of Capital, 1963] in *Operai e capitale*, pp. 57ff. [Trans.]

All these reasons lead us finally to conclude that the role played by populism in Italy is at once the product and cause of the absence of a strong, modern and advanced bourgeois culture. At this level, subjective and objective responsibilities intersect, correspond to one another and are muddled together until they form a knot that is undone only with difficulty. But some clear points can be identified and established. Despite progressive appearances, populism is a subaltern phenomenon in the broader picture of nineteenth- and twentieth-century European literature. The Italian intellectual stratum gives rise to it through a process that—also from this angle—reveals its substantive immaturity and its incapacity to open itself to the great problems of modern European and world history. Tied, as it is, to the particularity of the Italian situation, this intellectual stratum lacks the strength to raise itself above the limits of its education and specific social form. The affection and attention it shows the people are, from this point of view, nothing other than illusory attempts to search for redemption and greater openness through the exercise of its *good little provincial virtues*. The widespread sense of a social mission of writers and literati is not, as it might appear to the inattentive observer, the demonstration of a *high bourgeois* attitude. In Italy, more than elsewhere, populism and commitment are products of a mentality that is used to considering the world in typically petty-bourgeois terms. The ignorance of broader horizons than those provided by the writer's immediate, particular situations represents perhaps the most serious consequence of this fundamentally narrow literary and artistic outlook. The *high bourgeois* is always able to break the given conditions, reconstructing the process of knowledge and poetic representation in the most correct way, even from the historical standpoint. The petty bourgeoisie keeps to what can be touched with with their hands and see with their eyes, even when they do not go so fas as to presume, as often happens, that this small world is the real world, *the totality of feelings and human conditions*. The truth is that, in the twentieth-century, at the same time that the last great blaze of boldly critical bourgeois literature turned against the world that gave rise to it, Italy continued to produce generations of intellectuals naively confident in the socially regenerative function of art and poetry. The world (this world: the world of crumbling values and class struggle, the world of the most absurd and tragic inventions of spirit and capitalist mass society) was still open for them to the beneficial influence of popular feelings and virtues.

Until this point populism and progressivism have been described as objective echoes of a typically Italian sociohistorical situation and so, to some extent, as inevitable. But it is not possible even on this occasion to reduce everything to the usual justificatory discourse of historicism. The objective responsibilities become more precise when the role of populism is evaluated within the Italian literature of the last hundred years. One will then see that the presence of a powerful populist tendency is one of the reasons that make the establishment, in Italy, of a *high bourgeois* literature even more difficult. The populists and progressives did not limit themselves to reflecting the given conditions of a culture and society but pugnaciously defended their choices on the ideological and literary plane, fighting against all the manifestations of a seriously and consciously uncommitted art. The critical and polemical attitude of the Gramscians is from this standpoint significant. Setting out to overcome certain formalist tendencies of twentieth-century Italian literature, including those of provincial origin, they ended up lumping everything together, equating in their condemnation decadentism and avant-gardism, existentialism and expressionism, abstractivism and cubism. The appeal to popular virtues became in these cases openly and strictly conservative. The people was celebrated, represented, mythologized only to provide the pretext for the flatness of a taste disconnected from any European reference points. If Italian literature of the last hundred years can count on only four or five *high bourgeois* authors (Verga, Svevo, Montale, Gadda and—partly—Pirandello), it is also for this reason. The concrete possibility of a bourgeois literature in the highest and most profound sense of the term has been refused in favour of the idealist populist illusion. Some even believed that the 'literature of tomorrow' could be created on this basis. They failed to realize that, in the name of the people and its eternal virtues, the chance to create a serious, conscious and critical 'literature of the contemporary world' as it actually is, with its dramas and tears, its anguish and subterranean potentials for liberation, would be lost for ever.

PART II

The Crisis of Populism

Cassola

If we now turn to an analysis of Cassola's work, the first thing that strikes us is the stylistic qualities that distinguish it; qualities that are unmistakable and—in their own way—perfect. Quickly achieved and then enduringly maintained—save for some almost imperceptible but important internal modifications—his style is what best characterizes this writer who intentionally translated his ideal world into an intense, laborious and obstinate labour of form, as if trusting in *good literature* to give meaning and value back to a disaggregated and shapeless reality. Cassola's language is sober, pared-down and, at times, so naked as to be off-putting. Above all, it is a form of literary exercise that doubles as a subterranean polemic against all the experiments in the cross-contamination of life and art, of reality and poetry, that were attempted in the postwar years. Cassola is among those who still believe in 'literature'. This is a clue to his origins. He came of age in the shadow of that 'literary civilization' that developed in Italy between the wars and culminated in the years between 1936 and 1940, when, alongside attempts to 'reconstruct' a committed and progressive ideology, Hermeticism produced its theorists and made its extreme displays of taste.[1] Cassola never repudiated this youthful

---

1 The tradition of Italian Hermetic poetry that emerged around 1930 combined a Catholic spirituality with a vaguely existential attitude. Hermetic poetry is characterized by an obscurity of expression because—following the Decadent tradition—it develops a:

> [C]oncept of poetry as a closed, *formal universe* in itself, which as such was internally coherent (to the point that the problem of communication, although it remains—Hermeticism tends intentionally to relegate it to second place—loses all purely logical aspects and cogitating qualities, and is reduced to the pure flux of intuitively transmitted sensations and thoughts). [. . .] the recognition of the priority of the *word* over psychological, ethical and sentimental experience is a general [quality of this poetry] and, hence, predominant, and true feature of this period. [. . .] Poetry, from being the mirror of reality tends to itself become reality, which is to say, to have a life of its own—Asor Rosa, *Sintesi di storia*, pp. 435–6. [Trans.]

apprenticeship; on the contrary, today he reaffirms its importance. While many of its historical and cultural conditions have clearly altered in the meantime, Cassola vehemently retains its imprint, if in no other way than in how he treats his literary tools and establishes a relationship between creative experience and linguistic sign.

However, precisely because of the importance that style assumes in his work, it would be a mistake to consider the question in purely formal terms, to think that the problem ends with the acknowledgment and analysis of a tenacious will to *reduce* and *resolve* into linguistic signs the corresponding reality. If anything, this is the point of arrival of a long generative process and, in turn, the point of departure for a more developed judgement. The fact is that Cassola is a more ambiguous writer than he appears at first sight. His simplicity, achieved at the cost of heroic effort, reveals, under closer examination, a large quantity of hidden meanings. Allowing oneself be caught up in the idolizing of his prose would probably mean ignoring or touching only superficially upon essential and determinate parts of his personality.

But let us start by seeing what is meant by Cassolian prose. There is a passage from the novel *Un matrimonio del dopoguerra* which suits our purposes because it brings together some of the dominant elements of his style:

> Pepo was not happy at all about the girl's visit. He looked with hostility at that arched back, at the rhythmic motion of the arm as it scythed the grass. The shadow had already climbed further up, cutting a swathe across the artichoke field. As if to avoid having the wretched little figure before him, Pepo turned the corner of the cabin. 'Who talked me into this?' he wondered. And not even he knew whether he meant volunteering for the attack or even having joined the partisans in the first place.[2]

Note that Cassola is here far from the more extreme forms of his 'objectivism' (as it can be found in 'Rosa Gagliardi', 'Le amiche', etc.). This is all the more significant because of the effort he makes with regard to one of the themes (partisan life) that seem to have moved him to communicate with greater simplicity and humanity. Note also how, in this passage, he is reluctant to 'comment' on what takes place or to intervene directly. The protagonist of the episode, Pepo, a young partisan from Volterra on the verge of carrying out

---

2 Carlo Cassola, *Un matrimonio del dopoguerra* (1957); now in *Il taglio del bosco* (Turin: Einaudi, 1959), p. 376.

an assault, speaks for himself, that is to say, he judges himself at the same time that he makes certain gestures; and we, the readers, have the illusion that Cassola is merely referring to an episode which he has come to know about, without putting anything of his own into it other than that capacity to transport gestures and thoughts into this bare and schematic thing, that is, language: 'Pepo was not happy at all'; 'He looked with hostility'; '"Who talked me into this?" he wondered'. On the other hand, the objects are laid out just as they are, in all their hostility, as if they were enemies; or, better still, they are laid out just as they appear to the character but devoid of any concrete reality; they too are reduced to signs, to lines firmly drawn but without a body, like hieroglyphs written on air: 'that arched back'; 'the rhythmic motion of the arm'. The same landscape appears like a pared-down series of lines: 'The shadow had already climbed further up, cutting a swathe across the artichoke field', substantively amplifying the impression of descriptive modesty. (At other times, the landscape will be more extensively represented, but for reasons that are anything but stylistic, as we shall see). If the passage were to end with: '"Who talked me into this?" he wondered', the reader would have already grasped what Cassola wishes to convey: the feeling of uncertainty that dominates the relations between the character and the environment. But the author insists and confirms: 'not even he knew whether he meant volunteering for the attack or even having joined the partisans in the first place'. Here we touch upon an important characteristic of Cassola's prose. The stylistic objectivity—which he seeks even when (as in this case) a psychological or emotive element is the focus (Pepo's doubts and desire to be far away from the scene of action)—immeasurably increases the impression of isolation that surrounds the character and achieves the partially intentional effect of making *chance predominate* over the conscious choice of individuals: 'As if to avoid' (nothing more than a hypothesis); 'not even he knew whether' (Pepo has lost any notion of his actions). It would not be difficult to demonstrate the recurrence of this feature of Cassola's work, where the characters appear to waver as they search for a solution, which they are never able to discover in a *rational* relationship with the immediate environment. Pepo looks around as if lost, and each of the things he sees—appearing as though isolated within a picture devoid of all meaning—is unable to restore his lost equilibrium. Consider again the naturalness of the impression that makes him feel rejected by the hostile hardness of that 'arched back', by the insensitive mechanical-like 'rhythmic motion of the arm as it scythed the grass'. In this way even fear becomes a *case* to be registered. This is certainly a rationally explainable reaction (he must confront the fascists in an ambush), but it too lacks a 'meaning' when compared to the motion of things as a whole (that is, the hostility is reciprocal: Pepo looks to things and surrounding events in such a way that they seem separated from him as if by an invisible but consistent sheet of glass; in turn, things and events envelope Pepo in an enclosure beyond which he is unable to look). 'Reality' is reduced to a set of linguistic signs and the representation as a whole has something abstract and incorporeal about it.

Nonetheless, this passage reveals a stylistic element that originates elsewhere and has a different character, one that must be placed alongside another, less evident aspect of Cassola's personality. Doubtless it is significant that he writes: 'As if to avoid having the *wretched little figure* before him' instead of 'that *girl*' or 'that *figure*'. According to a rigidly objective stylistic tendency, this observation introduces a moral and subjective evaluation (*wretched*), even a lyrical one (*little figure*), which must linked to the writer's criteria of judgement rather than to that of his character. 'Wretched little figure' is, in other words, Cassola's assessment, his own moral and sentimental reflection. It is worth observing that in this case too, the protagonist, insofar as he is an autonomous thinking being, is deprived of the possibility of a judgement that might organize the substance of the surrounding reality. But it is even more important to underline that, in this way, Cassola shows himself to possess a less rigid and impassive personality than might seem at first sight. Yes, he is an 'artist', but only up to a point, if he feels the need and possibility of a direct intervention such as this, which is only partially consistent with the stylistic development of the overall picture. Even these opening glances reveal Cassola's moralistic and sentimental *animus*. But I shall return to this at length below.

Let us return to the so-called objectivity of Cassola's prose. It has a lengthy history and, as the author confesses, sinks its roots into the predilections of his childhood and adolescence.

In a piece from the 1940s, Cassola speaks of his youthful interest in natural history and, in particular, the classification of birds, citing more than once a text that was very dear to him and that he particularly appreciated at the dawn of self-awareness: *Ornitologia* by Luigi Figuier. In that same piece, itself entitled 'Ornitologia',[3] he recalls his attempt to write a *Storia dei papi* [History

---

3 This can be found in *Alla periferia* (Florence: Rivoluzione, 1942). Cassola has recently reissued the tales 'Alla periferia' and 'La visita', along with other stories, in an anthology

of the Popes] with an ink so diluted with water that shortly after drafting it, hardly anything remained legible. Only the chapter titles, which had been penned differently, stood out clearly: 'the sequence of pages, chapters and illustrations is very important; in fact, when I was little I attributed importance to this above all else'; consequently, 'I maintained that an extremely thin and colourless form of writing, leaving a barely perceptible, undecipherable trace, would confer beauty to the "typographical" look of the work'.[4] In another page composed at the time, Cassola confesses to an interest he had as an adolescent for those writer's biographies that prefaced works as a kind of instruction or were appended as brief notices on the inside covers: 'in half a page they contain all necessary personal data: born on the . . . in . . . from such and such a family; moved to . . . in . . . ; settling down in . . . '.[5] This ideal of essential simplicity is confirmed in other places with a clarity that leaves no room for misunderstandings: 'My primer and my first reading book were wonderful books. "It's Easter. It's Easter, children, celebrate!" So began and ended a poem in six verses under an illustration of some flowerbeds covered in daisies: was it possible to describe the joy of a holiday morning any better?'[6]

It takes a great effort to resist the temptation to spot, in many of Cassola's narratives, something of those stylized and unmoving hunting scenes that, as a child, the author admired in Figuier's volume; or not to identify, in this sketch of literary biography, the inspiration for many of the simple lives he subsequently described. It is hard also not to conclude that the first sign of the process of paring-down and denuding, so much part of his more mature style, can be found in his extreme and absurd desire to reduce literary and historical works to mere chapter headings, first lines and illustrations, eliminating the real text as superfluous or reducing it to a 'a barely perceptible, undecipherable trace'.

But even if one were to deny these links, which remain suggestive and surprising, there is no doubt that Cassola's statements are too distant in time not to contain a certain genuine plausibility. Underlining in this form, among others, his need for expressive nakedness, the Cassola of the 1940s—not yet revealed as a writer—exhibits the basic component of his human and stylistic

---

titled *La visita* (Turin: Einaudi, 1962). On the significance of this reissue, see Part 1, §17 in this volume.

4 Both quotations: Cassola, *La visita*, pp. 109–12.

5 Cassola, 'Storia e Geografia' [History and Geography] in *La visita*, p. 98.

6 Cassola, 'Il mio quartiere' [My Neighbourhood] in *La visita*, p. 79.

attitude, both the deepest and the least eliminable: the psychological one. Solitary and shy from the start, with a great desire to remain cloistered in his cocoon, Cassola decides to leave it only on condition that an exceedingly heavy and oppressive reality does not violently clash with his extremely keen sensibility; and, precisely at this time, he begins to construct for himself a spiritual world from which the sharp corners and coarser forms are carefully removed. In what subterranean and unconscious depths Cassola's psychology buries its roots it is difficult to say. *The fact remains that it is already fully formed before his first fundamental life experiences*, and will always remain anchored to these diffident and shy tones (reaching the point of prickliness, even disdain).

In the Cassola of 'Alla periferia' [On the Outskirts] there is also a suspicion of *crepuscolarismo* which is never completely eliminated in later years. Describing a stroll through the outskirts of Rome during which he observed a beautiful sunset, he speaks of his reluctance to return to the city:

> I almost can't find the strength to take the road that leads back to the city; *it would be better to remain forever at its doors! I love the suburbs more than the city. I love all the things at the margins.* When I was a soldier I only felt the barracks when I was close to the perimeter walls, facing the wood piled up to cook of the rations, next to the washhouses that are freezing wet in the twilight.[7]

Cassola's first, timid attempts to sketch a conception of the world and of poetry can be dated to this period. What do I mean by 'first'? In truth it is the only attempt the writer ever made. The reading of a small volume such as *Alla periferia* is unique precisely from this standpoint: in it we find a poetics that can be called basic but certainly not incomplete or organic. This is true in particular of the piece called 'Storia e Geografia' but also of others, such as 'Pensieri e ricordi su Monte Mario' [Thoughts and Memories on Mount Mario], 'Il mio quartiere' [My Neighbourhood] and 'Ornitologia'. In the other brief tales of a more explicitly narrative character, explicit allusions to general, human and literary problems are not lacking—more numerous even than in his later works (leaving aside *Un cuore arido*[8]). To my mind, this can only mean one thing: that Cassola comes to artistic creation with few but clear ideas. And he raises the problem of understanding why, having attempted it

---

7 Cassola, 'Pensieri e ricordi su Monte Mario' [Thoughts and Memories on Mount Mario] in *Alla periferia*, p. 40. The emphasis is mine, as it is in most of these quotations.

8 Carlo Cassola, *Un cuore arido* [A Barren Heart] (Turin: Einaudi, 1961).

only once, he definitively abandons the type of narration that lies somewhere between autobiography, essay writing and a narrative that, conversely, is prevalent here and seems to disappear in the contemporaneous volume, *La visita*.[9]

We have already seen, in analysing the passage from *Un matrimonio del dopoguerra*, how a judgement of value, an ideological schema—that of isolation—emerges from the assessment of style. It is surprising how this topic can be found fully developed in *Alla periferia* in a naturally more explicit and programmatic form.

It is clear that the 'ideology of isolation' cannot do without a particular conception of existence. What's more, it is precisely this original foundation that conditions all the others and sheds light on a way of experiencing and interpreting reality as a whole. Cassola is absolutely clear on this point:

> I wanted to construct a life a priori for myself: *an exceptionally naked, static life that would never become unaware of the only thing of value for me: the fact of existing* (with what followed from this, the coexistence of the sexes and then the activity of writer). I constructed this life for myself; I saw it and formed it through my exhausting fantasies.[10]

The concepts are so explicit that they barely require commentary. We should obviously underline the desire to place at the centre of life this pure and simple, naked and unchanging fact: life itself as existence. And when one speaks of 'will', we understand by this exactly what this word means: the continuous effort to construct the forms and modes of one's own life setting out from a schema devised a priori. We should no longer forget the a priori, voluntary nature of this operation. At the very time that Cassola's vital necessity tends to result in a naked objectivity, the shadow of a moral (or moralistic) attitude insinuates itself: the presence, that is, of a norm. But *it is now essential to understand that such a norm is not something more than the objectivist need; it is not an external superimposition that qualifies an attitude which is in itself neutral, that is, purely artistic.* On the contrary, it is lodged deep into the very process of denuding and stripping bare. It is the internal force that moves and justifies it. This is even more evident in the subsequent reflections:

---

9 We are not alluding to a chronological succession: the two books appeared in the same year and the stories they comprise may have been written over the same period. But their different character may have been down to the author's deliberate decision.

10 Cassola, 'Storia e Geografia', p. 99.

A similar way of proceeding, which is abstract and inhuman, aimed to turn me into a being without feelings and passions: a mannequin, a dummy, a silhouette, a figure without a third dimension stamped onto expected landscapes, struck by the low and rose light of the declining day. Indeed, I fanatically believed it necessary to destroy everything that was not the naked, simple, elementary fact of existence.[11]

It is important to note that the character Cassola models on himself resembles the human figures that he frequently represents later in his work. This also enlightens us about the origins of the particular form of autobiographical lyricism, bashful and reserved, typical of the mature Cassola.

The priority of the existential is restated in an even more immediate and basic form in 'Il mio quartiere'. But here Cassola adds a very important qualification to his conception of life. He recalls that as a child of three or four, the day he was 'aware of existing for the first time' was the day he escaped the 'chaos of instinctive existence'. The writer is convinced that he will never be as happy as he was at the time. Why?

Because in that moment I had my entire life ahead of me. Is there a word greater than this one, life? When one has said 'life', one has said everything! But reflect on this: after that moment, every hour that passed my life became evermore circumscribed; all the smallest facts from which it was woven came to define and hence to limit it; they were like so many mortgages taken out on my initially unlimited property. The more I advanced in time, the more the happiness of the first moment seemed unjustified.[12]

Here, for the first time, we encounter Cassola's typical formulation: 'When one has said: life, one has said everything!' Which is to say, there is no explanation for life outside of life itself—'it is life'—and, therefore, often recurs to mark, with its characteristic signature, the culminating points of his stories.[13] But there is also, for the first time, the sense of life as a limitation and diminution which will also return frequently in his work. That means life cannot

---

11 Cassola, 'Storia e Geografia', pp. 99–100.

12 Cassola, 'Il mio quartiere', pp. 78–9.

13 Some notable examples: from 'Rosa Gagliardi': 'Life is like that' (*Il taglio del bosco*, p. 59). From 'Il soldato': 'What do you want to do about it? That's life' (*Il taglio del bosco*, p. 539); 'that's how life is' (*Un cuore arido*, p. 295); 'That's what life is like' (*Un cuore arido*, p. 301).

really be explained, except by this single fact: that it exists. But life understood as a set of occurrences or facts represents a progressive impoverishment of the original, the extremely pure nucleus of life itself, which can be grasped in exceptional moments that is only plausible in childhood.

The problem of man becomes that of conserving as much as possible the lean and sober sense of existence against all the distractions and useless narcotics of life itself (and Cassola expressly points to vanity and lust as the most terrible forces standing in contrast to this need). In other words, the topic we have already analysed returns: 'I wanted to configure a life a priori: an exceptionally naked, static life that would never become unaware of the only thing of value for me: the fact of existing'. Cassola explicitly suggests two parallel paths, even if they are not perfectly analogous: fantasy and indifference. The former has the capacity to change the things that bring pain; the latter represents the condition of refusal, which is at the same time an overcoming of the worst feelings, that is, of the mediocrity of life. Both are linked to the search for solitude and isolation: a fervid life of the heart and the spirit can only ripen when untouched by the useless and damaging clamour of everyday occurrences, and when one remains surrounded by familiar objects and persons, integral elements of our human and geographical landscape. 'Men should live clustered together like me and Ernesto, me and Manlio, etc. They should never be forced to exit the circle in which they feel safe. If things could be like that, men would not be unhappy, they would not envy anyone, they would never hate their neighbour;'[14] 'During the afternoon my garden was always in the shade. I was happy there as only a caged animal can be. Everything that took place outside did not touch me.'[15] The idea begins to insinuate itself, which he takes up again and confirms more recently, that the perfect life is that of plants: 'In contrast to animals, trees go through life fixed in the same place. The life of a tree is exclusively one of contemplation. The life of animals is made up of distractions, narcotics and useless experiences.'[16]

---

14 Cassola, 'Gli amici' in *La visita*, p. 87. Even in this short story one can identify the origin of the autobiographical process that will lead to apparently objective creations some years later. The relationship with 'Le amiche' is evident here.

15 Cassola, 'Il mio quartiere', p. 79.

16 Cassola, 'Diario di campagna' in *La visita*, p. 87. Compare with the following passages from *Un cuore arido*: 'He would have never had enough of that view either. *Places never betrayed him*' (p. 165) and 'He should have hated those places that were full of sad memories. Instead he loved them; he loved them and would never have been able to leave them. "I am like a cat," he reflected, "*I am fonder of places than people.*"' (p. 308).

This way of conceiving existence means that our possibility of interpreting and understanding the surrounding reality is limited, not because of a short-coming on our behalf but, rather, a shortcoming of reality itself. And this because, seen as a purely external unfolding of facts and occurrences, reality seems to lack meaning or at least to be uncoordinated, incoherent. There cannot be meaning in something with which we cannot communicate. There is one way—and one way only—to recover a possibility of 'seeing' in the forms and the appearances that circle around us: having abandoned all hope of resolving the problem through recourse to general ideas (on this level the usual 'that's life' suffices), one can hope to know only when one is able to grasp the particular. This is the only element of reality that as such has meaning. Through this partial and limited, but certain and unmistakable meaning, one can even trace a path back to metaphysics (the need for which shows itself to be anything but overcome at this stage).

In 'Storia e Geografia', the writer recalls the day when, walking alongside his fiancée, he remembered her short-sightedness. Only then, thanks to this apparently insignificant detail which nevertheless distinguished and 'defined' her, he realized that he was about to marry her:

> This defect identified the girl beside me; I realized I was about to marry a short-sighted girl and, at the same time, I realized I was about to marry in an absolute sense. With this I mean that a particular fact generally remains unnoticed: but happy is he who notices it! The smallest, most insignificant detail gives him the sense of existence, which is to say, the meaning of eternity.[17]

It is clear that, having placed *the* detail at the foundation of reality, *every* detail considered in itself appears separated from all the others; because, as we have said, what is missing is a general law that would reunite them by providing a view of the whole. Hence, chance governs the unfolding of events: 'It is clear to me now that the accidents of time and space create and shape life. Today I no longer face an existence I can take for granted; today I have a life made up of unforeseen events and which I do not even think about; today I live one day at a time.'[18] This is yet another reason to remain closed within oneself, in search of something that is instead sure and inviolable.

---

17 Cassola, 'Storia e Geografia', p. 100.
18 Cassola, 'Storia e Geografia', pp. 100–01.

In those same youthful writings we have discussed up to now, there appears an idea of life and poetry that is closely related to the conception of the world we have analysed. It seems clear to me that the previous references to the young Cassola's penchant for ornithology, author's bios, childhood songs and so on, now assume a new character, one that is not only psychological, autobiographical or formal. On the contrary, they are expressions—even if only basic ones—of a developing literary problematic. On this point too Cassola has written explicit, programmatic pages. Remembering a conversation between friends on literary questions and, in particular, on the titles of books, he writes:

> I said only this: that on my part I would never have called a book of mine *Gli indifferenti*.[19] A title like that gives a signal and sets out a limit; it also adopts a moral standpoint. Well, I demanded that this signal, this limitation, this moral position should neither be in the title nor in the book. The book should consist only of the nexus between existence and the coexistence of the sexes. No psychological or moral content should be tolerated.[20]

This is without question a coherent position. If the surrounding reality appears to be based on particular facts put together by chance, how can we hope to base a judgement upon it? At best we can limit ourselves to some observations: *Alla periferia*, 'Le amiche', *Il taglio del bosco*, *La ragazza di Bube* and so on.[21]

But we have seen that the refusal to interpret (and so to judge) the surrounding reality came in Cassola's case not only from an ideological attitude but also, and perhaps above all, from a surge of psychological and (later) moral indignation. The obscure irritation he felt at the often humiliating mediocrity of existence tends to be transformed, in ways that never attain clarity, into a judgement that is more explicit and conscious: 'The life of animals is made up of distractions, narcotics and useless experiences';[22] 'Men should live clustered together [. . .]. If things could be like that, men would not be unhappy, they

---

19 Refers to Alberto Moravia's 1929 novel, first translated into English as *The Indifferent Ones* (Aida Mastrangelo trans.) (New York: E. P. Dutton and Co., 1932); and later as *The Time of Indifference* (Angus Davison trans.) (New York: Signet, 1953). [Trans.]

20 Cassola, 'Storia e Geografia', p. 101.

21 Not by chance, the only exception is *Un cuore arido*.

22 Cassola, 'Diario di campagna', p. 87.

would not envy anyone, they would never hate their neighbour';[23] 'Everything that took place outside did not touch me [. . .]. How could I have become timid and awkward if my eyes rested on things with such assuredness, how could vanity and lust push me to actions the memory of which sets my teeth on edge and makes my nerves tremble with unbearable shame? How can I have lost my serene way of advancing in the world?'[24] If I am not mistaken, one can find the embryo of a moral attitude that is as shy and diffident as the psychology of the one who expresses it and, therefore, is barely able to clarify itself through formulae and concepts. But refusal is also a form of judgement, even if it consists, as it does for Cassola, in the conviction that judgement is impossible. If one looks carefully, one will notice that Cassola's moralism is no less intense and perhaps even sharper and more exacting than Moravia's (to stay with his example). It has at times expressed itself in explicit form, but more often through the indirect form of judgement (we almost want to say, *of condemnation*) exemplified by his objective prose. And with that we return to ideas we have already encountered.

We can therefore draw some initial conclusions. The need to 'keep a distance' from the environment arises from the darkest and most remote depths of his personality, as manifest in the adolescent and youthful Cassola. This need is then clarified and systematized in a basically existentialist theory, which in turn expresses a search for essential truth that transcends the particularity of the single phenomena and is even intimately, inextricably tied to them. It does not thwart Cassola's sentimental yearning for a different world from the one in which we live, nor the unswerving need to judge what we are and how we behave; but he confines both within the limits of a psyche that is almost pathologically shy. Therefore, everything is expressed in the secret conviction that it is fundamentally inexpressible, and that truth lies elsewhere. On the other hand, this truth cannot be directly represented and hence one is forced to content oneself with what—exercising extreme caution—can be grasped of that truth in the casual play of appearances. The autobiographical character of Cassola's writing thus possesses meaning only if it is denied the immediacy of confession.

This appears to be substance of the genesis of Cassola's earliest prose. The autobiographical and subjective experiments of *Alla periferia*, while posing

---

23 Cassola, 'Gli amici', p. 97.
24 Cassola, 'Il mio quartiere', p. 79.

and clarifying these problems, self-destruct as completed results and obliterate the possibility for the writer to continue along that path. At this point, stylistic objectivism is shown to be the only possible solution for those who, like Cassola, have lost all faith in making explicit their judgement on reality, at the same time as they wish to jealously maintain this judgement intact within themselves, limited and precise, protected from the inversions and modifications that might provoke a cordial and extended relationship with a wider compass of humanity. It might appear that Cassola does not force reality to conform to his mental schema. However, in substance he is not willing to come to terms with reality and, while putting on a display of scrupulously respecting it, he disintegrates it at will in his literary transcription of it. Only an extremely sober and pared-down stylistic expression could perform the difficult balance that Cassola establishes between the survival of a will to communicate and the acknowledged impossibility for reality to be intelligible; between the secret but ineliminable survival of feelings and the distrust in the history of man, which is to say, in his struggles and efforts, in other words, his concrete actions. In this sense one can doubtlessly say that Cassola's style is more than mere formal expression; more correctly, it can be said to constitute the only legitimate way in his eyes to bring to bear a minimal level of signification to that which is considered to be without meaning in itself, or which, while it possesses meaning, is unable to manifest it. *The real assumes the appearance of coherence only once it is transformed into literature, even if the latter is schematic and ossified.*

This tendency is manifested to the highest degree in the author's earliest stories and short stories. We have tried to explain why immaturity pushes Cassola to exacerbate the abstract, almost incorporeal tendency of his prose. In some extremely brief passages (one or two pages long), he draws veritable metaphysical pictures (as in 'Bandiera rossa' [Red Flag] and 'Al polo' [At the Pole]). Other writings—the majority of those that make up the anthologies *Alla periferia* and *La visita*[25]—could be described as rough drafts, had they not lost any verist consistency and ambition. Instead they appear as tenuous graffiti on milky glass panels. The choice of themes generally appears random, to the point that what is typically defined as the 'meaning' of the story is missing. The writer appears to imply that one theme is as valid as any other and that the different characters are equivalent. By situating this observation

---

25 'La visita' (Florence: Parenti, 1942, Collezione di Letteratura-Romanzi e Racconti 42).

within the framework we have provided for thinking Cassola's conception of reality, we can immediately understand the continual return in his work of nigh-on identical characters (even in name and exterior attributes) and similar themes. What indeed counts is not the variety of existence, which is a purely external and hence insignificant fact, but the ways one reacts to it. And these, as we shall see below, are not as numerous as they appear: they can basically be reduced to one.

The most significant narrative of this period is probably the eponymous story from the anthology *La visita*. It begins *ex abrupto*, without a word of explanation, with the description of a tapestry hanging from the wall in widow Rosa Boni's home. Cassola represents the scenes in the tapestry as though it were a real story, the protagonists are: an English colonel Delfo and an American Murchison, resident of Australia. Then at a certain point, abruptly and simply, it is revealed that he was speaking about a tapestry. Only then does the short story begin. But its unfolding is not very dissimilar, quite the contrary, from the description of the tapestry: just as the tapestry gives an illusion of movement and life, life too has the rarefied immobility of a stylized drawing, as if written in the air. And yet the feeling that dominates the story and the relations—if they can be called that—between the two protagonists, Rosa Boni and her brother-in-law, is more explicit here than in the other writings from this period: the widow's attachment to her life, made up of memories and nostalgia. She is no longer prepared to 'take into consideration' the present, to work for it; she prefers to take refuge in her solitary nest and quietly await the end in the company of her thoughts. The conclusion of the story, which is pure Cassola, is extremely interesting:

> Rosa had done nothing all day except reflect on her past, with astonishment that so many things had happened in her life and that, ultimately, nothing at all had happened. And then she looked to where Andrea was buried and thought, as a conclusion and consolation for her day: 'How confusing and useless is life! And the more it is useless and confused the more we feel the need to entrust ourselves to divine mercy. The day the Lord wishes I too shall go to the cemetery and will sleep peacefully alongside my Andrea.'[26]

---

26 Cassola, *La visita*, p. 17.

This vein continues in the subsequent two stories, 'Rosa Gagliardi' and 'Le amiche',[27] although the former especially exhibits greater maturity.

Rosa Gagliardi differs from Rosa Boni only because she remains unmarried whereas the latter represents the condition of widows (which is so protracted, ten years, that she exhibits a sort of ideal spinsterhood). Aside from that, the two are very similar. Rosa Gagliardi also lives in solitude, which satisfies her completely, and carefully avoids being drawn away from it. Yet Rosa is not without human affection; for example, she very much loves her niece Anna, she follows through Anna's childhood, adolescence and youth to marriage and maternity. But she refuses the fate of her niece which seems to be richer but is simply mediocre. Her openness to the world never exceeds a certain limit; and her flights always conclude with so many returns to her home in the countryside, where she lives alone, full of memories and the past, desiring nothing but stillness, which is also spiritual peace, serenity and inner strength.

The opposite journey, the one taken by her niece Anna, reappears in the story 'Le amiche', whose protagonist has the same name. Young Anna, having grown up in the countryside, has a deep friendship with a girl called Franca. Briefly and simply, Cassola describes the nature of this relationship which, particularly in the case of Anna, is one of joy in relishing the spontaneity and disinterest of emotions in the early years of life. But the writer then runs quickly through the events of her life—she marries and has a child—almost as if to underline their lack of importance when compared to the problems of a more intimate and deeper life. In the course of a stroll with Franca, who by now has also become a young woman, they recall other promenades, other episodes from their recent past. And Anna, who is still very young, already begins to lament: 'They were good times [. . .]. It is useless, when we're girls, free.'[28] Her refusal to allow herself to be absorbed by the mediocrity of her present rests precisely on the fact that marriage has not altered her most jealously protected interiority of being. After all, even before she was engaged, she had intuited something of the sort while waiting in a clearing in the forest:

> Anna savoured the silence that reigned around her. How wonderful it was! How good it felt! It was impossible to be happier than this. And that happiness, so it seemed, would last forever, whatever

27 Now in Cassola, *Il taglio del bosco*, pp. 43–73 and 75–107.
28 Cassola, *Il taglio del bosco*, p. 107.

happened. She would get married and have children but would be equally happy. Why had Anita said that getting married would change everything? How silly! How could something that was inside her end?[29]

What begins to take shape in these female figures (Rosa Boni, Rosa Gagliardi, Anna) is the first type of positive Cassolian character. Its dominant quality is, as we have seen, the taste for solitude and diffidence towards the surrounding reality. This is accompanied by testimony to an intense inner life. But this intensity remains mysterious, secret, almost nothing of it appears other than here and there, a more intense vibration and the discovery of feelings and affections. Happiness is granted to these shy and remote beings, but only in the form of a dark, undefinable possession of a fundamental and unmodifiable nucleus of their personality. For those who know how to seek, happiness is therefore the conquest of nature.

As one can see, this positive character is always female. *Perhaps because virginity represents for women a more integral value than it does for men.* Perhaps because women are more sensitive, more attentive to the profound voices of existence and less distracted by all those occupations and commitments that externalize man through worldliness, often turning him into a coarse and primitive being. For these women, the ideal of love is not essential in an absolute sense; not even maternity is able to distract them from the contemplation of more important things. They have human affections but even these are overcome by nature at some point. That is to say, they are *sterile mothers* or *die-hard virgins* so that, even when they lose their physical virginity—which only takes place when they wish and always without the least pleasure or satisfaction—they rediscover a more profound and lasting virginity, which is that of the spirit.

Anna Mannoni from *Fausto e Anna*[30] is cut from the same cloth. She too awaits the arrival of love, that is, of life. And once she knows both love and life, she realizes just how insipid and painful they are. Moreover, love, a feeling so long awaited and vaguely dreamt of, betrays its objectionable and even disgusting aspects. After relations with her husband, Anna feels dirty, impure and

---

29 Cassola, *Il taglio del bosco*, pp. 92–3.
30 Carlo Cassola, *Fausto e Anna* (Turin: Einaudi, 1952).

nostalgically recalls the freshness of her adolescence. In the end, even she will rediscover spiritual solitude that means stillness and superiority.

However, *Fausto e Anna* is a much more ambitious novel than Cassola's previous works. I might even say the most ambitious in his entire career as narrator. Aside from the persistence of a certain thematic, it can be easily observed that Cassola attempts an entirely new path in this novel: that of narrating according to an explicit and intended meaning. Taking as his subject matter a well-defined dimension of history, he does not give up on his judgements or convictions; he only wants to experiment with them, thus turning them into elements of a battle of ideas and human actions with its own objective, historical reality. In this way, Cassola unwittingly commits what, from his standpoint, is a grave error. He accepts that the very existence of history is a problem that needs to be resolved. That is, he does not accept history as such (something he fails to concede in this work too) but the idea that it is necessary and interesting to reckon with it, even if only to arrive at the conclusion that history is neither necessary nor interesting. All of this is simply ideologically repugnant to Cassola, for whom history's lack of significance is undisputed and accepted as an incontrovertible fact. For the new dimension he locates his novel in to become poetically fertile, it would have been necessary to profoundly revise his ideological presuppositions—which he does not do at all. The result is that *Fausto e Anna* is disappointing, fragmentary and contradictory.

The least convincing figure is that of the protagonist, through whom the author unfolds his unusual theme of the moral, sentimental and ideal education of a young intellectual in the prewar years and those of the Resistance. The wavering of the protagonist between scepticism and religious faith, from faith to communism, from communism to indifference, and from indifference to the Resistance; his amorous torments and travails, always tipping to the opposing poles of sensuality and platonic satisfaction, purity and vulgarity; his incapacity to fix a pivot for his relationships and his consequent fruitless effort to make contact with other men and even with the woman he loves— all are described with a level of detail and doggedness that hardly ever feels real or poetically accomplished. Perhaps this is because at the root of the book there is an autobiographical truth. We shall not repeat the old formula that autobiography does not generate poetry except when it is overcome, etc. *It is enough for us to note that Cassola's autobiography* (that is to say, what defines the author as a man who lives in a historical and social milieu, with certain passions and ideas) *is unable to sustain the weight of a coming-of-age novel.*

Cassola would have had to overcome too much diffidence to achieve that result. On the contrary, we could say that violently confronted with a fact of considerable human and social import such as the Resistance, Cassola is pushed by the attributes of 'citizen' and 'intellectual' to an active participation in it, and yet he reacts negatively, as if to protect himself from the trauma this new reality might cause him. The expression of this attitude of incomprehension and self-defence is that moralistic condemnation of violence the origin and justification for which can be found in some acts of cruelty and ferocity perpetrated by a single partisan; but it can go so far as to throw a shadow of doubt over the entire experience of the Resistance. The old theme returns: faced with death and life, historico-political categories (such as communism or reaction) have no validity. But what was poetically valid and acceptable in the story of Rosa Gagliardi has only a limited and partial meaning when it comes to the figure of this young intellectual in search of a truth he will never be able to find.

Poor Fausto, trapped by the inner contradictions his creator is unable to resolve, moves like an unrealistic one-dimensional mannequin. Cassola, impotent in the face of the problem he poses but is unable to resolve, gives vent to an orgy of psychologizing. But since even this must turn on a certain interpretation of reality to be coherent, the orgy of psychology is resolved, in Fausto's acts and decisions, into an orgy of irrationality; and the (documentary, historical) weight of the social and intellectual origin becomes for Fausto a form of veritable inhibition, that can sometimes explode in pathological or infantile attitudes. All this is implied without the writer being fully aware of it; Cassola endures his character because, first of all, he endures himself.

The other side of the coin is, of course, moralism. While he is incapable of judging himself, Fausto (the writer) expects to judge others according to an *eternal* behavioural norm. This severely prejudices his ability to understand and *make friends* with the other members of the Resistance, the humble peasants and workers from the area around Volterra with whom he lives and fights. It is true that he experiences it as a limit, a privation. But Fausto's avowal of this always involves a moment of aristocratic satisfaction. And where is his struggle to overcome his limitations, to win himself over? The reality is that this struggle is destined to fail because it unfolds through a series of attempts, none of which is seriously and profoundly undertaken. *Fausto, the intellectual, when he puts his mind to it, is satisfied at being able to judge reality with a sharp and pitiless attitude from his solitary and unapproachable ivory tower.*

The apparently surprising fact that someone like Cassola supported and participated in the Resistance can be explained only with reference to the extremely generic character and the immensity of the movement. For Cassola embodies a typical attitude of cultural, political, ethical and ideological moderatism. His craving for isolation and his simultaneous excessive and almost illogical urge to judge, express that objective, historical dialectic between the jealous defence of individualism and the claim to intervene culturally and politically which takes root in the body of certain intellectuals and social strata. Anti-fascism also embraced this attitude, which powerfully marked the attitude intellectuals developed and deployed towards popular strata. For Cassola, as for many others like him, anti-fascism means a reverence for freedom and moral values, the abstract demand for a superior justice and the profound desire to distinguish between cultural and political life. His judgements on politics are fundamentally the same that as those he makes about history. To a spirit desirous of the absolute, practice always appears mean and limited. As soon as he turns to representing the dimension of human action, Cassola wavers between the shadowy indignation of *Fausto e Anna*, the elegy for the workers' defeat of 'Esiliati' and the twilight of a defeated socialist tradition in 'La casa di via Valadier'.[31]

The plebeian world has no place here other than as a negative point of reference—as when its primitiveness clashes with the 'highest ideals' of the writer—or as the expression of a historic failure which envelops the socialist hope in a better world. And yet the people are there, to remind even Cassola the Intellectual that history exists, even if he would much rather do without it. Despite this, as we have said, the problem of communication (in the socially progressive sense) between the intellectual and the world of popular anti-fascism is completely precluded for Cassola. Indeed, the author has no faith in the mediation of intellectuals (nor, consequently, in that of the party).[32] For the people to once again become a valuable field of observation for Cassola, it is necessary to take the intellectual (Fausto) out of the equation, thereby eliminating the *problem* of how to establish communication. Even the experience of anti-fascism and popular Resistance are brought under the aegis of stylistic objectivity. The world of the people is represented as a closed,

---

31 These last two short stories appeared for the first time in *La casa di via Valadier* [The House of Valadier Way] (Turin: Einaudi, 1956); now also in *Il taglio del bosco*, pp. 261–83 and 285–360.

32 On Cassola's attitude in this regard, see pp. 228–9 in this volume.

autonomous and socially isolated world. In this form they are already an 'object'; one of the many objects that pepper Cassola's horizon. This is not the only reason why Cassola renounces that fundamental postulate of progressivism, which is the search for a communicative and pedagogical relationship between the advanced intellectual and the people. He also happily does without the other pole of national-popular discourse that consists of a tendency to abstract from the people a set of positive values *that would then be put to work on the historical plane.* Cassola represents the people as a closed world simply in order to confirm its desperate autonomy and crushing isolation.

We can see how Cassola's standpoint becomes evermore defined. On the literary plane (in addition to the ideal one), *Fausto e Anna* represents Cassola's only concession to that explicitly fervent and 'experimental' climate characteristic of neo-realism; the subsequent works, even the most engaged, signal a return to a rigidly literary conception. On the ideal plane, his incapacity to move beyond his youthful convictions is fixed once and for all; the refusal of communism belongs to this recognition of the author's limits.[33]

Cassola's people (Tuscan workers and peasants) are evaluated and depicted within this framework from the start. They are more an aggregate of isolated individuals, than a social formation. It is not so much the force of ideas that moves them as the instincts, passions and feelings. Moreover, the political struggle becomes a natural phenomenon, like their daily life. Communism, fascism and socialism are words that mark instinctive reactions rather than rational choices. The morals of the poor person are ultimately no different

---

33 In support of this one could cite a statement from the short story 'La vedova del socialista' (*La visita*, p. 108), commenting on the life and convictions of an old militant who is attached to her ideals, he writes:

> She dreamt of a much more closed and depressing life than that the one she had. She dreamt of a world that one might have if—as I say—the dark clouds we find on ominous days, when it doesn't rain, came lower still over our heads (those days that I passed, not far from her house, in homes open to the public). Moreover, *I do not understand how one can desire the advent of a world built by us, and hence one that we have already taken for granted* . . .

Note that the writer's subsequent political experiences would appear to overcome and contradict this position taken in his youth. But to me it seems that his original thought, founded upon the refusal of 'a world built by us', remained very much alive even in the mature Cassola. One cannot attribute greater validity to his professions of socialist faith than the one which inheres a sceptical and disenchanted humanitarianism which in any case does not alter but, rather, corroborates his personality as a writer.

from those of the exploiter: violence against violence and little by way of reasoning on the forms of opposition.

Cassola draws this figure of the people from a well-defined tradition, that of Tuscan naturalism: think of Bilenchi and Pratolini, and, of course, via these or directly, Tozzi. He then shapes it, naturally, according to his sensibility, his taste, and his personal and sentimental preferences. Of the authors we have cited, he is the most distant—psychologically and humanly—from the popular characters depicted; the most reticent and aristocratic, the one least able to abandon himself to the impulses of the blood and the flesh (like Tozzi), to amiable attitudes (like Pratolini) or to the tender waves of memory (like Bilenchi).[34] In his descriptions, he shows no fondness for the natural form of anarchism that seems to form the most widespread political attitude among the Tuscan artisans and peasants. This coarse, basic sectarianism is not always redeemed by the represented authenticity of the feeling that moves it (at times there is something mean and obtuse at its root). And what accompanies this attitude is an equally coarse sort of bureaucratic deformation which is meant to be the attempt consciously to overcome the phase of the instincts and of spontaneous and blind rebellions, but instead represents its other face, symmetrical and censurable in equal measure. When Cassola touches upon these points, his characters are inhibited, wooden, as if blocked by them; or they react irrationally with a wilful and programmatic violence. This is true when it is a matter of representing the figure of a sectarian (as in the case of Piero in 'I vecchi compagni').[35] But it is all the more true when the subject is a minor

---

34 Some of Cassola's activities bear witness to a more direct and immediate, not merely literary knowledge of the Tuscan people he depicts in his writings. This is the case, for example, of the in-depth investigation carried out in *I minatori della Maremma* (Bari: Laterza, 1956), with Luciano Bianciardi. But, above all, we know that the way one looks at reality counts much more than the reality being looked at; and so the biographies of the miners at the back of the book (which we believe can largely be attributed to Cassola) already appear to be literary figures, protagonists of a novel. Second, we do not exclude the fact (as we will later explain) that Cassola's people possesses objectively verifiable characteristics. This however leads us to conclude, once again, that a partially or entirely exact sociological account is not always able to break a literary tradition and to bring out new formal and thematic values. On the contrary, it can end up restating them with the (apparently indisputable) force of its objectivity.

35 See *Il taglio del bosco*; in particular, p. 249: 'We needed to make a clean sweep of it— forget collaborating. I would have done it: get rid of the priests, get rid of the bourgeoisie, get rid of them all. But what were we thinking? That they'd understand? That they'd all become communists? They've already raised their heads again', etc.

local leader devoted to the party's slogans, to the point of abdicating independent thought. In such cases Cassola is vindictive, discarding the character's psychology and even his feelings. In the case of Baba, for example, stylistic objectivity can translate into moral and intellectual limitation.[36]

Moreover, it would be absurd to maintain that a relationship cannot be established between Cassola and his plebeian world. In order to understand the nature of this relationship it must be recalled—as we have said—that for the writer it is not a problem which can be resolved by enriching or substantially modifying certain antecedent theses; this is confirmed by his failure to grasp the political ferments agitating that environment. Equally, we should acknowledge that—in this case as well—Cassola encounters his people on the plane of feelings or nature. That is to say, he forges an image of the people or, better still, he selects a slice of popular reality that, within limits that are (probably) sociologically verifiable, is closest to his need for the objective translation of his most intimate and longstanding theme. In other words, *Cassola's people becomes the symbolism of his myths*. From this point of view, we do not see any difference between some of his so-called historical works and the metahistorical ones. The differences and contradictions re-emerge when Cassola is forced to recognize a minimal degree of substantive, objective validity to certain operating forces. Then, having opened this breach in his ideology of isolation, it will be a matter of recomposing it according to a completely renewed attitude or through a decisive return to the past. Meanwhile, in works like 'I vecchi compagni', 'Esiliati', *Un matrimonio del dopoguerra* and *La ragazza di Bube*,[37] the poetic effect is achieved every time there is a profound interpenetration of an individual destiny with a universal law of existence. Which is to say, the time that one can forget whether a certain commoner is a communist, a socialist, a fascist or a partisan, and instead simply identify him as a man.

One should note that the majority of historical events portrayed in these stories and novels are nothing but the transcription, in apparently objective terms, of the myths generated by Cassola's pessimism. The ideal–real relationship

---

36 See *Il taglio del bosco*, p. 226; and the conclusion to the story 'I vecchi compagni': '"How long is this interruption going on for", grumbles Baba. Certainly, it makes no difference whether there was light or not if one is to stay put not doing anything . . . But in the dark he was no longer even able to think.' (p. 259).

37 Carlo Cassola, *La ragazza di Bube* (Turin: Einaudi, 1960) / *Bébo's Girl* (Marguerite Waldman trans.) (London: Collins, 1962).

remains intact in this phase too. The ideals of the Resistance and of socialism are, for a brief instant and in exceptional situations, truly heartfelt and elevated (in this case even the cold Baba can be moved);[38] but then are drowned in the drabness of everyday life which naturally is itself a succession of banal, mediocre, disappointing events: the afflictions of poverty and hardship provide a real justification for this sense of uselessness that penetrates everyday life but fail to entirely explain it. Even these commoners feel, as does Cassola, the inexplicable harshness of existence and they too, like him, seek refuge in the nostalgic evocation of the past rather than in the confused and illusory expectation of the future. Going underground thus appears to be the happiest and the most consolatory moment of their lives, and the Resistance feels like a pause filled with enthusiasm and strength, a magnificent memory (however, as one lives it, it reveals its limits, its pettiness). In general, all that has been or could have been is preferable to what is: whether it be the poor marble worker Maggiorelli, who moved to Rome to escape fascist persecution and literally dreams the triumphant celebration that will signal the end of the dictatorship precisely as the police come knocking on his door;[39] or Baba who, despite having become a functionary of the party, feels the inner surge of nostalgia for that period of clandestine, dangerous struggle, when despite everything 'there was togetherness' and 'none of the jealousies and envies that emerge later';[40] or Pep who, in *Un matrimonio del dopoguerra*, having been forced to marry, as he contemplates a girl on the beech in Livorno, imagines that his life could have been different had he married a woman like that (about whom he knows nothing), rather than his wife (about whom he knows everything— which is enough to make her hateful to him).

Cassola provides these popular characters—reduced to his image and likeness—with a destiny of disappointment and defeat. He even brings this aspect of himself to this humble world: the conviction of the inanity of his characters' human efforts and the acceptance of the ineluctability of pain. Poor, afflicted, unhappy and destined to remain so, these workers and peasants struggle pointlessly under the weight of an adverse destiny. And since they are

38 In 'I vecchi compagni', when Baba brings a cargo of arms to the Partisans: 'A very young partisan holding a machine-gun confronted Baba, who was standing to one side: "We will take revenge for Nello Giannini," he said with a trembling voice. "Yes," said Baba, deeply affected' (*Il taglio del bosco*, p. 241).

39 See conclusion to the short story 'Esiliati' [The Exiled] in *Il taglio del bosco*, p. 283.

40 Cassola, 'I vecchi compagni', p. 259.

unaware either of themselves or of the world in which they live, their unhappiness appears all the more difficult, their sentence all the more inexorable. *At this point, Cassola renews that fondness for his characters with which he had been so miserly. In fact, only at this point was he able to recognize himself in them.*

At its worst, this fondness can show itself in sentimental effusion and explicit pity. But at other times Cassola displays a heightened force of penetration, to the point of recognition that the plebeian world has—enclosed within its shell and largely *incommunicable*—values distinct from those of its creator. Not even in this case is there a complete relinquishment of Cassola's position; nor are those plebeian values ever really in contradiction with the ethical and ideal presuppositions of the author. But unarguably a thematic expansion takes place, even if within it there is already the root of its overcoming and involution.

The first of these values is solidarity.

Un matrimonio del dopoguerra is the novel in which the theme is most fully developed (more lucid than 'I vecchi compagni'), and is one of Cassola's most interesting and successful attempts. He writes:

> The reunion of the cell was taking place. Pepo went to sit next to Zamir. Being there, among his comrades, he felt what for him was real family; because he now felt like a stranger at home or, worse, all those at home had become hateful to him.[41]

Pepo argues with his father; lives unhappily with his wife, whom he was forced to marry after he got her pregnant; he does not yet love his son; and both his sister and his sister-in-law are in league against him. Then there is unemployment, poverty and the sense of powerlessness stemming from all of this. On the other hand, there is the Party, or the 'meetings of the cell', the basic organ in which the Party becomes a set of human beings linked by the same fate, more than by the same ideas. To 'sit next to Zamir' is the concrete, particular, humble form through which this feeling is expressed. Zamir is just anyone, he is not even a particularly close friend of Pepo's. And yet Pepo, by sitting next to him, experiences the little flame of consolation that renders life bearable. This is even clearer in the novel's conclusion:

---

41 Cassola, *Un matrimonio*, p. 429.

At that moment the first siren sounded. Without speaking they crossed the square. They took care not to step in any puddles. Here and there was still a little snow, trampled and dirty. Pepo raised his eyes. A pale sun lit up the surrounding wall, the gate and the clock tower. For the first time, he looked at the factory with a sense of happiness.[42]

Pepo and his comrades, who find work in a factory in Saline, near Volterra, learn one morning that some of their friends who had remained unemployed had fallen in to a trap lain by the *carabinieri* while they were attempting to rob a deposit of old weapons. Right up to the minutes preceding the siren call, they were predicting what would happen to their fellow villagers, either condemning or justifying them. The siren returns them to silence. In that same instant, they, as characters, are returned to an atmosphere in which each of them appears to lose his personality along with his thoughts and feelings. While they move towards the entrance, they are merely animated figurines crossing the page, making particular gestures: 'They took care not to step in any puddles.' Immediately afterwards an almost entirely descriptive observation: 'Here and there was still a little snow, trampled and dirty', which further highlights the predominance of objects, blind and unintelligible, over the feelings of man. In this picture the figure of Pepo stands out. At first we get only a movement, a gesture: he 'raised his eyes'. After the short parenthesis of discussion, even he is imprisoned, like his comrades, in a web of insignificant acts. But Pepo's gaze manages to grasp an aspect of nature that the others, with their eyes fixed on the ground to avoid the puddles, were unable to see: the pale sun, which seems to promise the perpetuation of a distant, indefinite and unreachable hope, despite the surrounding greyness. Through this weak stimulus, an equally undefined and vague feeling surfaces in Pepo's simple consciousness: 'a sense of happiness . . .'. Nothing more is granted by this unbending creator to this plebeian character who is sunk in uncertainty and weakness as if in a cocoon which he will never know how to leave. But it is the factory that inspires in him this pathetic, sentimental rebellion against the mediocrity of his life: the factory, that is, the symbol (which is also vague, indeterminate, *not yet social*) of wretched human community, whose components are unable to do anything but desperately clinch one another so as to not fall apart.

---

42 Cassola, *Un matrimonio*, p. 471.

Closely associated with the value of solidarity is that of sacrifice. This motif is particularly evident in *La ragazza di Bube.*[43]

Here, as in other works by Cassola, the historical picture is ambiguous, contradictory and disputable. There is no doubt that with the story of Bube the author wished to represent, in a dramatic key (as he had done in *Un matrimonio del dopoguerra,* with regard to disillusionment and retreat), the crisis of a crude and infantile sectarianism which he considers to be the dominant political attitude among the Tuscan communist proletariat during and after the Resistance. At the same time, he holds the Communist Party responsible for not having restrained the violence perpetrated by its followers even as it was doing everything to play a legal and moderating role nationally. Not all of this need be rejected on the poetic plane. There are pages on the young Bube and on Mara's father, where the element of anarchic and blind protest assumes the spontaneous force of a conviction, through simple words, naked gestures and even oppressive silences. In this case too, Cassola, who as a 'historical' author shows himself incapable of sympathetically approaching the human indignation borne by the crude and violent rebellion of his characters, nevertheless reveals a basic understanding that allows him to participate in their suffering and defeats.

Certainly Cassola is a long way from being able to propose here or elsewhere a political or social alternative (his real alternatives are to be found in the characters Mara Castellucci or Anna Cavorzio). One cannot even affirm that he is able to pinpoint with full awareness this crisis of an objective, historical populism, which was one of the realities of the postwar workers' movement and among the sources of its defeats. Quite the contrary, when Cassola makes explicit judgements, in *La ragazza di Bube* as much as in *Fausto e Anna,* he reveals the conservative foundation of his thought—at times displaying the narrowness of his judgement. But the channels of his sensibility are all open to the problems of suffering and disillusionment; almost reluctantly, they reflect, albeit in a distorted and partial way, a painful popular defeat that originated in naive hopes and a political mindset that was crude and shapeless. And Bube, this dumb and blind character that nature has not yet reawakened from his torpid insensibility, ends up—precisely because of this extremely closed and inexpressive attitude—symbolizing the tremendous inanity of struggle.

---

43 The quotations are translated directly from the Italian edition. [Trans.]

Conversely, what we can in no way accept is the pedagogical use to which Cassola puts the life of the young partisan. The idea of regeneration through pain should be refused for at least two good reasons: first, because it has the stale odour of counsels too often repeated in the 'doctrines' of every creed; second, because it represents the clear superimposition of a thesis on the natural development of the story. In this respect, the last part of the novel is frankly irritating. Cassola's bourgeois moralism celebrates its splendours here.

Moreover, it would be an error to centre the reading on those elements of the historical framework which, however abundant they may be, are needed simply as a pretext and stimulus for a more substantive development, as is often the case in the work of this author. Indeed, the principal theme of the novel does not concern Bube, nor the historico-political facts, so much as Mara and her morals, her attitudes and *fate*. And Mara is a typical Cassolian character, born outside of history and *entering history only as a victim, never as a protagonist*. In this figure, one can rediscover many of the positive qualities that we have already underlined in Rosa Gagliardi and in the two or three Annas of the preceding short stories and novels: strength of spirit, superiority over the mediocre surrounding figures, genuineness and sincerity of feelings. But in her this is all turned to a different use.

It is very significant that she only reluctantly accepts the engagement to Bube. She feels no attraction to this closed and uncommunicative young man. And she does not sense a profound, long-lasting bond with him. Nevertheless, it is she who encourages him to take her while they are hiding for a few days in a hut, far from the eyes of the *carabinieri* and the police. Mara does so on the basis of a natural, sensual impulse; but, more profoundly, in this way she chooses her destiny (which she confusedly intuits). It is no coincidence that their union takes place precisely when she learns that Bube will have to flee overseas, during the first stage of his difficult expiation; from the start their love is closely tied to the idea of pain.

When Bube is in France, Mara becomes emotionally involved with a worker, Stefano, a very different proposition to Bube and the other coarse commoners like him. Stefano approaches communism through literature; he has artistic ambitions, writes short stories and poems. When he speaks, one notices his knowledge of romantic literature and comics. The sentimental and rhetorical part of Mara's popular soul leans towards him; moreover, due to her distance from Bube, she appears to have forgotten the amorous episode from her past and she asserts the right to choose freely and happily.

Different but ultimately related feelings prevent her from giving a lasting realization to her relation with Stefano. First, Mara—playing out her melodrama until the final act—experiences this relationship as beautiful, because it has no future; it is a fantasy without foundation. As soon as Stefano outlines their future life together (marriage, children, a room with access to a kitchen), all enthusiasm evaporates. Indeed, Stefano is her attempt to escape the harshness of reality, so it makes no sense for him to be transformed into a certain, definitive reality. Second, precisely while she flirts with the impossible dream of a happy life alongside him, Mara feels the unyielding imperative of duty rise up within her: she cannot abandon Bube, precisely because he is persecuted and unhappy. There is, of course, nothing ethical about this, in the lofty sense of the term, because for Mara *character and morality perfectly coincide*, and her strength really is instinctive.

Furthermore, even in this case Mara is reluctant to sacrifice herself because her natural disposition is to crave life, happiness. At first, she is almost forced by circumstances, by her father and her comrades to keep her promises. So, on the one hand, Mara is the victim that men sacrifice at the altar of convention, prejudice, violence and bigotry, while dressing it up as justice. For a while she suffers this condition of victimhood and would like to rebel against it. But, little by little, her conviction that pain is inescapable comes to be coupled with the intention to accept it thoroughly, conserving as much as possible her dignity, her force of character and her precise and fateful sense of things. Even this attitude of course cannot be explained except by heeding the serenely generous nature of the protagonist. Pain has no meaning, in the same way as a storm that bears down on a defenceless countryside has no meaning; and for this very reason it is futile to resist. Men have no pity for one another but know only how to demand and apply a tremendously impersonal justice before which each of us loses his real lineaments along with any true feeling and is reduced to a mannequin at the mercy of destiny. This is why there is no reason to struggle, curse or protest. On the other hand, everyday life has its own direction, moving forward all the same, with its habitual and meaningless gestures, despite the suffering of individuals. And vice versa, for those who suffer, the only true reality is the suffering, the disaster, which they carry along locked in their hearts.

In short, pain is the universal law and only those who experience it fully can hope to overcome their own egotism and indifference. But sacrifice is born of the conviction that one cannot escape one's fate and that to accept it is the only adequate response.

When Mara makes this choice (that is to say, she responds as best she can to the entreaty coming from the strongest and most secret part of her character), she takes on an unexpected stature. In the most difficult circumstances all the men around her, from her father to Lidori, from the lawyers to Bube himself become weak, uncertain and pitiful compared to her. It is she who instils strength, who suggests remedies and who provides the good example, like a slender and vigorous plant that bends but resists the storm that has uprooted trunks of much greater size and power. The truth is that in Mara—more than in all the novel's other characters—lives the spontaneous and incoercible force of nature; everything that happens to her can only render her resistance all the more resplendent and luminous. At the end of the novel, the sun that rose among the mists seemed to promise—to her as to Pepo—a distant hope as compensation for pain and sacrifice.

> At the first turning, Valdesca was revealed. There was a sea of fog below which emerged the summits of the hills in the shape of little islands. But the sun, crossing the fog with its oblique rays, sparkled in the valley. At no point did Mara take her eyes from the valley, slowly waking in the misty splendour of the morning.[44]

The character of Cassola's 'populism' should now be clear in its essential components. For this author, popular solidarity is nothing more than the instinctive recognition of the *fatal* commonality of afflictions and suffering into which pours the pale, subterranean current of a desperate hope, which every day History offends and disappoints. The joy of victory (or of love or serenity) rapidly gives way to the eternal exercise of sacrifice, which in turn is a *natural* and *spontaneous* duty born of the deepest fibres of a being that for centuries has become accustomed to resignation and to the virile or passive acceptance of pain. These feelings remain purely instinctive reactions; that is why Cassola could experience and appreciate them. But neither solidarity nor sacrifice are represented as dialectical elements of that closure of the people which at other times perfectly expresses them. In other words, solidarity and sacrifice are not the channels through which the primitive Tuscan people *presses* towards history, for the practico-political recognition of certain needs and certain rights. *Solidarity and sacrifice are both the cement that keeps popular autonomy solidly united and the disillusioned confirmation of its meta-historical isolation.*

---

44 Cassola, *La ragazza di Bube*, p. 236.

We must now correctly identify the 'novelty' of Cassola's practice. Italo Calvino has perceptively written:

[T]he beauty of Mara, who is perhaps the first positive human figure of great stature to appear in the new Italian literature (the word 'character' has bored me and I will not use it), has a contradictory foundation. Mara makes her decisions without escaping the canons of traditional morality, Christian resignation, the acceptance of renunciation and sacrifice; and this cannot fail to reveal a conservative vein running through Cassola's work.[45]

But that's not all, although Cassola unquestionably tries to restore certain Christian values in the spirit and customs of the people he represents. The truth is that characters like Pepo, Baba and Mara reveal the inability of a literary tradition and conception of reality to go beyond its constitutive limits.

The recurrent monotony of Cassola's characters can be attributed not only to the persistence of a characteristic motif of the author's (as we have repeatedly underlined) but also, and perhaps above all, to the restrictedness and poverty of the cultural and literary references from which these themes and figures have been drawn. How many times have we met these popular characters in nineteenth- and twentieth-century Italian literature, people who are *naturally* good, strong, tenacious and possess an indescribable capacity to endure and react in their secular, *eternal* suffering? It has sustained a host of writers: keeping them both in foreground and background, and within one's cultural horizon, the standpoint of a peasant and archaic Italy, which underplays the unfolding of history and remains forever immobile. Populism furnishes Cassola's original simplistic and reductive existentialism with a series of figures, a thematic and stylistic 'fabric', as well as an occasion to make the objectivist tendency denser and more consistent. However, at the same time it encloses it in a magic circle of ancient provincial myths: nature, simplicity, man and feelings. It envelops the same in a literary prison even more solid and labyrinthine than the one from which he had attempted to escape. Forcing it into the riverbed of an indigenous and provincial tradition, which Cassola seemed to repel in his youthful poetic declarations.

But such a position reveals another serious limitation. From the structural and stylistic standpoint, the need to poetically depict the human condition in

---

45 Calvino's response to a report on *La ragazza di Bube* in *Mondo operaio* 12 (July–August 1960).

broader and more meaningful ways is translated into the forms of the large novel. Cassola's attitude has not really changed internally: the widening of the theme does not mean, strictly speaking, a maturing of its underlying inspiration. The contradiction between the author's theoretical presuppositions and objective popular values is extremely limited and therefore does not exclude a re-composition on a different level, though one that is always rigorously bourgeois. For Cassola, escaping the ivory tower of prudent detachment means immediately falling into melodrama. In short, there is no middle course. And this is logical: *all existentialism, when it becomes popular, can only present itself in markedly sentimental forms, even in a naive glorification of well-meaning thoughts and positive choices.* From this point of view, *La ragazza di Bube* is unequivocal.

At this point it seems natural that the insignificance of history is fated to re-emerge, and to do so *within* Cassola's 'historical' representations themselves. The new historical motif basically takes the form of an occasion or episode: it leaves the door open to every explicit existentialist restoration. Populism again begins to melt into Cassola's ideology, in the same way that Cassola's ideology had for an instant given the impression of coinciding with the populist tradition. Ideology (all the more tenacious the less overt it is) shows itself to be stronger than any demand for regeneration. Moreover, the regeneration would not have been possible without discovering outside itself the mobile and dynamic world of history; *but Cassola's gaze is stubbornly turned upon himself.* A sudden surge of ambition, together with the desire to counter some aspects of our contemporary literature even more openly, will be sufficient for his prose once again to be entirely projected onto the past.

His latest novel, *Un cuore arido*, is replete with the past. It is the story of a girl who, after experiencing a number of sentimental episodes, is finally able to construct an indestructible inner isolation for herself.

If we loved clichés we would say that the circle of Cassola's human and poetic investigation closes here (at least for now). The analogies are extraordinary, not so much with his first stories, such as 'Rosa Gagliardi' and 'Le amiche', but with the theoretical statements of *Alla periferia*; and that is how they should be understood for anyone with a minimally good ear for such things. This juxtaposition with *Alla periferia* is not incidental but instead has a very precise significance in terms of our author's career. It is a fact that never as in this book had Cassola made explicit the existential position that he had sketched in his youthful writings, as much as twenty years earlier. At this point in his life, he obviously felt he had the strength to compose this work, where his *real* standpoint, his *real* conception of the world is not carefully concealed and translated into forms of naked objectivity. That is why, returning to the most cherished dreams of his youth with the entire weight and decisiveness of his established authority, he brings to *Un cuore arido* a clear demonstrative and ideological intent.

The nub of the story is the usual one. As the protagonist of the story, Anna Cavorzio, concludes: 'Life is like that'. But *what is fundamentally new is that Cassola presents us here with this judgement, not in its achieved and immobile fixity, but in its formation, as a process.* In other words, Anna is a Rosa Gagliardi from ten years earlier, who in the novel lives all that Rosa takes for granted. Certainly life remains in the background, inexplicable and inevitable. But the writer now seeks to understand *how* it exerts its influence over human beings who are at once protagonists and victims of it at the same time; and, above all, how one can save oneself from its nefarious influence. The writer's wish to provide a rational (within bounds) justification of his own attitude towards reality—which is to say, an ideological justification—weighs heavily on the resulting novel.

In the story of Anna Cavorzio we discover a concentrate of all the fundamental motifs of Cassola's *Weltanschauung*: it develops through three moments, each of which expresses an attitude that is already present in other characters and episodes from his books, and which are perfectly framed by the general economy of the novel. They are: the moment of waiting or of the *life hoped for*; that of disenchantment or of *lived life*; and that of the recovered feeling or of *contemplated life*. In the first moment, Anna waits to begin living, and does so with all the intensity that her introverted and stubborn character is capable of; in the second, she lives her love affairs, extracting from them only burning pain and profound humiliation; and in the third, she finally escapes from the painful, wretched and humiliating fray, which is the daily course of events, and rises above it, free at the very moment when she has renounced everything.

Across these phases and within each one, an obscure and irresistible law determines Anna's behaviour. In her enthusiasms as well as in her disappointments and defeats, she seems to act on behalf of something that is within her but is not her, is not only her, but is a 'meaning' deeper and vaster than can be contained in poor little Anna. It is true that Cassola, on more than one occasion, underlines the instinctive quality of the character (providing the psychological and pseudo-rational justification of events); but this instinctiveness in turn has a more distant as well as more elementary justification. It is required to explain (if this term can be used in this context) the necessary, mandatory character of the process through which Anna's adolescence and youth passes. Reading the book carefully, one discovers that the protagonist obeys a mechanical law of irrational impressions and reactions: the central theme of her story is represented by this total, absolute commitment to enthusiastically confront and overcome, one by one, the life experiences that she encounters, as if obeying an obscure need to arrive at a definitive conclusion as soon as possible, to come to rest among disenchanted but unbreakable certainties. This is what is intended by Anna's submission to the dangers of life or even her irrational impulse to throw herself into them. It is true that Anna succumbs too easily to the tenuous sensuality of a kiss. But it is even more evident that she makes use of the indubitable superiority of her moral and instinctive strengths only to yield to the weaknesses of others. It is she who pushes Mario, the young soldier engaged to her sister, to take her virginity (as Mara had done with Bube). It is she who throws herself into the arms of Marcello Mazzei, just when she had shown that she was able to keep him at a distance if she wished. One might say that Anna has no intention of resisting her destiny and instead pursues an unconscious desire for self-destruction and humiliation in order to re-establish, more easily and concretely, an equilibrium based on renunciation.

It is not difficult to articulate the content of this superior 'morality' which is embodied in the figure of Anna Cavorzio.

Life, Cassola argues in *Un cuore arido*, comes down to the exercise of feelings. The most important of them is love, the only chance granted to the individual to dissolve her solitary 'I' in a show of affections. But such a chance reveals itself to be cruelly illusory. The only possible love is that of waiting. When love presents itself in concrete, sensible form it too becomes a source of unhappiness, or becomes confused with one of the many aspects of a tainted reality. To free oneself from love means to free oneself from an onerous and painful weight which also has something off-putting and humiliating about it. But in love the future is condensed; so freeing oneself from love means freeing oneself from the irritation of a future one must await, escaping into memories and preparing oneself to acquire the final certainties (when Mario writes to her from America, Anna refuses to marry him although she still declares her love for him). At this point life (in the everyday sense of the term) no longer has meaning. Better still: the defence against reality, against a life that is but disappointment and pain, lies in denying that reality; life exists outside the one that each person is able to create for herself in her disenchanted heart. To arrive at the stage of supreme self-awareness, it is necessary to convince oneself through all the defeats and humiliations, that the abundance of feelings, which is to say, real life (clearly distinguished from everyday life), can be achieved in the intangible depths of our being, which the mediocre and disappointing flow of that simulacrum of existence formed by human relations lacks the strength to reach. In this vision, even love ceases to count for anything; on the contrary, it ends up being negative and counterproductive. Other values arise: before all else, the search for solitude, and then the contemplation of nature and places that appear to both reflect and nourish that charge of intangibility which is the most precious part of our soul. And indeed, these values do not flee, disillusion or change, and in remaining always self-identical they lend force and maturity to those who know how to understand and appreciate them.

But in *Un cuore arido* that ineluctable sense of destiny which Cassola elsewhere so fruitfully expresses fails to become poetically significant. Precisely because it intentionally constitutes the pivot of the tale—the thesis is too explicit, the necessity is revealed as extrinsic—Anna's obscure instinct reflects the (extremely clear) ideological intention of the author too overtly. As happens in other texts, Cassola's ambition to explain what he should serenely recognize as being unexplainable—his irrational feeling for the world—fails. Strictly speaking, the story of Anna Cavorzio is not so much a trial as an exemplary demonstration turning around a character who has been reduced to a paradigm. It is logical that as a paradigm, with all its ideal qualities put on show, Cassola's position reveals more clearly its limits. This is what always happens when an author with a narrow and limited theme claims to turn it into a general interpretation of the real or even, as in this case, a moral proposal.

On the level of style (in addition to that of structure), the emergence of these great ambitions provokes a greater complexity, often richer and more articulated than what had typified Cassola's work. But it is a merely apparent complexity. On closer examination it shows itself to be composite and fragmentary. The enrichment has not come about through the extension of his original stylistic signature but, rather, thanks to a process of simple juxtaposition. This level provides an even clearer demonstration of what we were saying about the theme of the novel: just as in the structure of the work the figure of Anna Cavorzio acts as stand-in for the author's ideology—causing the jarring incompatibility between the pages where the protagonist plays the part of a good Tuscan girl and the others where she assumes the shape of a symbol—likewise it is not difficult to distinguish in the book's style what belongs to the typical Cassolian character, objective and stripped down—from the immediate and explicit declaration of Cassola's own views. One example among many:

> Anna remained there, leaning against the ledge, with the fresh morning air coming through the wide-open window, and the sun warming her, making her sluggish. What did it matter if the future promised her nothing? The past counted for more. Then again, no life was poor in meaning; not even Ada's. The sun! The sun! It rose each morning, each morning its heat, its light would warm spirits. Each morning it returned to unveil the infinite beauty of the world, the beauty that the soul can contain but daily life cannot accommodate. Daily life was composed of many things, small and large: making beds and eating; getting engaged and married; but real life was like the light and the heat of the sun, something secret and elusive.[46]

The passage begins at an unusual pace, a few precise observations limited to a lyrical, contained, steady descriptivism: 'leaning against the ledge', the 'fresh air'; 'the wide-open window'; 'the sun', the source of simple sensations. Then we find a sequence of thoughts that we can immediately attribute to the character: 'What did it matter if the future promised her nothing?' But straight afterwards, they begin to slide into abstract generalizations: 'The past counted for more. Then again, no life is insignificant'—it is doubtful that Anna would fritter away her time with reflections of this order. The subsequent consideration, on the other hand, could reconnect the argument to Cavorzio's standpoint: 'not even Ada's'. In other words, what re-emerges is that famous motif of the particular-universal that Cassola had used to amplify the limited and modest thoughts of his popular protagonists, although he had done so from within and according to a criterion of objective faithfulness. The reflections that follow reveal a moment of uncertainty: 'The sun! The sun! It rose each morning, each morning its heat, its light would warm', we are left in doubt whether we are to assign the awareness of these sensations to the intellectual and cultural abilities of the author or of the girl. But immediately afterwards

---

46 Cassola, *Un cuore arido*, p. 308.

the narrative tips all the way over to the side of the author: 'spirits [. . .]. Each morning it returned to unveil the infinite beauty of the world', etc., etc. The intervention is blatant: 'the infinite beauty of the world'; 'the beauty that the soul can contain but daily life cannot accommodate'; 'real life'; 'like the light and the heat of the sun'; 'something secret and elusive'. Anna Cavorzio has disappeared from the scene and the author intervenes with the full weight of his culture and knowledge, as well as his difficult and ambitious vocabulary. Here we can *de facto* evaluate how disappointing the stylistic result is at this level: the most striking trait in this new Cassolian sentence is its generic character, its vagueness: 'no life was insignificant'; 'the infinite beauty of the world'; 'something secret and elusive'. The concepts escape their expression precisely because they are poor in content, so that the author, in order to save himself, hides behind naturalistic comparisons which are also quite generic and ineffective: 'its heat, its light would warm spirits'; 'real life was like the light and the heat of the sun'. The same terminology reveals this limited and, fundamentally, naively presumptuous ideological origin: 'the future', 'the past', 'spirits', 'beauty', 'soul', 'daily life'; 'real life'—this is the stylistic detritus of an unproblematic and hence easily overcome existentialism.

By way of conclusion, we could reiterate that the more Cassola's ideology is affirmed, the more disappointing and partial it is. What is true of the writings in *Alla periferia* is also true of *Fausto e Anna* and *Un cuore arido*, but with this difference: the youthful acidity of the early works and the resentful moralism of *Fausto e Anna* issue in *Un cuore arido* an attitude of refusal that is even more total and stubborn. Not even for Cassola have these twenty years passed in vain. But instead of leading him to soften his initial positions by developing a deeper cultural and human experience, they have exacerbated his convictions to the point that the reader may glimpse morbid symptoms. As an example, consider the way that in *Un cuore arido* Cassola represents love. On the one hand, he further accentuates its importance, its centrality in human life and especially in the life of women (as we have already noted). On the other, he attempts in all manner of ways to destroy every concrete, possible realization of it, devoting a fierce and obstinate effort to this task. Cassola is a writer who has always refused (for clear reasons of tradition and taste) the enticements of the sexual theme, so widespread in contemporary literature. On the contrary, he has waged a subterranean struggle against it whose traces (as noted) can be found in 'Le amiche' and then in *Fausto e Anna*, in 'Il soldato' and so on. But these indications are all taken up and exacerbated in *Un cuore arido*, where the unexpressed idea—which is perhaps unconscious to the author—is that love has no possibility of persisting and surviving because at some point it will inevitably become contaminated with sex. Given that sex is for Anna a form of duty and (with Mario) sacrifice or (as with Marcello) a dirty humiliation, she never allows her feelings of love to coincide with a composite and harmonious idea of spirit and the senses; and Cassola never tells us that she drew even the smallest amount of pleasure, be it purely sensual, from carnal union. When Anna thinks of the union of a man with a woman, she is always reminded of a tangle of coupling serpents that in distant childhood she saw a relative thrash and kill.

Then we find the meticulous description of interrupted sexual encounters, with particulars about sperm or obscene acts carried out by a poor disabled woman; an atmosphere of disgust, disapprobation, revulsion around everything that concerns sex; the conviction that this too was a filthy necessity of life and so on.[47] This attitude is evidently not accidental. What fifteen, twenty years earlier might have seemed a somewhat provincial devotion to chastity and purity now becomes a veritable morbid form in which the resentful refusal of relationships that lies at the heart of Cassola's latest work is exhibited to the highest degree. But as is often the case, the most forbidden fruits are the most desired; Cassola relieves himself of the temptation by showing how the forbidden fruits are horrifying and disgusting even only to look at. On another more complex level, the author's objectivism, having become an explicit ideological position precisely at the historico-literary time when it should perhaps have been deemed overcome by the very course of (literary and historical) events, is intensified and crystallized in a highly ambitious demonstration; whereas from the standpoint of narrative structures and stylistic signature it degrades, losing quality and purity. The circle closes, yes, but in a more worn, vacillating and contorted form than the initial one.

If our argument to this point has been clear, it will be easy to understand which of Cassola's works we prefer: generally, it is those that suffer least from the ideological and intentionally historical framing, while conceding nothing more to the cult of indifference and isolation than is objectively required by

---

47 These are Anna's words: '*Men . . . they all carry on like this* [. . .]. And so, while we're happy with words and caresses . . . they are not content with them. O it's ugly, I know, when they force us to do certain things. We . . . find those things disgusting; and then we are ashamed, and so we don't want to do them' (*Un cuore arido*, p. 288).

the narrated events. 'Il soldato' and 'Il taglio del bosco', in particular, stand out for their superior poetic and expressive qualities. The acerbically concise structure of these stories stands out (perhaps it is mere chance that the two works have the same page length); and it is clear that this brevity allows for the author's literary gifts, which are neither broad nor vigorous, to show themselves best. The framing of the events cannot be broken up into secondary episodes, many of which find a dubious necessity in short stories and longer novels. Instead, everything turns on the fundamental nucleus of the story, unfolding rapidly and concisely, something which Cassola—a writer more focused on the details than on the whole—has not always managed.

In 'Il soldato',[48] one is struck first by the absence of any spatial and temporal reference points. We know that the events take place in 'the land of pipes',[49] but why does that matter? Were we to suppress or modify some terms along with the allusions to certain modern customs, we would find ourselves before an episode of military life, aloof from any supposed reality, true in itself, as if dealing with an eternally valid human story. Cassola has gone out of his way to accentuate this atmosphere, leaving the character of Rita, the girl loved by the soldier Ghersi, in a state of mysterious and undefined separation. This confers on the story a more intensely lyrical rather than descriptive charge: all attention is led immediately, totally, to the knot of feelings and passions that both tie and separate the two protagonists.

Some of the fundamental motifs that inspire Cassola's writing return but in a more naked form, which is to say, in a form more fundamental and vital than elsewhere. Ghersi and Rita are figures pre-determined by their different and contrasting destinies. Ghersi's future is already unerringly determined: his father has died, leaving him with an establishment he must manage on behalf of his family; in other words, he is destined to spend the rest of his life in Legnano (he's very young, only twenty years old, and yet he already knows all this, confusedly intuiting how terrible that is). Rita is condemned by her reputation as an easy and immoral girl; although this is not clearly established in the story, it is enough that others consider her a whore for her to be automatically excluded from the category of women that can be loved.

The plot turns on the encounter between these two destinies. The relations between Ghersi and Rita are marked by a fundamental incapacity to understand one another, by an a priori impossibility of coming together and

---

48 'Il soldato' first published in 1958; now in *Il taglio del bosco*, pp. 473–50.
49 *Terra di pipe,* a disparaging reference to the Italian South. [Trans.]

opening up to one another. However, this is precisely the reason why they are not mediocre characters, because they are not yet reduced to the level of quotidian banality, the humdrum daily grind, without surprises for one another. Ghersi admits this to himself openly: he loves Rita because he is unable to possess her, to win her. In his eyes, she ends up being the materialized symbol—enormously attractive in its mystery—of those youthful dreams that never come true. The passion Ghersi feels for the strange and flighty Rita is akin to the final pathetic attempt to escape from the mediocre destiny that awaits him. She enters his heart in this profound and complete way because, in reality, Ghersi recognizes her as an integral part of his being, which he does not wish to renounce. To be more precise, his suffering and torment spring from the desperate reluctance he feels faced with the necessity of acquiescence, endurance and mediocrity. In loving Rita, Ghersi loves himself as a young man all the more violently and intensely the more he recognizes that there is no law or reason to explain why one suffers. Here too the protagonist's questions are destined to remain unanswered: '"Do you understand, Rita? I would have wanted to stay with you [. . .] always. I would have wanted to marry you. Why are you not a girl who can be married? Why? Tell me." He took her arm tightly, "Why are you not a girl that one can mary?"'[50] These questions are the eternal, insoluble questions about the destiny of humanity, the inevitability of pain and the irreparable precariousness of happiness.

Cassola takes up Ghersi's story with extraordinary chasteness, adopting a tone more of reserved elegy than flat description. Like his protagonist he accepts the bitter lesson that follows from the events; but in this bare recognition that pain has no explanation, there is always an aching tremor of protest, the painful awareness of having suffered injustice: '"What do you want to do about it? That's life." Ghersi looked at him, "Life, it's badly made," he said."'[51] The appeal of the story springs from the deeper exploration of this motif: the pathetic contemplation of a young life that turns back upon itself, crying and despairing as it discovers for the first time (the decisive and extreme one) just how difficult and cruel existence is.

These themes had already been given a more complete and superior expression in 'Il taglio del bosco',[52] Cassola's narrative masterpiece.

---

50 Cassola, *Il taglio del bosco*, p. 536.

51 Cassola, *Il taglio del bosco*, p. 539.

52 'Il taglio del bosco' first published in 1953; now included in the homonymous volume, pp. 109–76.

The plot of the story is composed of a few essential elements and there is neither development nor demonstration. The *fact*[53] leaps straight into the foreground, with the self-evidence of everyday things. Cassola does not even once attempt to universalize the protagonist's painful case; and yet the force of the poetry is such that here, perhaps for the only time, the author gives his conception of reality a sincerely convincing and persuasive appearance. That is because the human quality of the characters is determined unambiguously, without contrasting opinions or ambiguous allusions yet with extreme modesty and deep empathy. The distance between the writer and the popular 'level' he depicts, so evident in his other works, has been here reduced to a minimum: the essence of the peasant world is rediscovered in the sublime *humility* of the spirit; and the pained face of the author is plainly reflected in this humility. In other words, Cassola does not indulge in pure and simple literary invention; nor is the story of his characters used as a pretext for the explicit affirmation of his ideas. The balance between inspiration and objective story is fully achieved.

The story has a long beginning and the few events that take place are full of pauses, punctuated line-by-line and phrase-by-phrase. Guglielmo, a recently widowed woodsman, briefly returns to his home where his sisters live with his two young daughters; but he desires to leave again immediately because everything reminds him of the torment of loss and solitude. He hopes that work will assuage the pain in his heart. Guglielmo spends the entire winter with Fiore, a rough and insensitive chief woodsman; Francesco, an old drifter and fantastical storyteller; cousin Amedeo, colourless and normal; and the young and care-free Germano, in the deep forest, cutting down trees and brushwood, organizing the transportation of wood and packing the charcoal.

The scope of the story open up immediately with the description of this woodland. The labour of the five men, their interminably long days, the evenings spent around a fire recounting stories or playing cards, the slowly changing faces of nature enormously enrich the picture, shedding the light of truth on simple, basic but genuine feelings threaded throughout the story. The stylistic signature is unchanging: the narrative proceeds, fact after fact, without slippage or hesitation. Wanting to remain truthful, Cassola lends his characters commonplace phrases, fragments of conversation, expressions that truthfully express their basic psychology. More than anywhere else (although still sparsely) he inserts dialectal, idiomatic and slang expressions.

---

53 *Fatto*, fact, can also mean a deed, act, story or event. [Trans.]

At times when he narrowly delimits the elements of language and style, Cassola accentuates in an equally rigorous way the atemporal mood already present in his other writings: all contact with the outside world is broken, the small plebeian community lives alone with itself and nature. The tale has an atmosphere of enchantment: the story of Guglielmo and his workmates, of the solitary hardworking charcoal-burner, of the poor highlanders from Pistoia, lost in solitary encampments within the recesses of the forest—they appear as if suspended in a reality without borders or reference points.

And yet the separation from the world is unable to annul the play of feelings. On the contrary, isolated in this real, objective condition, they acquire an even greater purity: no external distraction intervenes to disturb and muddle them. The immense sadness that suddenly takes hold of people in the course of a rainy day or at the end of an evening chat is the clearest manifestation of this obscure sense of existence, aroused in them by solitude and the surrounding virginal nature. None of these humble human figures would be able to experience themselves so profoundly elsewhere.

Guglielmo soon realizes that his hope of smothering the pain through isolation and work is but an illusion. In fact, in the forest he too is more of a man than in the village, his home. Hence his suffering chafes all the more, because it is more continuously present. Once again we come across the themes dear to Cassola. But here they are free from any sentimental self-satisfaction and psychological exaggeration. The search for indifference takes place here too, but how much more human and poetic it is than in *Un cuore arido*! 'To fall into sleep's darkness was the best that was left to him. When Guglielmo felt sleep come on, he was happy, because for a few hours he would be freed of all thought, and because another day had passed.' The desire to overcome pain harks back to its source in the instincts, and is translated in terms of an elementary sensibility: Guglielmo, the woodsman, finds indifference in the very fabric of sleep which suffocates with its soft and restful blanket all activity tormenting the mind and the heart, and makes one suddenly aware that another fraction of this odious time has passed. ' "O God, I'll become worse than Fiore," he thought. After all, it would not have been bad. At least Fiore didn't feel anything. He had not even felt the death of his son. It was much better to be like Fiore; or like Francesco, who had no one.' The awareness of his condition of unhappiness and pain stems from empathizing with those near him (and not from an a priori self-valorization; recall the dialogue, the first part of which is beautiful, between Guglielmo and the old charcoal-burner, who is also a widower); likewise, the attempt to escape the sting of his feelings is rendered in equally concrete terms, in the form of *models of life that already exist in the shape of men and are no longer simply ideas*. The love that Guglielmo feels for his wife is clearly extremely important or, rather, an essential element of his personality—yet it is never named directly, nor could it be, because in reality Guglielmo does not experience it as such, nor does he know that his feeling bears that name. *Instead it is a dark and natural force of attraction for a creature that is close, supportive and friendly*; and the loss of his wife is, consequently, angst at the isolation and futility of life, which is equally indefinable and natural. Inspired by the conversation with the charcoal-burner, Guglielmo is able to give a timidly metaphysical interpretation of his state of mind: 'How many stars there are! How many distant, unknown worlds . . . ! Was there work, suffering, death, pain up there?' But ultimately this, too, is a brief interlude. The truth—simple, naked, and yet terrible—is suffering, a suffering that even strenuous work, or physical labour, is not able to extinguish. All chance of consolation is lost at this point. All that remains is pain and a question to which no one is able to respond. Clinging to the gate of the cemetery, Guglielmo 'thought that Rosa should have helped him. It was not possible to continue like this. Up there in the sky, she should give him the strength to live. And he looked up. But everywhere was dark; there was not a single star.'[54] No unnecessary words are used even for the schematic texture of feelings and gestures. Only one thought stirs Guglielmo's mind: that life like this is unbearable; looking around oneself is a concrete, physical way of looking for help, solidarity; but the dark night sky rejects his appeal with the self-evidence of things themselves. And yet, the naked prose is animated as if by an interior life, more intense than the one unfolding on the surface and that the author describes: 'And he looked up. But everywhere was dark; there was not a single star'; gestures and things, but full of a secret and profound emotion; between the character and the surrounding world, no rational communication is possible, instead something like a mysterious circle of recognition is established. *Sunt lacrimae rerum*,[55] even if Guglielmo is not able to recognize it, and he only *feels*; but he feels with the indefinite and hence total force that is within him, as it is in all phenomena, in all the essences of nature. Objectivity is sublimated in a melancholic and contemplative lyricism: the particular discovers

---

54 Cassola, *Il taglio del bosco*, p. 149, 151, 174 and 176, respectively.
55 '[T]here are tears [for things]', from Virgil's *Aeneid*, 1.462. [Trans.]

here its *true* transcendence in an overcoming of itself through pain; and pain in turn becomes poetry because it is effectively a man's pain.

This conclusion leads us back to our starting point: this knowing combination of autobiography, lyricism and descriptive minutiae, despite its typically Cassolian qualities, can be understood historically only by reconnecting it to the intellectual and cultural climate that shaped the early life of the author. Let us leave aside the quality of the result, which in this is case is truly excellent; but how can one not feel that the formula for his work stems largely from the infinite series of analogous attempts in the Italian literature of the 1930s and 40s? Here we find not exactly a reprise but a pure and simple continuation and development—in the terms of a more profound and genuine human truth—of that twentieth-century Italian literary tendency that placed the problem of the 'I' at the centre and mediated the solution by affirming, more or less explicitly, the dominance of literature over life or, rather, by sublimating life in literature. In Italy, this reflected an ontological intellectual attitude (with a decidedly bourgeois backdrop) not without a display of provincial and conservative resentments.

If Cassola's most poetically successful work must be located within this historico-literary moment (it goes without saying that the publication date of the works count only to a point), one can well understand how this also doubles as a comprehensive judgement on him as a contemporary artist. The truth is that Cassola is all the more a poet, as in 'Il taglio del bosco' and in 'Il soldato', the more his gaze is turned to the past; whereas the more he is concerned, in one way or another, with current themes, the more he diminishes. This is understandable since everything shows that Cassola is constantly and obstinately engaged in a polemic with the *whole* of the contemporary world. And he conducts his polemic by arguing for the human and literary dimensions of a civilization which is imperfect and contradictory, and which the history of the last twenty years has irreparably eroded and consumed. This does not mean that the (literary, human, social) world of today is in the abstract, better than that of yesterday to which Cassola remains nostalgically wedded. It is simply different from it, and in order to comprehend it, it is therefore necessary to recognize the laws that govern it. To refuse it and hide in a peripheral area of reality—which appears objectively to reproduce certain archaic ideal characteristics preferred by the *laudatores temporis acti*[56]—is only to accept one's own limits and even to hold them dear.

We hope to have shed light on how much this attitude of prejudiced refusal is due to the character of the man in the course of the analysis of his works and of his piecemeal development. In addition, we must signal a conspicuous cultural limit that weighs heavily on Cassola's activity. For reasons we have mentioned on a number of occasions, there is no doubt that he remains very much tied to his origins. It is important to highlight that this fidelity, suitably enriched and deepened, is the source of his more successful works. However, these origins are marked by a powerful provincial emphasis: essentially linked to the milieu around the journal *Letteratura* which continued and impoverishes in various ways the formal research of the literary journal *Solaria*; and, within that same journal, to the group of Tuscan writers that hark back to a literary tradition that we have more than once indicated as the most tenaciously conservative tendency in our literature across the nineteenth and twentieth centuries. We have already alluded to Tozzi, who Cassola admired not so much as a writer of robust and sanguine complexion, as for being the interpreter and representative of a literature limited to the neighbourhood, the lane, the family and the primordial contrasts of feelings and passions;[57] and to Bilenchi, whose contribution to *strapaese* literature we have already touched upon, and whose importance time has done much to diminish. We should also add here the name of Alessandro Bonsanti,[58] the editor of *Letteratura*, to whom Cassola was perhaps closer than anyone else, with his semi-metaphysical efforts and his search for suspended and immobile settings.

More recently the names of Franz Kafka and James Joyce have been mentioned; and Cassola has been spoken of as a precursor to *l'école du regard*.[59] Cassola has unwaveringly referred to his debt to Joyce (to the early Joyce, which should be a warning sign to the attentive reader). But in our judgement these associations are unfounded. Cassola's 'objectivism' which is the aspect

---

56 'Praiser of times past', from Horace's *Ars Poetica*, line 173. [Trans.]

57 Cassola declared (in an interview in the magazine *L'Espresso*, 17 July 1960) that: 'I remain unfazed by the accusation of being regional, provincial, limited to a small world. Tozzi, the Italian twentieth-century author that I love most is also accused of this.'

58 Alessandro Bonsanti (1904–1984), writer, politician and founder of *Letteratura*; was elected mayor of Florence in 1983. [Trans.]

59 More commonly known as the *nouveau roman*. The most celebrated representatives of this tradition are Alain Robbe-Grillet, Nathalie Sarraute and Michel Butor. [Trans.]

closest to the works of Kafka, Joyce and *l'école du regard*, never achieved the level of absolute and undisputed purity. Over and again we have demonstrated how in Cassola the ideology of solitude does not preclude the worship of 'good intentions'; and it is precisely this aspect that reveals our author as the typical representative of a provincial, petty bourgeois, conservative world. One cannot allude to writers such as Kafka and Joyce, or even to minor or miniscule figures such as Alain Robbe-Grillet and Michel Butor, forgetting that in their case the novelty of the literary result is parallel and convergent with the tragic (or parodic) destruction of all sentimental detritus, of all manifestations of the heart or natural positivity. Certainly, one should not completely reject the hypothesis that something of *Dubliners* has stuck to the pen of our writer. But what else does this acknowledgement mean if not that in this case, too, Cassola has wanted to hark back to an archetype of twentieth-century art only so as to deny all its subsequent developments and to confirm that his gaze is turned back to the nineteenth century, that mythical period when characters still had well-defined feelings, simple and clear features, and a profound disposition to live a life without ideal or practical complications? The truth is that Cassola lacks the inclination to understand the meaning of a contemporary reality confronted and dissected at the level of the great European cultural experiences. It is no coincidence that the only literary discovery that counted for anything after his youthful experiences (and which I believe is behind the shift exemplified by *Un cuore arido*) is *Doctor Zhivago*, namely, a book that commendably lends itself to being appreciated by a mind little inclined to look seriously and consciously at the present, because it is the work of an author who also constructs his entire world on the basis of the refusal of contemporary man and his history.[60] Moreover, it should be noted that Cassola reads Pasternak in a particularly tendentious and one-sided fashion; for this reason he misses many elements of the real ordeal of the protagonist, Zhivago, whereas others are over-emphasized, such as the poetry of nature and sentimental education. The conservative aspect of this reading can be clearly seen when Cassola enlists it in a fierce diatribe against the whole of contemporary literature and, in particular, against the 'literature of crisis' (which the author proposes to define more correctly as the 'crisis of literature'), for which he forecasts a speedy end. The writers Cassola bundles together and condemns without distinction (with a surprising level of nonchalance) are, one after

---

60 We refer to Cassola's response to a questionnaire by the journal *Il ponte* 14 (1958): 528–36, into *Doctor Zhivago* and Boris Pasternak from which these quotations are drawn.

another, 'Camus, Sartre, Green, as well as Mann and Malraux'. The theoretical declarations are no less hasty and naive, but in their assertiveness and conviction they reveal a basic intellectual arrogance we have observed elsewhere. So for him 'the faults of Decadentism' are not only technical or stylistic; they exist, above all, in the 'loss of the *simple human basis* of the poem'; indeed, 'literature is the expression of feelings, and without feeling, or with bad feelings, one makes bad literature'. For that reason, Pasternak had been right 'to only follow the law of inspiration', since '"*modern*", "*contemporary*", is only *what is fresh, genuine, poetic*'.

In the light of such statements—which display a popularizing and superficial Croceanism that re-emerges alongside typically petty-bourgeois spiritual and moral needs—Cassola's guiding themes are put in a new perspective. In other words, we realize that Cassola's existentialism, founded on the glorification of good intentions, on poetry and inspiration and so on, is nothing but a resentful provincial claim against the modern world itself.

Conversely, one cannot deny that there are aspects of modernity in Cassola's work, although more often than not only as passive echoes of situations and largely unwitting. The obstinate refusal of a rational attitude and of history, along with a meta-historical and literary evasion—these are also, clearly, forms of the Decadent Movement and more broadly characteristic of *Novecentismo*. But Cassola is unable (that is, he lacks the strength) to use these points in his favour, to turn them into instruments of penetration and further exploration of contemporary reality. One must nevertheless admit that there is a difference between someone who theorizes isolation as the shortest road to the dissolution of the world (of *this* world) and someone who turns it into a shield to hide in his own pale Limbo, *which nonetheless serves to console*. Ironically, those works where Cassola develops a broader and more demanding narrative demonstrate that he is unable to cope with the *true* reality of the twentieth century. It becomes clear, then, this attempt to bring together his personal ethical and ideological ideas with certain demands of the contemporary world results only in low-level popularization. *In a particular configuration of the publishing market, even the ideology of isolation can become a genre for widespread consumption.* Cassola's sentimentalism degenerates either into melodrama or ethico-political manifesto, revealing its worst—most extrinsic and superficial—aspect.

Faced with this phenomenon, 'old style' cultural explanations alone are no longer sufficient to justify certain choices; instead, one must trust in more broadly sociological explanations. From 1955 or '56 onwards, the Italian literary world cannot be judged without examining the complicated interweaving of cultural, pseudo-cultural and industrial-cultural factors that underlie many shifts that appear merely poetic or linguistic. From this standpoint (which of course is not singular or paramount, and which we examine here from a rigorously phenomenological and not moralistic standpoint), the leap that Cassola takes from the short story to the long novel and, later, from a theme of (literary as well as ideal) retreat to a theme that *broadly exploits* the original nucleus of inspiration, is also an episode displaying the growing evolution of the Italian publishing and cultural market. The latter offers the author the possibility of reaching a previously unimaginable public (*La ragazza di Bube* and *Un cuore arido* were sold in tens of thousands of copies). In exchange, it demands that his point of view be made more *explicit* and take a more *popular* form. Naturally, this phenomenon is not absolutely conscious on one side or the other (although on both sides there are conscious elements). That does not mean it doesn't exist or manifest itself with a certain degree of clarity (the same can be said for all of Giorgio Bassani's later works, from *Il giardino dei Finzi-Confini* [The Garden of the Finzi-Continis] to *Dietro la porta* [Behind the Door], a work in which the approach of the *Storie ferraresi* [Tales from Ferrara] is elucidated and 'explained to the people', not without melodramatic ploys or cinematographic effects). Here, we can merely point out the great interest of this theme. It is undoubtedly remarkable that the bourgeois culture industry of the 1960s should so openly and decisively support the bourgeois literary position of the 40s (Bassani and Cassola are not mentioned by chance); or, vice versa, that the latter should lend itself, with its technical and formal refinement, to act as a shield for the brutal aggressiveness of the former. But it can also be completely explained in the light of the bourgeoisie's unchanged historical drive for cultural and literary hegemony. One might object that Cassola knows nothing of such things. But it is precisely not knowing anything that leads to acquiescence and *service* (it is barely necessary to remind the reader that we are using these terms in an absolutely objective sense).

That is how Cassola's name can be employed today in literary disputes in an almost exclusively conservative way, to designate a regressive passatismo.[61]

---

61 *Passatismo* was a disparaging term coined by Italian futurists to castigate past-oriented cultural and intellectual forms. [Trans.]

In many ways this is correct, although we refuse to believe that the opposition, Cassola–Pasolini, which is often brought up in these disputes, represents anything more than the clash between two different ways of taking up and cultivating old traditions.

We are tempted to conclude by stating that the original nucleus of Cassola's poetics lies in its capacity to express an extremely tenuous and contradictory vein of Leopardi-ism. But Calvino has already observed that the Recanatis of the spirit[62] must not be loved, whereas Cassola and all the others writers of the country and the provinces passionately love the sites of their solitude and pain. *Cassola, too*—like Pasolini, for example—*is unable to relinquish the idea of the redemption of his own unhappiness.* In this sense, to turn to the people, or to popular figures, means only one thing: that in the rediscovered humility of the subaltern world, in its exceptional capacity for suffering and feeling, the writer discovers a particle of consolation for his perennial pain. The endpoint of the investigation is never rebellion or the urge to act but only a profound feeling of passivity or refusal.

Among other things, this is necessary to explain why in Cassola, as in so many other writers of twentieth-century Italy, the undeniable decadent or romantic ferments tend always to be arranged in a literary or ideal structure that is neither decadent nor romantic (spasm, revolt, even a formal break) but, rather, neo-classical (acceptance, even outer dignity). The all too easy and vague statement according to which Cassola is a 'minor classic' is only correct if by this one is alluding to the climate of renewed formal composure which absorbs, calms, blunts and dulls the confused fruit of his inspiration. Fundamentally, what springs from this literary effort is Cassola's dignified. 'pessimistic vignettism'. Beyond this sober, essential and opaque screen, the vibrations of the poetry are muffled and smothered. But that is what the allusion to Leopardi means. Unable to go beyond these limits, Cassola has nonetheless sometimes been able to recognize and find himself in a painful and modest contemplation of human suffering. Cassola's voice is most effective when it comes to us through a world that has disappeared, as the final appeal of a spiritual civilization that is no longer accessible, and that in his own work struggles to re-emerge from the ruins of a limited and by-now useless culture. But when the author lacks any other ambition than to express the 'pain of

---

62 Recanati in Province of Macerata, Marche region of Italy, is the hometown of Giacomo Leopardi. [Trans.]

life', his subdued tones return pathetic heart-rending echoes from that world. Even the petty bourgeoisie can move itself to tears, when it does not turn its ills into myths or hopes but only exposes them as the objective reflections of a painful common fate.

Pasolini

If we limit ourselves solely to those works from Pasolini's early years that he deemed worthy of publication, we see they are teeming with varied efforts and experiments. Bearing in mind that he was born in 1922, the somewhat exuberant and often fantastic precocity of this poet's production is evident: his collection of poems in Friulian dialect *Poesie a Casarsa* (1941–43);[1] in 1945 he composes a journal in Italian [*in lingua*];[2] in 1945–47 the series *Dal diario* [From the Diary], which takes up only a few of the poems from the preceding work; in the years between 1944 and 1953, the works in dialect are *Suite friulana* [Friulian Suite], *Il testament Coran* and *Romancero* [Ballads]; in 1949–50 we find the novel on peasant life *Il sogno di una cosa* [The Dream of a Thing]; and, taking a few steps back, we come across the poems in Italian *L'usignolo della Chiesa Cattolica* [The Nightingale of the Catholic Church, 1943], *Il pianto della rosa* [The Cry of the Rose, 1946], *Lingua* [Language/Tongue, 1947], *Paolo e Baruch* (1948–49), *Italia* (1949), *Tragiques* (1948–49) and *La scoperta di Marx* [The Discovery of Marx, 1949].

A novel and around 150 poems, in all likelihood accompanied by a vast set of unpublished drafts, bear witness in the 20-something Pasolini to a frenzied activity, an immoderate desire for confession. At this time, speaking and writing must have been more important than living. Or, to put it another way, life—even at its most painful and traumatic—must have appeared as a vast field for experimentation in which Pasolini's sole aim and possibility of meaning lay in nurturing poetic expression. This is a common condition for writers from the period 1920 to 1945, when many were influenced by the myth of a rigorous and exclusive literary ontology. Pasolini's attachment to

---

1 Casarsa is the Friulian town where Pasolini's mother moved the family in 1926, and where he began to write poetry as a small boy. [Trans.]

2 *Parlare in lingua* means to speak 'correctly', in a more standardized Italian. [Trans.]

Literature and Poetry is very visible in his early works. As a worthy devotee of the twentieth-century tradition that runs from Sbarbaro to Onofri to Ungaretti to Montale and Penna to Caproni,[3] his work stands out in that it blossoms precisely when the climate of that tradition was beginning to wane. Pasolini's education takes place in those years (1940–45) in which things greater than poetry and literature were maturing and unfolding. It is not by chance that his poetic education was immediately eclipsed by seismic global events which, while leaving the former initial framework implicit, is in turn transformed thematically and stylistically. It is true that Pasolini himself has written that a 'literary formation conditions an entire literary existence'.[4] Yet there is no doubt that between this early Pasolini and the mature one there is a breach that far exceeds that of normal internal evolution, of linear and logical development. To the various personal traumas, Pasolini can also add this historico-cultural one: the failure and objective closure of his poetic apprenticeship, which corresponds to the violent arrest of a certain internal development of the general theoretico-literary discourse. Notwithstanding the individual turmoil that characterizes it, Pasolini's poetry moves, at least until 1948, within the furrow of the *novecentesca* tradition. His turn to mature literary production takes place through the deliberate refusal not of his earlier poetry (which on the contrary Pasolini considers of aesthetic and documentary value), but instead of the principles and poetics that influenced and sustained his early practice. And as everyone knows, what marks this passage is, as we shall see, Pasolini's shrewd poetic meditation on the character of an entire literary civilization.

However, the significance of the early Pasolini goes beyond such a historico-literary reconstruction. It is curious that, for the most part, these early works did not become public until Pasolini had become known as a poet and narrator stirred by very different ambitions and aims. We are in the

---

3 Camillo Sbarbaro (1888–1967), Ligurian poet, writer, aphorist and translator. Arturo Onofri (1885–1928), metaphysical poet. Giuseppe Ungaretti (1888–1970), leading figure in twentieth-century Italian poetry—his collection of war poetry *Allegria di naufragi* (Florence: Vallecchi, 1919) also a second edition *L'Allegria* (Milan: Preda, 1931) is regarded as a turning point in Italian literature. Sandro Penna (1906–77), poet, known for his erotic gay poetry, *Remember me, God of Love: Selected Poetry and Prose* (Blake Robinson trans.) (London: Carcanet, 1993). Giuseppe Caproni (1912–90), poet, literary critic and translator, his work is discussed in Giorgio Agamben, *The End of the Poem: Studies in Poetics* (Daniel Heller-Roazen trans.) (Stanford: Stanford University Press, 1999). [Trans.]
4 Pier Paolo Pasolini in the note to 'La posizione', *Officina* 1(1956): 249.

presence of a writer who voluntarily opts to reconstruct his own literary past before everyone's eyes, at a distance of a number of years from the composition of these works, as if polemically challenging all the conjectures and assumptions of his critics. Those who have condemned these re-exhumations, judging them counterproductive in light of the more recent image of the writer, should recognize that Pasolini does not fear but, rather, craves scandal. Indeed, he is frequently animated by a desire to appear before the world's judgement weighed down with all sorts of faults and sins. This is much more evident and naively explicit in the youthful works we have listed than in the later ones. These early works furnish us with the proof (something like the barely covered trace of poetic speech) of an entire series of secret psychic processes, of very powerful natural inclinations through which the poet constitutes for himself a character with a definite human and passionate attitude that outlasts the early literary convictions. This criterion of interpretation, the one most suited to Pasolini's literary production of the 1940s and 50s, does not exclude the possibility that the poet was already capable of producing accomplished works, perfect in their own right. However, we will see that even in these cases the impetus is to be sought in the poet's assertive and exclusive subjectivity, in his propensity to place himself at the world's centre and remain there with a painful and often unfulfilled desire for the absolute. The entirety of this earliest and least well-known period of Pasolini's practice can be understood from within the same parameters of interpretation, even though (or precisely because) the results oscillate between a crude autobiographism and an exquisite, almost exhausted lyricism.

The vigour of Pasolini's poetry during this phase stems from the experience of the Friulian language. From the start we must dispel the possible misunderstanding concerning the widespread parallel that is drawn between dialect and the popular. Pasolini is drawn to Friulian, his mother tongue, by a host of reasons that he has admirably outlined, the last of which is the will to speak in the name of the people, to become the voice of the voiceless peasantry. Conversely, it is readily understood that the objective environmental stimuli, while preserving—as we shall see—a precise function and consistency, are reshaped and transfigured in a poetic vision that is anything but weak and immature. The 'regression' of which Pasolini speaks from one language to the other, from a civilization in crisis to a civilization immersed in primitive purity, is in practice nothing but a process of absolutizing the real, where the new language and the different (more genuine, more virginal) environment simply constitute instruments in which well-defined subjective moods and sensations are analogously expressed. Pasolini himself has taught us that dialectal poetry very rarely (and never in the twentieth century) means popular poetry. It is not this obvious truth that we wish to underline here. More importantly, amongst all the dialectal poets of the twentieth century, it is Pasolini who reaches the highest degree of literary exquisiteness and poetic transfiguration; although he is also the one who, more than all the others, feels the need for an objective *stimulus*, for an instrument of analogical expression. This archaic Friuli, understood as primitive language and humanity, both dream and reality, moves between the absoluteness of the 'I' which ultimately summarizes and transforms everything within itself, the fleeting but decisive presence of objects that seem to lend themselves to the violence of Pasolinian love. The complexity of the relationship is symbolically summarized in the poem by Peire Vidal set as epigram to:

> With my breath I draw towards me the air
> that I feel coming from Provence
> everything that comes from there gives me pleasure.[5]

If one is far from the motherland, as was Vidal,[6] one breathes in the air of one's country as if to enjoy its distant pleasures. If one is not far from one's motherland, as in the case of Pasolini—but one is, like him, tormented and sad—one invents a fantasy country to superimpose on the real one, giving it the geographical shape of one's own spirit, the layout of the inner roads and deep rivers that plough a furrow in to the unfathomable darkest depths of the 'I'.

In this climate, nature becomes merely a tremor, a continuous waterfall of undefined sensations, euphuisms all the more effective the more modest they are. This is the dedication:

> Fountain of water from my village.
> There is no fresher water than in my village.
> Fountain of rustic love.[7]

---

5 Pasolini's poems in Friulian dialect are now collected in *La meglio gioventù* [The Best Youth] (Florence: Sansoni, 1954), from which nearly all the following quotations are drawn. [English translations are made from the Italian version that Pasolini supplies at the bottom of the page, and which Asor Rosa reproduces in the original.—Trans.]

6 Peire Vidal was a twelfth-century Old Occitan troubadour from Toulouse. [Trans.]

7 Passolini, *La meglio gioventù*, p. 15.

Note not so much the extreme sobriety of the language, something too evident to require underlining, as the subtle knowingness of the feeling, graduated, punctuated in three brief but fundamental moments. First, the naked recognition of the memory, which stretches into an affectionate pause towards the end of the verse: 'fountain of water from my village'. The feeling, initially contained in a modest and severe possessive (from *my* village), is raised in the second verse into a statement of naive and virile pride: 'there is no fresher water than in my village' (which should not be read, for that matter, in a declarative key but, rather, with the same tranquil, meditative tone characteristic of basic certainties). But here too the boasting is softened and made more intimate by the significant repetition of the possessive that punctuates and supports the final part of the verse ('from my village—in my village'). The third verse uncovers the analogical key that inspires it: the motif of 'water' ('fountain of water—there is no water') can be found entirely in the vibration of the feeling: 'Fountain of [. . .] love'. And the love is 'rustic', not so much in light of the customs of the *país* as in terms of those inclinations towards purity and primitiveness that the poet begins to discover in himself as he advances in his Friulian explorations. Another example:

> Luminous evening, the water rises
> rises in the ditch, a pregnant woman
> walks in the field.
> I remember you, Narcissus, you had the colour
> of evening, when the bells toll
> for the dead.[8]

'Luminous evening'—Pasolini's Friulian poems are filled with such colours, sometime more precise and intense, but much more often indeterminate, like vague halos around things.[9] It is easy to detect here the particular meaning and function of the use of dialect, in preference to literary language. There is no doubt that the musical resonance of *imbarlumida* / 'luminous', and the undertones contained in such words are much richer and deeper than *luminosa* / 'illuminated'. Moreover, it should be noted that Friulian (Pasolini's Friulian, to be more precise) exhibits an unusual wealth of vocabulary of this

---

8 Passolini, *La meglio gioventù*, p. 16.
9 'The sun dark with smoke'; '(T)he serene evening tinges the shadow on the old walls; in the sky the light blinds'; 'Down there the sky is all serene'; 'When the evening is lost in the fountains, the colour of my village is lost'; 'One can see the distant hamlets under the pale hills'. There is hardly a poem in this collection without a note of this sort.

sort, which is destined to animate with its mere presence the sober words of the poet: *soreli* / 'sun'; *sèil* / 'sky'; *cuàrp* / 'body'; *lun* / 'light'; *ciera* / 'earth'; *rosada* / 'dew'; *ciamp* / 'field'; *ploja* / 'rain'; *roja* / 'brook'; and *moràr* / 'mulberry'. Even death, *muàrt*, seems to become pure sound in this ancient and noble language. *Sera imbarlumida* / 'luminous evening', opens the first tercet of this composition, introducing the reader, with surprising immediacy, into an ambience full of echoes and resonances:'the water rises in the ditch', is already a living act, whose sound and movement we can grasp, precisely because of the enduring suggestion of the first two words. But the subsequent image: 'a pregnant woman walks in the field', is like the finale of this lyrical intuition: the mysterious sense of procreation passes slowly through the picture, like that pregnant woman walking across the field among the early evening shadows. The analogical procedure becomes magnificently clear in the relationship between the first and second tercet: the motif of Narcissus, which we won't linger over here as it will be examined below, leaps out of the picture we have described, like the image of an intimate melancholy ('you had the colour of evening') reflected in a deep dark mirror. The realism of some precious images was only of *service* to the poet. In the background the dull (but very sweet) echo of the bells brings to a close in a musical mood the composition that began with the feint colours of an evening still bathed in light.[10]

The figure of the poet appears submerged in this atmosphere, but in reality is present in every vibration, every image of nature. Let us recall that, for Pasolini as a young man, Friuli is a Provence of the spirit.[11] The relationship of the poet with the world is, at least in origin, a pure feeling of nostalgia or, rather, love: 'I am the spirit of love / who returns to his village from afar'.[12] But this love is also an exorbitant possessiveness, a dark craving for identification. Take note, for it is possible here to rediscover the root of a process through which a spirit sick with the absolute plunges into reality and discovers the world. As we were saying, fundamentally we find an obscure, original,

---

10 Lights, colours, sounds and silences are tightly woven in Pasolini's Friulian. The bell is the faithful friend of the decadent melancholy spirit. See 'Ciant da li ciampanis' in *La meglio gioventù*, p. 27: 'I died in the sound of bells'. And 'over the fields what silence the bell brings!'; 'the bells beat in another sky'; 'today is Sunday, and the bells ring like a flock'. More significantly: 'Bell, you're always the same, and with dismay I return to your voice'.

11 On the significance of Provençal verse and song in Pasolini's early poetic work, see Massimo Cacciari, 'Pasolini provenzale?', *MicroMega* 4 (October–November 1995). Available at: https://goo.gl/Hr4iQn (last accessed on 7 March 2019). [Trans.]

12 Passolini, 'Ciant da li ciampanis', p. 27.

unconscious tendency to rediscover within this nature the sources of being itself:

> I am born
> in the scent the rain exhales
> from the fields of
> living grass. . . I am born
> in the brook's reflection.[13]

The poet is born as the voice of nature, as a creature of the water, the grass and the rain. Slowly re-emerging into consciousness, without ever conquering it completely (if we take consciousness to be synonymous with full dominion and clarity), along his path he discovers men and things. The things of the landscape and the environment take shape in the immediacy of sensations and states of the soul, which easily take the place of rational and reflective processes. Men too assume the semblance of feelings. But their raw physicality, their full-bodied individual and social existence are not completely lost. Ultimately, the poet's relationship with the Friulian peasant is also constituted by a natural affinity, a primal identification. Like the poet, even the peasant is made of earth and light:

> Laugh, you, light-hearted youth
> feeling in your body
> the warm and dark earth,
> and the fresh, clear sky.[14]

When he's handsome and cheerful, he's handsome and cheerful like an animal: 'You, David, are like a bull on an April day';[15] 'handsome like a horse'.[16] Hence his life—unfolding like that of nature—knows no anxieties, nor any of the animosities and rebellions of those who pass through History and make use of consciousness on a daily basis. The step from the life of nature to peasant ethics is a small one: it is enough to live and to be, without effort, *what one is—what one has always been*:

> But we live
> calm and dead

---

13 Pasolini, 'O me donzel' in *La meglio gioventù*, p. 19.

14 Pasolini, 'A Rosari' in *La meglio gioventù*, p. 50.

15 Pasolini, 'David' in *La meglio gioventù*, p. 24.

16 Pasolini, 'Bel come un ciaval' in *La meglio gioventù*, p. 107.

like water passing
unnoticed through the hedges
[. . .]
Time does not move
it looks at the laughter of fathers
like rain among the branches
in the eyes of youths.[17]

Like the water flowing past, like the rain among the branches . . . Read *La not di maj* [A Night in May]: an archaic, almost proto-Romance conception of peasant life tends to assert itself in generic maxims and a narrative devoid of a historical dimension.[18] The old peasant with a face marked by pain and toil sinks into nothingness as though he were part of a collective existence without individual qualities:

I do not see
a past in your eye
consumed by a web
of bloody wrinkles.
But only dark years
and forgotten nights
and buried passions
in a time without days.

I no jòt un Passàt ['I do not see Past']—but 'a Past' is History, and History is the history of men. In a way, the peasant is not yet a 'man': he is land, a clump of earth, the bud of a tree. He is also 'representative' of a chain of generations, which absorb and erase him as an individual, just as the chain of seasons absorbs and erases, in the life of nature, the significance and importance of individual years:

Life without destiny,
carried away with the body:
from son become father
between the hearth and the clods of earth.[19]

---

17 Pasolini, 'Tornant al país' [Returning to the Village] in *La meglio gioventù*, p. 26.
18 'A Night in May'. 'Proto-Romance' is a linguistic term referring to the kind of Vulgar Latin that served as a precursor and transition to Romance languages. [Trans.]
19 Pasolini, 'La not di maj' in *La meglio gioventù*, p. 52 and 54, respectively.

Simplicity, purity and spiritual virginity are the positive traits of this 'life without destiny', of this 'unknown living',[20] of this world where 'living is certain'.[21] The adolescent Pasolini sinks into the contemplation of this primitive and atemporal existence with the ardour of a mystic who has glimpsed the image of Salvation. The peasant archaism thus reflects a much vaster relationship of religious communion with Nature of the world, which the poet feels he partakes in. Yet once its autonomy is revealed, it becomes the luminous and illusory mirage of the overcoming of this painful and contradictory spirituality. Let us not forget this first discovery but, in the meantime, let us specify the connotations of the other pole of the discourse: the poet, in his intimate—or, rather, private—history.

We have said: voice of nature, creature of water, grass and rain, spirit of love. But these too are nothing but metaphors for the illusions that the voice of the poems has already developed and affirmed. Beneath the myth of the poet as 'voice of nature', which would suggest innocence and simplicity, hides instead a highly tormented psyche, a knot of feelings and passions only some of which come to the surface. As in *Diari* (1945 and 1954) and *L'usignolo della Chiesa Cattolica*, it is easy to grasp in the more openly documentary-type poems of *La meglio gioventù* a condition of laceration and self-contradiction, experienced either as suffering or the relish of masochistic pleasure. The fundamental motif is that of offence-love by (and towards) the world. The metaphoric form typically assumed by this motif is that of the adolescent poet condemned to unhappiness by an excess of zeal and innocence.[22] The relationship to external reality is thus formed in two contrasting ways: an aesthetic of passion (beauty, youth, love) and an obscure consciousness of sin (breaking the norm, scandal) sometimes united and sometimes separated by the unsettled ambiguity of the spirit that expresses them. The twenty-six-year-old Pasolini, possessed by a kind of religious lewdness, writes:

I fall in love with bodies
that have my same
filial flesh—loins
burning with modesty—

---

20 Pasolini, 'Lied' in *La meglio gioventù*, p. 51.

21 Pasolini, 'Tornant al país' in *La meglio gioventù*, p. 25.

22 'Only you (mother) gave solitude to he who, in your shadow, felt for the world an overly powerful love'—for the motif of the 'overly powerful love', see Pasolini, *L'usignolo della Chiesa Cattolica* (Milan: Longanesi, 1958), p. 105.

mysterious bodies
of a pure and virgin,
honest beauty, trapped
inside unknowing games
of smiles and grace [. . .],
(the air that brightens them
and their lovely hair
in impure meadows
of their innocence),
bodies drained in shudders
of the flesh, spectre
of pitiless heartbeats,
sword thrust deep
in the blown rose
of the bleeding throat
bodies of sons
in happy trousers, with their mother's dark
or fair hair in their steps
and too great a love of the world
in their hearts.[23]

But then, grasped by an equally religious fear, he confesses:

Under the clear face of the sky,
I abide in my life, which in its distance
endures among the bustle of crickets
and the clouds, always inclined
towards risk, towards an inhuman limit
for reasons increasingly obscure, absurd [. . .][24]

And he reiterates, with flagrant brazenness, in an internal dialogue:

It's pointless, can't you see
the pale compromise?
Be then the obsession
that does not seek remedies

---

23 Pasolini, 'Memorie' in *L'usignolo della Chiesa Cattolica*, p. 106 / 'Memory' in *The Selected Poetry of Pier Paolo Pasolini* (Stephen Sartarelli trans.) (Chicago: University of Chicago Press, 2014), p. 111.
24 Pier Paolo Pasolini, *Dal diario* (1945–47) (Caltanissetta: S. Sciascia, 1954).

> The illicit is in your heart
> and only it counts,
> laugh at the natural,
> millennial prudishness.[25]

But immediately after he reveals his defencelessness in an infantile tremor of fear:

> I cannot overcome
> the iciness of anguish, and I
> cry and I used to in the heart of
> the earth and the sky.[26]

In this 'dusky atmosphere', pervaded by the 'warmth of the night', of 'lukewarm half-light', of 'fragile air' and 'tremendous space', where the poet's room 'has the charms of the palm tree' and the flesh of the youths bares the ambiguous colours of primroses and violets, the natural aestheticism of the spirit and the acquired one of literature meet and perfectly correspond.

However, Pasolini's inner feelings in this period cannot be fully grasped without penetrating into the nature of the relationship between the young poet and his mother: for she is both the source and the object of his thirst for love; at once a source of the greatest consolation as well as a stimulus for the most painful remorse. From the solemn tone of the sacred depiction 'La Domenica Uliva' ('Son, your voice is not enough to make you like the fathers . . .'), one moves to the rapid and violent expression of 'Il diaul cu la mari' [The Devil with the Mother], where the song circles around the dramatic experience of madness and theft.[27] The son, a mad thief, finds his torment in the night and discovers his death in the yellowish gleam of a bulb. Meanwhile the mother, in a nearby room, listens to the solitary and furtive sounds of her irredeemably different young son:

> Your son goes back up the steps
> walking softly like a thief
> You don't know, but in his breast
> he keeps a Madman without a mother.
> The Thief enters the bedroom

---

25 Pasolini, 'L'illecito' [The Illicit] in *L'usignolo della Chiesa Cattolica*, p. 72.

26 Pasolini, 'Himnus ad nocturnum' in *L'usignolo della Chiesa Cattolica*, p. 88.

27 'Palm Sunday', and later, 'The Devil with the Mother'. The phrase in brackets is from Pasolini, 'La Domenica Uliva' in *La meglio gioventù*, p. 41.

and is left aghast in the light:
now his death is this light
that fills the room with yellow [. . .][28]

In the beautiful 'Suspir di me mari ta na rosa' [My Mother's Whisper to a Rose][29]—its rhythmic melody set by Pasolini's agile use of septenarius and senarius metres—he returns to the theme of betrayal ('both forgotten, / —the mother and the rose!') with a hint of the cheerful melancholy (or melancholic cheer) he revealed and theorized elsewhere in his analysis of cheerfulness.[30] But the particular elegance of the composition does not exclude its basic sadness, which is all the more intense as, here, it appears to be unquestionably accepted. Elsewhere, the mother is a mystic symbol, though not shorn of ambiguous but evident sexual characteristics (as in 'Annunciazione' and 'Litania').[31] In 'Memorie' one retraces the steps of this love from its origins, discovering how Pasolini continues to see the mother as the figure of the *fanciulla*, the *giovanetta* / 'young girl', in which memory assumes an itinerary that leads beyond his own birth to the fount of the mother's virginity. We are thus made aware that Pasolini's ideal dream is to see himself as an adolescent alongside his mother as a young girl, in a process of regression that leads them both to a condition of innocence that neither of them enjoys any longer. But that is not all. The mother's face in which the poet finds his reflection is *his own*; a twinned image with which he, raving, tends to completely identify. Writing of his mother, Pasolini says:

A beauty deep
with shadow in the smooth
brow and the youthful
wave of the hair—
lean in the bones
of chin and cheek,
hard in the tender
curve of the face—
a boyish, thieflike

---

28 Pasolini, 'La Domenica Uliva', p. 70.

29 Pasolini, 'La Domenica Uliva', pp. 79–80.

30 See Pasolini's essay 'La poesia popolare italiana' [Italian Popular Poetry] in *Passione e ideologia* (Milan: Garzanti, 1960), p. 197.

31 Pasolini, *L'usignolo della Chiesa Cattolica*, pp. 59–60 and 63–5 / 'Litany' in *Selected Poetry*, pp. 94–8.

beauty—limpid,
turbid—full of
an old innocence,
hardened by the years
but still meek, perhaps [. . .][32]

And speaking of himself, whom he had called 'thief' while underlining the ambiguous character of his youth, he repeats:

There burns a lifeless spring
Bored or upset, I write of it
on the sheets where my aged
adolescence persists in its purity [. . .][33]

It is not insignificant that the young Pasolini's lament (at twenty-five) was for lost adolescence;[34] and that the adolescent Pasolini looks to his childhood and to children with such sweetness. On this path one encounters the mother, symbol of an intangible, now dissipated heritage that is forever nostalgically recalled. Over and above youthfulness, adolescence, childhood, this path back in time leads *into* her, into the pre-natal peace the poet has lost by being born. The young Pasolini, already wounded by an irreparable blow, moves towards life with his head turned back, his gaze fixed on that point where the darkness that precedes life brushes against the darkness that accompanies death. Only then can one understand what 'Provence' means to him, and what the peasants, youths and animals of Friuli represent for this soul covetous of the past.

Some specific motifs reunite this scattered theme and present it to a gaze that is fundamentally self-identical, even when it appears to become lost or deviate. Death and Beauty are probably the most important. As we have said, the contemplation of life cannot separate itself from the thought of death in those who, in truth, have never begun to truly live. In 'Il dí da la me muart' ['Day of My Death'], the idea of death is indissolubly conjoined with that of youth and adolescent virginity:

---

32 Pasolini, 'Memorie' in *L'usignolo della Chiesa Cattolica*, p. 103 / 'Memory' in *Selected Poetry*, p. 107.

33 Pasolini, *Dal diario*, p. 15.

34 'Like a man unharmed by a shipwreck I turn behind me and see, softened by the past, oceans of rare violets, of silent primroses'—Pasolini, *Dal diario*, p. 18. In the same collection, see the Rimbaud-esque poem 'Io non so più parlare' [I No Longer Know How to Speak].

I will still be young,
    with a pale shirt
and soft hair that rains
    down on the bitter dust.
I will still be hot
and a child running
    over the warm tarmac of the road
will lay a hand
on my crystal lap [. . .]³⁵

In many many other compositions—'Li letanis dal bel fí' [The Litanies of the Handsome Youth], 'Ciant da li ciampanis', 'Aleluja' [Hallelujah] 'Ciants di un muàrt' [Song of a Dead Man], 'La not de maj'—death penetrates the peasant universe, assuming the same indifferent naturalness as any other normal life-event (see in this regard even the prose piece 'Davide' in *L'usignolo della Chiesa Cattolica*).³⁶ Moreover, the anguish of a psyche dominated by the senses seems only to be placated by visions of sweet youthful beauty. We have already explained the non-banal motifs of this attraction for what is adolescent or childlike.

Narcissus is also a symbol, like the mother, of something good that has been lost, something that was originally extremely pure and chaste but which now—in the poet's laboured investigation—tends to oscillate ambiguously between perversion and cruelty. Alongside the various 'Danse di Narcis', see what are perhaps the more significant 'Il nini muàrt' [The Dead Boy], 'Ploja tai cunfíns' [Rain on the Borders], 'David', 'A Rosari' and 'Soreli' [Sun].³⁷ In light of this poetic discovery, Friulian youth assumes a new function that sheds light on the entire complex relationship that ties the poet to his chosen people. An extremely sweet aura, even if always a little too soft and wan, falls on the weave of feelings and passions. Reading Pasolini, one might conclude that there is no language richer than Friulian in words for children and youths, each of which brings into these poems—already so tender and precious in themselves—an even sharper sense of gracefulness and affection: *fantassùt, fantassín, frut, frutin, fruta, frututa, donzèl, fantal, fantata, fí, zuvinùt*. And

---

35 Pasolini, *La meglio gioventù*, p. 72.
36 Pasolini, *L'usignolo della Chiesa Cattolica*, pp. 55–6.
37 'Danse di Narcis' in *La meglio gioventù*, pp. 60–4 / 'Narcissus Dancing' and 'Sun' in *Selected Poetry*, p. 77 and 63, respectively.

even more sweetly: *bambín* (which Pasolini translates as 'love'). But this is nothing compared to the quantity of terms of endearment and affectionate epithets that Pasolini gathers or invents to crown with sweet love the favourite protagonists of his poetry. In this gallery of peasant narcissism, we encounter 'golden hair' (*La meglio gioventù*, p. 109); 'sweet hair' (p. 72); 'white and pink faces' (p. 122); 'a pretty blonde lock' and 'eyes like burning roses' (p. 110); a 'face of rose and honey' (p. 17); a 'graceful head' (p. 24).[38] A world of sensuality unfolds in vibrations, in hinted caresses, actions at once shameful and daring.

However, sensuality is a term that fails to capture the nature of Pasolini's feelings; indeed, it implies an element of satisfied pleasure, and hence of becalming of the passions, which does not exist in his poems. For Pasolini sensuality is always brutally and directly sexuality: it is the never placated projection of a violent and mysterious fascination that attracts the poet towards sin as an existential act, a manifestation of the absolute. The peasant world, which exists as a set of relations reduced to their elementary and pure components, nourishes this hunger. Between birth and death, facts of nature, we discover a set of impulses that are themselves natural: a naive desire for enjoyment, an absence of (or insensitivity towards) moral scruples and an unconscious celebration of genital forces.

One can well understand that in a universe such as this, where life's strength is nothing but a primitive survival impulse, life and death meet and beauty fades continually into the void of absence.

> I'm a handsome lad,,
> I cry all day;
> I beg you Jesus,
> don't let me die [. . .]
> I'm a handsome lad,
> I laugh all day;
> I beg you Jesus,
> O let me die [. . .][39]

---

38 Similarly, in the peasant novel *Il sogno di una cosa* (Milan: Garzanti, 1962): 'the blonde's face just a little red' and 'the capricious and resplendent smile' (p. 13.); 'Milio, white and red, with very blue eyes as hard as glass' (p. 110); 'curls as black as coal' (p. 17); 'the strawberry colour of their cheeks [. . .] the drop of light in their cheerful eyes' (p. 194).

39 Pasolini, 'Li letanis dal bei fî' in *La meglio gioventù*, p. 21.

cries the lost young man, who *feels* these boundaries to be too close and unstable; but on these uncertainties he reaffirms his humble desire for pleasure:

> Today is Sunday
> tomorrow one dies,
> today I will dress
> in silk and in love [. . .][40]

And Narcissus, a figure soaked in grace, is driven by a tremor of melancholy to linger over the threshold of the void:

> I remember you, Narcissus, you had the colour
> of evening, when the bells
> ring for the dead [. . .][41]

and

> You, David, are like a bull on an April day
> in the hands of a laughing boy,
> gently bound for slaughter [. . .][42]

Pasolini's pan-sexual mysticism is located—as we have suggested—on the vast border granted by this religious kindling of the senses; Nature and men are looked upon with an anxious desire for possession by those who realize they are nothing but 'one who has come into the light'.[43] This mysticism, this fervent and total leap, assumes different guises according to whether the poet is attempting a leap towards men and the world. Certainly the best poetic effects remain those tied to spontaneous communion with states of nature, whereas the more ideologically committed forms are often spoilt by superficial aesthetic decisions. For example, the relationship with Catholicism is profound where the young poet reproduces and recreates *within himself* the threadbare, centuries-old dialectic between purity and sin, temptation and salvation, innocence and corruption, as happens with the relationship of identity-contradiction vis-à-vis the Mother. But when the Mother is the Virgin Mother of God, the symbol, instead of being brought to life and generalized, becomes sterile, in a schema that oozes ambiguity and capricious complacency:

---

40 Pasolini, 'Li letanis dal bei fî', p. 22.
41 Pasolini, 'Il nini muart' in *La meglio gioventù*, p.16.
42 Pasolini, 'David' in *La meglio gioventù*, p. 24 / 'David' in *Selected Poetry*, p. 63.
43 Pasolini, *Dal diario* (1945–47), p. 14.

TURRIS EBURNEA. Breast of ivory,
nests of lilies,
no father's hand
has ever forced you.
Luminous contours
of black clouds
our rain
does not darken you.[44]

The figure of the *fanciullo contadino* [Peasant Lad], so recurrent in Pasolini's Friulian poems, is nothing but a translation of the religious symbol of the Saviour, whose primitive innocence and virginity it replicates. But when Christ appears on the scene in person, the clear attribution to him of the Peasant Lad's adolescent qualities has the unwholesome quality of a Black Mass, laden with all the imaginable suggestions of sexual scandal, but stripped of an original mystical charge.

Christ, thy body
like a girl's
is crucified
by two foreigners.
They're two strapping
lads with shoulders
red and eyes,
a heavenly blue.
They hammer the nails,
and the cloth upon
Thy belly trembles [. . .][45]

One should instead note that at another level the relationship with Christianity can become objectified through an extra-subjective contact. This happens when the poet rediscovers, in the deep crevices of peasant existence, the tenacious persistence of a belief in otherworldly justice and a hope in salvation. The border separating a certain spontaneous animism from real devotion to a revealed truth is doubtless very uncertain in Pasolini, no less

---

44 Pasolini, 'Litania' in *L'usignolo della Chiesa Cattolica*, p. 64. / 'Litany' in *Selected Poetry*, p. 97.

45 Pasolini, 'La Passione' in *L'usignolo della Chiesa Cattolica*, p. 17 /'The Passion' in *Selected Poetry*, pp. 85–7.

than among his peasants. But the feeling of this remarkably *weak* title to an overcoming of earthly suffering is *very strong*. Recall the analysis of 'Not di maj', where, in contrast to that vision of life immersed and almost obliterated by the anonymous flow of generations and seasons, we find, in conclusion, the reference to the Unknown God who has promised and testified to his promise with his sacrifice:

> Bow down, Christian folk,
> to listen to a feeble voice,
> that descends from the cross,
> among all this silence [. . .].[46]

In the face of all this absence and tremendous immobility, one can find the faint but lasting appeal of peasant religion, of popular Christianity. It too is sunk in the archaic origins of this secluded Romance people; constituting its humble, subterranean consciousness, which exists *barely* above the deep strata of unconscious survival. The Church is not that of the priest and his law, but the meeting place and space of encounter, which marks with its simple solemnity the fundamental dates of human existence: baptisms, weddings and funeral ceremonies. That is the sole possibility these humble people have to mark man's time outside the spontaneous unfolding of nature: 'Men sing Church Latin with the voices of the dead. But the singing of the Miserere is in crisp dialect. And you, young lad, leaning against the pillar, have the voice of the dead but the fragrance of April.'[47]

The set of literary attitudes described so far are thrown into crisis around 1947–49. Aestheticism, decadent religiosity, elementary vitalism and sexual attraction are gradually assimilated into a more historically and ideologically mature outlook. Traces of them, at times decisive ones, persist even in later years but in a less pure form, where the lyrical impulse of the earliest compositions will never be revived (at times at the expense of the aesthetic result itself). Without question the most relevant factors in this evolution are the war and the Resistance. The establishment of a populist cultural and political ideology forces Pasolini to critically revise his relationship with the people, which originally was spontaneous and individualist. If our analysis is right, it will be clear that at the beginning of his personal and poetic life, for Pasolini

---

46 Pasolini, 'La not di maj' in *La meglio gioventù*, p. 54.
47 Pasolini, 'La Chiesa' in *L'Usignolo della Chiesa Cattolica*, p. 38.

the people purely and simply compensate for his ills (let us set aside for now the fact that he fails to realize that thereby he *recreates* them in his image, projecting his own ills upon them). It is extremely significant to note that now (only now) does Pasolini begin to situate the peasantry [*popolo contadino*] in a historical dimension, where suffering and injustice are no longer considered to be the product of nature but of oppression. See the verse sequences 'Il testament Coran' (1947–52) and 'Romancero' (1953); see also the novel *Il sogno di una cosa* (1949–50).

In 'Viers Pordenon e il mont' [Towards Pordenone and the World], 'La miej zonventút' [My Youth] and in *Il sogno di una cosa*, problems like poverty and emigration are tackled explicitly. Narcissus dons the red neckerchief and naively tries to conquer the world. Naturally, the break is not so clear-cut as might at first appear. The peasants still preserve the characteristics and inclinations of old. Naivety and purity remain their best qualities. In *Il sogno di una cosa*, that mix of cheerfulness, melancholy, shame, audacity, innocence and desire for sexual pleasure—which from this time on will characterize adolescents in Pasolini's works—is depicted for the first time. In this phase too, then, the *humble consolations* of the poor man remain much more important than his *naive hopes*—for Pasolini as much as for his peasants, no party meeting will seem preferable to a cheerful vigil next to the fire. But while the psychological and environmental coordinates remain the same, the range of actions and the field of ideological ambitions become much more varied. Peasant naivety is not a *fact*; it is an indictment to throw into the faces of the rich and powerful.[48] Popular Christianity is no longer underground, a very ancient display of spiritual life; it is the claim for a justice promised *also* on this earth and the discovery of the religious nature of working-class redemption.

> He was a lad with dreams,
> a lad in blue overalls.
> The real Christ will come, and he will teach you, worker,
> to dream.[49]

---

48 So, for example, in 'Il testament Coran', a young partisan who was hanged by the Germans speaks: 'I bestow my image as an inheritance on the conscience of the rich. The empty eyes, the clothes that stink of my crude sweat. I was not afraid with the Germans of leaving my youth. Long live the courage, pain and innocence of the poor!'—Pasolini, *La meglio gioventù*, p. 114. [Trans.]

49 Pasolini, 'Vegnerà el vero Cristo' [The True Christ will Come] in *La meglio gioventù*, p. 108.

Beyond death is no longer the void of absence or the anonymous flow of collective life, but simply the confused intuition that something, a *thing* will one day be realizable.[50] For the ancient qualities of the people, Pasolini *does not substitute but superimposes* other, new qualities discovered in the atmosphere of an overall historical drama. To naivety, purity and simplicity he adds hope; a hope in the guise of a *dream*, which, from this time on, will be ambiguously confused with *nature*, forming its fleeting and illusory antithesis.

On the subjective level this discovery of a new popular dimension leads to an overcoming of the exclusively *intimistic* relationship that Pasolini had entertained towards Friuli-Provence up until that time. This separation occurs without contrasts. From this time onwards, Pasolini harbours a typical revenge complex towards everything that refuses his possessive embrace (think of *La religione del mio tempo*). In 'Cansion' e 'Conzèit',[51] the accusation of 'Christian Friuli' could not have been more explicit. The 'too great love' of the poet for his people and his land was repaid with ingratitude and rejection:

[A]fter so much around them agonized with love
in order to understand them,
to understand their poor, shining and hard existence,
your men have shut themselves away with you
under a cloudy sky.[52]

At bottom there remains the nostalgia for the 'true, blessed, distant existence' of this land.

But the separation and offence mean that this nostalgia and this love are done for, allowing the poet to escape enslavement to this adolescent bond. And yet Pasolini does take from Friuli a ready-formed image of himself, one fixed in the words and formulae of a definitive maturity. He leaves the archaic and meta-historical frame of the peasant milieu and language, already knowing everything of his future destiny: 'I who am still a youth, cannot in my solitary joy be cheerful about what is not within me.'[53] Strengthened by his 'innocent and pure love', he bears a 'a heart warm with sin', 'a heart clear

---

50 In *Il sogno di una cosa*, the death of Eligio: 'Suddenly, he pointed to Nin, but his arm fell straight back while he again moaned meaningless words. "A thing" he said, "a thing!" And he hinted, winking, to something that he, Nini and Milio knew well [. . .]' (p. 213).
51 See Pasolini, 'Envoi' in *Selected Poetry*, p. 80. [Trans.]
52 Pasolini, 'Cansion' in *La meglio gioventù*, p. 88.
54 Pasolini, 'Cansion', p. 89.

and young' for the world. And finds there—or thinks he does—history, ideology and civic passion.

The stylistic instruments change along with the evolution of this theme. In 'Spiritual', 'Fiesta' and 'Mi Contenti' [I'm Content], his attention is focused on the peasant festival, with one's twenty or hundred lire to spend, the rough and reckless dances, the innocent drunken binges, the ultimately naive and defenceless cockiness. The rowdy atmosphere, like that of a frontier encampment, is rendered with lively folksy motifs, even imitating metrically North American models (folklore and jazz). But the more important novelties found in *Romancero* are in the poem cycles *I Colussi* and *Il Vecchio Testamento*. It is easy, here, to understand how the overcoming of the lyrical or melic phase leads to an epico-lyrical and narrative one. The Friulian *villotta*[54] is replaced, as a model, with the popular genre of the epico-lyrical canto, from which Pasolini also takes certain themes and even whole situations in an interweaving of influences from Friuli, Piedmont, Emilia Romagna, etc. What should be forcefully underlined here is the philological-cultural motif, an index of one of Pasolini's persistent attitudes. Rarely are any of his stylistic or thematic choices not justified in properly philological terms. Very often philology remains the only valid element of Pasolini's literary attempts as, for example, in 'Il soldato di Napoleone' [Napoleon's Soldier], 'Beppino e Fiorina' and 'Ricciolin d'amore' [Lovely Curl]. In other words, when it is called for, Pasolini is able to compensate for a failure of inspiration with a dose of doctrine. That is why the poetry of this 'passionate' poet is often cold and artificial, *willed*, like an examplar of style. Furthermore, these are the years when he dedicates himself to the study of popular and dialectal forms of poetry, publishing two important articles, respectively introducing two important collections: 'La poesia dialettale del Novecento' (1952) and 'La poesia popolare italiana' (1955).[55] In this essayistic and almost academic atmosphere, other cultural elements assume much lesser significance. One section of the *L'usignolo della Chiesa Cattolica*, 'La scoperta di Marx' (1949), betrays what will come

---

54 A polyphonic composition originating around the fifteenth-century; typical of the Friulian popular tradition. The structure of the modern villotta entails four hendecasyllabic lines of verse followed by a refrain. [Trans.]

55 See Mario Dell'Arco and Pier Paolo Pasolini (eds), *Poesia dialettale del Novecento* [Twentieth-Century Poetry in Dialect] (Parma: Guanda, 1952); and Pier Paolo Pasolini (ed.), *Canzoniere italiano. Antologia della poesia popolare* [Italian Songbook: Anthology of Popular Poetry] (Parma: Guanda, 1955). [Trans.]

to be a popular misconception: that the mere observation that in existence there is 'something other than love / for one's destiny' is flaunted as if it were a discovery of Marxist ideology. I repeat, what is much more important is that in this period, through the literary and philological development of the concept of the 'people', Pasolini begins to delineate his own original ideological position, a vision of social reality that is both complex and mature. The reference to the ideologies of the workers' movement remains a mere tendency for now: more a source of stimuli and suggestions, than a complete and convinced participation.

The first hints of this type of poetic production can be found in the short poems 'Europa' (which is from as far back as 1945–46) and 'La marcia della gioventù' [The March of the Youth] (which the author dates from 1950). But the peculiar tone of this poetic moment is reached in the first compositions gathered in *Le ceneri di Gramsci*: 'L'Appennino' [The Apennines], 'Il canto popolare' [Popular Song], 'L'umile Italia' [Poor Italy] and 'Quadri friuliani' [Friulian Tableaus], all of which were composed in 1951–55 (as we have noted, these were particularly exhilarating years for Pasolini). In these works, the passage from the instinctive phase to the deliberately populist one is already complete. The poet is animated by the desire to give Italy a different complexion: the long passages dedicated to the past (the medieval and proto-Romance origins of popular song; the descriptive episodes regarding the pre-Roman, Greek and barbarian periods; the sense of the civilization of the *comuni* that was still alive if somewhat decayed; the textual citation of ancient songs) aim to create a climate of almost religious anticipation, from which springs the fatal need for a presence that for many centuries remained *pure* and has finally now become an *expectant waiting*. The people 'ready since the freshest and most inanimate epochs'[56] but 'whose clamour is nothing but silence'[57] exists within History like a mute but inexorable claim upon the future. It has always waited, 'never removed from time', and hence not blinded by *modernità*: 'the people has always been the most modern'.[58] Always anchored to the Past (the Past? rather to itself, which is to say, to its life, that can be neither eliminated nor suppressed), it is nevertheless only alive in the Present. But, living or surviving, they project their formidable instinctive force forward, assuring

---

56 Pasolini, 'Il canto popolare' in *Le ceneri di Gramsci* (Milan: Garzanti, 1957) p. 22.
57 Pasolini, 'L'Appennino' in *Le ceneri di Gramsci*, p. 18.
58 Pasolini, 'Il canto popolare', p. 21.

themselves a permanence unknown to reason. The people camps on solitary, crumbling hillside villages composed of hovels and shacks, in monstrous suburban districts, laying siege to the meagre citadels of civilization and history, armed only with their senses, happiness and their animal cheerfulness.[59]

> At the heart of the race of the dispossessed,
> a barbarous breed still living
> in primordial times, unblessed
> by the secret affairs of Christianity's light
> in the inexorable course of the ages[60]

nests the irrational force of an irrational warmth of life; each is 'enclosed in the heat of sex , / their only measure'; and in the extremely sweet and corrupt Italian nights, from one end of the peninsula to the other, along the long spine of the Apennines, the impetuousness of naive adolescent sensual delight is nothing other than the continuing festival of not yet exhausted vital energies:

> sarcastic cries of hot-blooded
> violent youths . . . odours of hot, wet rags . . .
> old Southern voices . . . wisecracks
> in the dark . . . Weightless Emilian choirs
> among villages and ruins.[61]

At this point the mystical process of communion with the popular soul is no longer enough for our poet. It is not enough to observe and love, nor is it enough—as we have noted—to bear witness; instead, it is necessary to praise and proclaim the new gospel. The starting point is obviously the *purity* of the primitive condition we have just described; in the people, we rediscover objectified and macroscopically reflected the ancient individualistic dialectic of sin and salvation, love and hate, purity and corruption:

> among a people
> given to the most genuine cynicism,
> the most genuine passion, brutal both
> in withholding and sharing themselves, clear
> in their mystery, because at once pure and corrupt.[62]

---

59 See the sixth verse of 'L'Appennino' *Le ceneri di Gramsci*, p. 15 / 'The Apennines' in *Selected Poetry*, p. 163.

60 Pasolini, 'L'Appennino', p. 17 / 'The Apennines', p. 165.

61 Pasolini, 'L'Appennino', p. 13 / 'The Apennines', p. 159 [translation modified.]

62 Pasolini, 'L'Appennino', p. 18 / 'The Apennines', pp. 165 and 167 [translation modified.]

At the bottom of this abyss is longer only a mystical lighting of the senses or the tremor of youthful passion. Instead, we find the ideologically extremely explicit conviction that a possible liberation of Man may be realized through the alliance—it too of religious origin—between a rationally progressive desire and a popular impulse that is fundamentally instinctive and irrational. The poet, speaking to a boy from Rebibbia, writes:

> In your recklessness, your unconsciousness,
> is the consciousness that history seeks in you;
> this history where Man has nothing but the violence
> of memories, not a free memory . . .
> And by now, perhaps, he has no other choice
> but to give to his urgent desire for justice
> the strength of your happiness,
> and in the light of a time that is beginning,
> the light of one who is what he does not know.[63]

The light of justice will only have meaning if the light of natural happiness illuminates it; and the light of the future—so much of this picture is hypothetical!—can only be the reflection of this light which is born in darkness.

If the examples given in this analysis are insufficient to convince the reader, Pasolini comes to our aid with words that belong more to the essay than the poem. The religiosity of the world is to be found in a condition of primitive purity: 'More sacred where more animal-like is / the world'.[64] Force and poetry (take note: poetry) are the characteristics of this animal-religious state, of which the people are witness and custodian. The problem is one of recapitulating these characteristics in history without losing or repudiating them: [W]ithout betraying the poetic / the original force, / we must—for good or ill— / exhaust its human mystery.' It is not possible to split these two aspects of the world, other than at the cost of a part of truth. Hence we must convince ourselves that the true and rightful lie above all where it seems that there is only negation of truth and justice:

> This is and is not
> Italy:
> its pre-history and history

---

63 Pasolini, 'Il canto popolare' in *Le ceneri di Gramsci*, p. 24.
64 This and the following quotations are from Pasolini, 'L'umile Italia' [Poor Italy] in *Le ceneri di Gramsci*, p. 52.

should coexist within it, if
light is the fruit of a dark seed.

At other points, the argument becomes clearer and more ambitious. The welding together of this assertive and exclusive populism with one even more ideologically and politically mature is established in the conclusion to the first part of 'L'umile Italia'.

Rome, the centre of a millennial oppressive power, is surrounded and squeezed by the corrupt grip of the villages. '[T]he jungle of dark souls [. . .] like a flood rises over the broken embankments'. And this poor and humble Italy, depraved, impure, unwholesome and totally unaware of itself does not know it aspires to recognition, and yet it forcefully and painfully does:

[. . .] in its impotence
the still plebeian Rome
feels the *national craving* for power.

I believe that this is the first time that Pasolini uses this easily identifiable terminology.

Pasolini outlines this material in deliberately objective forms, mindful of the lessons imparted to him by 'popular song'. Lyrical moments are not lacking but they are much reduced when compared to the overall development of the subject matter. But objectivity, in this sense, remains a merely negative connotation; it is a way of establishing from a very first reading that the dimension of the 'I' is forcefully shunted into the background. We draw closer to the centre of the problem by noting that Pasolini attempts to produce a parenetic discourse, not uninfluenced by the civic and progressive literature born of anti-fascism and the Resistance. In the moments of greatest incandescence, which is to say, when the poet is in the presence of acts of popular life (sex, song, cheerfulness), an epic tone penetrates the exhortation or reproach, forming its opposing axis, the ever-available internal variant (that is, from ['Ilaria's closed eyelids' to 'ironic cries of hot, blood-thirsty, violent youths']). And yet the entire poetic discourse ends up marked, at least in the cited poems, by a constant monotony, an almost completely uninterrupted dreariness in which one can find the imprint of a powerfully intellectualized, which is to say, fanciful, origin. Without immediately drawing drastic conclusions, it is perhaps already possible to indicate some stylistic and thematic motifs that lead us to underline a permanent fracture between Pasolini's most pronounced poetic qualities and his ambitions, which from this time onwards are pre-eminently concerned with civic literature and ideology. Too often, for example, epic and oratory turn for him into rhetorical emphasis and grandiloquence. The tone of Pasolini's poems (we are referring to 'L'Appennino', 'Il canto popolare', 'L'umile Italia') is never relaxed or contemplative. Even when it becomes more elegiac (like at the start of the second part of 'L'umile Italia': 'Oh, swallows, the humble voice of humble Italy'), it never escapes an excess of tension. The motif of oratory as such is only partially able to explain how this grandiloquence can be found in descriptive passages as well as epic-popular ones. The greatest break with sobriety takes place when we come across the people in its active existence; we then witness a veritable orgy of low-grade expressionism:

> Under the closed eyelids, a little kid
> from Cassino, sold by his parents,
> laughs; he's being fed
> by a killer and a whore
> on the raging banks of the Aniene,
> on colonial nights as Ciampino,
> dazzled under faded stars, shakes
> from the roar of our rulers' airplanes
> and along the Tiber the sentries of sex
> pace about on their nightly campaigns,
> wearily waiting by earthen latrines
> from San Paolo to San Giovanni and
> to Rome's hottest streets, and nineteen
> fifty-one slavishly chimes
> its hours, shattering the serene
> air round the shanties and basilicas.[65]

Naive imaginings more ridiculous than scandalous endlessly constellate the verses: from the 'earthen latrines' to the 'sentinels of sex'—that is to say, prostitutes—from the 'caves slimy with faeces and children' to the 'mud-covered tables in pigsties'. Conversely, there are numerous scholarly, philological inlays: 'seedy bars', for example. Occasionally, the poet repeats as if from a podium—we can almost hear the rolling tone of his voice, the hand gestures accompanying his words—the accents of a veritable oration, soaked in a poorly digested ideology:

---

65 Pasolini, 'L'Appennino' in *Le ceneri di Gramsci*, p. 12 / 'The Apennines' in *Selected Poetry*, p. 157.

O, it is not the time of history,
this, of life that is not lost,
these are not the highs, colourless
regions of a motherland that has become
conscience beyond memory [. . .][66]

One could say there is a breathlessness to the voice of the poet, engaged in a tremendous effort to surpass himself. Certainly the path from the 'water' of Casarsa to the exhortatory and moralistic spirit of *Le ceneri di Gramsci* must have been anything but straightforward or natural. Having stood before the world, Pasolini swells with the effort of encompassing it whole, of giving his words the force of conviction. But the trace of the effort remains very visible on every page.

The extremely frequent use of adjectives (which endures into the later poetry) is a signal of this. Some have spoken of Pasolini's spontaneous penchant for the Baroque and the Alexandrine. This psychological aspect should not be underestimated; but we have also seen how the poet knows how to be sober when a determinate literary forms demands he remain within particular limits. So there must be a deeper explanation. The truth is that Pasolini, having moved from Friuli to Italy, gives to the *attempt* to achieve the dominance of the ideal the *form* of instinctive possession. He is unable to imagine an external reality that is not full of colours and smells, to be looked at with one's eyes and touched with one's hands. It is almost as though the fear of losing or losing again this vaster world gripped him furiously every time he approaches it with a naive familiar impulse. The infrequent adjectivization among poets of the twentieth century, in particular the Hermeticists, testified to a conception of the world that was wilfully limited to the confines of a rigorous lyricism: reality was skeletal, naked feeling. In the face of this, Pasolini wishes above all to reconstitute the possibility of a logico-parenetic language that develops in terms of an exclusively lyrical order; he intuits that the first precondition for the success of the attempt lies in restoring the world he represents to its true dimensions. The high frequency of adjectives (there are copious examples of two or three adjectives applied to the same noun), serves only to fill the spaces left empty by the energetic reduction and contraction of the Hermeticists, pouring into them the variegated clots of his passionate appetite for the world. This is clearly an extremely dangerous operation. Thus configured, the world

---

66 Pasolini, 'L'umile Italia' in *Le ceneri di Gramsci*, p. 51.

overflows with lights, sounds and colours. But in this superabundance there is something approaching proof that Pasolini's realism opens onto a vast superficial contact or a passionately empathetic embrace rather than to a penetrating exploration of depth. The impression remains that the accumulation of adjectives reveals a loosened grip, slipping and passing away without imprinting the mark of poetic judgement upon things.

We are led to similar reflections by the stylistic and metric models that Pasolini chooses as part of his new poetic ambitions. The problem he faced, in its simplest terms, was the following: given that the language of Hermeticism and that of twentieth-century literature more generally was not merely a matter of stylistic formulae, but the expression of a specific conception of the world, the extra-literary origin of the refusal of this general conception meant the refusal of that language and style. Different solutions were tried. Pasolini chose first to remain within the Italian tradition. Then he decided to turn his attention back to earlier epochs and stop only where he discerned the possibility of a language and style that could still be used for narrative, epic-lyrical, parenetic and descriptive ends. To anyone who accompanies Pasolini along the stages of this investigation, Carducci and the Carduccian poets spring spontaneously to mind. While justified, the reference to the last great father of civic Italian poetry is doubtless also extrinsic and tendentious. There certainly is Carduccianism in Pasolini, specifically in the over-emphatic character of the language and its populist and Jacobin-like attitude. But it is a Carduccianism generally filtered through the lessons of Pascoli, a poet with whom Pasolini shows a human and literary kinship. Besides, we have proof that Pasolini has studied Pascoli attentively: the journal *Officina* was inaugurated with an exegesis of Pascoli's work. But the traces of this relationship are scattered throughout Pasolini's poetic production. Certain metric structures already present in his Friulian poems could be traced back to literary models from Pascoli. Consider the use made by Pascoli of the *ottonari* quatrain,[67] which is particularly precious and musical, particularly in the 'Dolcezze' [Sweetnesses] section of Pascoli's poetry collection *Myricae*: in the poems 'Benedizione' [Blessing], 'Il mendico' [The Beggar] and 'A nanna' [To Sleep]. Pasolini often employs the same metre in the collection *La meglio gioventù*, with similarly exquisite skill. Compare 'Ploja tai cunfíns' with

---

67 The *ottonario* is a verse in which the principal accent falls on the seventh syllable. [Trans.]

'Benedizione'. The hendecasyllabic rhymed couplets which can, for example, be found in Pascoli's 'Piccolo aratore' [The Little Ploughman] and in the 'Piccolo mietitore' [The Little Reaper] returns in 'Ciant da li ciampanis', with kindred meanings and effects. It is clear, however, that in this first phase, the richly impressionistic qualities (colours and sounds) of the very young Pasolini bear witness to the echo of experiences analogous to those of Pascoli. Neither the Provençal language nor that of twentieth-century literature could have taught the Friulian pupil more in this field. When Pasolini makes the decisive thematic shift, the old master once again comes to his aid, in a manner perhaps even more decisive and evident. But this does not take place without an extremely shrewd rethinking, which must be borne in mind both for what it reveals and still more for what it hides. In the article 'Pascoli', Pasolini shows he is well-aware of the importance that the poet from Emilia Romagna can have for him and his friends, engaged in an effort to overcome the experience of twentieth-century literary modernism: 'Consider the amazing "descriptive" possibilities of Pascoli's stylistic form for a group of ideologists, like us, who define ourselves as outside the field of an ontologically literary morality typical of the twentieth century'.[68] After having carefully analysed the reasons that make Pascoli into an archetype for the *Novecento* literary movement (his impressionistic approach, the use of formal Italian and everyday speech, the poetics of the 'little boy',[69] etc.), Pasolini examines the limits of Pascoli's work, basically identifying them in the prevalence of the *obsessive* element (psychology, affective life, subjectivity) over the rationally pursued *tendency*. We will for now omit discussion of this point, but we shall return to it. Instead we want to point out that, for Pasolini, only the elaboration of an autonomous and coherent ideological attitude allows us to overcome Pascoli's shortcomings. Pascoli's linguistic discoveries are themselves crippled by the absence of this dimension, for his 'is not the linguistic broadening that characterizes Manzoni

---

68 Pasolini, 'Pascoli', *Officina* 1(1956): 1. A slightly modified version of this article has been published in *Passione e ideologia*, p. 267.

69 'Il fanciullino' or 'Little Boy', is a prose essay in which Pascoli develops his poetics. Drawing on the Platonic myth from the *Phaedo*: 'Probably even in us there is a little boy who has these childish terrors'—Plato, 'Phaedo 77e' in *The Complete Dialogues of Plato* (E. Hamilton and H. Cairns eds) (Princeton: Princeton University Press, 1989), p. 61. He states that this is the condition for us to look at the world with astonishment. While typically the charm is lost as we age, the task of poetry is to reawaken the 'little boy' and to gaze at the world again as if for the first time. See Giovanni Pascoli, 'Il fanciullino' in *Pensieri e discorsi* (Bologna: Zanichelli, 1907), pp. 1–55. [Trans.]

or Verga, which is instead due to a realism of ideological origin, to a vision of the world that presupposes a standpoint outside of the world, from which the world thus appears both enlarged and united in its vast complexity'.[70] Hence, salvation from the obsession of the 'I' and knowledge of the world are entrusted to a 'realism of ideological origin', which Pascoli—the prisoner of a certain culture and sensibility—lacked the courage to develop. It is implicit that Pasolini has the ambition to succeed precisely where Pascoli failed. But Pasolini does not say that his poetics nevertheless recommence from Pascoli himself. The refusal of Pascoli does not mean choosing anything substantively different from Pascoli. The refusal of Pascoli is the attempt to recreate *a Pascoli enriched by ideology (that is, fundamentally, by a richer, more articulated and mature populism)*. On the personal level the affinities remain powerful: like Pascoli, Pasolini is easily moved to tears; like Pascoli, he loves feeling sorry for himself and enjoying the sensual pleasure of pain. On the plane of metre and style, the relationship appears extremely tight. Pasolini's predilection for colourful and impressionistic adjectives continues to bury its roots in Pascoli's teachings. The 'genres' he explores and their metres (songs and epic-lyric *poemetti*[71]) do not depend any less on popular compositions than they do on models drawn from Pascoli. The most frequent form in Pasolini is now the *poemetto* in tercets of hendecasyllables. To explain their use one can look back as far as Dante and descend all the way down the ranks of later didactic and satirical poets. The fact is that such a metre is used extremely frequently by Pascoli and particularly in a set of compositions that were to interest Pasolini precisely in this period of his literary activity. The *Primi poemetti* and *Nuovi poemetti* are all (except for 'Pietole'[72]) in tercets. As are the famous compositions 'Il giorno dei morti' [The Day of the Dead], 'Il cuore del cipresso'

---

70 Pasolini, *Passione e ideologia*, p. 275.

71 Stephen Sartarelli describes *poemetto* as:

> [T]he Italian diminutive of *poema*, a term that specifically designates a long narrative composition such as a *poema epico* or a *poema cavalleresco*. A short lyric composition, on the other hand, is called a *poesia*. A *poemetto* is thus something shorter than an epic or a romance, but longer than a *poesia*, and usually employs *endeasillabo*, the "noblest" verse line in Italian. The notion of *poemetto* used by Pasolini as a midlength form of meditative poem derives directly from Giovanni Pascoli, who wrote a great many of them . . . —See Introduction to *Selected Poetry*, p. 21n35. [Trans.]

72 A poem based on Pietole, a village near Mantua, thought to be the birthplace of Virgil. [Trans.]

[The Heart of the Cypress], 'Il lauro' [The Laurel] and many others of the *Poemetti conviviali* [Convivial Poemetti], from 'Alexandros' to 'Gog e Magog'. In Pascoli, the chain of tercets is brought to a close by an isolated verse, which rhymes with the middle verse of the final tercet. The same isolated verse can be found in Pasolini, but in general it does not reach the standard of the hendecasyllable but remains a mere stump, with a much less musical but sometimes more incisive character than the same verse in Pascoli. In Pascoli the verse is found only at the end of the stanza, while in Pasolini it can be found within it as well, with an accentuated function of scansion and pause. Pasolini's verses are, of course, much more irregular than those of Pascoli: it is not difficult to find assonances in place of rhymes, quantitatively anomalous verses and so on. The versification of the metric-stylistic pace of the composition, on the whole, loses the sweetness and musicality of Pascoli's composition, becoming more agitated and aggressive. However, even this nonchalance when it comes to metre results in an increase in emphasis, pursued and willed through the repeated disruptions of the voice, which end up producing a merely intellectual hurdle for the reading instead of a more or less ideal tension. This breathlessness, of which we have already spoken, is also reflected in this aspect of Pasolini's poetry; it is as if the metric-stylistic measure ends up being disproportionate to the task that the artist-ideologue sets himself.

Similar considerations can be made for other metric forms adopted by Pasolini. 'L'umile Italia' is composed of stanzas of ten nine-syllable verses. The famous 'La mia sera' [My Evening] is composed of stanzas with seven nine-syllable verses, plus one closing six-syllable verse that rhymes with the penultimate nine-syllable verse. Other similarities suggest an even closer relationship to Pascoli, a direct reading of his texts. In 'L'umile Italia' we find: 'joy is light' (a typically Pasolinian expression); in 'La mia sera': 'a light joy'. In Pascoli: 'What flights of circling swallows! / what cries in the calm air!'. In Pasolini the motif of swallows flying and screeching over Italian piazzas is taken up and amplified in the third and fifth stanza. Let us add, in conclusion, that the *poemetto* composed of loose hendecasyllables, employed in the *La religione del mio tempo* is very frequent in Pascoli's *Canzoni di Re Enzio* [Songs of King Enzio] and *Poemi del Risorgimento* [Poems of the Risorgimento]. 'Recit' in *Le ceneri di Gramsci* is composed of rhyming couplets of either twelve or fourteen syllables; it has a pace that reminds us, in a more fragmented and corrupted form, of 'La sacra di Enrico Quinto' [The Consecration of Henry V] by Carducci, composed in rhyming octosyllable couplets. Carducci himself had used triplets in hendecasyllables in 'Idillio maremmano' [Maremma Idyll].

What we have said so far about Pasolini's stylistic and metric (but also personal and psychological) predilections constitutes merely an introduction to the analysis of the most essential elements of his literary and poetic attitude. The references to Pascoli and Carducci, the evident harking back to a pre-*Novecento* tradition, lead us directly to a discussion of Pasolini's poetics in the period ranging broadly from 1953 to 1957, when the poet, in a series of now fully mature writings, seeks to define his standpoint in all of its aspects. In these texts he is able to elaborate a set of judgements and clarifications that remain perhaps the richest and most intelligent among those proposed by postwar and Resistance Italian writers.

It should above all be noted that Pasolini's populism now takes another step towards coherence and completeness. If the phase of the first *poemetti* represented the passage from an instinctive populism to a conscious one, now populism begins to be infused with a precise political meaning. Behind the ideology of populism there looms the presence of a culture that acts as guarantor and in a sense objective historical witness to Pasolini's vision of the people. The names of Croce and Gobetti are mentioned, as if to attest to the appearance of a moral dimension; and, above all, the name of Gramsci and behind him one can identify the active, revolutionary role of Marxist ideology:

> Today there exists a new culture, that is to say, a new interpretation of reality, and this is certainly not thanks to the belated attempts of our bourgeois avant-gardists to update our culture. It exists *potentially* in Marxist thought; 'potentially' because its activation can be envisaged once Marxist thought (*if such is fate*) will have become Marxist historical praxis in the history of a new social class undertaking the organization of life.[73]

Let us not linger over the doubtful 'Marxist' rigour of Pasolini's formulations and seek instead to grasp their meaning in light of his poetics. What Pasolini takes to be the positive impulse of Marxism is its ability to uncover the wounds of the society in which we live, tearing from it the veil of the (moral, ideal, *linguistic*) hypocrisies that carefully enfold and protect it:

> [I]f Marxist thought can bring about a political struggle and hence a crisis of society and the individual in our Western countries, then [a new culture] already exists and acts today—even if only potentially.

---

73 Pasolini, 'Osservazioni sull'evoluzione del '900' [Observations on the Evolution of the Twentieth Century] in *Passione e ideologia*, p. 330.

It exists within us, whether we support or reject it; and it does so pre-cisely in our impotent support and our impotent rejection.[74]

One might claim that from this moment Pasolini puts the emphasis dra-matically on the crisis of the individual rather than that of society. But in the 'impotent support', in that 'impotent rejection' there is the root of all that is most convincing and positive in Pasolini attitude. We should not forget that Pasolini does not yet identify with any of the 'official' ideologies. On the con-trary, he is—to borrow one of his expressions—not possessed by any of them. Pasolini is well aware that he and his friends have remained bourgeois, 'remained such with the violence and inertia of a psychology determined by history'. Nevertheless, precisely 'this situation [. . .] of a choice not made, of a drama unresolved due to hypocrisy or weakness',[75] constitutes for him the fertile seed of an ideological creation as yet not crystallized or formulated. On a number of occasions, Pasolini underlines the difficulty, the discomfiture of this attitude: 'it is an independence that costs incredibly dear. How we would have wanted—as one says—*to have chosen*'.[76] But he always reiterates that only in this freedom and independence from ideologies—which does not of course exclude a passionate interest in them and, in general, in any ideologically com-mitted position—is it possible to rediscover the condition of stylistic freedom, which is to say, of poetic independence. 'Do not [. . .] adapt the horizon to the periscope, but the periscope to the horizon, the immense horizon of phenomena'[77]—that is the foundational principle of this poetics. The poetic practice of experimentalism springs from it in a direct and consistent manner:

> In the 'experimenting' [. . .] which we recognize as being our own
> (to differentiate ourselves from the current neoexperimentalism),
> there persists a contradictory or negative moment. That is to say, there
> is an undecided, problematic and dramatic moment that coincides
> with that ideological independence we alluded to and which requires
> a continuous, painful effort to remain at the height of an actuality
> that is not ideologically possessed, as it could be for Catholics,
> communists or liberals.[78]

---

74 Pasolini, 'Osservazioni sull'evoluzione del '900' in *Passione e ideologia*, p. 330.

75 Both quotations: from Pasolini, 'Osservazioni sull'evoluzione del '900' in *Passione e ideologia*, p. 330.

76 Pasolini, 'La libertà stilistica' [Stylistic Freedom] in *Passione e ideologia*, p. 488.

77 Pasolini, 'La posizione' in *Passione e ideologia*, p. 250.

78 Pasolini, 'La libertà stilistica', pp. 488–9.

Taking a step back, we can identify all the literary solutions that Pasolini discards as unusable for the novelty that he seeks. In this period, he still appears conscious of the danger posed for a bourgeois writer by the fanciful attempt to overcome his bourgeois existence. He therefore refuses what he defines as 'populist messianism', attributing it to poets such as Mucci, Vivaldi and Baglio;[79] because he views as sterile and self-destructive 'the ambiguous flight from oneself that cannot but appear as [. . .] the passage of a bourgeois writer into the party of a class that, having passed through tremendous difficulties, aims to gain possession of the world, to re-establish it through its own actions'. But he also refuses a poetry that 'as an aesthetic choice is merely an inner story' and that would therefore appear to be 'pure introversion, the fruit of an egotism that is no longer necessary'.[80] This was true, in its final developments and in the work of its epigones, of the experience of the *Novecento* literary movement—completely bound, on the one hand, to a conception of style as a class privilege and, on the other, locked within the solitary contemplation of intimate, almost private motifs. Faced with this alternative, not even the path proposed by communist critics in their journals seems acceptable. That is because their use of ideology takes place in naively futurological ways, that is to say, in a mechanical and ultimately sterile fashion. Pasolini writes:

> As far as the so-called 'tactical' positioning of the communists is concerned, or more precisely of *L'Unità* and the *Contemporaneo*, it would be a needless act of cruelty, worthy of a Maramaldo, to stick the knife in.[81] The ideologico-tactical crudity and harshness of Salinari and others was tainted by what Lukács—in an interview given to a correspondent from *L'Unità* during the PCUS congress—called perspectivism. The naive and almost illiterate (and even bureaucratic) theoretical coercion stemmed from the conviction that a realistic literature should be founded on that 'perspectivism'. Whereas, in a

79 Velso Mucci (1911–64), poet, critic and translator, editor of the PCI journal *Il Contemporaneo*; Cesare Vivaldi (1925–99), poet, art critic and translator; Gino Baglio (1923–), Resistance poet, editor of the poetry journal *Momenti*. [Trans.]

80 Both quotations are from: Pasolini, 'Osservazioni sull'evoluzione del '900', p. 331.

81 *L'Unità* is a newspaper founded by Antonio Gramsci in 1924, which for much of its history was the daily of the Italian Communist Party (PCI). *Il contemporaneo* was founded in 1954 as a politico-literary magazine, focused on Marxist culture and theory. In 1965, it became a supplement of *Rinascita*, the PCI's cultural magazine. Fabrizio Maramaldo was a soldier of fortune, who in the sixteenth century fought for the Holy Roman Emperor Charles V in Hungary, taking part in the Sack of Rome as well as laying siege to Florence in 1530, where he became a byword for savagery. [Trans.]

society such as ours, we cannot simply repress—for the sake of a compulsory and prefigured perspective of well-being—the state of crisis, pain and division [. . .].[82]

The enduring distinction between an ideologico-literary proposition, from an almost-official form of a highly-qualified sector of the workers' movement, and Pasolini's personal attitude, is certainly very interesting. There is no doubt that Pasolini expresses a valid concern, particularly in relation to the naivety of Soviet 'socialist realism' or Italian efforts such as *Metello* (which appeared the year before Pasolini wrote this article). The discussion always returns to that 'state of crisis, pain and division' that for Pasolini represents the necessary, and not easily ignored, corollary of a new poetry and culture.

As we have mentioned, from this awareness stems 'the necessity of a genuine experimentalism which is not just gradual and intimate but also sunk in inner experience, which is not only attempted in relation to oneself, of one's unrelated passions but also in relation to our own history.' More concretely, it means a return to stylistic and linguistic instruments that leap beyond that literary absolute, that poetic ontology that had distinguished the literary experiences of the *Novecento*; and it directly signals the will to a new, open and diffuse form of expression which is widely communicable and bears within it extra-subjective and historical values. 'Language, which had all been raised to the level of poetry, now tends to be lowered to the level of prose, that is of the rational, the logical and the historical'. Pasolini continues: 'There flows from this a probably unanticipated re-adoption of pre-twentieth century or traditional (in the current sense of the term) stylistic modes, to the extent that they are naturally brought back to the bounds of rational, logical and historical, if not instrumental, language'. Nearly all the observations we made concerning Pasolini's relation to Pascoli and more generally to late nineteenth-century Italian poetry are valid here too.

> But such traditional stylistic methods become means of an experimentation which in its ideological consciousness is instead absolutely anti-traditional, thus putting violently in question, by definition, the structure and superstructure of the state and condemning, with what is probably a tendentious and passionate act, the tradition which, from the Renaissance to the Counter-Reformation to

---

82 Pasolini, 'La posizione' in *Passione e ideologia*, pp. 249–50.

Romanticism, accompanied its social and political involution, all the way up to fascism and our current conditions.[83]

There intervenes here a philological spirit formed prior to the crisis of 1945, in keeping with Contini's lesson[84] about the 'illogical and restless presumption of logicality' and now surviving with the aim of guaranteeing a 'continuous verification', a 'continuous struggle against latent tendentiousness'. Philology acts as a custodian and guide for Pasolini's mobile will to never remain closed within a crystallized position. The same philological spirit 'presides over the political attitude as well, over the difficult, painful and even humiliating attitude of independence that accepts no historical and practical form of ideology'. The conclusion is that one cannot establish any point of contact between this form of Passolinian experimentalism and the various forms of *Novecentesco* literary experimentalism, and the variety of attempts at a new poetry that Pasolini defines as neo-experimentalist precisely inasmuch as they are epigonic with respect to the *Novecento* movement. Pasolini's experimentalism 'presupposes an innovative struggle not in style but in culture— in spirit. The freedom of research it requires consists, above all, in the awareness that style, qua institution and object of vocation, is not a class privilege; therefore, like all freedoms, it is endlessly painful, uncertain, without guarantees, *anguished*'.[85]

We prefer to test the validity of a poetics via the analysis of the poetry that can be derived from it. Nevertheless, some observations of a general character can be made straight away. The first and perhaps most fundamental one concerns the possibility of developing a novel discourse through the adoption of 'traditional stylistic forms'. This is not to affirm the old formula 'the form is the thing', but simply to note that the espousal of 'traditional stylistic forms' is, above all, the *adoption of a certain model of literary opposition, restricted to the path of a typically Italian custom of moralistic and parenetic discourse, which is powerfully ideological and whose most obvious characteristic is its incapacity to*

---

83 Pasolini, 'La libertà stilistica' in *Passione e ideologia*, p. 486 and pp. 489–90.

84 Gianfranco Contini (1912–90), literary critic, historian of literature and philologist, author of studies on Dante, Petrarch, Gadda and Montale, among others. A significant influence on Pasolini, who wrote several essays on Contini's *oeuvre*, beginning with an appreciation of his dialectal poetry in 1943. *La meglio gioventù* is dedicated to Contini. [Trans.]

85 All three quotations: from Pasolini, 'La libertà stilistica', p. 491.

conceive a revolution in language that would be analogous to and follow upon a hypothetical revolution in themes. The consequence is that Pasolini, despite attempting to escape the *lingua franca* of the middle classes in poetry as well, realizes a type of formal-stylistic solution which appears—in its all too easy sententiousness, emotiveness and arousal—to be directed at the petty bourgeoisie that dominates our intellectual strata. When Pasolini writes in the poemetto 'Picasso',

> O, this ruthless Peace of his
> this idyll of white orangutans,
> is far removed from the feeling of the people.
> The people is absent from here[86]

he betrays the prejudice according to which revolutionary art is necessarily popular art. And what else does the rejection of Picasso mean if not the wholesale refusal of the avant-garde, which fails even to have a glancing impact on Pasolini's art? Pasolini throws a bridge between the humanitarian exigencies of late-nineteenth-century radicalism and socialism and post-Resistance populist ideologies. The language he draws upon is a function of this attempt. Only through paraenesis could Pasolini make space for the mythological figure of this people (historically, objectively) *filled with petty-bourgeois spirit.* In other words, Pasolini's formula—'traditional instruments + new ideology' —represents the process typical of all moralistic and rhetorical positions. It goes without saying that this ideology is nothing other than the confirmation of a tradition or of a traditionalist or conservative politics. This is evident in Pasolini's singular solution to the problem of representing 'a society such as ours', in which 'we cannot simply repress—for the sake of a compulsory and prefigured perspective of well-being—the state of crisis, pain and division'.[87] In 'Picasso', Pasolini remarks, in words that reiterate the refusal of an extremist and tendentious art:

> The exit
> towards the eternal is not in this desired
> and premature love. Salvation
> is to be found in remaining
> in hell, with the iron will
> to understand it.[88]

---

86 Pasolini, 'Picasso' in *Le ceneri di Gramsci*, p. 33.
87 Pasolini, 'La posizione' in *Passione e ideologia*, p. 250.
88 Pasolini, 'Picasso', p. 34.

But what (touching, for the time being, only upon the surface of the phenomenon) does this 'with iron will to understand' mean, if then everything is resolved in the process of pure mimesis, 'in a violent and absolute environmental mimesis', as Pasolini will later theorize?[89] In this case too, rejecting the vanguardist solution means accepting the less threatening solution (despite appearances) of an easily vulgarizable naturalism (if we replace the term *mimesis*, drawn from stylistic forms, with its historico-literary equivalent). Yes, 'remaining in hell', but only in order to represent it for edifying purposes. There is nothing less revolutionary.

Passion, which constitutes the other pole of Pasolini's poetry, presents us with similar ambiguities. Pasolini explains:

> 'Passion *and* ideology': this *and* is not intended as a hendiadys (ideological passion or passionate ideology), if not secondarily [. . .]. It wishes instead to be at least disjunctive if not oppositional, in the sense that it posits a chronological gradation: 'First passion, *but then* ideology'.[90]

His position on the relationship between the two terms develops beyond the mere recognition of their existence. He concludes: 'Passion, which is by its nature analytical, makes way for ideology, because its nature is synthetic'.[91] The fact remains that, right up to the more recent essayistic formulations, like in the poetic and narrative works, Pasolini never holds an ideological attitude without a passionate, irrational stimulus. This would be without question justifiable or even commendable, as it is in so many twentieth-century authors, were it not for the fact that that passion ends up losing its vital, irrationalist charge precisely in the shallows of a 'screen' ideology that crystallizes it in obviously artificial intellectual formulae. We must reverse the judgement that has most frequently been used to attack Pasolini's poetics, namely, that Pasolini is never able to free ideology from its passionate register. The truth is that this passion is never strong enough to nourish and dynamically overcome ideology; it too is a passion generated by traditional feelings, which pushes the writer to rebel against a contemporary world that is locked within the expected boundaries of protest and disgust (so that society ultimately has no difficulty absorbing them). The motif of the 'inner crisis' also loses much of

---

89 Replying to an enquiry on the novel in *Nuovi argomenti* 38–39 (May–August 1959): 45.
90 Pasolini, *Passione e ideologia*, p. 493.
91 Pasolini, *Passione e ideologia*, p. 493.

its significance if we see it in practice as an elegiac self-commiseration of limited historical proportions. *The abhorrence of society and of bourgeois conformism
is blunted if the polemic turns within the closed atmosphere of popular penury.*
The demand for upheaval appears extremely weak if made in the name of that
ancient but still surviving 'will to identification' and 'yearning for possession'
whose roots go back to Pasolini's adolescent trauma. The logical conclusion
of Pasolini's argument, which is studded with an awareness of the inevitable
contradictions that accompany its unfolding, cannot but be the reference to
the validity of a permanent, meta-historical and absolute law in which all
efforts converge, taking on the form of faith: 'We defend ourselves against all
mysticism and hence also from the courage of historical thought itself', writes
Pasolini. And yet he cannot help replying to himself: 'but we know that, in
the end, the series of experiments will end up being a path of love—physical
and sentimental love for phenomena of the world, and intellectual love for
the spirit, for history—which will enable us to always be "with feeling, at the
point where the world is renewed".'[92] Here, in the symbol of Love, that same
formulation 'Passion *and then* Ideology', or 'Passion, *but then* Ideology', seems
inadequate. Here, 'Passion *is* Ideology'; it is taken up immediately into the
heaven of ideas, identified as a perspective, used as an instrument of knowledge. Among the numerous bad cases presented by contemporary literature,
the worst is when passion, unable to put ideology in crisis, itself becomes
ideology—which is to say, formulaic crystallization and schematicism.

There is no doubt that Pasolini attains the pinnacle of his poetic work
when he is still able to keep the two terms separate, to hear and represent them
as the poles of a dialectical opposition that are taken up by the forces of instinct
and history, reason and the unconscious. That is to say, in the 'impotent support' and the 'impotent rejection' of a situation of widespread discomfort,
which is immediately reflected in a dramatic inner contradiction, a struggle
without possible escape routes. We now find ourselves in the *poemetto* 'Le
ceneri di Gramsci' (1954), the only work by Pasolini—leaving aside the
Friulian poems—where the degree of tension reaches its purest and most indisputable result. However, this in no way modifies the fundamental elements
of our argument hitherto.

The *poemetto* opens extremely slowly, with observations of minutiae pro-
longed for two entire stanzas. The author's old impressionistic ability emerges

---

92 Pasolini, 'La libertà stilistica' in *Passione e ideologia*, p. 491.

again in these pages, although blurred and obscured by an atmosphere that is no longer serene and idyllic, where objects, things, figures emerge as scattered detritus from a large swamp (it should be noted that this change does not represent a loss of quality). The frequent use of adjectives or words to give 'colour' does not issue in a quasi-vertical accumulation of descriptive sensations but, rather, in a cadenced and captivating rhythm, unfolding around things like the sinuous coils of a soft snake:

> It's not May that brings this impure air,
> makes the darkness of the foreign garden
> darker still, or dazzles with the glare
> of blind sunbursts . . . this frothy sky
> over pale-yellow penthouses
> in vast semicircles that deny
> a view of the Tiber's meanders
> and Lazio's deep-blue hills [. . .][93]

The picture comes together through a circular movement that *seeks* it own centre. When the poet *discovers* the theme, it is already sufficiently mature to be understood and savoured:

> Between these old
> walls the autumn May extends
> a deathly peace as unloved as our destinies [. . .]

From here it is a short step to the contemplation of ruin, of historical disintegration:

> It carries all the grayness
> of the world, the close of a decade where
> we saw our keen, native attempts
> to remake life end up among the ruins
> and a sodden, sterile silence [. . .]

The decade of Christian-Democrat ruled Italy, the betrayal of the Resistance, the dissolution of hopes and vivid affections are indicated in immediate, instinctive images; we see here that the analogical procedures of Decadent and *Novecentesca* poetry—which Pasolini had made such skilful use of in the past—have never entirely ceased to flow from his pen.

---

93 This and the following two quotations: from Pasolini, *Le ceneri di Gramsci*, p. 71 / 'Gramsci's Ashes' in *Selected Poetry*, p. 167 [translation modified].

The meeting with the shadow of Gramsci is not, in truth, without rhetoric; and that hand with which the dead man indicates, in the manner of a Marxified Silvia,[94] the 'ideal that illuminates [. . .] this silence',[95] exhibits the coldness of a bas-relief, the likes of which one might see at a cemetery for patriotic heroes. But from the start, and then increasingly clearly, another figure detaches itself from the rhetorical image of Gramsci the ideologue and party man, one more congenial to the nature of Pasolini's talent. The elements of contrast between which Gramsci the witness and martyr is placed are, on the one hand, the secular bourgeois cemetery,[96] with its air of dignified egotism, and, on the other, the sound of beaten anvils that reaches it from the popular quarter of Testaccio, not so far from there and yet already another world, another planet. Between the cold, tedious atmosphere that surrounds the grave, almost as if to suffocate its memory and allure, and that warmer but equally indifferent presence of the people, that is where we find Gramsci: 'young', 'not father but humble brother', apparently disarmed, defenceless. Not the Gramsci of struggle and resurgence, but the Gramsci of prison and suffering, 'reduced to pure and heroic thought'; an adolescent betrayed by his very audacity, confined to solitude, in death as in life, by the offences of men and the cruelty of history. This Gramsci as a young man—or, rather, an adolescent—humiliated and offended, is in truth not a historical character but a creature of Pasolini's sensibility.

The motif of hope is linked to this figure through the symbols of a meagre and unadorned faith:

A red cloth like those the Partisans
once wore around their necks;
beside the urn
on softened ground, two geraniums [. . .][97]

In this unquestionably mystical synthesis of sacrifice and tenacity lies the possibility of a sentimental and ideological relationship between the poet and Gramsci. But this relationship is not simply, as it might seem, between a stim-

---

94 Refers to the protagonist and addressee of Giacomo Leopardi's poem 'A Silvia' (1828). Silvia was a young woman from the poet's youth who had died of consumption; she symbolizes the unhappiness of the human condition and the futility of hope. [Trans.]

95 Pasolini, 'La libertà stilistica' in *Passione e ideologia*, p. 491.

96 Gramsci's grave is in the Cimitero Acattolico of Rome, which is also known as the 'Protestant' or 'English' cemetery.[Trans.]

97 Pasolini, *Le ceneri di Gramsci*, pp. 74–5 / 'Gramsci's Ashes' in *Selected Poetry*, p. 173.

ulus to reason and praxis, on the one hand, and an enduring survival of instincts, on the other. If that were the case, the question would be entirely resolved in an objective historical dialectic. The truth is that Pasolini, once he has overcome his initial rhetorical inclination, looks to Gramsci with a much more fraternal attitude, with seriously embodied sympathy and love. In a number of places this involves the expression of a morbid individualist sensibility, manifested in a kaleidoscopic movement, an unlimited psychological unpredictability:

> Torn
> between hope and old distrust, I draw near,
> having chanced into this spare green corner,
> before your grave, your spirit here at rest
> among these trees. (Or perhaps it's something
> else, more ecstatic but more modest
> too, some drunken adolescent
> symbiosis between sex and death . . .).[98]

But on closer inspection, we note that the weight of Pasolini's love for Gramsci is not even exhausted in this morbid attraction for the figure of the young martyr. Other deeper and darker motifs intervene to form and nurture it. There is no doubt, for example, that in the fraternal Gramsci of which we have spoken, Pasolini feels he has rediscovered his own brother, who had fallen as a partisan fighting against the fascists, and is now reborn in this symbol of perennial testimony (think back to the final verses of 'Comizio' ['Rally'],[99] where the memory of the martyr has the same Gramscian air of disappointed and betrayed youth). While the more problematic Gramsci, caught between offence and forgiveness, reason and instinct, is nothing but the *alter ego* of the poet who talks and cries with him as if standing before a mirror, attempting to distinguish *himself from himself* (and hence objectifying his rational conscience in a historical 'figure'), but always ending up assuming *in himself* all that surrounds him (even the 'figure' he created in order to objectify, to historicize his own consciousness). Notice how, from the verses in the third

---

98 Pasolini, *Le ceneri di Gramsci*, p. 75 / 'Gramsci's Ashes', p. 173.
99 'He asks for pity, with his modest, unbearable gaze, not for his fate but for ours [. . .] And is he the too honest, too pure one who needs to go with his head bowed down? To beg a little light for this world reborn in a gloomy morning?'—Pasolini, *Le ceneri di Gramsci*, p. 41.

stanza 'And here too I am',[100] until the end of the fourth, the focus of poem's argument shifts towards the poet. The *poemetto*—which began as a kind of objective reconnoitring and then circled around the symbol of Gramsci, taken up and abandoned more than once, in a syncopated rhythm that bears witness to the difficulties of a precise definition—now begins to assume a freer, more intense and passionate pace, as if the poet, turning his gaze directly upon himself, acquired greater strength and interest. The preeminence of the poet in a poem dedicated to 'Gramsci's Ashes' will not diminish in the other sections of the *poemetto*. It is characteristic that, in the two subsequent stanzas, when the discussion returns to the semi-objective initial dimension, this happens only as a function of the final questions, where the personal situation of the poet re-emerges as a concluding, determining fact ('You will ask me, in death unadorned . . .' and 'But I, with the conscious heart').[101]

What strikes one in Pasolini's self-reflection is not—as we have said—the strength of the contrast between reason and instinct, passion and ideology but, rather, the force with which passion stands its ground against ideology, refusing to be subordinated to it. From here, first, stems the clarity of analysis:

> and if it's
> true I love the world, it's only with a violent,
> ingenuous, sensual love [. . .][102]

But also the harshness of the choice, which for now leaves no opportunity—except marginally—for languid commiserating in one's fate:

> And yet, lacking your rigor, I get
> on by not choosing. I live by not wanting
> as in the postwar years now past.

There is a courage in confessing the irrational, subconscious root of his attitude:

> loving
> the world that I hate
> in its misery, scornful and lost
> by some dark scandal
> of conscience [. . .]

---

100 Pasolini, 'Gramsci's Ashes', p. 175. [Trans.]
101 Pasolini, 'Gramsci's Ashes', p. 183 and 187 [translation modified.]
102 This and the following two quotations: from Pasolini, *Le ceneri di Gramsci*, p. 76 / 'Gramsci's Ashes', p. 175, 175 and 177, respectively.

All this leads to the limit being experienced as force, as glorification. There is no discouragement in these by now famous verses of Pasolini's; there is no surrender of the poet to Gramsci, but there is a surrender of Gramsci to the poet:

> The scandal of self-contradiction—of being
> with you and against you; with you in my heart,
> in the light, against you in the dark of my gut.
> Though a traitor to my father's station
> —in my mind, in semblance of action—
> I know I'm bound to it in the heat
> of my instincts and aesthetic passion;
> drawn to a proletarian life
> from before your time, I take for religion
> its joyousness, not its millennial
> struggle—its nature, not its
> consciousness. It is man's primordial
> strength, having been lost in the act,
> that gives this faith the joy of nostalgia,
> the glow of poetry. More than that
> I cannot say, without being right
> but insincere, expressing abstract
> love, not heartbreaking sympathy [. . .][103]

In a moment of absolute sincerity the people become again what they are and can only be at the core of Pasolini's poetic inspiration: a religious symbol, the object of psychological and spiritual attention, of projections of love and hate, motived by the 'heat / of my instincts and aesthetic passion'; a living creature, even if an entirely arbitrary one, in which Pasolini cannot help but reflect his yearning for identification with the world. On this basis, not only can one distinguish oneself from all that is 'insincere, expressing abstract / love' but also voice the brazen demand, which denied and refused:

> Poor as the poor myself, I cling tight,
> like them, to demeaning hopes;
> like them, every day of my life I fight
> just to live. Yet in my disheartening
> condition as one of the dispossessed,
> I still possess—and it's the most thrilling

---

103 Pasolini, *Le ceneri di Gramsci*, p. 77 / 'Gramsci's Ashes', pp. 174–6.

of bourgeois possessions, the ultimate
state of being. Yet as I possess history,
I am possessed by it, enlightened by it:
but what good is the light?[104]

The topic of the naively obsessive and impurely virtuous 'I' that bears 'that sense of life as poignant, violent / oblivion in my breast' continues in the fifth stanza. Lowering the tone, Pasolini passes through a literary memory of Shelley, and his 'fleshly / joy of adventure, aesthetic / and puerile'.[105] And so he gazes broadly across the *umile Italia* as in a tracking shot from one end of the peninsula to the other, surveying the objects of his populist disposition. This 'prostrate' Italy, 'as though in the belly of a giant cicada', with its age-old characters: "young ciociaro', who 'sleeps in a Goethian dream, / member swollen under his rags']; 'kids (. . .) their brown faces / dripping wet', who 'hotly / call out to their friends among the people / of the shore'; and the eternal dazzling landscapes: the 'blindly (. . .) dry bends of Versilia's shore', the 'scented panic' of the coast, the 'airy throngs of evergreens, baroque' of Lazio. All this to again conclude, with a dash of youthful arrogance, in the obsessive question, which is as eternal as this earth and this Italian sex:

Would you, in death unadorned,
have me abandon my desperate
passion for being in the world?[106]

The final stanza opens with the poet's farewell to Gramsci, as he plunges back into the life of Testaccio, a district swarming with sounds, voices, gestures and colours. From the first lines the profound contrast between the serene or, rather, severe but immobile and infertile peacefulness of Gramsci's cemetery, and the unbridled vitality of the Roman people glimpsed in one of its most ancient and yet intact districts . . . This contrast is in the end one between life and death, between icy rationality and burning passion, between a serene invitation to truth and the profound, total participation in error. The people returns to the fore; but this time it do so not in the rhapsodic and still literary form of the preceding stanza ('*il giovincello ciociaro*' with its echo of Goethe), but instead in the already tested form found in the central nucleus of the fourth stanza. That is to say, as the enlarged projection of the state of the poet

104 Pasolini, *Le ceneri di Gramsci*, pp. 77–8 / 'Gramsci's Ashes', p. 177.
105 Pasolini, *Le ceneri di Gramsci*, p. 79 / 'Gramsci's Ashes', p. 179 and 181.
106 Pasolini, *Le ceneri di Gramsci*, p. 182 / 'Gramsci's Ashes', p. 183.

and, at the same time, as his hypothetical sociological validation. There is no life 'in this historic void',

> but subsistence [. . .]
> as if they
> were a race of animals whose arcane
> orgasm lay in no other passion
> than that of daily labour [. . .][107]

Even here there is no lack of literary interventions, decadent disconnections, the repetition of phrases that have become commonplaces in Pasolini's poetry: from the allusion to the 'the splendid / sunburnt, almost Alexandrian / sensuality illuminating all, / igniting everything impurely', to the 'hidden little trollops, angrily / waiting above the aphrodisiac filth', to the 'dark adolescents' who 'whistle down the sidewalks'. But for that reason the tension of the poetic discourse does not dissipate until the final lines, until the end of the *poemetto*:

> Life is commotion; and these people are
> lost in it, and untroubled when they lose it,
> since their hearts are full of it. There they are,
> poor things, enjoying the evening, helpless;
> yet in them and for them, myth is reborn
> in all its power [. . .]

Here the repudiation of Gramsci appears to diminish, whereas in reality it becomes more powerful and total. Standing in opposition to the myth of the ideologue is that of 'proletarian life', which is a good deal more powerful and genuine. This is the myth of a people which hides beneath its indifference, cynicism and intoxicated sensuality such a charge of purity and love that it can objectively posit the need, albeit mute and obscure, for redemption from injustice and pain. Finally, for the first time the Christian vision of being is welded here to the Decadent but progressive spirit of the author, who only discovers the sacred-positive character of the world in, the unscathed force of the instincts, refusing any other kind of commitment. Indeed:

> But I, with the conscious
> heart of one who lives only in history,

---

107 This and the following quotation: from Pasolini, *Le ceneri di Gramsci*, p. 102 and 84, respectively / 'Gramsci's Ashes', p. 185 and 187, respectively.

> can I ever act with pure passion again
> when I know that our history has ended?[108]

The limits and virtues of the *poemetto* are evident from the analysis provided so far. It is interesting to turn (or turn again) our attention to two of its aspects. The one concerns the ideological attitude of the poet in this particular phase of his development. The other is focused on the original, mature stylistic results attained at this juncture. With respect to the former, we will merely repeat that in this particularly successful small composition, Pasolini's populism shows itself to be (at least for now) nothing other than the ideologization of a complex of passionate feelings and impulses that have not been disciplined by history. The discussion of Gramsci is a discussion of Pasolini. Gramsci represents, if you will, a progressive historical dimension whose validity is rejected, although it is certainly not ignored. What counts is the irrational course of the world, the secret existence of this animal populace in which the poet reflects his Narcissistic image. Only later will he attempt to travel the road that unites (but does it really?) meta-history to history.

The tone of 'Le ceneri di Gramsci' is not dissimilar in quality and accent to the analyses we gave of 'Canto popolare', 'L'Appennino' and 'L'umile Italia': there is always one note higher than necessary, at times approaching mere oratory and rhetoric. But it is also one of the most personal works that Pasolini has created in this genre. This way of circling slowly and confronting problems only to then explode in a set of burning questions, of clear-cut, certain, even exclamatory statements, is entirely his own. Also unique to him is this softness of speech, in which only here and there, in an effort of vengeance and virility, is he able to encase himself in harder almost brazen attitudes. His too is the ability—so rare in him as well—to summarize in phrases that are interwoven and wedged one within the other, the polymorphous feeling of a semi-animal sexual life. There is no doubt that Pasolini is able to embrace his subject matter with direct physicality. I do not speak only of his love for it but, rather, of his full-bodied discourse, rich in humours, brimming in vital juices. Here too lies his skill; he is still able, where necessary, to achieve ornamentalism with sobriety, to extinguish the burning pyre of sensations in the simple essence of an eternal emotion.

---

108 Pasolini, *Le ceneri di Gramsci*, p. 84 / 'Gramsci's Ashes', p. 187.

One can already see that the tension begins to diminish and the themes to repeat themselves in the final *poemetti* of the collection *Le ceneri di Gramsci*. In 'Recit', the motif of the 'humiliated and offended', turns into an autobiographical outburst, a feeble and infantile protest. Pasolini reacts tearfully to the accusation of obscenity directed at *Ragazzi di vita*, seeking sympathy and asking for clemency and pity. To the moralism of the accusers the poet opposes his own moralism. What other term is there for the bewilderment and indignation he feels in the face of this wickedness and incomprehension? Pasolini does not think, does not *feel* that the bourgeois world saves its hostility for its enemies; he does not accept the ineluctability of this condition. For him to request a truce is for him to confess his inferiority and *to acknowledge the bourgeoisie as possible judges*. The continual allusion to the immense and misunderstood capacity of love, which he manages to express, is in this order of feelings an appeal to be understood and loved by the enemy as well. Pasolini depicts himself as a poor martyr, cowed under the blows and yet faithful to his nature as lover:

> But why force me to hate, I,
> who is almost grateful to the world for my pain,
> for my being different, and for this reason being hated,
> yet I know only how to love, faithfully and wholeheartedly [109]

'Il pianto della scavatrice', which is an extremely long and complex, even overabundant, poem, oscillates between an excessive and forced expressionistic descriptivism—

> [I]n a world of sad, *bedouin* suburbs,
> *yellow* grasslands lashed
> by a wind *forever restless*; swarms
> of *withered* and *tough* little children
> screaming in their *ragged* T-shirts
> *and their drab, faded* shorts,
> the *African* sun, the *violent* downpours
> that turned the streets into rivers
> of *mud*, the city buses *foundering*
> in their corners at the terminus,
> between the last strip of *white* grass
> and some *acrid, burning* garbage heap

---

109 Pasolini, 'Recit' in *Le ceneri di Gramsci*, p. 91.

and the elegy of private confession ('stunning, wretched city, you've taught me'), not without obliging narcissists.[110] Here we see the poet present himself as 'Poor as a cat in the colosseum', 'a little soul' that

> was growing in that boundless
> world, nourished by the joy of one
> who loved, though unrequited.[111]

The nostalgia for Rebibbia, from the tranquil, monotonous and bourgeois district of Monteverde Nuovo, where the poet later moved, gradually turns into epic self-glorification, an unbalanced, abnormal egocentrism that approaches a kind of madness; and the centre of the world is this shapeless 'Bedouin' district:

> This was the centre of the world, just
> as my love for it was at the centre
> of history.[112]

Almost as if smiling with satisfaction at this happy image of himself reflected in the mirror, he writes:

> [T]he few friends who called on me
> on forgotten mornings and evenings
> up by the Penitentiary,
> saw in a brilliant light: a *gentle, violent revolutionary*
> in the heart and language. A man in bloom

The motif of a regression to animal purity does not appear either more genuine or novel, even if it is imagined here in the complicity of sleep and bed:

> And in the same oblivion
> is light . . . in that unconsciousness
> of infants, beasts, or naive libertines
> is purity . . . in that flight
> the most heroic frenzies, the most divine

---

110 Pasolini, 'The Cry of the Excavator' in *Selected Poetry*, p. 195, 197 and 191, respectively. [Trans.]

111 Pasolini, 'The Cry of the Excavator', p. 193 and 195, respectively. [Trans.]

112 This and the following two quotations: from Pasolini, 'Il pianto della scavatrice' in *Le Ceneri di Gramsci*, p. 103, 105 and 114–15, respectively / 'The Cry of the Excavator', p. 197, 205 and 213, respectively [emphasis added—Trans.].

emotions—in a lowly human act
performed in the sleep of a morning.

The highest moment of the composition is in the sixth stanza, where the poem takes up again the motif-symbol of the excavator. The excavator begins its work anew and sends forth an almost human cry. But it is not only it that cries and screams in torment. Everything in the past that is dying also cries and screams. Even if it is in order to become better, adds Pasolini. It is clear, however, that his voice is entirely occupied with that lament and commiseration; whereas even here the future is nothing but abstract faith or concrete pain. Indeed,

> What cries is all that ends
> and begins again. What used to be
> a stretch of grass, an open expanse,
> and is now a courtyard white as snow
> enclosed within walls of resentment [. . .];
> What cries is whatever changes, even
> for the better [. . .][113]

It is enough that the poet be faced with the (entirely literary) temptation to take up again or begin the argument about this hypothetical future, for him to then fall back into hackneyed and irritating rhetorical-populist inflections:

> The light
> of the future never stops wounding us, not even
> for an instant: it's right here, burning
> in our every daily gesture,
> tormenting even the confidence
> that gives us life, the passion of Gobetti
> for these workers as they hoist,
> in this street on the other front of humanity,
> their red tatter of hope.[114]

In 'La terra di lavoro', the long descriptive introduction demonstrates that Pasolini's mimicry is nothing but the new face of the old naturalism. Although in this case there is an ever-present—if not always visible—veneer of human-itarian pity and Christian emotion (the small child, 'a creature that sleeps in depths / of a lamb's life'; the young man that 'does not see the foreigner, / does

---

113 Pasolini, 'The Cry of the Excavator', p. 217.
114 Pasolini, 'Il pianto della scavatrice', p. 118 / 'The Cry of the Excavator', p. 217.

not see anything, collar raised up against / the cold, or against the treacherous mystery / of a delinquent, a stray dog'). The central motif of the canto lies in the reaffirmation of the impossibility for these 'souls marked by twilight' to communicate with others; their innocence is detachment from the world and condemnation (and inviolability). The rediscovery of this theme is imbued with the atmosphere of 1956 and the Hungarian revolt. But the polemic against the 'others' and the implicit exaltation of these 'souls' ring hollow, like the lines of a newspaper editorial on current events:

> Those who rip the flag
> red with the blood of the murdered,
> are his enemies, as are those
> who faithfully defend it from the white assassins.
> The boss who hopes in their surrender
> is his enemy, as is the comrade
> who demands that they fight for a faith
> which is now the negation of faith [. . .][115]

The poet's refusal of the world—a world in which he seems to believe men exist only to provoke his emotive reactions—is too easy here: 'So, in a day of blood, the world is restored to a time that had seemed finished'. And the return to the old passion, to the old 'inner paradise', is this time less genuine than normal, precisely because the poet would like it to be driven by this general historical and political distaste.

The most coherent and complete application of Pasolini's poetics can be found in his narrative experiments. In effect, the lyrical mediation that survived until that time in the *poemetti* of *Le ceneri di Gramsci* is intentionally extinguished in them. What remains is the pure and total connection with the represented reality. This adaptation of the inspiration to the object, which Pasolini posits in order to rediscover the genuine foundations of existence, means in practice being able to *gather together* the exact contours of a determinate cross-section of reality (without the falsification of language and tradition), while remaining convinced that the tendentious choice of object and its amorous embrace are much more than a merely neutral reflex. That the environment of *Ragazzi di vita* and *Una vita violenta* is that of poor working-class Roman suburbs is not, therefore, merely incidental or autobiographical.

---

115 Pasolini, 'La terra di lavoro' in *Le ceneri di Gramsci* p. 137.

There is a further transition to account for—from the still fundamentally emblematic people of the Apennines or of Rome, as found in the *Le ceneri di Gramsci,* to the lumpenproletariat of the Roman working class suburbs, which is historically and existentially formless, lacking even a tradition of poverty, itself also born from a historical trauma, a still recent obstruction, and hence prey to a far more wretched and pitiful precariousness. There is no doubt that Pasolini wanted to take a step towards the knowledge of an essential and definitive truth, acquired from the lowest point of human existence. There is a dual justification for this attempt. The first, historical and rational, seems to us quite fictitious, especially if one stops at the first of the two abovementioned novels: in this light to regress to the lumpenproletariat means identifying the extreme form of the state of crisis and pain by which we are all possessed. Only once this work of discovery had been carried out could one attempt a cautious recovery of the historical dimension, rediscovering humanity where the author had initially placed the inhumanity (if not the animality) of an existential condition. One can link the proposal of a national-popular literature in the Gramscian sense to this return journey to the regions of the highest level of social injustice. Inter alia, it is evident that an implicit politicized moralism (the 'scandal of penury') leads the poet to protest against this humiliation of man perpetrated in the monstrous agglomerations of hovels, shacks and decaying buildings that surround Rome, the capital of Italy and Christianity.

On the other hand, it is impossible to reduce the source of Pasolini's choices to these motifs of a political, historical and ideological character. This truth, achieved at the lowest level of human existence, is not so much cause and object of knowledge, as the ecstatic contemplation of an immobile foundation of being. The descent into Hell does not always involve a resurfacing. The light of terrifying but satisfying certainties can be discovered in those very depths. The dismay and shame are compensated for by the basic observation that it is not always necessary to know. Pasolini is certainly not the first writer to discover the equivalence of 'maximum corruption = maximum purity', but he is perhaps the first to attempt a historico-sociological 'demonstration' of it with such effort and breadth of methods. The abstract categories of his youthful poems (we are thinking of the anthology *L'usignolo della Chiesa Cattolica* in particular) assume a real face and specific shape. The instincts and passions, freed from their last subjective bonds and autobiographical restraints, become objectified in a gallery of characters and episodes: pederasts, pimps, thieves, prostitutes, alcoholics, killers and thugs perform a human comedy of unexpected proportions on the apparently narrow stage of their world of wretchedness and oppression. In reality, they are but 'figures' whose significance is not purely literary. While they act and live for themselves—and do so with the intensity that comes from having no thoughts beyond material survival—they hint at something other than themselves, which could even be the very sense of the world, its extra-temporal kernel.

It was Pasolini who wrote: 'Beyond division there will be also a "historical tone" (to coin an irrational definition), a *soul* of time, if nothing else precisely in the drama and pain of division; it can be drawn upon—if we're permitted to moralize a little—through a great inner intransigence or a great compassion for the external world'.[116]

The limit of this attempt lies, at least in theory, in its lack of purity; that is, in an ambiguous mixture of elements that contradict one another. The descent into the Underworld demands a firmness of nerve, a violence of passion, a lucid refusal of all intellectual and sentimental *recompense*, which Pasolini here more than elsewhere shows he lacks. He appears violent and aggressive, but in reality is easily moved to commiseration and lament. He should display a firm and boundless cruelty, whereas in the culminating moments of his works he is unable to hold back pitiful tears that turn tragic scenes into instruments for the expression of his timid and fearful soul. He adopts the lumpenproletarians of the working-class Roman suburbs as figures of a total, aberrant sub-human condition, with the aim of rediscovering in them the essential precipitate of life, of *every* life; and he often stops at the self-satisfied or soft description of a vital chronicle, frayed and shapeless, which does not escape the well-defined boundaries of a historical situation devoid of prospects. He is also caught within the recurrent contradiction that, on the one hand, leads him to ride obsessively across the dark roads of being and, on the other, suggests to him the ideological aim of assuming this subject as the foundation for a historical and progressive discourse. In this way Pasolini dulls his most genuine sources of inspiration (the craving for possession and identification with the world) without being able to reconstruct an organic (though not necessarily homogeneous) picture of the various passages from the pre-historic to the historic world, from the sub-human to the human world. We should not be surprised if the welding together of these two aspects of being

---

116 Pasolini, 'La confusione degli stili' [The Confusion of Styles] in *Passione e ideologia*, pp. 348–9.

is then fictitiously realized by that moralism of which we have already spoken in relation to the *Le ceneri di Gramsci*, but which is here the more querulous and annoying the more it pretends to present itself as the voice of a general historic conscience.

Ragazzi di vita[117] represents what we might call the philological and cultural moment of this investigation. It has not been noted, for example, that the form itself of the book is that of the literary essay. The fact that it is lacking a central story (Riccetto is only one of the many *ragazzi*; in some chapters he even becomes a secondary character), justifies this impression. But there is also an essayistic character to the pace of many of the passages, where the life of the popular suburbs and districts of Rome is described with a folkloric precision that is only a little enlivened by the careful inlaying of dialectal and semi-dialectal lexicon. Taking a single characteristic example, that Pasolini's long 'tracking shot', extending over several pages, on a Rome drenched in the summer sun and buzzing with an elemental but passionate life: 'The heat wasn't sultry and it wasn't dry—it was just hot. It was like a warm coat lain on the light breeze, on the yellowish walls of the district, on the fields, the carts, the buses with bunches hanging from the doors.'[118] The tone of this prose attempts in places to raise itself to a moderate epicality. But the passage, like many others, has an essentially descriptive value, which is of interest to the degree that it serves as a kind of inventory of the places where typical Roman people can be found.

In other words, *Ragazzi di vita* appears to be clearly constructed with materials drawn from the scientific survey of the customs and ways of the Roman people and, in particular, of the suburban lumpenproletariat. Pasolini, though he arrives with excellent philological and linguistic knowledge, is fundamentally a stranger in this environment that nevertheless holds for him an irresistible fascination and attraction. Initially, he cannot undertake that deeply desired process of identification of the 'I' with the object without resorting to

---

117 The expression refers essentially to young 'lumpenproletarians' but more specifically rent boys, hustlers, petty criminals or street urchins. We have therefore retained the Italian. [Trans.]

118 Pier Paolo Pasolini, *Ragazzi di vita* (Milan: Garzanti, 1955), p. 212 / *The Ragazzi* (Emile Capouya trans.) (London: Carcanet, 1989), p. 195. [See also a new translation by Ann Goldstein, *The Street Kids* (New York: Europa, 2016). All quotations are from the 1989 English edition.—Trans.]

instruments of a more cultural or poetic order. In this way, *Ragazzi di vita* reveals a singularly sincere and traumatic vocation towards the sub-human, which is translated in the inert coldness of an entomological labour, of an entirely constructed and artificial narrative procedure.

Whoever wishes to can retrace, page by page, episode by episode, Pasolini's meticulous labour of linguistic collation, as he goes from working-class suburb to working-class suburb, from street to street, notebook in his pocket, in search of the *ragazzi di vita*, of their fathers and mothers, chatting, joking and laughing with them, all the while *studying them*. Here is a brief anthology, simply covering the typical gestures and attitudes of these lumpenproletarian characters, where the semi-scientific (but poetically inert) origin of this method of investigation appears immediately obvious: '"Well, how about it?"'; 'Giggetto burst out, thrusting his arm towards them with the hand held wide open to emphasize how unbecoming their conduct was'; '"Get a load of me, will you?"'; ' "Look", said Marcello, pushing out his open hand in the same gesture that Giggetto had made earlier'; "And he made the gesture for nothing doing, shaking his hand with the thumb and forefinger extended"; 'Nadia came forward smiling, bashful, keeping one hand at the neck of her gown and stretching out the other to them'; 'He stood up and delivered an address all in gestures, weaving back and forth, lifting his hand two or three times from breast-level to his nose, then making his fingers do a pirouette as if to indicate that some highly original idea was going through his mind'.[119]

The same mimetic-philological procedure is used in the description of more complex psychological relations as, for example, in the conversation between the Neapolitan gambler and Riccetto:

> The Neapolitan began his explanation again, and he warmed up as he talked and got as red in the face as a plate of spaghetti. He got up, facing Riccetto—who kept saying yes—staring at him with a rather irritated expression, talking for a moment, in order to lend greater emphasis to what he was saying, looking half-questioning, half-inspired, kneeling with his legs apart, his belly sticking out, and his hands raised and spread, like a goalie getting set for a high one.[120]

119 Pasolini, *Ragazzi di vita*, p. 13, 15, 15, 21, 80, 149 and 207, respectively / *The Ragazzi*, p. 18, 20, 20, 25, 78, 139 and 190, respectively. [For the last, one should read the entire passage on Alduccio's drunken father.]
120 Pasolini, *Ragazzi di vita*, p. 31 / *The Ragazzi*, p. 35.

Observe how each moment in this passage is drawn from the unique character of a pre-constituted popular typology whose elements slot together like the pieces of a puzzle. It originates from curiosity rather than from real human and poetic interest. (In other words, by now Pasolini knows, and his observations confirm it, that the plebeian becomes red in the face with the effort of thought; that his expression assumes the air of anger when he seeks to lend his words the force of conviction, even if in reality he is not angry with anyone; that a particular fixity of the eyes in moments of respite stands for the intense continuation of his attempt at persuasion; and so on. But the 'truth' of all this neither surprises nor excites because it does not overstep the bounds of the psycho-sociological survey).

Individual characters are constructed piece by piece through an effort of this sort. Amerigo, the powerful and violent crook from Pietralata is typical: 'His jacket collar was turned up; beneath his curley hair, matted down with dust, his face shone green and his big dark eyes stared glassily. He shook hands with great force, without seeming to, as if there couldn't be the least doubt that both of them were great people.' Here the tacit psychological trait is grafted onto a description of external appearance that is also derived from a thoroughly developed typological observation. As one proceeds, these mechanical traits become increasingly striking: 'Amerigo jumped down from the footboard, taking up the shock with his knees like someone who has spent time in the gym, without moving his hands from his pockets'; 'he walked on, setting one foot in front of the other, looking so evil that you felt you'd get a shock if you touched any part of his body.'[121] This last passage is particularly interesting because we can glimpse how Pasolini treats this documentary-style material to draw out impressionistic effects, i.e. artistic and psychological colours. The last observation ('you could tell he was ready', etc.) is in fact justified only if it is referred to the particular visual perspective of the poet. But this artistic 'use' of the document, which here appears legitimate because of the relationship established between the description of the bully and the psychologically erudite metaphorical impression it provokes, more often than not results in strident contradictions or with surprising ingenuity.

Adding a natural, popular expressionism to the much more tenuous and soft (but also more artificial) taste of the writer, can lead to weak stylistic

---

121 Pasolini, *Ragazzi di vita*, p. 91 and 92, respectively / *The Ragazzi*, p. 88 and 89, respectively [translation modified].

results, in which the desired deformation of the image produces caricature-like rather than grotesque effects. For example: 'Alvaro, a youth with a bony ... face, and a big head that would make a louse die of old age before it could finish the round trip'. Or in relation to the moon: 'It was as if it were not showing the world only its backside, and from that silvery rear end a great light streamed down, suffusing every object'. Or through the forced poetic rendering of an originally instinctive and penetrating figure of speech: 'The thunder came in crashes that sounded as if six or seven of St. Peter's domes, put into an oil drum that could hold them all, were being banged together up there in the sky, and the concert could be heard miles away, behind the rows of houses and the outer districts, toward Quadraro or toward San Lorenzo or wherever, *maybe even over there in that little patch of blue sky where sparrows were flying*'.[122]

Inserting erudite words and citations into the context of documentary materials does not serve to deepen the expressive character hidden in the roughly described elements, but flattens them and renders them impotent through an irritating intellectual nudge and a wink. Pasolini writes of some prostitutes 'that [they] had crouched down *diplomatically* amongst the bushes, in *pious retreat and reflection*'; and of Riccetto: 'on Sunday, playing his part to the hilt, he *mystically* gave up roaming around with Lenzetta and others in Centocelle or in Rome itself, and took his girl to the movies'; or ' "You see this?" Riccetto added *didactically*'.[123] This tendency to 'rework the data' in literary form culminates in pages where the lyrical intent prevails decisively over the descriptive. But in these cases one wavers between the smug poeticality of crisp and decadent origin, and a syntactically complex and stylistically affected discourse in which the old Pasolinian colour often surfaces albeit in a deteriorated and threadbare fashion. We will provide just one example of this:

As the houses spread out, among the piazzas and overpasses silent as a cemetery among subdivided lots where there was nothing but build-ing sites with steel frameworks five stories high or filthy little open stretches, you could see the whole sky. It was covered with thousands of pimply little clouds, in every shape and colour, descending to the

---

122 Pasolini, *Ragazzi di vita*, p. 8, 145 and 160–1, respectively / *The Ragazzi*, p. 14, 136 and 149, respectively [emphasis added—Trans.].

123 Pasolini, *Ragazzi di vita*, p. 77, 158–9, and 135, respectively / *The Ragazzi*, p. 75, 147–8 and 127, respectively [emphases added—Trans.].

saw-toothed disappearing summits of the skyscrapers in the distance. Black sea shells, yellowish mussel-shapes, bluish moustache-shapes, yolk-coloured gobs of spit, and farther off, beyond the streak of blue, as clear and glassy as a river in the polar regions, a big white cloud, curly, fresh, and so big it looked like the Mount of Purgatory.[124]

The story of the *ragazzi di vita* is unable to assume the human intensity that Pasolini wanted to extract from it, on the basis of a still uncertain and immature stylistic and narrative texture. Its chronicle-like aspect remains too much in evidence and at the same time too circumscribed to permit the reader to leap into that dimension of general truth to which the writer ambitiously aspired. Nevertheless, Pasolini achieves his best results in this very field—that of the essential data and documentation. When he is able to strip himself of his ideology, both of the mystical-decadent side as well as the historical-progressive one, he furnishes limited but convincing images of reality. Far as this might appear from his most cherished beliefs, there is no doubt in our mind that the success of the *ragazzi di vita* as characters is due to the temporary absence of any attempted idealizing transfiguration. Hence they *at least* appear true whenever they are, in the most limiting sense of the expression, what they are, whereas they appear false and unrealistic every time that the writer burdens them with his own hidden intentions. To avoid easy misunderstandings, it should be said that the truth of which we speak is above all a sociological truth.

We refer back to what has already been said concerning Pasolini's systematic documentation of the uses, customs, milieus and language of the suburban lumpenproletariat. If there is one objection that cannot be made of Pasolini, it is that of having 'invented' characters and milieus. We can take nothing away from the sociological verisimilitude of his narration. The more the writer remains faithful to this trait the more his achievement at least appears genuine (we have said, and we reiterate, *at least*, since it should be clear that sociological meticulousness is not by itself synonymous with poetic achievement). Pasolini roots his most rigorous pages in the trinity of lumpenproletarian life: hunger, sex and money. Some of the irresistible cries of the *ragazzi di vita* are born precisely of these perpetually unsatisfied, aggressive and exclusive like those that represent all life within the narrow horizons of heart and intellect that poverty has granted to these wretches: "'I'm so hungry I could shit my pants",' yells Begalone, with the air of someone stating the most blatant truth in the

---

124 Pasolini, *Ragazzi di vita*, p. 163 / *The Ragazzi*, pp. 151–2.

world; and another time, more dejected and in pain: "'We ought to get ourselves committed to the poorhouse, that's what. Jesus, how I'd like a piece tonight. Fat chance of that'; and Riccetto, in one of his moments of happiness: 'sang [. . .] at the top of his lungs, completely reconciled with life, full of big plans for the immediate future, feeling all that cash inside his pocket: cash, source of all pleasure and all satisfaction in this cockeyed world'.[125] When Pasolini faithfully follows the direction of this elemental vitality, the narration as a whole assumes a rhythm and a naturalness that are anything but superficial. See, for example, the chapter 'Dentro Roma' (Inside Rome), in which Alduccio and Begalone's adventures—involving the few hundred lira they need to wangle so as to eat something and go to the brothel—are drawn with a speed and ferocity unusual in Pasolini (despite the fact that Riccetto's return to the suburb where he had spent his childhood awkwardly breaks the smooth development of the picture).

Pasolini is less successful when he philosophizes; even less so when he allows himself to be won over by emotion and invents tear-jerking stories of *ragazzi di vita* who die in their collapsing homes, sad children swept in the river's undertow, or violent and heartless young men moved to pity by the fate of a little swallow. We will linger on these aspects in *Una vita violenta*, where they not only persist but are ideologized and inserted into what we might call an organic context. From the start we should note that we cannot simply charge these aspects of lumpenproletarian custom and sensibility with sociological implausibility—as has frequently happened. We know that this type of sentimentalism is a genuine attribute of the 'popular soul'. What we are not willing to concede is that the melodrama is any less insignificant or false as an attempt to grasp social reality merely because it takes place in the Borgata Gordiani or Quarticciolo.[126] If anything, this is the element that *objectively* welds a certain lumpenproletarian (or popular) custom to a petty bourgeois one. The fact that Pasolini reflects this with sympathy, as the 'positive' aspect of this world, means only that he does not realize how much his *ragazzi di vita* are integrated into the bourgeois world that he apparently so detests— the aggression against the 'world' turns out to be much weakened by this.

---

125 Pasolini, *Ragazzi di vita*, p. 173, 217 and 85, respectively / *The Ragazzi*, p. 159, 199 and 83, respectively.

126 Roman neighbourhoods where Pasolini's novels are set. [Trans.]

Una vita violenta takes up many of the characteristics and aspects of *Ragazzi di vita*. The texture of the plot is still shaped by the minute labour of analysis and direct observation of which we have spoken at length in relation to the earlier novel.[127] Even here the text is often interrupted by learned, intellectual formulations that enact a kind of ideal transfiguration—though one that is ambiguous and suspicious—of the behaviours and often contemptible characters being depicted.[128] At other times, the lyrical aim that is openly and directly inserted into the fabric of the narrative takes it away from its apparent objectivity, revealing the substantial survivals of Pasolini's 'poetic spirit' (in the *Novecentesco* sense).[129] But above all, in *Una vita violenta*, the current of compassion and commiseration—that is, of sentimentalism—continues to expand in relation to the openly progressive intent of the work. The entire novel is innervated with stubbornly resurgent seams of populist pity, where even the fiercest details are dampened, as in a great, inexhaustible reservoir of tears. The story of Tito and Toto, the protagonist's little brothers, is truly exemplary. Having lived together like little animals, yielding and docile in their wretchedness, they die in quick succession precisely because they are clearly unhappy living separately. Pasolini finds the most affectionate, even cloying, expressions for them, as though he had met two good subjects for his thirst for sweetness and love. Tito and Toto are not in truth children, they are little angels who

---

127 For example, Pier Paolo Pasolini, *Una vita violenta* (Milan: Garzanti, 1959), p. 46 / *A Violent Life* (William Weaver trans.) (London: Carcanet, 1985), p. 42:

Ugo faced him; he put his hands together like he was going to say an Our Father. Then with a rapid gesture he turned them, still joined, but towards his knees, the tips of the fingers against his chest: when there were in that position, he pressed the finger-tips together, waved his hands rapidly against his chest and under his chin, five or six times, interrogatively, then translated the gesture: 'Whadda you care?'

128 For example: 'The other character was beginning to enjoy himself. He stood up, his face bold, a blissful smile creeping into his narrow eyes, staring forward, absorbed in his pleasure, *in profound and spiritual ecstasy*'—Pasolini, *Una vita violenta*, p. 22 / *A Violent Life*, p. 21 [emphasis added—Trans.].

129 For example: 'Shitter got out: there was a pine tree, and, behind it, a little wall: four sheds around, *crushed by the silence*, among the muddy garden patches, and over it all, a little mound of black muck'—Pasolini, *Una vita violenta*, p. 70 / *A Violent Life*, p. 61. And: '[T]he peace was so complete that you could hear a dog barking three or four miles away away, beyond all that damp earth and those filthy mounds, towards Rome, or towards the sea, you couldn't tell which: and *it sounded like a lost soul, crying*'—Pasolini, *Una vita violenta*, p. 71 / *A Violent Life*, p. 62 [emphasis added—Trans.].

have descended as if by chance into this inferno of shacks and who speedily return into the heavens, adorned with all their filth and innocence (only to then reappear to Tommaso in a dream, dirty as before but even more good and loved, dressed in rags that seem embroidered silk). Tommaso Puzzilli, a creature of mud, has in the depth of his heart a cluster of pure and rich feeling. It might not seem like it, but it only takes a star-studded sky spreading out above his head for this *ragazzo di vita* to be moved like a child or a decadent intellectual:

> The sky above was cloudy and whitish: only here and there a clear patch could be seen, much darker. In one of these patches, just above the roof of corrugated iron and tarred paper of Sora Adele's shack, at the tips of some shredded clouds, there were a few little stars, shining all alone. And around the wretched pile of huts there was a silence, a peace, a solitude that were frightening. After a little while, without even realizing it, while he stood there alone and downcast, Tommaso felt something like a tear rising in his throat. But he promptly swallowed it again.[130]

Pasolini could not show greater skill in measuring out the ingredients of this mixture: the contrasts between clear and cloudy; the appearance not of stars but, take note, 'little stars' that 'shimmer and shine' in solitude (the verb extends and confirms the sense of the diminutive); encircling the picture of misery, a ring of silence and reflection that arouses a tremor of dismay. Tommaso's tears are both too natural and too anticipated to be true. Pasolini's attitude towards his popular characters is here marked by that disposition of spirit that can be summed up in the rendering of the 'poor' plebeian as 'poor devil', with all the ethical and ideological implications borne by these terms. We do not mean this just in a generic sense. On the contrary, the use of these terms is notably frequent in the two novels, not so much in a connotative sense as in the ethico-affective one. In *Ragazzi di vita*: '[the watchman] *poor bastard* began to yell for help'; 'the *poor devil* was so hungry'; 'two eyes that made him look like a *poor suffering* Christ'; 'Riccetto [. . .] *poor bastard* [. . .] got up rubbing his eyes, and stumbled down the stairs after the cops'; 'his *poor* mother'; 'Genesio, who was good-hearted and an easy prey to his own emotions and affections, *poor boy*'.[131] In *Una vita violenta*: 'Some of them, like

---

130 Pasolini, *Ragazzi di vita*, p. 152 / *A Violent Life*, p. 128.

131 Pasolini, *Ragazzi di vita*, p. 162, 164, 166, 171, 140 and 255–6, respectively / *The Ragazzi*, p. 150, 152, 154, 158, 193 and 234, respectively [emphasis added—Trans.].

Tommaso and his crowd, were *poor* kids who lived in the shacks'; 'All *poor* slum women'; 'Toto, however, didn't keep it up for long, and after two minutes, he was already pacified too, *poor* thing'; 'dragging those *poor* feet along'; and 'with that *poor*, rubbery face'.[132]

Despite these affinities, it is clear that *Una vita violenta* can be considered far more complex than the other novel. In the period that goes from *Ragazzi di vita* to *Una vita violenta*, Pasolini further develops his subject and his ideology. *Ragazzi di vita* belongs to the moment that we elucidated theoretically with reference to the articles from *Officina* and the poems of *Le ceneri di Gramsci*. This phase was characterized by the lack of a historically determinate and ideologically committed engagement and by literary experimentalism. Subsequently, Pasolini tries to buttress his position by leaving behind this phase, in which the overall problematic is continually shifting. With regard to ideology, this means moving decisively towards Marxism. In relation to his literary choices, it means developing a type of narrative that has at its heart a story, that is to say, an axis, a nucleus of fundamental interests that unites the scattered fragments, and thus appears much more determined by a thesis and a precise intention. As far as his political attitude goes, it means drawing closer to the Communist Party, almost without any further qualms or doubts. Setting aside a consideration of this last point—which relates more to the general choices shaping the cultural politics of the left—we can say of the other two points that they advance in tandem, although not always in an organic or convincing manner. Pasolini's Marxism, for example, is one of the most curious and artificial to be encountered in the recent period of literary progressivism. And yet, there is no doubt that he aspired to take up just such an ideological position if—in conclusion to a set of answers to a 1959 interview (the same year that *Una vita violenta* was published)—Pasolini could affirm, almost jocularly: 'I believe only in the "historical" and "national" novel, in the "objective" and "typical" sense. I do not see how any others can exist, given that "purely individual destinies and events outside historical time" for me do not exist: otherwise what sort of Marxist would I be?' We can see here how Gramscian terminology and references of a Lukácsian type merge in an easy and surprisingly futile combination. Moreover, the same ease can be detected when Pasolini goes on to delineate the content of a literary experiment linked to

---

132 Pasolini, *Una vita violenta*, p. 15, 128, 151, 167 and 296 respectively / *A Violent Life*, p. 16, 109, 127, 141 and 250, respectively [emphasis added—Trans.].

this recent, but passionate, socialist faith. One can see that Marxism is for him everything that cannot be defined as irrational or decadent: ' "socialist realism" as a still ideal formula that needs to be clarified in theory and realized— this, I believe, is the only working hypothesis. And for a very simple reason: *socialism is the only mode of knowledge* [sic] *that allows one to place oneself in an objective and rational relationship with the world'*.[133] The truth is that of all the possible variants of Marxism, Pasolini has grasped—perhaps through the mediation of the official communist interpreters—only the Gramscian theme of the national-popular, which is in fact the only one that matters in his fictional works.

Very probably, it is to this 'Marxism' of Pasolini that we owe the inspiration behind the story of Tommasino Puzzilli, the protagonist of *Una vita violenta*—the *ragazzo di vita* who, after a variety of experiences, gradually develops an almost imperceptible glimmer of historical, political and personal awareness. In this case too, we will not ask whether Tommaso's story is plausible. On the contrary, to avoid pointless debates, we will simply accept that such a story, with its intentionally gradual transitions, can take place within a lumpenproletarian life. Yet Tommaso remains one of those characters whose origins are entirely intellectualistic and 'opportunistic'; in other words, they are ideological in the most restrictive and debased sense of the term. Pasolini presents him initially as a *missino*[134] thug, morally insensitive, sexually bestial; then, through the experience of his engagement with Irene and of the sanatorium, he becomes a communist and ultimately a hero thanks to his spirit of bravado and ancient, subterranean generosity. He originates in that well-known cliché of left politics which is entirely founded on the theme of the 'elevation of the masses' and on the presupposition of the *human* progress embedded in the people's initiative. There is nothing in him that could not be found in the pages of local Roman news in *L'Unità* or *Avanti!*. We even witness his rediscovery of the decisive role played in the formation of a consciousness that has ceased to be simply animalistic by popular housing—by the theme of universal housing and the controversies around the shantytowns on the edges of the capital.

---

133 Pasolini, 'Inchiesta sul romanzo' [Inquiry into the Novel], *Nuovi Argomenti* (1959), p. 48 and p. 46, respectively.

134 A follower of the Movimento Sociale Italiano (MSI), the principal postwar neo-fascist party. [Trans.]

The attempt to build the entire novel around Tommaso Puzzilli would have been even more fantastical and artificial had the author not balanced (in this case too) his ideological constructions with the evermore intense and abnormal strivings of his darkest passions. Indeed, it is remarkable that *Una vita violenta*, despite being based upon a progressive aim, also constitutes a step towards those deep and dark zones of existence where it is difficult to distinguish the human from the sub-human or even the animal level.

Pasolini presented his stylistic and narrative programme in the interview to which we have already referred:

> Practically speaking, for me the question presents itself as follows: to make things speak one must resort to a regressive operation. In fact, 'things' and the men who live immersed in them, whether proletarians—among 'things' understood as work and the struggle of existence—or bourgeois—among 'things' understood as the totality and compactness of a cultural level—all this lies *behind* the writer-philosopher, the writer-ideologue.
>
> Such a regressive operation translates into a mimetic operation (given that the characters use *another* language from that of the author, which serves to express *another* psychological and cultural world).

And this 'mimetic operation' is perfectly summarized in the phrase: 'immediate physicality: that is, the character in action, the landscape as a function, a violent and absolute environmental mimesis'.[135] Just how well this operation sits alongside Marxism, is a question that will strike anyone who observes the contradiction between the fundamental rationality of the one and the peculiar passion of the other. And the fact that the two terms now coexist peacefully in Pasolini's mind without struggling with or attempting to overcome one another, can be explained only on the basis of a real cultural ambiguity that has no other root or end if not those determined by the desire to win a place in a politico-cultural-ideological camp. Moreover, this remains the most vital and operative part of Pasolini's inspiration, over and above his intentions as a writer, even when the latter have been rendered theoretically explicit.

We are not only referring to the enormous importance that the sexual act, in all its forms, assumes in this framework (although the significance of the

---

135 Pasolini, 'Inchiesta sul romanzo', p. 47 and 45, respectively.

obsessive insistence with which Pasolini returns to the milieu of prostitutes, pimps and pederasts cannot be ignored). Even more important is the persistent use of animal symbolism to characterize the acts, feelings and impressions of the characters. It is doubtful whether he fully realizes this, but when Pasolini thinks of his lumpenproletarian figures, he cannot do so without drawing out a corresponding animal root or analogy. The result is that in its best moments, the novel becomes a veritable bestiary, animated by completely uncontrollable vital impulses. The owner of the table football is 'thin as a sardine'; two sailors observed while having sex with two prostitutes resemble 'two lizards hit on the back with a stone'; Tommasino as a child appears as a 'little spaniel', and has 'his eyes owl-like'; a harmonica player displays a row of teeth like those of a 'dead cat's'; a waiter looks like as a 'werewolf'; a certain Nazzareno has a 'chicken-head'; Cagone resembles a 'cod'; a petrol station attendant wears his hair like a 'crouched bird'; Ugo shows his teeth 'like a rabid dog', and then slinks along the pavement 'like a snake'; when among girls Tomassino turns 'as red as a rooster'; Irene keeps her elbows alongside her hips 'like a pair of plucked wings'; an old homosexual has 'a dog face'; a priest has 'lips pale as a cat's'; Tomassino angry with Irene shows his 'teeth sticking out like a corpse's'; the aforementioned Nazzareno laughs 'like an ape'; the *ragazzi di vita* move about like a 'pack of old jackals'; the chronically-ill patients of the Forlanini are 'thin as finches'; a pederast at the cinema remains as still as 'a cat watching a dog'; Tommaso and the pederast, who are silenced during an argument at the cinema, immediately become still 'like those animals who play dead'; the shape of Tommaso's head is 'round like a bird-dog's'; Scintillone [Sparkler] yawns 'like a tiger'; under the rain of the storm one can see a shadow that looked 'like a dog or a kid'; Tommaso throws himself into the sludge 'like a hog'; and the women saved from the storm are 'naked as worms'. The use of animalistic terms is not limited to these grotesque and expressionistic aspects. Affection and sentimentalism flow between these same banks. The old lady, 'meek and mild', ashamed and scared in the middle of the assault by the police of Pietralata, is 'a bed-bug, an ant'; Settimio, Tommaso's good friend, is 'tiny and quick as a mouse'; even Tommaso, in a moment of calm while he wets his hair, resembles 'a duckling'.[136] When he then turns to children and the

---

136 Pasolini, *Una vita violenta*, p. 16, 20, 21, 26, 39, 39, 40, 41, 72, 82, 82, 95, 101, 158, 219, 246, 252, 253, 257, 327, 332, 332, 344, 369, 374, 377, 143, 225 and 347, respectively / *A Violent Life*, p. 16, 19, 21, 24, 36, 36, 37, 37, 62, 70, 70, 81, 86, 133, 185, 208, 213, 214, 218, 275, 279, 287, 289, 310, 313, 316, 121, 191 and 287, respectively.

young, Pasolini reveals a rich vein in diminutives, where his excessively soft and sentimental sweetness reverberates. Roman, like Friulian, shows itself to be a language rich in words for infants and youth: *pipelletto, mignoletto, pisellino, piccoletto, ragagnattolo, pischello, pivello, pivelletto, ragazzino, giovenco, mino,* etc. For this gang of *pischelli,*[137] Pasolini concocts a series of gentle, animal references: we will come across 'an unweaned puppy'; a 'puppy-like forehead'; 'arguing like puppies'; 'like a heard of goats'; 'a flight of sparrows'; a 'pile of kittens'; and, naturally, in relation to Tito and Toto, he speaks of: 'the way a dog does', 'puppy', 'real puppy' and 'two little monkeys'.[138]

When a man does not resemble an animal, he resembles a thing, a vegetable, an object: a young man will appear as 'a fresh bunch of lettuce'; a hand is 'like a cabbage stalk'; the prison guard, is defined in slang as an 'asparagus' [*sparagio*]; a group of people resembles a 'handful of dried leaves blown by the wind'; the face of the pederast is 'like an ear of corn'; and the tongue moves between lips 'like a piston'. It is no surprise that when Tommaso swims he moves mechanically 'like a puppet'.[139]

When these beings are gathered together, the impression is even more brutal and total. At this point Pasolini's images display undertones of intense morbidity, blinded by the disgusting mystery of this life. It is no coincidence that Tommasino's search for the pederast he's tapping for money takes place in a popular cinema that is depicted as follows:

> Under the bright light, the room looked like a stone when it's been lifted up and you find it was covering a pile of worms: one coiled around the other, moving and crawling all around, twisting their heads and their tails, half-crazed, struck by the light like that.[140]

Coming to the worm after passing through the dog and the pig is to reach the lowest level of the search that Pasolini had begun so many years earlier. Note that the tenor of this observation is not ethical but aesthetic. It refers to Pasolini's inability to now bring to conclusion the argument he had earlier

---

137 Like the terms in italics here, *pischello* is a diminutive, somewhat affectionate term for 'youngster'. [Trans.]

138 Pasolini, *Una vita violenta*, p. 25, 176, 215, 297, 317, 377, 29, 151, 260 and 260, respectively / *A Violent Life*, p. 24, 148, 102, 250, 269, 316, 27, 127, 220 and 220, respectively.

139 Pasolini, *Una vita violenta*, p. 55, 101, 204, 317, 327, 362 and 373, respectively / *A Violent Life*, p. 49, 86, 172 [translation modified], 267, 275, 304 and 313, respectively.

140 Pasolini, *Una vita violenta*, pp. 325–6 / *A Violent Life*, p. 274.

established. The motif of purity, which should have been grafted onto that of corruption, gushing from it like virginal and vital water, appears now to crumble like a tower unable to withstand the assault by the muddy flood. One might say that Pasolini is overcome by his very craving to always go to the base of things, to always reach towards the essence of the good through the essence of the bad. The bottom of this well into which he has sunk is nothing but a slimy magma in which everything is stifled. That same populist content from which Pasolini draws inspiration, shatters and falls away as though under the pressure of more substantial forces. The anger, the violence, the unconscious protest of these lumpenproletarians is nothing but a mechanical gesture confined by a deaf and opaque nature, the nature of brutes.

To regain altitude is not possible, particularly because Pasolini now—despite all his declarations—continues to look behind himself, towards the darkness from whence he comes. It is therefore both logical and suggestive—while being destructively contradictory of the novel's principal assumption—that Tommaso's story ends with the recognition shown him by the *ragazzi di vita*, his first comrades and friends, at his deathbed. After the communists, who visit Tommaso in his agony, leave, there remain Zucabbo and Lello, the final and most appropriate witnesses of the violent end of Puzzilli's violent story; almost as if to affirm that the heavens of eternal and wise lumpenproletarian corruption are preferable to the heavens of immature politico-ideological purity. Logical and suggestive too is Tommaso's reaction to their care, vouching for the indomitable and sacred persistence of sub-human vitality.[141]

But the combination of populism, progressivism, aestheticizing decadentism and animal-like morbidity does not coalesce, if not by virtue of the usual moralizing and intellectualizing operation. In *Una vita violenta* as well, Pasolini's accomplishments are laudable whenever he forgets his ideological armoury and can put a brake on his subconscious spasms. The most successful pages of the book display a taut and moderately passionate realism, as in chap-

---

141 Pasolini, *Una vita violenta*, p. 382 / *A Violent Life*, p. 320:

> 'What the fuck are you crying for? If anybody's gotta cry around here it's me,' said Tommaso.
>
> 'You're not dying are you?'
>
> Their eyes glistening in their crooks' faces, burned by the sun and by hunger, Lello and Zucabbo kept standing there, not moving.
>
> 'Fuckoff!' Tommaso said. 'Instead of staying here and keeping me company, go outside and screw around. It's Sunday!'

ters like 'La battaglia di Pietralata' [The Battle of Pietralata] and 'Che cercava Tomasso?' [What did Tommaso Seek?], where the writer keeps to things and their movements without pouncing on them ravenously. The mass scenes where the single protagonists lose their individual faces and once again become anonymous particles of lumpenproletariat are those that the author pulls off most persuasively. Perhaps the most beautiful pages of the book are those on the revolt in the Forlanini sanatorium, with these skinny and emaciated rebels, like images of death that are nonetheless animated by a great, indomitable anger.

These observations are confirmed by a linguistic analysis of the work. It is well known that Pasolini bases his use of dialect on the conviction that the social fracture that still persists in Italy stands in the way of a homogeneous national language at the literary level. Besides, mimicry in this sense also means the word fitting the object. When a common [*popolare*] person speaks, it is absurd to make him speak in proper Italian. Analogously, when it is a matter of expressing a feeling, a psychological element, the typical act of a character who comes from the common people, one cannot but refer to the word in dialect that best matches it. 'Given that the characters use *another language* to that of the author, which is used to express *another* psychological and cultural world', writes Pasolini, it will become necessary to 'use dialect either completely or partially'. We believe we have demonstrated how this operation remains caught in its philological origins, revealing the role of research in determining and fundamentally characterizing it on the linguistic or poetic plane. Moreover, the narrative mixture in *Una vita violenta* no less than in *Ragazzi di vita* reveals a refined literary disposition, in which Pasolini's supposed realism is scaled back to the level of a game or a precious inlay. Pasolini shows himself to be aware of this when he states: 'The mimetic operation is [. . .] the operation that requires the most able and dogged linguistic investigations,' adding immediately afterwards: 'certainly one must let things speak, physically, immediately: but to allow "things to speak", it is necessary "to be writers, and even be so conspicuously".'[142] The existing and unhealed fracture between the world of the author and that of his characters can, I believe, be clearly seen in the different treatment reserved, on the one hand, for the dialogues, and on the other, for the narrative itself. The *ragazzi di vita* do not speak in dialect but in the slang of the local districts and the criminal

---

142 Pasolini, 'Inchiesta sul romanzo', p. 47 and 48, respectively.

underworld. Here mimicry is pushed to the point of reproducing short-lived terms or expressions that, while presumably in use while Pasolini was researching these two novels, today are no longer in circulation simply because of the social upheaval of the extremely restricted groups that had shaped the expressions for the purposes of internal communication in slang. Pasolini operates here on an extremely narrow linguistic plane, with an obstinate faithfulness that further diminishes the communicable human significance of his characters. In the course of the narrative he alternates passages in which he maintains the structure of an extremely developed and complex literary syntax, limiting himself to occasionally grafting elements of the popular lexicon onto it, and other denser and more tangled passages that display a tendency—even at the level of syntax—to try and convey a more immediate and unreflexive expression. But in both cases the author is never able to hide behind the 'monument' erected to the Roman lumpenproletariat. Each time the exquisite erudition of the operation or the 'mixed' character of the subject matter reveal that the real protagonist of the work, the genuine speaker of *Una vita violenta*, is the author's culture, his philological and linguistic knowledge.

Pasolini's creative history ends, at least for now, here. This is not only because in the subsequent years Pasolini only published one volume of poetry,[143] *La religione del mio tempo*, whose dominant characteristic is the explicit confession of the poet's coming to a halt and undergoing an extremely severe crisis. Above all, it is because ever since the appearance of *Una vita violenta* Pasolini does not appear to have been able to further develop his stance, overcoming the obstacles he had run up against fruitlessly, time and again. Despite his cinematographic productions—which retrace the narrative experiments without any great innovations—the impression is that over these years Pasolini has been occupied with gathering up and meditating upon the (spiritual and literary) consequences of an aesthetic adventure that on the whole can be deemed a failure. The author had attempted to construct a project of civic and progressive literature by activating a lyrical-parenetic form of discourse in

---

143 The collection *Poesia in forma di rosa* [Poetry in the Form of a Rose] (Milan: Garzanti, 1964) appeared when this study had already been completed. We did not feel the need to alter our opinion in the light of this. To our eyes, *Poesia in forma di rosa* does not provide new material but simply confirms our investigation into the entirety of Pasolini's character, particularly our forecast of the growing prevalence of the narcissistic motif of self-affliction and the theme of the 'return to the past'.

his poetry and a realism founded on a mixture of styles and on the psycho-sociological truth of the setting and the characters in his prose. In both cases, what was presupposed was a certain ideological choice that we have discussed extensively. Perhaps no other writer has suffered such a collapse, within his own work, of an ideological standpoint that was not only personal but also historical and objective. Pasolini had arranged his entire investigation around a determinate conception of the world that particularly highlighted the moralistic condemnation of bourgeois evils and the demand for a more humane humanity for all—also or, rather, especially, for the destitute, the offended, the unfortunate, gathered together in the theoretico-sociological concept of the people. While he did so, *this anti-bourgeois moralism of bourgeois stamp, this remarkably traditional humanitarian petitioning, this extremely accommodating and convenient concept of the people were thrown into crisis* in the context of the crisis of a 'left-wing culture' that had by this point clearly shown itself to be an integral and necessary part of bourgeois culture.

A retreat and return to the past become inevitable after the loss of that impulse of protest that the poet had practised throughout the 1950s, however confusedly, as a reflection of the much wider climate of agitation and mobilization of the masses. It must be said that, on this subject, Pasolini makes an error typical of moralists or of writers who have strongly egocentric temperaments. They confuse a process of historical development, which as a whole is positive or logical and even inevitable, for an evermore accentuated form of decadence and corruption. If the world no longer understands Pasolini, this does not happen—he thinks—because Pasolini does not understand the world, but because this world is evil, corrupt, etc. Moreover, the world is evil and corrupt because Pasolini's ideologico-literary experiment does not prevail over other positions. Therefore, one cannot be surprised that the only poetic notes articulated by Pasolini after *Le ceneri di Gramsci* and the novels, concern this condition of humiliation and pain in which the poet finds himself in the wake of the acknowledgment that what he had believed to be right and positive turned out to be ineffective and unproductive. The collection *La religione del mio tempo* bears witness to this passage from the enduring (if ambivalent) populism of the *poemetto* 'La ricchezza' [Riches], to the already raised doubts about the composition from which the book draws its title, through to the harsh outbursts of the 'Epigrammi' [Epigrams] and the disheartened reflections of the 'Poesie incivili' [Uncivil Poems].

The civic and historical theme survives only in the initial phases of the collection. 'La ricchezza' (1955–59), on the other hand, can be traced back to the years of *Le ceneri di Gramsci* and *Ragazzi di vita*. The affinities are particularly evident with the latter work. But what a decline in tone, what a naive, almost disarming superficiality in so many of the reflections about the figure of the lumpenproletariat and his ilk! Who could ever think that verses such as these are the works of an expert and refined writer like Pasolini?

> The whore is a queen, her throne
> a Roman ruin, her hand a patch
> of shit-strewn field, her sceptre
> a red patent-leather handbag.
> She barks in the night, dirty and fierce
> as an ancient mother, protecting
> her domain and her life [. . .].[144]

More authentic (as well as more sombre and restrained) tones can be sought elsewhere: where Pasolini specifies and elaborates once again the nature of his relationship to this disaggregated and shapeless people of which he speaks and sings. If anyone still has any doubts about whether the people act as objective stimulus for the poet, read about how he has no compunction in admitting the literary basis and aesthetic-passionate nature of his feelings for them:

> Our hopes are equally obsessive:
> mine aesthetic, theirs anarchic.
> The aesthete and the lumpenproletarian
> are subject to the same hierarchy
> of sentiment. Both stand outside history,
> in a world with no outlets
> but sex and the heart.
> Where joy is joy, and sorrow sorrow [. . .]

Of course, this figure of the people continues to be of great importance in Pasolini's work. But it is not insignificant that when the writer is more heated and emotive towards it, it is due to the presence of children and adolescents, as if the generic purity of popular corruption were not enough for

---

144 This and the following quotation: from Pier Paolo Pasolini, 'La ricchezza' in *La religione del mio tempo* (Milan: Garzanti, 1961), p. 42 and 52, respectively / 'Riches' in *Selected Poetry*, p. 249 and 259–61, respectively [translation modified].

him and it was necessary to dig even deeper, to go even further back to satisfy his thirst for love.

The initial part of *La religione del mio tempo* assumes the tones of sweet and intense melancholy, precisely because the poet's gaze is fixed on two plebeian adolescents, already a little roguish, but still cheerful, still fully possessed 'the poor force / of their almost animal heart,'[145] who pass beneath the windows of his sickroom.

We have already noted that the interest of this collection is not to be found in the repetition of populist themes, which by now have become commonplace in Pasolini's works. The dominant tone of the work is provided instead by a need for revision, which not only attaches to the present, but even to the past and future of the writer. This motif is present in all the compositions brought together here, leading one to suppose that some of them, featuring a double date of composition (such as 'La ricchezza', 1955–59, and 'La religione del mio tempo', 1957–59), were taken up again precisely in order to submit them to a revision of this type. (One can see that new motifs, linked to the author's sense of crisis, can be found inserted into the structure we encountered previously in *Le ceneri di Gramsci*). This revision is turned above all towards the past (given Pasolini's character, not at all inclined to accept guilt for a particular course of events, this can only with difficulty be called a self-criticism). Here we see the poet retracing all the stages of personal development, describing himself as child and adolescent, sensitive and passionate, animated by a limitless ardour for the world.[146] The first religious experiences are presented in their strictly literary genesis ('And yet, Church, I came to you, / clutching Pascal and the Songs of the Greeks / in my passionate hands'[147]); the distance from the Church is described as the latter's betrayal of Pasolini (in line with the particular *animus* that leads him to view this historical phenomenon or institution as a function of his subjectivity). The discovery of the Friulian peasant is seen objectively, in its mythic-religious motivations.[148] The apprenticeship in life that the

---

145 Pasolini, *La religione del mio tempo*, p. 87.

146 Pasolini, *La religione del mio tempo*, pp. 82–3.

147 Pasolini, *La religione del mio tempo*, p. 87 / 'From the Religion of my Time' in *Selected Poetry*, p. 281.

148 From Pasolini, *La religione del mio tempo*, p. 87 / 'From The Religion of My Time', p. 281: 'Pascal and the *Songs of the Greeks* / in my passionate hands, as though / the mystery of peasant life, hushed / and deaf in the summer of '43 / between the village, the vineyards / and the Tagliamento's banks, were / the centre of the earth and heavens'.

then still poor poet undergoes in the libraries, the working-class districts and the Roman galleries also has the underlying sense of a literary and aestheticizing experience. But the break between the old and new world of the spirit is produced by the Resistance, with its ideological legacy, the discovery of rationality and progressivism.

However, the past for Pasolini only serves the purpose of regret or deprecation. He constructs an image of himself as an innocent enamoured of the world, driven by hope and salvation, only in order to make his present condition all the more searing and pitiful. The Resistance is remembered above all to make it clear that it has been betrayed, that the ideal inheritance of this historical experience has succumbed to the accumulation of contemporary hypocrisies and errors. Pasolini exhibits that typical anti-fascist vision that judges the events from 1945 to today according to a standard of decadence, almost as if history since then had followed an arc of increasing degradation (which is undeniable if one's point of reference is that particular type of bourgeois-progressive ideology, according to which there exists nothing positive outside of 'popular passion'). The viewing of *Roma città aperta*[149] unleashed in the poet this quake of memories, this merely sterile commiseration for a form of anti-fascism that was rightly punished by the inexorable movement of history for its moralistic presumptions. The ghost of the dead brother resurfaces, and it too assumes a literary colour, the creature of an exhausted ideology. To shed tears for him is to shed tears for himself, for the literary illusion of 'winning' the world with the strength of his words.

The poet becomes all the more querulous, lost and uncertain when he begins to speak of himself in the present tense. What we might go so far as to call Gozzanian[150] tones issue from his pen when he presents himself as

---

149 Roberto Rossellini's *Rome, Open City* (1945), a neo-realist film depicting Nazi occupation and the Resistance in Rome. [Trans.]

150 The reference is to Guido Gozzano (1883–1916), poet and writer associated with the Decadentist movement. In a later work, Asor Rosa describes Gozzano as a writer who:

> [G]ives voice to the disquiet of a small town petty bourgeoisie, which is extremely civilized but passive before a social reality undergoing great changes, such as the rapidly industrializing Turin of the early years of the century. [. . .] Gozzano fails to [. . .] systematically oppose the dominant poetic forms of his time. The humble language of Gozzano's poetics and the complacent contemplation of his own withdrawn and defeated character cannot, against this background, give way to a new poetics able to compete—so to speak—with the older forms, but is instead realized through the destructive filter of self-irony, which is the

wounded by the magnified cruelty of fate: 'I'm like a child groaning / not only for what he can't have, but also for what he shall never have'.[151] He is more penetrating and cruel in his description of all the ways in which, one after another, he is abandoned by the consolations he relied upon up to this point. First of all, the one through which—though never fully at peace—he had survived the aggression of external evils: 'the hopeless / gift of sex has all gone up / in smoke'.[152] At this point it is not difficult to confess to the failure of that initial burst of kindness and love with which the young poet, intoxicated by poetry, had surrounded himself as with an angelic halo, because

the devotion of an adolescent [. . .] was destined
to turn into vice: for age corrodes
meekness, and makes an obsession
of mournful self-giving [. . .].[153]

Even more precious, because it strikingly confirms our earlier diagnoses, is the admission of the intentional (that is to say, alien and fanciful) character of Pasolini's ferocity: "But the violence of the senses and the intellect / *that has confounded me for years / was the only way*'. When this protective integument falls away—and we should not be surprised, since we are indeed dealing with an integument, laboriously maintained around the soft nucleus of Pasolini's elegiac soul—the love for the world can easily turn into resentful incomprehension or moralistic condemnation. In some of the ugliest pages he has written, Pasolini indignantly describes that Christian Democratic Italy where 'nobody knows how to feel real passion'; 'there is no longer anything but nature, which only gives off the fascination of death, nothing in this human world that I love'.[154]

---

conscious sense of a hopeless discomfort.—*Storia europea della letteratura Italiana, Vol. 3* pp. 174–5. [Trans.]

151 Pasolini, *La religione del mio tempo*, p. 79 / 'From The Religion of My Time', p. 273. The Italian poem as quoted by Asor Rosa differs from the one contained in the English edition. This might be a case of a poem that Pasolini reworked in later life. The translation of what Asor Rosa provides would read as: 'I'm like a child / who does not cry for what he shall not have'].

152 Pasolini, *La religione del mio tempo*, p. 79 / 'From The Religion of My Time', p. 273.

153 This and the following quotation: from Pasolini, 'La ricchezza', p. 57 and 59 / 'Riches', p. 263 and 265 [emphasis added—Trans.].

154 From Pasolini, *La religione del mio tempo*, p. 102.

In short, it is fated that the oldest motifs that inspired him return to the surface. Pasolini too now sets out to close his circle. The motif of death ('Frammento alla morte')[155] rises up fully formed from the obscure depths, whereas in earlier works and years Pasolini had only treated it as a dialectical element of reality—as in the novels—or as the source for a lively intellectual contrast. It is no coincidence that Pasolini should underline the pre-natal, sub-conscious origin of this feeling, having perhaps first rediscovered it precisely by being unable to bury it under the accumulation of rational historical experiences. Do you recall the 'aged adolescence][156] of the twenty-four-year-old Pasolini? Do you recall the 'Madman' which he described himself as, once he found himself so crazily different from the rest of the world?[157] Fifteen years proved insufficient to wipe from his heart the stigma of his adolescent ordeal. A crack opens in that well-articulated but fictitious ideological construction—a construction where even passion becomes ideology, as we have indicated on more than one occasion—and Pasolini rediscovers within himself, now turned to stone, the feelings of the past: 'Inside me is a poet's black rage. / A crazed adolescent's old age.'[158]

Even the very impulse to civic poetry exhausts itself in this atmosphere, not so much defeated by the iniquities of the times (as the poet would like to make us believe in the verses of 'In morte del realismo' [On the Death of Realism]), so much as overcome by his very ambiguity and inconsistency. The epico-lyrical *poemetto* and its dignified and elevated ways are replaced by the epigram in a form that is more irascible and desperate than aggressive. But it too is a way to testify that Pasolini is on the ropes, that he no longer has the strength for a wide-ranging, extensive ideological debate and is forced to scream, to use invective, sometimes even pure and simple swearing.

Behind the epigram one can see the outlines, in the form of a logical and immediate consequence, of the solution proposed by poems like 'La rabbia' and 'Il glicine', which reveal the closure of a long phase of Pasolini's literary experience without however being able to propose any sign of a new and more fertile path. With them we return, in forms that are certainly broader and of course murkier, to the lyrical experiments of his youth. The canto replaces the

---

155 Pasolini, 'Frammento alla morte' in *La religione del mio tempo*, pp. 167–9 / 'To Death: A Fragment' in *Selected Poetry*, pp. 295–9.

156 Pasolini, *Dal diario* (1945–47), p. 15.

157 Pasolini, 'Il diaul cu la mari' in *La meglio gioventù*, p. 70.

158 Pasolini, 'Frammento della morte', pp. 167–9 / ['To Death: A Fragment', p. 297.

poemetto. The elegy shows itself to have survived behind the paraenesis. Pasolini's pained soul, disheartened by an accumulation of complexes that each line of poetry now uncovers and clusters together in a succession that is even too sincere, encounters again—if only for an instant and thanks to an almost miraculous combination—the correct tone for its expression, one that is both intimate and personal.

The dominant motif here is that of crisis, of desperation. But, more precisely, it now assumes the countenance of anger ('from now on the demon / of rage is inside me';[159] 'At almost forty years of age, / I find myself in a rage like a young man / who knows nothing of himself but his youth'). The poet does not pause, however, to acknowledge his anger or vent it against his real or presumed enemies. He has the courage to press on farther than he had been able to go with the civic ideology of the preceding *poemetti.* The canto is shifted all onto Passion:

> because,
> there is an ancient heart,
> that exists prior to thought [. . .]
> between body and history
> there is this wonderful, jarring musicality,
> where what is finished and what begins
> are the same, and remain as such
> over the course of centuries:
> a fact of existence [. . .][160]

The shadow of History appears to show itself again only because the suspicion is that one can ascribe to it the terrifying resurgence of instincts that are not only victorious but triumphant over the poet's resistance:

> *Something* has widened the abyss
> between body and history,
> weakening me, withering me,
> reopening my wounds.

The affinities with his youthful poems are not limited to this thematic tendency to look to the past, to mourn it or generically recriminate against it.

---

159 This and the following quotation: from Pasolini, 'La rabbia' in *La religione del mio tempo*, p. 171 and 172, respectively / 'Rage' in *Selected Poetry*, p. 301 and 303, respectively.
160 This and the following quotation: from Pasolini, 'Il glicine' in *La religione del mio tempo*, pp. 175–6 and 177, respectively.

Ancient symbols crop up all over the place, populating Pasolini's imagination, which is no longer limited by its allegiance to ideology. We have already observed how the figure of the brother returns persistently in order to signify the memory of the Resistance and to ward off its betrayal. But, above all, the Mother reemerges from the darkest recesses of Pasolini's consciousness, assuming again the function of judge and witness that he had attributed to her during his adolescence and youth. Although less felicitously represented when Pasolini burdens her with those sentiments and ideals he considers positive— meekness, faithfulness, heroism, purity, sweetness—she assumes a deeper meaning in those moments where one finds, alive in her, the poet's traumatic, obscure and tormented inability to communicate peacefully with the world, and his love of being attacked and offended. This transference of Pasolini's self-consciousness to the archetypal symbol of the Mother is often unable to go beyond autobiological truth. But it is in any case a vital psychological motif within the creative destruction that distinguishes the most recent works of Pasolini.

However, we should not seek the true poetics of the post-Gramscian Pasolini here either. It can be discovered—fragmentary, uncertain, frayed— where the author even more decisively reconnects with the pre-Gramscian phase of his poetic inspiration. It has been insufficiently noted that in poems like 'La rabbia' and 'Il glicine', there reappear analogical procedures through which Pasolini recovers the irrational and instinctive dimensions of existence. It is true that behind the poet's crisis there is, as we have noted, the crisis of a culture and an ideology. But it is significant that no sooner does he turn inwards again that he discovers natural symbols in which to recognize and 'explain' himself. In 'La rabbia', it is the solitary rose of the bare garden of the poet that raises in him an irresistible wave of feeling and bittersweet sadness:

> I draw closer still, smell its scent . . .
> Ah, there's no point in shouting, no point in silence
> nothing can express an entire existence!'[161]

The vegetal creature is the only one that the rage of the poet can still attempt to communicate with or approach. Those who recall the beautiful Friulian poem 'Suspir de me mari ta na Rosa' cannot be surprised that, having recovered this existential kernel at the level of instinctual and subconscious analogies, Pasolini can then use it to attempt to establish a minimum of indi-

---

161 Pasolini, 'La rabbia', p. 171 / 'Rage', p. 301.

rect communication with the world; which is really to say with that part of
the world that survives the collapse of the love that once was felt for it—the
mother and the rose turn out to be joined by a symbolic affinity of characteristics and existences:

> I forgo all action . . . I only know
> that in this rose I inhale,
> in a single, wretched instant,
> the scent of my life: the scent of my mother [. . .][162]

However, from the perspective outlined here, what is even more significant
is that the occasion for this crisis to explode and issue into an explicit confession is given by the sudden, overwhelming, sensual flowering of a plant like
the wisteria. Contemplating this extraordinary exhibition of a life without limits, neither past nor future, the poet finds himself sinking into the darkest and
most satisfying abysses of being. As he declaims:

> You, with your dark perfume,
> deciduous and climbing,
> are sufficient to purify me of history,
> like a worm, like a monk [. . .][163]

Everything that is positive about this natural vitality is felt like a rapture
without remorse. Pasolini discovers himself as the brother of the wisteria, and
he shouts, as though ascribing to the plant the realization of a hope that he—
inasmuch as he is a man and so to a degree thinking and rational—will never
be able to accomplish:

> Happy
> you who are only love, a vegetal
> twin reborn in a prenatal world [. . .]

In the face of the wisteria, of its existential violence, the poet's weak soul
that seems to bend, as if overcome and lost, incapable of resisting this orgy of
the senses.

> [. . .] here I am: wisteria covers
> the rose-coloured surfaces
> of a neighbourhood that is the grave of every passion

---

162 Pasolini, 'La rabbia', p. 171 / 'Rage', p. 301.
163 This and the following quotation: from Pasolini, 'Il glicine', p. 177 and 176–7, respectively.

affluent and anonymous, warm
under the April sun that decomposes it.
The world escapes me, I still do not know
how to dominate it, it escapes me,
O, once again it is another [. . .][164]

Following the momentum of this achieved identification, Pasolini writes verses that are like the decadent *summa* of his spirit, the essential concentrate of his incurable aestheticism:

You who brutally return,
not just rejuvenated but even reborn,
a fury of nature, so sweet,
you break me because I am broken
by a sequence of miserable days;
you lean over my reopened abysses,
your virginal perfume over my eclipse,
ancient, crumbling, sensuality, fearful pity,
desire for death [. . .]

But the tone is at this point so sincere and unguarded that it is difficult, once again, to distinguish how much of it is pure literature or instead a belated burst of poetry. Be that as it may, having returned to elegy, Pasolini rediscovers the path of inner truth, where ideology persists in the form of brute cultural fact, similar to a crumbling, unsteady boulder that breaks the escaping waters but cannot determine their course. There could be no more negative conclusion to his story, which everything leads us to believe has fully returned to the furrow of aesthetic passion, of instinctive and elementary pantheism [*panismo*].[165] But one must credit him with having found his own epigraph with which to stamp (probably definitively) the vital course of his turbulent experience:

I have lost my energies;
I no longer know the meaning of rationality;
my decayed life runs aground

---

164 This and the following quotation: from Pasolini, 'Il glicine', pp. 178–9 and 179, respectively..

165 *Panismo*, or the 'panic feeling for nature' (*sentimento panico della natura*), refers to an intense perception of the natural or external world as fusing with the human. In Italian poetry, it is associated with Gabriele D'Annunzio's efforts to revive a Pagan worldview. [Trans.]

—in your religious transience—
desperate that the world
has only ferocity, and my soul only rage [. . .][166]

These are clear, exemplary phrases. One might say that, having arrived at
the point of no longer knowing what to express, Pasolini has rediscovered
sobriety and ferocity, which ill suited him when he was driven by the will to
say great, important things about the world. For that matter, this is a typical
situation for the artist who is more a man of letters [*letterato*] than a poet. If
we faithfully retrace the various stages of Pasolini's practice we will notice that
at the origin or foundation of each of them there is an impulse of literary character, an excessive desire to involve and reabsorb all of reality in literature. We
have tried to note this phenomenon each time it arose, underlining its presence
not only where it was most obvious—as in the Friulian and youthful poems—
but also in the realist novels and in the ethical-civic poems of his maturity.
The figure of Pasolini is fundamentally that of a brilliant man of letters; perhaps the last great man of letters of the Italian tradition, with the traits and
errors typical of this figure: egocentrism, heightened sensibility, technico-stylis-
tic refinement and extremely powerful ideological ambitions that do not grow
in line with the formal investigation but, rather, overlay it as though *allied* to
it. Pasolini's very 'leftism' can be explained by resorting to the nature of this
tradition and custom: there is nothing more typical than the petty-bourgeois
man of letters who seeks to compensate for the fear of his isolation (which he
would in any case be unable to give up) through contact with the popular
masses and its *harmless* official representatives, which here too is ideologically
prefigured and worked through intellectually. From such a figure poetry can
only spring forth through literature. This too is extremely typical of the Italian
tradition. Pasolini comes to be a poet (in the Friulian compositions, in *Le
ceneri di Gramsci*, in 'Il glicine') when he is able to turn his proud self-suffi-
ciency as a man of letters into a motif of drama and desperation. The truth is
that when Pasolini cries and despairs, we never hear vibrate the chords of a
wholly self-sufficient human feeling, because he is hidden behind passions and
impulses that find their origin in a literary myth: abstract and evanescent, in
the same way as the suffering of the poet is always abstract and evanescent,
that is to say, ambiguous, rarefied. Like so many men of letters throughout
Italian history, Pasolini knows how to be a poet, when he allows us to feel that

166 Pasolini, 'Il glicine', p. 179.

literature, as such, can also be the occasion for pain and scandal. This certainly does not mean that he is entirely conscious of this aspect of his poetry. On the contrary, it is natural to think that he mistakes his literary suffering for human suffering, just as it is certain that he mistakes himself—a decadent and patently conservative man of letters—for a progressive writer open to the broadest dramas of the modern world. But it is certain that the truest Pasolini is really the one who is able to more or less knowingly refuse the enticements of a possible ideological or historicist disguise, presenting himself instead in the guise of aristocratic refinement. The Pasolini, in other words, who, faced with *Le ceneri di Gramsci* or the failures of his life, dares to cry out that nothing counts more in his eyes than 'aesthetic passion', the obsessed and obsessive love for the spoken word and its graces.